ISLAMISM AND ITS ENEMIES IN THE HORN OF AFRICA

ALEX DE WAAL

editor

Islamism and Its Enemies in the Horn of Africa

INDIANA University Press

Bloomington & Indianapolis

First published in North America in 2004

Indiana University Press
601 North Morton Street
Bloomington, Indiana 47404-3797, USA

http://iupress.indiana.edu

Telephone orders 800-842-6796
Fax orders 812-855-7931
Orders by e-mail iuporder@indiana.edu

Printed in India

Cataloging information is available from the Library of Congress.

ISBN: 0-253-34403-4 (cloth: alk. paper)
ISBN: 0-253-21679-6 (pbk.: alk. paper)

1 2 3 4 5 09 08 07 06 05 04

FOREWORD

This book has been several years in the making. It initially arose from conversations between Mohamed Salih and myself on Islamist voluntarism, in the context of research we were both conducting into different aspects of this growing phenomenon. In my case, this was spurred partly by a realisation of how inadequate was the way the subject was treated in my ongoing writings on famine, sharpened by observing the undeclared regional war between Sudan and several of its neighbours. Surveying the growing array of literature on militant Islamism, especially after September 11, 2001, the lack of a study of north-east Africa became evident.

Fully acknowledging intellectual and other debts for this kind of work is an impossible task. The book's chapters represent reflections on very long engagement with the issues by each of the authors. Some of the sources of information are unattributable, but several individuals stand out as important influences on myself and A. H. Abdel Salam. Among these we must mention Sid Ahmed Bilal, Ordesse Hamad, Yasin Miheisi, Muna Khugali, Suleiman Rahhal, Tajudeen Abdul-Raheem, the late Yousif Kuwa Mekki and, above all, Abdul Mohammed and Yoanes Ajawin.

We have tried to use reason to study the phenomena of extremist Islamism, which claims that through the use of the revelation of Allah's will in politics, economics and philanthropy all problems will be solved. We have not hesitated to argue that there is a liberal alternative which is better. This book was completed on the eve of what appeared to be an inevitable war between the United States and Iraq, with a sense of trepidation that history was about to take another dramatic turn with wholly unpredictable consequences. The book holds no answers. But implicitly it argues for a more measured and far-sighted response to extremism and terrorism in place of the bellicosity that marks so much of the Western world's reaction. We dedicate it to all those who struggle for reason and tolerance in every country.

London, September 2003   ALEX DE WAAL

CONTENTS

Foreword   v

Glossary   ix

The Contributors   xii

Chapters
1. Introduction   *Alex de Waal*   1

2. On the Failure and Persistence of *Jihad*
                               A. H. Abdel Salam and Alex de Waal   21

3. Islamism, State Power and *Jihad* in Sudan
                               Alex de Waal and A. H. Abdel Salam   71

4. Islamic Political Dynamics in the Somali Civil War
                                                  Roland Marchal   114

5. Islamic N.G.O.s in Africa: the Promise and Peril of Islamic
   Voluntarism   *M. A. Mohamed Salih*   146

6. The Politics of Destabilisation in the Horn, 1989–2001
                                                  Alex de Waal   182

7. Africa, Islamism and America's 'War on Terror' after
   September 11   *Alex de Waal and A. H. Abdel Salam*   231

Bibliography   258

Index   271

GLOSSARY

ADF	Allied Democratic Forces (Islamist resistance movement in Uganda)
ahl al hal wal aqd	'Men of authority,' the informal ruling class in the Islamic Caliphate.
Ahle Sunna wa Jama'a	Somali Islamic Group. The term is used historically in the Sunni tradition to refer to refer to the dominant and often the conservative viewpoint among Moslems school of thoughts.
al Azhar	An ancient mosque and university in Cairo. It has no formal status within the government structure, but the views expressed by its leaders have a profound popular weight.
al Gama'a al Islamiya	'The Islamic Group', radical Egyptian Islamist organisation led by Sheikh Omer Abdel Rahman.
al Itihaad al Islaami	'The Islamic Union,' Somali Islamic radical group
al Qa'ida	'The base', the organisation led by Usama bin Laden.
al Majma al Islam	'The Islamic Assembly', an Islamic institution formed in Somalia.
Amir	Prince
Ansar	Supporters, a name given the the followers of al-Mahdi call in Sudan in the 19th century.
da'wa	'Call to God', Muslim evangelism
dhikr ceremony	Sufi traditional ceremony held to praise God, involving dancing and chanting.
ELF	Eritrean Liberation Front
EPLF	Eritrean People's Liberation Front
EPRDF	Ethiopian Peoples Revolutionary Democratic Front
Fatwa	The Islamic position in a certain subject issued by an established authority.
FLN	National Liberation Front, Algerian ruling party
Hezb al Tahrir	'Party of Liberation' that calls for the restoration of the Islamic Caliphate.
Hudud	Punishments for severe crimes under Islamic law.
IGAD	Inter-Governmental Authority on Development, the subregional grouping of north-east African states

ix

Ijma	'Consensus', one the sources of Islamic provisions according Islamic jurisprudence
Imam	The one who leads Muslims in prayers. It also means an Islamic religious leader.
Jahiliyya	Literally, 'ignorance' or 'anger': a name given to the times in Arab peninsula before Islam, and now used to mean the antithesis of Islam.
Jama'at Ahlal Islam	'Society of the People of Islam', Somali radical Islamic group.
Jama'at Islah (Islaax)	'Society of Reform', Somali radical Islamic group.
Jihad	Arabic for 'struggle'.
Jihad-ists	In the context of political Islam, jihadist refers to revolutionary political Islam or the use of force to implement the provisions of Islam.
Khilafa (Caliphate)	'Succession', name given to the Islamic Empire after the death of Mohamed until the demise of the Ottoman empire in the 1920s.
LRA	Lord's Resistance Army (Christian fundamentalist-syncretist resistance movement in Uganda).
Mawlid commemorations	Commemoration of the Prophet Mohamed's birthday
Mufti	A Muslim scholar appointed by the state to articulate the Islamic position in important and controversial matters.
Mujahidiin	'The strugglers': those who pursue the *jihad*.
NDA	National Democratic Alliance, Sudanese opposition umbrella.
NIF	National Islamic Front (the ruling group in Sudan).
OIC	Organisation of the Islamic Conference.
OLF	Oromo Liberation Front (Oromo nationalist movement founded in 1973 in Ethiopia).
ONLF	Ogaden National Liberation Front (Somali resistance movement in Ethiopia).
PAIC	Pan Arab and Islamic Conference.
PDF	Popular Defence Forces-Sudanese government militia.
Qadiriyya	One of the biggest and oldest Sufi groups in the Islamic world. Named after its founder Sheikh Abdel Qadir al Gailani
Qiyas	'Analogy', one the sources of Islamic provisions according Islamic jurisprudence.
RCC	Revolutionary Command Council, the military officers who took power in Sudan in 1989.
Republican Brothers	Sudanese Islamic group, which call for peaceful transformation into an ideal Islamic society.

Saar ceremony	A healing ceremony for women to drive out bad spirits.
SAF	Sudan Alliance Forces, an armed opposition group within the NDA.
Salaf (*salafi*)	'Predecessors', refering to the early generations of Muslims The belief of salafiist Muslims is that the closer a generation was to the time of the Prophet the more correct it was its understanding of Islam.
Shari'a	Islamic law.
SNM	Somali National Movement (Isaaq-dominated Somali faction).
SPLA/M	Sudan People's Liberation Army/Movement. The main rebel group engaged, in Sudan's civil war since 1983.
SPM	Somali Patriotic Movement (Ogaden-based Somali faction)
SSDF	Somali Salvation Democratic Front (Majerteen-based Somali faction)
sunna	Prophet Mohammed's saying and deeds
Tablikh (*tabligh, tablik*)	'Informing'; refers to the informing of the Islamic provisions and is the name of a movement that originated in Pakistan and has many branches in African countries
takfir	Accusing a Muslim of being infidel, excommunication.
takfir wa al hijra	'Excommunication and migration', a radical Egyptian Islamist group led by Shukri Mustafa in the 1970s.
Tanzim al Jihad	'Organisation of *Jihad*' a neo-fundamentalist jihadist organisations in Egypt led by Ayman al Zawahiri
tariqa	Sufi group or sect, literally 'way'
TNG	Transitional National Government of Somalia
ulama	Scholars of Islamic doctrine and law
Umma Party	The political party of Ansar Sect in Sudan.
USC	United Somali Congress (Hawiye-based Somali faction)
Wahhabi	Reformist reactionary Islamic group, named after its founder Ahmed Abdel Wahab. Wahhabism is the formal ideology of the Saudi state.
Waqf	Islamic trust or foundation.
zakat	Donation to the poor, one of the seven pillars of the Islamic belief.

THE CONTRIBUTORS

Alex de Waal is a writer and activist, who has worked for eighteen years on issues of war, famine, human rights and governance in Africa. He is currently working on the impact of HIV/AIDS on governance, including political stability and food security. He was born in Britain and educated at Oxford, where he obtained a DPhil in social anthropology. He is author of eight books and numerous articles, including: *Famine that Kills: Darfur, Sudan, 1984–1985* (Oxford: Clarendon Press, 1989); *Famine Crimes: Politics and the Disaster Relief Industry in Africa* (Oxford: James Currey, 1997); and *Demilitarising the Mind: African Agendas for Peace and Security* (Tronton, NJ: Africa World Press, 2002).

Alex de Waal is a director of Justice Africa, a London-based organisation that supports human rights, peace and democracy in Africa, and serves as adviser to the UN Economic Commission for Africa in Addis Ababa on issues of HIV/AIDS and governance. Formerly he has worked for African Rights, Inter Africa Group and Human Rights Watch, as well as being chairman of the Mines Advisory Group.

A. H. Abdel Salam was born in Sudan and educated at the Egyptian university in Khartoum. He has been an active member of the Sudanese bar, and served as secretary-general of the Sudan Human Rights Organisation in 1994–9. Abdel Salam was also chairman of the Steering Committee for Human Rights in the Transition in Sudan, and co-editor of the volume, *The Phoenix State: Civil Society and the Future of Sudan* (Tronton, NJ: Red Sea Press, 1999; published in Arabic as *al Mashru' al Medani*). He has published numerous articles on different aspects of human rights and law reform in Sudan and serves as legal adviser to Justice Africa.

Roland Marchal is senior research fellow at CNRS (National Centre for Scientific Research) attached to CERI/Sciences-Po (Paris). Has published extensively on the Horn of Africa, especially Sudan and Somalia and on theory of conflict. Among his publications are *Dubaï, Cité Globale* (Paris: CNRS Editions, 2001) and, with Christine Messiant, *Les chemins de la guerre et de la paix. Fin de conflit en Afrique orientale et australe?* (Paris: Karthala, 1997).

M. A. Mohamed Salih is Professor of Politics of Development at both the Institute of Social Studies, The Hague, and the Department of Political Science, University of Leiden. He is vice chairman of the International Human Dimension of Global Change (IHDP) of the International Council for Social Science (ICSS) and the International Union of Sciences (IUS). Among his recent books are *African Democracies and African Politics* (Pluto Press, 2001); *African Pastoralism: Conflict Institutions and Government* (Pluto Press, 2001); *Environmental Politics and Liberation in Contemporary Africa* (Kluwer, 1999); and *Ethnicity and the State in Eastern Africa* (Uppsala: Scandinavian Institute of African Studies 1998).

1

INTRODUCTION

Alex de Waal

North-east Africa has been a laboratory for political Islam. The Nile Valley has been the incubator of radical Islamist theory and practice. After 1989, Sudan became the Arab world's sole militant Islamic state. Meanwhile, the Horn of Africa became one of the main theatres of conflict between jihadists and their enemies. This struggle was intense, violent and complex. By 2001, militant Islamism's 'big project' in the region was exhausted, left with just the capacity to block progress towards democracy and peace. A far-reaching attempt to create an Islamic state and society had, in the words of its own architects, come to a standstill. Its failures were rooted more in the contradictions of political Islamism itself than in the power and skill of its adversaries, whose parallel and opposing projects also reached an impasse at the same time.

However, from the perspective of 2003, in the midst of the global confrontation between the US 'war on terror' and its militant enemies, jihadist Islamism has gained a new global relevance. North-east Africa is a sideshow in this war, and a cockpit for others' battles. However, the region will undoubtedly be transformed by this conflict, whose dimensions are as yet unclear. The failures of political Islam in the region must also be seen in tandem with the failures of alternative social and political projects, notably leftist revolutionary militarism, which rose and fell in parallel with the Islamist project.

The shortcomings of Islamism are intellectual, social, political and military. These failures are evident not just to political scientists and analysts, but to the citizens of the countries concerned. For example, at the time of writing there is widespread popular support in Sudan for an American-led initiative to end that country's civil war and establish a more representative and less Islamist government. The disastrous experience of political Islam is part of every Sudanese's personal experience. Yet, Usama bin Laden is a figure of cult adoration for many Africans, and political Islam continues to raise the banner of resistance against US global hegemony. And the nature of Islamist writing, specifically its attachment to a Utopian ideal of political community fixed in the past, makes it very difficult for Islamists to admit their failures. Meanwhile, Islamism has been adept at the 'little projects' of delivering public services and mobilising the piety of young Muslims for social change in Muslim communities. Islamists are likely to improvise new forms of political mobilisation.

Most writing about political Islam relegates north-east Africa to a footnote to the confrontations being fought out in Egypt, Palestine, Afghanistan and other parts of Asia. Islamists themselves write little other than polemic and newspaper commentary on the region. This is despite the fact that for a few significant years, radical Islamists of all shades met in Sudan. Khartoum is where the Iraqis, Iranians and al Qa'ida converged in the early 1990s. Meanwhile, most English-language analyses of the protracted political crises of the Horn of Africa are rooted in political science traditions that have, at best, passing familiarity with political Islam. Even studies of the Sudanese civil war, the crucible of Islamism's confrontation with Africa, suffer from this bifurcation. This book seeks to bridge this divide. In the Nile Valley and the Horn of Africa, political Islam has been fused with local political struggles to create new manifestations, which have lasting consequences for the countries concerned, and which also have a wider impact upon political Islamism.

Islams and Islamisms

Islam in north-east Africa is hugely diverse and it is inviting trouble to try to simplify its many manifestations. Michael Gilsenan rightly cautions against the tendency, among Muslims and non-Muslims alike, to simplify and homogenise 'Islam' (1982: 18–19). He also reminds us that for two centuries (at least), there has been an ongoing process of Islamic 'revival', so that contemporary Islamic militancy should not be seen as a wholly new phenomenon but rather as a continuation of an established tradition of renewal. Only some selected issues and locations have been brought into focus in this book, with a few references to wider questions across Africa and the Middle East. The principal focus is on the confrontation between militant Islam and its political and ideological adversaries, especially in Sudan and Somalia. These adversaries include popular Islam, which in Africa is mostly Sufi sects. This selective focus has its dangers, for example in that it neglects the rich complexity of Islams in Ethiopia and Kenya. It seeks to provide narrative and analysis to fill important gaps in the contemporary history of the Horn of Africa and the Nile Valley.

Writing on this issue also has its political perils. A focus on militant Islamism runs the danger of feeding into the 'clash of civilisations' hypothesis, and presenting Islamism as a monolithic phenomenon with an inevitable tendency towards violence. Scholars have laboured to correct Western misapprehensions about Islam (Esposito 1995) and many have been at pains to argue that the core meaning of *jihad* is personal, non-violent struggle (Fazlur Rahman 1982, Sachedina 1996, Bassam Tibi 1998, Abou El Fadl 2000). In no way does this book contradict these arguments. The overwhelming majority of Muslims are peaceable and tolerant, and most political parties that identify themselves as 'Islamic' are likewise. Public opinion surveys in Africa do not show significant differences in support for democracy and tolerance between Muslims and non-Muslims (Afrobarometer 2002). Our concern here is with a particular strand of militant Islamism that developed out of the Muslim Brothers in Egypt, which has repeatedly incubated a violent jihadist fringe, and which took control of the Sudanese state in 1989, and confronted other states in the region shortly thereafter. The political significance of this fringe is wholly disproportionate to its numerically small following of committed *mujahidiin*. But we must also face the reality that the political claims of the extremist fringe and even its 'propaganda by deed', such as terrorist actions, have been applauded by a larger constituency. Much has been written on the core terrorist organisations such as al Qa'ida, most of it journalistic (Bergen 2001), some of it excellent and detailed (Cooley 2000, Benjamin and Simon 2002) and some of it less so (Bodansky 1999). There are also numerous studies on political Islam and the Muslim Brothers themselves (Sidahmed 1996, Roy 1999, Weaver 1999, Sullivan and Abed-Kotob 1999, Abdo 2000, Kepel 2002), and analyses of the political philosophy (or lack of it) of Islamist writers (Esposito ed. 1983, El-Affendi 1991b, Choueiri 1996, Bassam Tibi 1998). However, in this opus there is little that focuses on the ideological, sociological and political threads that link Islamism in its Egyptian birthplace to its manifestations in the rest of Africa, particularly the Horn. And, despite much writing on the Sudanese civil war, there is little that puts this conflict in the contexts of the Islamist project and regional politics. This book tries to fill parts of this vacuum.

At the risk of oversimplification, we distinguish between Islam as it is lived and practised by most Muslims in north-east Africa ('popular Islam') and the major strands in political Islam that have emerged over the last two centuries, some of which are vibrant today. Popular Islam encompasses diverse phenomena. The Sufi sects, mainly peaceable, that dominated the allegiance of most African Muslims in the Sahel, Sudan and Horn fall comfortably into this bracket. Sufism is also vibrant in Egypt. Similarly it has spread among the East African Muslims, many of whom had developed syncretic forms of popular Islam. In these contexts, Islam was a private faith and also a set of values for a community: Muslims were people who sought to live their lives with a sense of decency and dignity.

Islamic revival movements have recurred since the eighteenth century. Several concern us here. The Mahdist millenarian movements in West Africa and Sudan broke with Sudanic traditions to create what has subsequently been mythologised as a revolutionary protonationalism. However, they are more accurately seen as pre-modern millenarianism, a Sufi-inspired jihadism, based upon the mystical vision of a charismatic leader. As with other cases of primary resistance to imperial conquest, all were defeated, and modernist nationalism drew its cadres and philosophies from a different source. In the Sudanese case, the last and most threatening to the colonial order, the Mahdi's posthumous son, Sayyid Abdel Rahman al Mahdi, sought to transform the Mahdist Ansar movement into a sectarian political party, accommodating British rule, with considerable success. Significantly, contemporary Sudanese militant Islamism has appropriated the Mahdist mythology in pursuit of its legitimacy.

A non-African revivalist movement that has recently had major impact on Islam in Africa is the Wahhabi movement of eighteenth-century Arabia. This was a puritanical reformist movement characterised by a certain intellectual rigour and adherence to conservative Bedouin social practices. The Wahhabis sought to return to the original Islamic sources for inspiration, trying to emulate the first generation of Muslims, the Salaf. They were militant and through the military victory of the Saud family they almost conquered the Arabian peninsula with extreme violence. They were intolerant too, especially of the Shi'a minorities and Sufis. Wahhabism is one of the earliest forms of modern Muslim fundamentalism, and subsequent revivalists of widely differing ideological colours have described themselves as Salafi.

'Islamism' is the response of Muslim theoreticians and freelance activists to the challenges of modernity. Its immediate ancestry lies with the

Salafi reformist thinkers of the late nineteenth century. Like the Wahhabis, these reformers sought to return to the roots of Islam for guidance, rejecting the tradition of imitation (*taqlid*) in favour of authenticity. Unlike the Wahhabis, their method was not conservative literalism, but a reinterpretation of the sacred texts (*ijtihad*) in the modern context—at that time, dominated by the brute reality of Western imperial rule. They were modernisers. Jamal al Din al Afghani is recognised as the founder of this movement. His disciple Mohamed Abduh rejected polygamy (on the basis of the impossibility of a man following the Prophet's injunction to treat all his wives on an equal footing) while Qaasim Amin advocated the equality of the sexes. Abduh's student, Rashid Rida, was however more pedestrian and conservative: he provides the link to the Islamic activism of the Muslim Brothers. At this time, the distinction between secular anti-imperialism and modernist Islamist revivalism was somewhat blurred.

Islamism as a movement developed in the 1920s, spurred by the collapse of the Ottoman empire and the abolition of the Caliphate. It was a creative approach to the challenge of how Muslims could live in the modern world, and how they could respond to the political challenge posed by illegitimate political authorities, at that time colonial rule. Indeed, the questions of sovereignty, constitutionalism, law and ethics and democracy—all modern political concerns—are among the main themes of Islamism. In important respects, early 'Islamism' was a child of its times: the 1920s and '30s were an era of economic and political crisis, matched by universalising ideologies. Hence, the Islamism of that era can be interpreted as a sibling of fascism and communism. Again, we see many variants, from the 'moderate' Islamism of Egypt's Islamic Trend to the militancy of Sayyid Qutb to the 'Islamology' of Ali Shari'ati in Iran. All are 'modernising'. However, a focus on the 'modernity' of Islamism should not overlook the varieties of political modernisation—both fascism and communism were also 'modernising' (Utvik 2003). This book is concerned overwhelmingly with the Sunni Islamism of the Egyptian Muslim Brothers and its various offspring, the most intellectually and organisationally influential in Africa. The basic argument of chapters 2 and 3 is that in Egypt and Sudan, the Islamist project has failed to overcome some major theoretical and practical weaknesses. An abiding problem has been the readiness to use violence, which, once embraced, has led its proponents into an intractable logic of conflict. Islamists have resorted to the suppression of dissent and the adoption of violent *jihad* with disastrous consequences.

However, while the political project of constructing Islamic states has failed, one of the themes of this book is the successful adaptation of

Islamism to the micro-level challenges of life in much of Africa. The Islamists have been dynamic at a local level in proposing practical solutions to the real day-to-day needs of people, for health services, education, access to micro-credit, and freedom from sexual harassment. In Somalia, the concern of chapter 4, Islamists have been able to respond well to the demands of social service provision, commerce and administration of justice in a collapsed state. Their success has been directly proportional to their accommodation to traditions of Somalia's 'popular Islam' and their readiness to work with, rather than against, the dominant militarised clan factions. Chapter 5 examines some of the ways in which Islamism has developed a traditional of voluntarism, and accommodated to other agendas, more resonant with 'popular Islam'.

'Neo-fundamentalism' is an awkward but useful neologism that describes the forms of political Islam that have emerged from the failures of modernist Islamism. The term is usefully elucidated by the Muslim scholar Fazlur Rahman:

The current postmodernist fundamentalism, in an important way, is novel because its basic élan is anti-Western (and, by implication, of course, anti-Westernism). Hence its condemnation of classical [Islamist] modernism as a purely Westernizing force.... [T]he neo-fundamentalists, after... borrowing certain things from classical modernism, largely rejected its content and, in turn, picked upon certain specific issues as 'Islamic' par excellence and accused the classical modernist of having succumbed to the West and having sold Islam cheaply there.... Thus while the modernist was engaged by the West through attraction, the neo-revivalist is equally haunted by the West through repulsion. (1982: 136)

A priori definitions of neo-fundamentalism are unhelpful. Rather, it is better to identify its chief characteristics. Along with anti-Westernism, the dominant characteristic of neo-fundamentalism is its anti-intellectualism and resort to argument from authority. Fazlur Rahman continues: '... the greatest weakness of neo-revivalism, and the greatest disservice it has done to Islam, is an almost total lack of positive effective Islamic thinking and scholarship within its ranks, its intellectual bankruptcy, and its substitution of cliché mongering for serious intellectual endeavor.... [The neo-fundamentalist's] consolation and pride are to chant ceaselessly the song that Islam is "very simple" and "straightforward" without knowing what these words mean.' (1982: 137) However, the term 'scholar' is elastic. Neo-fundamentalism has its own canon of scholarly works, including the writings of Yusuf al Qaradawi and Mohamed Salim al 'Awwa. These contend that a 'return' to the purity of the first Qur'anic generation will resolve every social and political ill. The influence of Wahhabi Salafism, backed by Saudi cash, has been instrumental in the rise of neo-funda-mentalism. In a liberal environment such intellectual vacuity would not survive long, but it has become protected by the structures of intimida-tion of the Islamists themselves and the patrimonial states that dominate the Muslim world. The use of force to protect the intellectually indefensi-ble lies at the heart of the current Islamist impasse.

Neo-fundamentalism has differing political manifestations. Olivier Roy, writing in the early 1990s, saw this as an abandonment of political ambi-tions of the Islamist thinkers to create a modern Islamic state, and a reversion to forms of voluntarism and evangelism (Roy 1999). Here, we use it to encompass another parallel phenomenon as well, which shares many of the same intellectual and social characteristics, but also em-braces violent *jihad*. This has been labelled 'Jihadist-Salafism' by Gilles Kepel, drawing on the terminology of the movement's own spokesman, Imam Abu Hamza (Kepel 2002: 219). In this book, we use the variant term Salafi jihadism, identifying both national and global variants.

Despite their differences, there is also continuity between modernist Islamism and neo-fundamentalism, found in the concept of violent *jihad*. The role of violence in political Islam, in theory and practice, is pro-foundly controversial. Chapters 2 and 3 try to locate the role of violence in Islamist political thought and practice. The most influential Islamist thinkers in North-East Africa—notably Sayyid Qutb and Hassan al Turabi—have explicitly advocated violent *jihad*. Their theorisation of violence is located on a moral or transcendental plane, and it has not proved to be a mechanism for bringing about the social and political change they desire. The practice of violence is more pragmatic, and also has not succeeded in its major aims. However, one of the themes of this book is the complexity of the theory and practice of *jihad*, and the elusive-ness of its definition of victory.

Studying jihad

Social and political scientists have been uncomfortable with the study of violent *jihad*. There is an emergent discipline of the study of conflict in the context of development, alongside a growing body of practice and theory of conflict resolution. As this book seeks to show, the study of *jihad* does not fit easily within these paradigms.

There are different, if inadequately theorised, concepts of success in *jihad*. The core Islamist theory of *jihad* is transcendental: victory is pro-vided by God alone, rather than being an obligation on the *mujahid*

himself. This operates both through the miraculous or apocalyptic establishment of the Kingdom of God and through the individual *mujahid*'s
attainment of paradise. The logic is transcendental: just as Islam itself collapses the distinction between ethics and law, absolute *jihad* obliterates
the division between the right to wage war and rights within war. Even
though Islam has a long history of humanity in warfare (Boisard 1985:
259), this form of *jihad* is fundamentally antipathetic to the exercise of
restraint or respect for the laws of war. In his apologia for Usama bin
Laden's attack on America, Hassan al Turabi can only quarrel with the
number of casualties inflicted on September 11, not with Usama's *right* to
conduct this mode of warfare (al Turabi 2002).

Yet at the same time, the irreducible logic of war imposes a certain discipline on the practitioners of *jihad*. If they are to survive and prevail,
mujahidiin must match their adversaries, mobilise fighters, exercise command, control locations (preferably though not necessarily countries) and
master military tactics. *Jihad* is a real insurgency, usually grafted onto
other agendas such as national resistance against an oppressor or invader.
One of the persistent themes of this book is that political Islam in its various manifestations—organisational, philanthropic, military—is poor at
moving from a micro-level to a wider national level. Islamism appears to
operate well as an ideology of resistance, nourished by allegations of conspiracy and by the martyrdom of its adherents, but fails when it exercises
power. For the practical *mujahidiin*, victory is the most dangerous moment.
This is when they are tested, by what the Prophet Mohamed aptly called
the 'greater *jihad*', namely the struggle for one's own internal purity.
Islamic warriors who have achieved power, whether in Sudan or Afghanistan, have found this to be their greatest challenge and their greatest failing.

Contemporary *jihad* is also exceptional in that there is a special band of
mujahidiin, cut off from their own societies, and schooled in a universalist
Salafi jihadist ideology. These are the 'Afghan Arabs', the graduates of the
Peshawar-based anti-Soviet *jihad* in Afghanistan in the 1980s. Together
with Muslims moulded by their alienating experience of Europe, they
have coalesced into al Qa'ida. Chapter 2 includes passing reference to
their aspirations and the nature of their organisations. It is extraordinarily difficult to reach an objective judgement about their capacity.
There is a remarkable disjuncture between the trajectory of the Islamist
project of constructing Islamic states and societies, which was fading in
the late 1990s, and the growth of this extreme fringe and its distinctive
new form of terrorism. Al Qa'ida has demonstrated that it is not necessary for an organisation to have an organised political constituency or the

protection of a state for it to operate and inflict damage that is massively disproportionate. Arguably Usama bin Laden's embrace of 'apocalyptic terrorism' (Gunaratna 2002: 92–3) is both exceptional and symptomatic of his abandonment of an organised political constituency. No state could connive with this agenda and survive. Alternatively, Usama has touched the nerve of the Muslim world, and is articulating the rage of a generation of young Muslims that feels humiliated by America, Israel and the bankrupt autocracies that rule across the Arab world.

Jihad in its highly-coloured ideological forms has been rare in contemporary Africa. Two overlapping instances are examined in this book: the Sudanese civil war, specifically with reference to the military offensives of 1992, and the regional terrorist campaigns of international jihadist organisations based in Sudan in the 1990s. Unsurprisingly, we will find that neither are theorised at all by Islamists, not even by the region's most prolific theoretician, Hassan al Turabi. In fact, Militant Islam's encounter with Africa has been marked by confusion and ambivalence, and insofar as it has made progress, this has been by embracing local agendas.

The call for *jihad* may be analysed within a broader context of understanding African wars. The dominant paradigms focus on the instrumentality of violence as a mechanism for the consolidation of state power and economic gain. These approaches are well-theorised in the work of David Keen (1998, 2000), Mark Duffield (2001) and William Reno (1998). An important strand of this analysis has grown out of studies of the Sudanese conflict (cf. de Waal 1994), and a variant has been applied to analysis of the Algerian civil war (Martinez 2000). In some protracted wars, such as Angola, Liberia and Somalia, the adversaries accommodate to one another and in important senses need one another in order to pursue their political and economic strategies. Studying the roles of militant Islam in the north-east African wars allows us to focus on the instrumentality of jihadism, and also on the ways in which its ideology influences the conduct of war. In this context, 'victory' may consist solely in escalating the struggle itself.

However, it is important in following this analysis not to lose sight of real political and ideological differences between belligerents: wars can be fought to win as well as for profit and control. Moreover, jihadism has its own logic of justification for war, and escalation once war has begun. In this context, Clausewitzean theories can be pressed into service, enabling us to identify the particularities of *jihad* in its different manifestations. For example, Islamist ideology can be important in mobilising forces and instilling discipline in the context of a weak state (de Waal

1997b). It is also a contributor to the militaristic political discourse and style of governance that marks states that engage in war. This is the 'political imagination' of militarism, or what Luis Martinez (2000) calls the war-related *imaginaire*. Organised violence can serve to legitimise both political and economic entrepreneurism, the 'brute causes' of many conflicts. Militant Islamist war has its own particular variant logic.

These themes are all picked up in succeeding chapters, concerned specifically with the Sudanese civil war, the international dimensions of the Sudanese conflict, and the role of political Islam within the ongoing civil war in Somalia.

Islam and civil society

From its earliest days in the 1920s Islamist mobilisation has been focused as much on society as on the state. In the 1930s the Society of Muslim Brothers in Egypt was a 'state within a state' or, perhaps more accurately, a 'society within a society'. The Muslim Brothers organised not only as a political party, but set up schools, hospitals and factories as well. In the 1970s the breakaway Islamist movement Takfir wa al Hijra tried to create a pure Muslim society by obliging its members to withdraw from the wider Egyptian society. This was an abortive experiment that was crushed by the state. Subsequently, the Muslim Brothers have organised through non-governmental organisations, including professional associations, voluntary agencies, mosques and schools, and humanitarian agencies. This has been described as mobilisation in the civil society sector (Sullivan and Abed-Kotob 1999), and it undoubtedly represents a major and highly effective investment in providing practical solutions to many of the immediate problems facing Egyptian society, as well as furthering the agenda of Islamising society from below.

Outside Egypt there has been a bold experiment in creating an Islamic society in Sudan, utilising concepts including 'Islamic social planning' and the 'comprehensive *da'wa*' (call to God). These are one of the main concerns of chapter 3; they are the civil counterpart to *jihad*. The experiment has not succeeded. In Somalia, Islamists have provided important services, but have worked within a framework that is not theirs (chapter 4). Across Africa, they have set up Islamic voluntary agencies, a phenomenon analysed in chapter 5. These exhibit much variety, reflecting the circumstances in which they operate, and the orientations of their directors and funders. They too have been caught in the trap that their effectiveness has been compromised by the political and religious agendas they seek to promote.

Do these experiments represent an Islamic civil society? We need to tread carefully. Secularist conceptions of civil society can be misleading in the Islamist context. Western models identify civil society with regulated voluntary organisations and associations, newspapers and other non-state institutions that stand distinct from the state and mitigate its powers, and which promote freedom of speech and social, cultural and political plurality (Keane 1998). Secularist Egyptian academics such as Saad Eddin Ibrahim have endorsed this definition, holding that 'civility' in the management of difference is a crucial ingredient in 'civil society' (1995, 2002: 245). In Sudan, many human rights activists and democrats see civil society as holding the potential for rejuvenating free political life in their country (Abdel Salam and de Waal 2001). These views of civil society echo the experience of Eastern Europe in the 1970s and '80s, when the term was reinvented as a means of carving out a free space under the threat of totalitarian domination. It was, in the words of Vaclav Havel, a way of 'living in truth', and drew upon a political-cultural archive of cosmopolitan liberalism that had flourished before the Second World War.

After the triumph of Western liberalism in 1989 and the 'democracy wave' that rolled over Eastern Europe and Africa, 'civil society' was elevated to play a new role in global governance. It was recognised as a component of both liberal democracy and a free market economy—in the latter capacity, as a means delivering welfare while simultaneously rolling back state institutions (Abrahamsen 2000, Jenkins 2002). International donor enthusiasm with 'civil society' has meant that governments in Africa have been obliged to encourage civil society, and funds have been available to organisations that can define themselves as such, so much that the operational definition of 'civil society organisation' is now 'what international donors can support'. The 'civil society' they create is in their own image.

Islamist approaches to 'civil society' need to be seen in the context of the particular circumstances of different countries, and also of characteristically Islamist models of social organisation (Zubaida 1997, 2002, Salih 2001). In Egypt, they do stand against the power of an authoritarian and increasingly incompetent state. Islamist-run professional organisations not only meet the needs of their members, but also challenge the state (usually in an implicit way), carving out spheres of action in which they can act autonomously (Sullivan and Abed-Kotob 1999, Abdo 2000). Islamic NGOs are often well-run and effective at responding to real needs for education, health care and disaster relief. They are popular. They are also skilled at evading state control, exercised through regulations that strictly control registered NGOs, for example by registering as *waqf* ('pious endowments') or taking over mosques. Because of their scale and vigour in filling the space between individuals and the state, Islamist organisations must be included within 'civil society' (Ibrahim 1995). In Sudan, with the state supporting them, Islamic voluntary agencies mobilised the enthusiasm of many young Islamists to reach remote villages and undertook educational campaigns in pursuit of the comprehensive *da'wa*. In all cases, their overwhelming concern is delivering social and spiritual services, sometimes linked to establishing commercial enterprises.

The Havelian concept of 'living in truth' resonates in the principles and practice of Islamic voluntarism. In its political form, as explored in this book, Islamist volunteer cadres seek to live as virtuous Muslims. The cultural archive they draw upon is primarily the original sources of Islam and the example of the first generation of Muslims, the Salafa, along with the example of the contemporary 'guide' or teacher whom they are following. This is where they diverge dramatically from the liberal conception of civil society, in that their Utopian vision is one of conformism and the suppression of dissent and all forms of political or cultural pluralism. This applies to the other institutions of an Islamist 'civil society', including universities and the media, as well as NGOs. In the current neo-fundamentalism climate, this means not only suppression of dissent, but an often fierce anti-intellectualism.

Does this count as truly 'civil society'? Let us compare John Keane's definition, that civil society is founded on 'respect for the multiplicity of often incommensurable normative codes and forms of contemporary social life. The term "civil society" is a signifier of plurality.' (1998: 53) We do not need to agree with Keane's post-foundationist normative definition to concur that civil society cannot be based on a monist, totalising conception of society, and to acknowledge the key role of free expression and intellectual production. Insofar as neo-fundamentalist intellectualism is marked by argument from authority, truncated political imagination, and intolerance of dissent, it is the antithesis of this kind of civil society.

The analysis of 'Islamic' civil society arrives at a familiar paradox. It is characterised by micro-level dynamism combined with an incapacity to address the wider problems of society. This incapacity is more than a weakness, it is a flaw that challenges the very rationale for regarding Islamist voluntarism as a manifestation of 'civil society'. Islamist neo-fundamentalists are often actively engaged in the suppression of the very forms of creativity that are central to allowing society to find its way in a rapidly changing world. Liberal Islamists' civil society is more tolerant, but susceptible to the bullying of their neo-fundamentalist brethren. Islamist civil society remains 'civil' as long as it is without political power. But—as with many leftist movements in earlier decades—civil society activism is often displaced political mobilisation. And when it attains power or influence, it becomes decidedly uncivil. Hence, while Muslim countries need civil society, an 'Islamic' civil society is not an escape from their impasse.

Islamic humanitarianism

The concept and practice of Islamic humanitarianism have gained particular relevance in Africa in the last quarter century. Starting in the 1970s, various factors came together to create new forms of institutional *da'wa*. One of these was Islamists' rediscovery of an authentically Islamic charitable practice. As Jonathan Benthall notes,

Unlike other great sacred books, the Qu'ran sets out the basic headings of the budget and expenses of the state, and historically anticipated by some 12 centuries the principle of what we call social security.... Some ideologues such as Sayyid Qutb claim that *zakat* is a specifically Islamic concept superior to Christian charity because, being in principle mandatory, it neither exalts the giver nor demeans the recipient. (Benthall 1997: 15–16)

Two other factors were Islamic finance in the Gulf states and a growing expertise in relief and development in Muslim African countries (especially Sudan). Sufism, because of its reliance on the charismatic authority of the *sheikh* of the order and the spiritual blessings provided by his *baraka*, is ill-suited to the emergence of institutionalised philanthropy. International Salafi philanthropic organisations have become a central aspect of Islamism's encounter with Africa. This is a new dimension to Islamic 'civil society', and is the main focus of chapter 5. The same agencies and practices that were first developed in Muslim Africa were subsequently transplanted to Bosnia, Afghanistan and elsewhere. Muslim humanitarians face a major challenge if they are to retain the authenticity of their own charitable tradition, while also avoiding the perils of militant politicised Islamism.

Islamic NGOs are fond of pointing out that the majority of the world's refugees are in predominantly Muslim countries. In these same countries Western relief institutions, including donor governments, UN agencies and NGOs, are also encountering political and philanthropic Islamism. It is an encounter marked by incomprehension and distrust on both sides. The Islamists fear the political, economic and cultural influence of

Western agencies and their donors. The US government's readiness to fund and promote American 'faith based' NGOs, many of whom have strong Christian associations, gives rise to Muslim suspicions about what is the 'real' agenda of these agencies. And, especially, they note with alarm the readiness of many Western relief agencies to call for Western military intervention, and occasionally obtain it. Islamic agencies are quick to fasten upon any perceived double standards in their Western counterparts.

For Western organisations, there is a temptation to fall back upon existing categories for humanitarian organisations—categories that are themselves problematic—and label their Islamic 'partner agencies' as either 'good' or 'bad', depending on how well they appear to meet Western criteria. Thus, for example, the British-based Islamic Relief is widely regarded as credible and independent, akin to a Muslim version of the broadly secularised church-based Western agencies, and is therefore considered an acceptable partner. (Ironically Islamic Relief is more particular about its funding sources than many of its secular or Christian counterparts, for example refusing to accept state funds.) In other cases UN agencies have found themselves funding organisations that have subsequently been blacklisted by the FBI for alleged links to terrorist networks. (It is unsurprising that organisations with jihadist connections are less scrupulous about their sources of funding.) Overwhelmingly, Western and Christian humanitarians simply seek to fit Islamic agencies into their established frameworks, rather than examining the philosophical basis for their activities. Too many of them don't know what questions to ask, nor how to understand the answers they receive.

The study of 'complex emergencies' has emerged as a major strand of international (i.e. Western) engagement with political crises and their humanitarian ramifications. The concept of a 'complex emergency' was initially an ad hoc response to the institutional difficulties of operating relief operations in a war zone, its 'complexity' referring to the mixture of war and natural disaster, but has since taken on a life of its own (de Waal 1997a: 69 ff). Complex emergencies are primarily *political* emergencies. Islamist political agendas, in both violent (*jihad*) and philanthropic (*da'wa*) manifestations are intimately engaged with many of these crises, from Sudan to Bosnia to Afghanistan. Complex emergencies are also complicated, with their causation and potential responses operating at multiple levels and in diverse ways. Political Islam, as a totalising philosophy and practice, engages with many of these different processes, including ideological inspiration, political and military mobilisation, commercial activities and humanitarian response. However, the understanding of

Islamism in its various manifestations has thus far remained marginal to the study of complex emergencies and the training of professional humanitarians. This will doubtless change. Several chapters of this book are relevant to the enterprise of writing an account of a complex emergency that integrates such Islamist elements.

Political imagination and the role of the intellectual

An abiding theme in any discussion of political Islam is the marginalisation of intellectual discourse that has occurred progressively over the last thirty years. For various reasons, some of which are addressed in chapters 2 and 3, political Islam not only lacks a political science, but is actively hostile to any form of social science whatsoever. In fact, Islamist intellectualism reproduces two key aspects of European Orientalism, albeit in new forms. One trait is essentialism, the 'myth of the arrested development of the Semites' (Said 1991: 307). Neo-fundamentalist writers insist on treating Islam as unchanging and unchangeable. They do not judge Islam by its relevance to solving the problems of human beings and societies, but rather evaluate human beings and societies according to the impossible perfection demanded by Islam. Bassam Tibi notes:

Such an argument leaves no room for the study of history, and historical discourse is eliminated: Islam, as a pure principle expressed in the scripture, is immutable, regardless of history, time, culture, location, or whatever. Muslims may change, but Islam will not. Muslims have only themselves to blame for their deviation, for that is the source of all incongruities between scripture and reality. These deviations are in fact depicted in fundamentalist writings as the source of the current Islamic malaise. (1998: 161)

The second aspect of Orientalism is the use of scholarly discourse as a part of an apparatus of power. European Orientalism was an integral part of imperialism (Said 1991). Neo-fundamentalist Orientalism utilises the discourse of *takfir* (labelling disagreement as apostasy, leading to excommunication) in a similar way. This makes entering into any sort of intellectually rigorous dialogue with such people difficult. It is unsurprising that neo-fundamentalist Islamists' response to intellectual challenge is censorship, by moral sanction and ultimately by violence.

The Islamist tradition of violent direct action by individuals is rooted in examples of the Prophet instructing his disciples to correct injustices by immediate action, to the extent of killing on sight (An-Na'im 1990: 184). The most famous contemporary case is Ayatollah Khomeini's *fatwa* against Salman Rushdie, but this is only one manifestation of intellectual intimidation, and sometimes terrorism, practised by neo-fundamentalists. Introducing a scholarly work by the modernist Muslim Pakistani scholar Fazlur Rahman, Ebrahim Moosa decries this intellectual intimidation: 'Dozens of Muslim intellectuals are either regularly hounded by frenzied mobs of religious activists and zealots or are censored by governments with sometimes an unholy alliance between the zealots and dictatorships.' (2000: 27) One of the militants' most famous victims is the Egyptian writer Farag Foda, murdered by extremists in 1992, after the thoroughly establishment *sheikhs* of al Azhar had condemned his writing. Another is Nasr Hamid Abu Zaid, hounded from his country by the same coalition of violent militants and reactionary *ulama*. He has said 'I advise the president [of Egypt] to push forward the intellectual battle [against the fundamentalists].' (quoted in Bassam 1998: xi) Any intellectual discussion of the role of political Islam is a form of intellectual combat, and censorship is the Islamists' first and most effective line of defence. One of the greatest misfortunes of recent decades is that some governments that are avowedly hostile to Islamist extremism, such as the Egyptian government, join hands with their supposed adversaries in enforcing this censorship—one example among many of the tacit collusion of enemies.

The degradation of intellectual discourse about Islam is profoundly destructive. It deters serious scholarship and fragments the intellectual community. To cite Ebrahim Moosa again,

Proponents of radical Islam argue that the intellectual pursuit of Islam, especially in non-traditional institutions such as universities and colleges, is a new form of Orientalism. Those who advocate the reconstruction of Islam, such as Fazlur Rahman, are in particular singled out as being subversive. The paranoia is pervasive. The valuable books that both insiders and outsiders write mainly in Western languages hardly make it to the shelves of the intelligentsia of the Muslim world. If these ideas do reach those shores they appear in the form of banned or restricted literature and can hardly be acknowledged since their contents may to be too explosive to be tried out in a living social laboratory. It is also true that only a handful of Islamicists working in the West read the works of their counterparts in the Muslim world, especially those written in indigenous languages. (Moosa 2000: 27)

With its disabled intellectual immune system, political Islam is highly dependent on striking fear into its critics, whether they are 'outside' scholars or 'insiders' from within the Muslim community itself. This is as true of the 'moderate' neo-fundamentalists as of the militant jihadists. Reformist Muslim scholars argue: 'The toleration of unorthodoxy and dissent is vital for the spiritual and intellectual benefit of Islam itself.' (An-Na'im

1990: 184) It is also essential for the reinvigoration of the political life of Muslim countries.

Studying the Muslim Brothers' political theory requires analysis at two completely different levels: at a high, abstract philosophical level, and at the level of practice in communities, student organisations, professional associations and voluntary agencies. The pivotal case for the theory and practice of Islamism is Egypt. Chapter 2, which is concerned with the intellectual, social and political conditions that have produced a theory and practice of *jihad*, is of necessity concerned in large part with the Egyptian Muslim Brothers. Egypt's intellectual, social and political dominance in the Arab world, and its powerful influence over political Islam in north-east Africa, mean that this focus is inescapable. However, Egypt is also the exceptional case, whose lessons do not transfer to other countries. Egyptian Islamism has a universal aspiration that is not matched in Sudan or other predominantly Muslim countries in Africa.

A proper study of political Islam in Egypt is beyond the scope of this book. Rather, our goal here is to situate the goals of the Islamist struggle in Egypt and the means to achieve that goal in the context of the 'political imagination'. This is an imprecise concept, located at the point where political theory meets popular culture and elite discourse. It refers to the motivating ideas in a political culture, which arise from these different sources and which are made salient by the prevailing political environment. Our conclusion is that, since the execution of Sayyid Qutb in 1966, the theorisation of political Islam in Egypt has remained stuck. One reason why this is so important is that Qutb leaves unresolved the question of how the Islamic state is to be achieved, excepting by *jihad*, and moreover, his theorisation of *jihad* is extremely superficial. Over the succeeding decades, owing to state repression and the increasingly restrictive public debate on political affairs, Egyptian Islamism has merely developed variant tactics for responding to the immediate dilemma of its illegality alongside the legitimacy deriving from popular Islam and community-level programmes. One of these tactics has been incremental embrace of state and civil organisations, another has been violent *jihad*. Neither of these approaches has resolved the Islamists' impasse or addressed the paralysis of the Egyptian state.

If we are to seek an Islamist political theory grounded in historical realities, we must look either to Iran—where Shi'a Islamism has had a rather different political manifestation—or to Sudan. In the latter case, we seem at first to have a different picture. For almost four decades the dominant figure in Sudanese Islamism has been Hassan al Turabi, who is responsible

both for a theoretical Islamist revolution (El-Affendi 1991a) and for helping stage a successful coup d'état. In contrast to the Egyptian brethren,
Turabi has both a theory and a practice of politics, manifest in his writings and career and culminating in the programmes of 'Islamic social
planning' and 'comprehensive *da'wa*'. But this project also has fatal weaknesses, and once again we see jihadist violence as symptomatic of both
ideological impasse and political failure. Many studies of Islamism neglect the Sudanese experience: chapter 3 demonstrates that as well as
being significant in its own right, the Sudanese case has far-reaching theoretical importance for understanding political Islam. There is, fortu-
nately, more of a real intellectual debate on Islamism in Sudan. But again,
we see that the Islamists have managed to dominate the high ground,
both by moralism and through intimidation.

Africa has a limited role in the Islamist political imagination. If Islamist theorising about Islam is 'Orientalist', its theorising about Africa is
similarly essentialist, marked by stereotypes, often derogatory, about African cultures and traditional religions. Arab Islamists' 'discovery' of African Muslims is a theme in several chapters. Meanwhile African Islamists'
encounter with their Arab brethren has been uneasy, marked by misunderstandings and conflicts of motives, and in some cases descending into
outright conflict. The split in the Sudanese Islamists is one case, and the
difficulties faced by Arab Islamists in penetrating and co-opting Somali
Islamism is another. We can narrate the frictions of these encounters, but
Islamists as yet lack the theoretical apparatus to analyse them. This is a
striking example of how the domination of Muslims' political imagination by a sterile neo-fundamentalism is depriving African societies of the
means to discuss their crises and their responses. But again, paradoxically,
the Islamist worldview strikes a chord in a world dominated by American
military, economic and cultural power, in which the life chances of hundreds of millions of Muslims are arid and constrained.

Writing current history

Writing contemporary history poses many challenges, including choice
of analytical frameworks and sources (Ellis 2002). This book tries to syn-
thesise a range of materials, in different languages and from different
sources, to try and provide an overview of the trajectories of political
Islam in north-east Africa in the last decade. This is an exercise that inevi-
tably leads to an uneven coverage, both geographically and thematically.
It also raises methodological issues. One of the starkest of these is a reli-

ance on unattributable sources for key points in the narrative, especially in chapter 6. Much of the history of the regional conflict of the 1990s remains unwritten. Contemporary newspapers are unreliable sources, most of the archives of the governments remain secret or do not exist at all, some of the key participants are dead or incommunicado, and few have written any memoirs of the period. On the grounds that it is better to record something, albeit incomplete and contested, than leave important events and processes in complete darkness, a narrative has been compiled that leaves many of its sources unnamed. This is partly a challenge for others to explore these events in greater detail. Perhaps some of the evidence that comes to light will mean that the accepted narrative of these events needs to be radically changed.

The story of the Islamist project and its adversaries is not finished. It is hazardous to write a narrative while events are still unfolding, but it is a risk worth taking. The reaction to the atrocities of September 11 and the American 'war on terrorism' have already had important consequences throughout north-east Africa. It spurred the Sudanese peace process out of its slumber. The Lord's Resistance Army, classified as a 'terrorist organisation' by the United States in December 1999, lost its Sudanese sponsorship in consequence, and briefly looked as if it might be defeated. The al Qa'ida attack also provoked renewed US interest in Somalia, manifest in the closure of the international operations of al Barakaat, Somalia's largest company.

More widely the cult of Usama bin Laden and the repercussions of America's 'war on terrorism' have magnetised the question of political Islam in dramatic new ways. As a token, global *jihad* is now fixed in the political imagination. Usama's spectacular act of terrorism, and his rhetoric that pits the dispossessed Muslim world against America and its puppets, resonate across much of Africa and the Middle East (cf. Doran 2002: 41). In one hospital in Kano, northern Nigeria, 70% of the baby boys born in the last months of 2001 were given the name 'Usama'.[1] After September 11 there were street celebrations in many northern Nigerian cities, and T-shirts bearing pictures of Usama bin Laden sold quickly. It is unlikely that the people of Kano would welcome Usama as their *amir*. But, in the context of domestic power struggles configured around the issue of Islam, support for Usama's attack on America has become a focus for expressing popular opposition to President Olusegun Obasanjo and his highly pro-US policies. While global Islamism is refracted into

[1] BBC, World Service News, Africa, 'Osama baby craze hits Nigeria', 3 January 2002.

local politics, one of the lessons of al Qa'ida is that local political grievances can have much wider repercussions.

The struggle between militant Islam and its enemies has entered a new
phase, making new demands on the peoples of the Horn of Africa and
their leaders. In this context, a vigorous and informed debate on the
events of the recent past and their significance can contribute to facing
the future.

2

ON THE FAILURE AND PERSISTENCE
OF *JIHAD*

A. H. Abdel Salam and Alex de Waal

Political Islam, like all social and political projects, is shaped by circumstance and adversity. Insofar as *jihad* is an integral part of Islamist theory and practice, it too is a product of its time. Has political Islam failed, as influential writers have argued? (Roy 1999, Kepel 2002) Certainly, the project of building Islamic states and societies in north-east Africa has not succeeded. Despite the vision of its advocates, that Islamism is a vibrant alternative, with the potential to promote democracy and civil society, contributing a comprehensive and humane vision that mixes private enterprise, community and social welfare, the record of its 'big project' has ultimately been one of failure. And this failure is eroding the gains of its 'little projects'. Our analysis is that neither modernist Islamism nor its 'neo-fundamentalist' successors have moved beyond snatching micro-remedies to small-scale problems to being able to construct a coherent political programme for a country.

But two caveats are in order. The first is that Islamism's enemies in the region have also failed. Authoritarian patrimonial states such as Egypt have nothing to offer. The radical militarised left that took power in many African countries between 1986 and 1997 briefly offered an energetic alternative, but also failed, descending into a series of wars. The second is that time has moved on, and in a world dominated by US power in which poor countries in Africa and the Middle East have little or no latitude for developing their own authentic social and political agendas, Islamism too is fated to take on new forms. Undoubtedly, new variants of political Islam will continue to appeal to Muslims, especially the young and marginalised. They will translate into political agendas of resisting a global order that is currently offering them nothing.

21

A similar argument applies to violent *jihad* as a means of enacting political change. As a method of building a real Islamic state and society in a
real country, *jihad* has exhausted itself. The pure Islamist theory of transcendental struggle and divinely sanctioned violence to achieve the Kingdom of God is theoretically bankrupt and politically impossible. The
north-east African *jihads* of the 1990s did not defeat their enemies, including the Egyptian state and the secular regimes of north-east Africa—
though it did help to exhaust them. But, as erstwhile practical projects in
Africa and the Middle East, such as achieving democracy and development, recede into the indefinite future, heroic resistance to an oppressive
world order becomes more meaningful. Now the Islamists' overriding
enemy is the United States, and jihadism is undergoing another muta-
tion. If prospects for worldly success are vanishing, then victory can be
redefined to mean escalating the struggle against the ungodly and martyrdom in the path of God.

The ambiguity of the jihadist impasse is captured by Hassan al Turabi's
apologia for the crimes of September 11. (al Turabi 2002) Turabi is a lawyer, but his analysis of al Qa'ida's attack on America studiously excludes
any reference to international humanitarian law. The destruction of the
World Trade Center and the crash on the Pentagon were, he concedes,
crimes, in which an excessive number of civilians were killed. But Turabi
argues that Usama bin Laden's attack on the symbols of American power
was well-justified, and that the US retaliation in Afghanistan is a greater
crime. The argument fails to rise above this level of the justification of
rage, and the iteration of who is responsible for what. It reflects the rage
and despair of his followers.

This chapter examines the practice and theory of *jihad*. It develops a
narrative that locates *jihad* within various liberation struggles and inter-
state wars in North Africa and the Middle East, the organisational practice of the Muslim Brothers and other Islamists (and their adversaries),
militant Islam as a youth movement, and the development of Islamist
political philosophy. It has a major focus on Egypt, a country that is at
once pivotal for any analysis of Islamism, and exceptional in many
respects. One of Egypt's exceptional characteristics is the universalism of
its political philosophers, which both broadens their appeal and limits
their practical relevance to other Muslim countries. Egyptian-led and -in-
spired jihadism has been present in Sudan and elsewhere in the Horn.
Another focus of Islamist practice is Saudi Arabia. The puritan Wahhabi
Islam of Saudi Arabia is intellectually impoverished in comparison with
Egypt's rich tradition of Islamist thinking, but it has lavishly exported its

particular brand of Salafi fundamentalism. In Africa, Saudi influence is mediated through philanthropic organisations, some of which also have contributed to militant jihadism.

Despite the a-historical essentialism of its thinkers, Islamist history and philosophy are intertwined. Among Islamist ideologues, Sayyid Qutb has gone furthest in encouraging his intellectual biographers to interpret his writing through the lens of his personal experience. In his seminal book *Milestones*[1] he writes:

> The writer of these lines has spent forty years of his life with books and research on almost all aspects of human knowledge. He specialized in some branches of knowledge and studied others due to personal interest. Then he returned to the fountainhead of his faith. He came to feel that whatever he had read was as nothing in comparison to what he found here. He does not regret spending forty years of his life in pursuit of these sciences, because he came to know well the nature of *jahiliyyah*, its deviations, its errors, and its ignorance, as well as its pomp and noise, and its arrogant and boastful claims. Finally he was convinced that a Muslim cannot combine these two sources—the source of Divine guidance and the source of *jahiliyyah*—for his education. (Qutb 1990: 96)

This is helpful to understanding Qutb. It is also important to know that Qutb was imprisoned by Gamal Abdel Nasser for a decade and tortured, an experience which must have radicalised him. *Milestones* was written in prison, and much of Qutb's writing can only be understood in the context of political and ideological competition with Nasser's pan-Arabism. (Abu Zaid 1992) One reason for the power of Qutb's writing is the modern language that he uses, in contrast with most of the Islamist writers but in common with his Nasserite opponents. But, as Charles Tripp has warned, we must also interpret Qutb's writing in its own terms (Tripp 1994). Since his execution in 1966, Qutb's ideas have had a powerful autonomous influence. Similarly, in this chapter we seek to draft an intellectual genealogy of contemporary *jihad*, using the framework of Muslim experience and Islamist agendas, and their encounters with their adversaries and one-time allies.

The dialectics of jihad

Militant Islamism and its neo-fundamentalist offspring have been incubated by war. Contemporary *jihad* is the sorcerer's apprentice of the wars that have afflicted the Middle East and the Horn of Africa for as long as

---

[1] *Ma'alim fi al Tariq*, also translated as 'Signposts on the Road'.

the historian cares to examine. Moreover, these wars have become more intense and bloody in recent history, and for most countries they have become part of what constitutes 'normality'. Even in countries at peace, there is a pervasive culture of militarism, brought about in part by the values imparted by military governments. One of the threads running through this chapter is the argument that war has its own logic, that the fear, abuse and violence associated with militarism and war have distorted political processes and even political theory itself. The Society of Muslim Brothers, founded by Hassan al Banna in 1928, was a rival to the totalising ideologies of fascism and communism. The continuing violent occupation of Palestine has been a festering sore in the Arab political consciousness, leaving a perennially uncompleted agenda of national liberation. Nasser's concentration camps were the living manifestation of what Qutb described as *jahiliyya*—perhaps best translated as 'pre-Islamic barbarism'. A partial list of wars includes the Arab-Israeli wars, the Ethio-Somali wars, the Sudanese civil wars, the Eritrean war of liberation, the Afghan *jihad*, the Iran-Iraq war, the 1990–1 Gulf War, the Algerian wars, and the battles between American Special Forces and Somali militias in Mogadishu. Given that Islamism aspires to regulate all aspects of human behaviour, it is unsurprising that Islamists should require a theory of war. And arguably political Islam is simply more frank than liberal political theory in recognising the centrality of violence to political process.

Muslim scholars vigorously debate the true meaning of '*jihad*'. Its literal meaning is 'struggle', and many academic writers contend that *jihad* should be interpreted as non-violent struggle in the path of God. From many examples, we can single out Abdel Aziz Sachedina: 'In its Koranic usage [*jihad*] denotes a moral endeavor to work for peace with justice—a component of the quest for restorative, not purely retributive, justice.' (1996: 113) He and other writers point out that the Prophet Mohamed distinguished between the 'lesser' *jihad* (fighting Islam's enemies on the battlefield) and the 'greater' *jihad* (striving for personal virtue) (cf. Fazlur Rahman 1982, Bassam Tibi 1998, Abou El Fadl 2000). *Jihad* is often used for social and political mobilisation, for example in literacy campaigns or by Ugandan Muslims in their efforts to overcome HIV/AIDS. (Badri 1997: 277) Islamic scholars have also distinguished between 'defensive' *jihad*, where an obligation to fight is imposed upon all Muslims, and 'offensive' *jihad*, which is a lesser duty on the political leadership. Among Islamists, Sayyid Qutb is the most prominent of those who have sought to reverse this order, and focus on *jihad* as *both* violent combat and personal purification. In *Milestones* Qutb famously dismissed those who would restrict *jihad* to 'defensive war' or 'solitary inner combat of the believer against temptation' as 'defeatists' (1990: 46–7). Qutb's theory of *jihad* has powerfully influenced a succession of militant Islamists, including Mohamed Abdel Salam Farag (who provided the justification for the assassination of Sadat), Abdalla Azzam (the Palestinian militant who joined the Afghan *mujahidiin* and first called for global *jihad*), Omer Abdel Rahman (leader of the Egyptian militant organisation al Gama'a al Islamiyya and convicted of 'inspiring' the 1993 bombing of the World Trade Center), Hassan al Turabi (*sheikh* of the Sudanese Islamists), and Usama bin Laden.

Our purpose in this chapter is not to decide whether it is 'correct' that the Qur'an calls for violent *jihad* or not, but rather to chart how concepts have evolved in the last half century. In fact, we shall see that the most significant concepts of *jihad* have been poorly theorised, or not theorised at all. Unlike the scholars of Islam who write their learned books from universities, the practitioners of *jihad* usually write, if at all, in response to pressing circumstance. Sayyid Qutb is virtually the only one to have written a truly philosophical essay, which he did from the hospital wing of a prison. Hence we must deduce the theory of *jihad* from its practice as well as the writings of its advocates. Modern Islamists' approach to *jihad* has emerged and been transformed over the eighty years since the abolition of the Ottoman Caliphate. For most of the period we can see shifting and uncertain coalitions between emergent political Islam and secular liberationist ideologies, with the latter dominant most of the time. Only in the 1980s did the Islamists take the ideological and political lead, and appropriate the *jihad* concept exclusively for themselves, and in the last decade we can see variant Islamist concepts of *jihad* in operation.

Before the 20th century '*jihad*' had a range of uses. At different times it encompassed reformist struggle and both defensive and offensive war. The *jihads* of the Prophet and his successors were against non-Muslim peoples and empires. The medieval scholar Taqi el Din Ibn Taimiyya, who grew up in the aftermath of the Mongol devastation of Baghdad, introduced the important innovation that *jihad* could be conducted against an ungodly ruler who was nominally Muslim. This remained a concern for historians only until the transformation of the Muslim political world in the aftermath of the First World War.

Despite its political decline and unpopularity, the *khilafa* remained a symbol of the spiritual unity of Muslims and a source of legitimacy in the political sphere. (Haider 1996: 55) Its abolition by Kemal Ataturk in 1924 was the culmination of a crisis of political legitimacy throughout the Arab and Muslim world, which had been set in train by Napoleon's conquest of Egypt. Modernist Islamic revivalism, led by the Salafi reformers, notably Jamal al Din al Afghani, Mohamed Abduh and Rashid Rida, paralleled this political crisis. Theirs was a modernising, anti-imperial ideology of Islam, seeking justification for political independence in the first generation of Muslims (the Salafa). They neither theorised nor advocated violent *jihad*.

Egypt's first nationalist uprising took place in 1919. Its leaders spoke of '*jihad*', but a cursory examination shows that the concept was used in a wholly secular manner. Saad Zaghlul's Wafd party was described by the British as having a 'Bolshevik tendency' and commanding the 'sympathy of all classes and creeds'. (Fromkin 1989: 419) Copts and Muslims alike— including priests and Imams—demonstrated under the banner 'Long Live the Unity of Cross and Crescent!' The strikers and rebels called themselves '*mujahidiin*' without offending any Christian sensitivities.

Nine years later, the modern Islamist movement was initiated by the Egyptian schoolteacher Hassan al Banna. The Society of Muslim Brothers was a remarkable innovation: the usurpation of moral authority by a freelance activist with a Sufi background and no formal qualifications as a member of the *ulama* (scholars of Islamic doctrine and law). Within a few years, the Muslim Brothers had developed into a major social and political force in Egypt. Al Banna's innovation, and the theory and practice of *jihad*, have to be seen in the context of the abolition of the Ottoman Caliphate and the ensuing void of political legitimacy. For the first time since the age of the Prophet, Islam became a stateless religion. Moreover this coincided with overt European military and political domination and the settlement of Jews in Palestine. Arab Muslims were now face-to-face with the reality of domination by European powers that had no claim on legitimate Islamic succession. As Karen Armstrong (2000) has argued, religious fundamentalisms have developed as a response to the challenges of modernity. Armstrong's thesis focuses on the way in which the power of scientific rationalism has challenged the ambitions of revealed religion to provide a comprehensive world-view. Fundamentalism springs from attempts to provide literal cause-and-effect explanations that can compete with science for 'objective truth' rather than providing mythological coherence. There is a tradition of scientism in Islamic fundamentalism,[2] but more pertinent to our concern here, the triumph of the (Western) secular state, and its military, organisational, legal and edu-

---

[2] It is generally called 'Bucailleism' (Golden 2002). This holds that the Koran anticipates modern scientific findings, thereby demonstrating not only the compatibility of Islam and science, but also the fact that the Holy Book could only have been revealed by God.

cational frameworks, similarly threw down a gauntlet to religions that espouse a socio-political order. In pre-modern days, the literal reading of the social order envisioned by the Holy Book was not a meaningful exercise, but when a secular imperial power administers a society with unprecedented effectiveness using rule books, some devout religious thinkers are challenged to interpret their own texts so as to provide answers to *every* human and social condition.

It is within this context that we must see the development of proposals and movements for reconstituting Islamic authority. The abolition of the *khilafa* and the creation of the Muslim Brothers marked a redefinition of the extent of obligation on individual Muslims. (El-Affendi 1991b: 83–5) Hitherto, duties such as establishing the state and protecting the faith fell on *ahl al hal wal aqd* ('men of authority'), thereby absolving others from actively pursuing these goals. Ethical guidance was provided by the *sheikhs* of al Azhar, the highest religious authority in the Sunni world. Now, freelance activism such as that initiated by Hassan al Banna redefined the obligation of *all* Muslims to struggle for these goals.[3]

Al Banna did not theorise *jihad*. His key contribution was to provide an example of Islamist political mobilisation. This had militaristic elements, such as the Scouts, which resembled the youth wings of fascist and communist parties in Europe (Commins 1994: 146), and the 'Special Apparatus', which was involved in violent acts such as assassinations and which set up an underground network that could survive state repression. The organisational structure of the Muslim Brothers had distinctly Islamist elements, such as its reliance on the charisma of the *murshid* (guide) and the *bay'a* (oath of loyalty) given by members. But in most respects it was a thoroughly pragmatic model of organisation that proved both durable and adaptable.

The first instances of violence instigated by modern Islamists occurred when the Muslim Brothers mounted a campaign of violence against the British occupation of Egypt in the late 1940s. The 'Special Apparatus' assassinated British army officers and Egyptian government officials, sparking off a spiral of repression and retribution that culminated in the closure of the Society in 1948 and the assassination of al Banna himself in February 1949.[4] Egyptians had practised political assassination as a

---

[3] There are intriguing parallels with the 1920–2 protests in India, led by Mahatma Gandhi, which involved both Hindus and Muslims, and which were motivated in part by religious sensibilities and Muslim shock at the dismantling of the power of the Caliphate (see Akbar 2002: 175–6). The vital role of south Asian Islamism will not be discussed here.

[4] Al Banna's views on violence are uncertain and controversial. Before he died he publicly

moderator of tyranny for some time: this was the first occasion on which the Islamists had tried it. At this stage, however, it was not given a specifically Islamist justification. Along with most other nationalists, the Muslim Brothers welcomed the 1952 coup, and co-operated with the Free Officers. However, this cohabitation proved to be short-lived. Following a plot to assassinate Nasser in 1954, the leaders of the Muslim Brothers were arrested and the organisation was banned. It became both actor and victim in a cycle of violence and repression, with thousands of its members imprisoned and tortured. Sayyid Qutb was one of these: he was released, re-arrested and then executed in 1966. The cycle of political violence, repression, detention, selective execution, negotiation with the government and release, has become familiar in modern Egypt. The different strands of contemporary Egyptian Islamism—the gradualist Muslim Brothers and the violent jihadist groups—are still grappling with the question of how to deal with a powerful repressive state whose power base lies in the army. In this context, the Qutbist idea of extending the realm of *jahiliyya* to include states ruled by self-avowed Muslims becomes critically important. To make a parallel with neo-Marxism, Qutb was the first *anti-neo-colonialist* Islamist philosopher.

Returning to the Muslim world's anti-colonial struggles, the Algerian war of liberation demonstrates the convergence of the agendas of Islamist and secular anti-imperialism. The FLN's struggle against the French was the prototypical African nationalist liberation struggle. When the insurrection was launched in 1954, the use of the word *jihad* to describe a movement of national liberation was unproblematic. It tapped into the legitimacy provided by the Algerian tradition of resistance to the French over the previous century. (Laremont 2000) The French policies of cultural imperialism meant that Arabism and Islam were readily pressed into service as components of resistance ideology, even though Algeria's most prominent Muslim leaders came rather late to the struggle. The FLN fighters were known as *mujahidiin*, and its journal was entitled *El-Moudjahid*, though its articles' orientation was overwhelmingly leftist-third worldist. The FLN's seminal political thinker Ramdane Abane, '[b]eing himself neither a Marxist-Leninist nor a devout Muslim theologian, wanted the F.L.N. to fill a critical void by adapting its own ideology to embrace both creeds without being committed to either.' (Horne 1977: 133) On the other hand Houari Boumedienne, who subsequently became

---

disavowed the killings and condemned their perpetrators as neither Brothers nor Muslims. Many believe that this statement was made under pressure from his interrogators.

president, had no difficulty in being simultaneously an 'Islamic socialist' and an adherent of Frantz Fanon. The nationalist-Islamist alliance was forged partly by the ferocity of the French counter-insurgency, and partly by the Algerians' abandonment by the French Communist Party, which ruled itself largely irrelevant by insisting that the national contradiction was secondary to the class contradiction—i.e. liberation could only follow a successful proletarian revolution in France. Subsequent attempts to retrospectively 'Islamise' the war of liberation tell us more about the struggle for political legitimacy in contemporary Algeria than about the ideology of the independence war itself. (Kepel 2002: 172)

The Algerian liberation war is also a nexus at which we can examine the confluence of Islamism and secular liberation ideology. The FLN borrowed organisationally from the French Resistance, Marxist-Leninism and the Viet Minh. This convergence is also evident in Franz Fanon's writing on violence, which developed from classic Marxist revolutionary violence to an incompletely-theorised but compelling idea of violence as personal and collective liberation during the war. In *The Wretched of the Earth*, Fanon wrote that for colonised people, violence 'invests their characters with positive and creative qualities' and 'At the level of individuals, violence is a cleansing force.' (Fanon 1967: 73, 74) Fanon's writing on violence is often opaque and his methodology confused—perhaps why his influence has been so broad, ranging from the Iranian Islamist Ali Shari'ati to Hutu Power advocates in Rwanda. His account has clear parallels with Qutb's theory of *jihad*, and indeed has been called 'holy violence' by one biographer. (Perinham 1982)

For almost a century the Palestinian struggle for self-determination has been the central event in the Arab world. More than anything else, this injustice has shaped (or perhaps, confined) the Arab political imagination. The betrayal of the Palestinians by the British and then by a succession of Arab leaders has justifiably contributed to the dominant school of political theory in the Arab world that attributes causation to conspiracy plus force of arms. Palestinian nationalism has been led by secularists and, with few exceptions, until the rise of the Islamist Palestinian organisations in the 1980s, this was not described as a *jihad* but rather as a nationalist struggle. The Mufti of Jerusalem, Hajj Amin el Husseini, was an opportunist and never an Islamist. Yasser Arafat has been secularist throughout his long career. The leftist Popular Front for the Liberation of Palestine, led by George Habbash, initiated international terrorist spectaculars by hijacking aeroplanes in the late 1960s. (Chaliand 1985: 77) The presence of the state of Israel in Palestine, and the crucial supportive

role played by the United States, have subsequently enabled Islamist militants to label their struggle a defensive *jihad*, thereby increasing the obligations on all Muslims to join or support the fight against Israel and its
allies.

Sayyid Qutb and the theorisation of jihad

All the conflicts mentioned above were rooted in particular national predicaments. In each case, the political strategies and ideological justifica-
tions followed from the practicalities of mobilising resistance. On some
occasions, the struggle was called '*jihad*'. On other, comparable occasions,
jihad was *not* invoked. An example is the early years of the Eritrean
nationalist struggle, which was led mostly by Muslims, some of whom
had close links with Arab nationalists. (Eyob 1995) However, with the
publication of Qutb's *Milestones* in 1964, the Islamists for the first time
had a universal manifesto for *jihad* and a theorisation of why national liberation was not enough. Sayyid Qutb is single-handedly responsible for
the Islamist re-theorisation of *jihad* as a central element in the struggle for
an Islamic order.

Of all Islamists Qutb's writing is the most direct and accessible. *Jihad* is
both practical and transcendental: 'It is a movement to wipe out tyranny
and to introduce true freedom to mankind, using resources practically
available in a given human situation, and it had definite stages, for each
of which it utilized new methods.' (1990: 50) 'True freedom' for Qutb is a
situation in which all barriers to the embrace of Islam by all humanity
have been destroyed. He agrees with more pacific Islamists that Islam's
first and preferred option is preaching and exposition (*da'wa*). But when
obstacles are put in the way of Islam, 'it has no recourse but to remove
them by force so when it is addressed to peoples' hearts and minds, they
are free to accept or reject it with open minds.' (p. 51) This removal by
force is *jihad*, in Qutb's revolutionary sense. He scorned those who failed
to see this:

When writers with defeatist and apologetic mentalities write about 'jihad in
Islam' and try to remove this 'blot' from Islam, they mix up two things: first, this
din [faith] forbids the imposition of its belief by force, as is clear from the verse:
'There is no compulsion in religion.' Secondly, it tries to annihilate all those political and material powers that stand between people and Islam, which forces some
people to bow before other people and prevent them from accepting the sovereignty of Allah. These two principles are independent of each other, and there is
no justification for mixing them up. These defeatists, however, mix the two
aspects confining jihad to what today is called 'defensive war' (pp. 46–7).

Among other things, Qutb is taking *jihad* out of political or historical context, and creating it as a universal. This is a fascinating and important example of the impact of a pure idea on political life: these universalised components of Qutb's *'jihad'* have since become the foundation of the 'global' *jihad* of a succeeding generation. With *Milestones*, militant Islamists located a route from the imperfect *jahili* present to the perfect future. An act of *jihad* is simultaneously a blow against tyranny and the fulfilment of a transcendental duty. While the *mujahid* is obliged to utilise all means practically available, the outcome lies with God alone. As Olivier Roy explains, 'There is no "obligation to produce a result" in *jihad*: it is an affair between the believer and God and not [only] between the *mujahid* and his enemy.' (1999: 66) This can serve as a rationalisation of futility: 'The shade of swords is not an invitation to kill, it is an invitation to die.' (Akbar 2002: xv) This concept fills an important void in Islamist political theory, which, as we shall examine below, lacks a political science. The new meaning Qutb gave to *jihad* has important implications. One of the abiding theoretical problems with the idea of the Islamic state is the paradox that, on the one hand, Muslims can only achieve virtue if they live in an Islamic state governed by the *shari'a*, while on the other hand, *shari'a* and an Islamic state are possible only if there is a community of virtuous Muslims already in existence. Qutb indicates that the effort to achieve personal virtue is the same struggle as to achieve the Islamic state. The two are to be achieved simultaneously.

Qutb enjoins Muslims to respond to the practicalities of circumstance. And jihadists have been supremely practical, grafting *jihad* on to a variety of causes. But the utopianism of Qutb's aims and the concluding pages of *Milestones*—which are concerned with the Muslim's unconcern for outcomes, these being in the hands of God—make for a tempting interpretation that *jihad* needs *no* political strategy, only faith. Putting the Qutbist theory of *jihad* into practice is both enticingly simple—it requires just one or three devout *mujahidiin*—and quite impossible. It is evident how those whose only battleground is the theatre of mass terrorism can justify their crimes with reference to Qutb.

Sayyid Qutb's theory of *jihad* may make sense within the transcendental logic of Islamism. Does it make sense as a strategy for fighting a war or overthrowing a government? War dictates and follows its own logic: it is a mode of action and organisation apart from those of civil politics. Clausewitz famously noted that war tends to the absolute and described the various processes whereby this happens (Clausewitz 1968). Having embarked upon war, a state will progressively call upon all available resources in pursuit of victory. Clausewitz was concerned mainly with the material aspects of this process of escalation, involving greater human mobilisation, greater spending, greater technology, a broader battlefield and wider alliances. But ideological escalation is also commonplace during war. As conflicts continue, war aims tend to inflate. Additional claims are made to prove the correctness of the cause, the enemy is more horribly demonised, and more ideological sanctions are invoked to justify the sacrifices made. God usually figures on both sides of any protracted war. Meanwhile, war-thinking displaces the rationales of civil politics and normal human decision making, creating a new and sometimes mystical psychology in which human beings are means rather than ends, and victory at any cost becomes the ultimate goal. (Grossman 1995, LeShan 2002)

It has been fashionable to decry Clausewitz as relevant only to 'old' inter-state wars. (Van Crefeld 1991) Much of his analysis is indeed rooted in a nineteenth century realist school of international statecraft. His dictum that 'war is the continuation of politics by other means' meant, in the context of his time, that war was the continuation of inter-state struggles for supremacy or survival. But the logic of conflict that Clausewitz identified transfers remarkably well to 'new' or irregular wars (Kaldor 1999). This was acknowledged by none other than Mao Zedong, who approvingly cited Clausewitz's observation that 'every period must have its independent theory of war' (Mao Tse-Tung 2000: 49). In recent internal wars, war can be a continuation of economics and commerce by other means (Keen 1998, 2000; Berdal and Malone 2000) and a continuation of social and political policy by other means, by insurgents as well as governments (de Waal 1997b). For nationalist *jihad* Clausewitzean logic remains intact. In the Algerian or Palestinian struggles for independence, the invocation of religious legitimacy has served as a tool for mobilising support and justifying sacrifice. In Sudan and Algeria in the 1990s *jihad* again became part of this mundane, instrumental logic of violence.

Does Qutb's transcendental *jihad* differ from secular war? Qutb certainly believed so: 'The Islamic jihad has no relationship to modern warfare, either in its causes or in the way in which it is conducted.' (p. 47) But that perhaps betrays Qutb's failure to analyse contemporary wars. Mysticism and illogic have characterised the decision-making of many secular war-makers. Military psychologists have long puzzled over the fact that some men and women *enjoy* war. Lawrence LeShan (2002), for example, argues that engaging in war allows individuals to simultaneously fulfil their needs to gain individual meaning for their lives, and also be part of a larger entity. He argues that 'war is most typically an assertion of self-transcending drives' (p. 84). Dave Grossman (1995) analyses how difficult it is to train men to kill, and notes the far-reaching behavioural implications once this conditioning has been achieved.

Virtually no wars have yielded the outcomes expected by those who initiated them: *all* major wars defy the sober logic of comparing costs and outcomes. (Kolko 1994) Much literature demonstrates how those who initiate wars rarely if ever envision their actual results, how military decisions are made on poor information and flawed analysis, and how governments often persist in failed policies long after their inadequacies have become clear. (Tuchman 1984) For example, Gabriel Kolko's study of the twentieth century's greatest wars concludes: 'When Europe's rulers embarked so casually upon war [in 1914], few among them even remotely imagined the compounding difficulties and challenges they would encounter.' (1994: 106) He argues that they simply did not possess the command of facts and analysis that would have allowed them to predict the disastrous outcomes of their decisions, notably the extent to which embarking upon a foreign war would entail massive domestic social upheavals. 'To anticipate all those factors that decide the results of war would have required an analytic clarity and honesty that political and military leaders rarely possess, and even when useful knowledge and intelligence existed, precisely because it often revealed unfavorable conditions for attaining victory at acceptable costs, the career-oriented men who run states preferred to ignore it.' (p. 20) Kolko was referring to rulers and generals schooled in Clausewitz and other theoreticians of war. How much more does this myopia and flawed political logic apply to Islamists, who scorn the study of social and political science?

If we turn to guerrilla war, we find that it demands a quasi-mystical belief in the power of violence, enacted by a few individuals, to enact grand political change. (Laqueur 1977: 23, 126–7) How else would a small band of guerrillas in the forests of Bolivia or Congo explain that their cause is not hopeless? Successful guerrilla forces have usually been led by individuals with remarkable charisma and stubbornness, who have persisted when all seems lost. Mao's Long March is the *locus classicus* of heroic refusal to admit defeat. In north-east Africa, most outside observers argued that the Eritrean struggle was doomed to oblivion at various points in the 1970s and '80s, but yet it managed to overcome its setbacks and eventually triumph in 1991. The National Resistance Army in Uganda in 1983 appeared to be facing certain defeat, but managed to survive and emerge victorious. Similar stories can be told for a number of other guerrilla struggles. Some have explicitly invoked traditional religious authority, to the extent of involving ancestral spirits directly in their struggle (e.g. Zimbabwe, see Lan 1985). One common factor in guerrillas' victories is that they manage to inflict sufficient political damage on the governments they are fighting that those regimes reach the point of internal collapse. Thus for example the Algerian FLN never controlled significant territory and was brought to the brink of military defeat by the French army, but still achieved all its war aims. Similarly, the Somali National Movement, decimated by the Somali army's counter-offensives in 1988, still managed to take power in north-western Somalia because of the implosion of the government in 1991. Mao and Che Guevara similarly theorised the guerrilla's best chance of success as wearing down the enemy to a point of exhaustion, whereupon victory could be seized by moving from the guerrilla phase of warfare to the conventional phase. (Mao 2000: 66–9, Guevara 1998: 13) Against these stories of victory, there are even more instances of failure: but it is the faint hope of ultimate triumph that sustains guerrillas in the bush. In short, the apparent irrationality of most guerrilla war-making has not stood in the way of its occasional ultimate success.

Where Qutb's transcendental *jihad* differs is that the mystical or irrational element is not a contributory factor to the struggle, but is its central component. At an elementary level, Qutb's *jihad* is undoubtedly the pursuit of a political aim (the Kingdom of God) through other means. But because the gap between action and outcome is so vast and can only be filled by divine intervention, Clausewitz's logic has become unrecognisable. In this context we can appreciate why Islamist *mujahidiin* seem to invert Trotsky's argument against terrorism:

If it suffices to arm oneself with a revolver in order to reach our goal, then to what end are the goals of the class struggle? If a pinch of powder and a slug of lead are enough to destroy the enemy, what need is there for a class organisation? If there is rhyme or reason in scaring titled personages with the noise of an explosion, what need is there for a party? (quoted in Laqueur 1977: 67–8)

The *jihad* of Qutb aspires to provide precisely the 'rhyme and reason' that the unbeliever Trotsky could not see. At the point of true *jihad*, it would appear, history stops: to borrow a term from physics, there is a 'singularity'. God Himself grants victory, and through Islam, consolidates it and achieves His sovereignty.

Pure *jihad* in Sayyid Qutb's sense is an abstraction, comparable to the 'absolute' war of Clausewitz. Subsequent to Qutb, we can identify three distinct poles of jihadist practice, with most manifestations consisting of a mixture. The first is nationalist *jihad*, as in Palestine. This retains an enduring imprint from leftist theories of revolutionary violence, guerrilla struggle and national liberation. Its principal contemporary practitioner, Hamas, is primarily a national liberation movement, and Islamist theorists (who are otherwise hostile to nationalism) have been careful to acknowledge that this is quite legitimate in the special context of Palestine. The second and third are variants of neo-fundamentalist *jihad*, militant manifestations of the anti-intellectual Islamist movements of the 1980s and '90s. They are hybrids of Qutb's 'absolute' *jihad* and the necessities of circumstance.

Neo-fundamentalism: discourse and power

During the 1950s and '60s, Islamism made practical and ideological compromises with third worldism. But the two diverged sharply in the 1970s. Nasser's defeat in the 1967 war and Black September in 1970 marked the secular nationalists' failure to win dignity for the Arab peoples. Anwar Sadat attributed his (relative) success in the 1973 war with Israel to the fact that he was the 'Believer President'. This was not declared a *jihad*, but it was an important step in the Islamisation of political discourse in the Arab world. The war was also the occasion for the Gulf states, including Saudi Arabia, to use the oil weapon, and the extraordinary flows of money to these countries transformed Islamism. Unimagined wealth in the hands of the pre-modern Saudi monarchy, wedded to its own conservative Salafism, brought a new dimension to political Islam.

Saudi Arabia's official Islam is the puritan fundamentalism of the school of Mohamed Ibn Abdel Wahab, the eighteenth-century conservative reformer. The Wahhabis are militant, their intolerance based on a reading of the medieval writer Ibn Taimiyya.[5] A hitherto obscure sect based among the Bedouin of the Arabian interior, the Saudis succeeded in conquering the Holy Places (with British assistance), establishing a dynastic state with no constitution other than the Qur'an, and through geological accident becoming grotesquely wealthy. Through this fortuity, an intellectual and spiritual backwater of Islam came to exercise a wholly disproportionate influence on the development of Islamism from Afghanistan to Nigeria to the Philippines. King Abdel Aziz al Saud was ready to use extremes of force in his subjugation of the Arabian peninsula and was violently intolerant of any Shi'a communities he overran, destroying

---

[5] Some scholars dispute this reading. For example, Fazlur Rahman argues that Ibn Taimiyya's basic precept was that Muslims must not under any circumstances kill other Muslims. (Fazlur Rahman 2000: 132, 161)

their mosques and tombs. Wahhabism is also strongly hostile to Sufism. His successors have developed what Said Aburish calls 'royal fundamentalism', assuming a litany of rather absurd titles including 'Guardian of the Holy Places' (Aburish 1997: 240–1, 359).[6] The term 'absolutism' might be more appropriate: Saudi rule is a reversion to, at best, early modern forms of despotism.

Wahhabism has subsequently become impaled on the contradiction that the avowedly Wahhabi state is famously corrupt and was only able to stay in power during the Gulf War courtesy of the American army. Saudi Arabia's Islamists are split between those (such as the Mufti, Sheikh Bin Baz) who support the regime, and those who condemn it for its violations of Salafi principle (such as Mohamed al Mas'ari, Safar al Hawali and Salman al Auda). Both camps are equally neo-fundamentalist. Earlier, in response to Nasser's alignment with the socialist bloc, the United States and Saudi Arabia sought to promote Islamism as a conservative alternative to nationalist pan-Arabism. The CIA's Miles Copeland has written of his search for a 'Muslim Billy Graham' to oppose Nasser.[7] (Aburish 1997: 325) At the time, this did not succeed, but Islamism's relationship to national liberation was becoming more profoundly ambivalent.

In passing, we can note that Islamism in Iran has followed a different trajectory. For a number of complex reasons that are beyond the scope of this chapter, Shi'a Islamism has been more strongly influenced by the rationalist philosophy that Qutb and other Sunni Islamists have so strongly rejected.[8] Ali Shari'ati, for example, can be characterised as a believer-leftist, and Ayatollah Khomeini placed constitutionalism higher than Islamic doctrine in the political affairs of the Iranian state. Islamist parties with ties to Iran, such as Hezbollah in Lebanon, have tended to retain this leftist-nationalist legacy, which has otherwise become rare in the Muslim world.

The divide between Islamism and national liberation was further deepened by the lack of any theorist of the stature of Sayyid Qutb who could follow in his footsteps. None have combined Qutb's simple and elegant style of writing and his ability to draw on rationalist philosophy

[6] Subsequently revised to 'Servant of the Holy Places'.
[7] The notion of 'good Islam' and 'bad Islam' subsequently influenced US policies after the downfall of the Shah of Iran (see Hunter 1998: 14).
[8] For example, while Shi'a jurisprudence includes the principle of reason, Sunni schools rely only on the principle of analogy. It is also intriguing to note that the pivotal figure of Salafi modernism, Jamal el Din al Afghani not only studied in the Shi'a colleges of Persia, but later concealed this fact (see Keddie 1994).

(while rejecting it as a discipline for his followers). Below, we shall examine the impasse in the Islamist movement created by the self-imposed limits on its intellectual scope and political imagination. Our key point here is the emergence of a reactionary Salafism as a guiding ideology within Islamism. Unlike the modernising late nineteenth-century Salafis, these reactionary Salafis refer to their sources in a generally uncritical and wholly unhistoricised manner. While the reformist Salafis used religious texts to re-think tradition, the new Salafis use argument from authority to impose dogma and brand dissent as deviance from 'true Islam'.

Each generation of Islamists has been shaped by its adversary. As Nasr Hamed Abu Zaid details, Qutb's *Milestones* is in significant part a direct challenge to secular Nasserism:

Qutb directly challenges the slogans of the 1960s regimes: 'Freedom, Socialism and [Arab] Unity.' With the exception of 'Freedom', Qutb's discourse aims to obliterate these slogans. He negates their legitimacy on the grounds that they are not derived from the belief in [Allah's] sovereignty. Socialism or social justice and unity are merely earthly tyrannies or idols that Islam came to destroy. [Quoting *Milestones* (Qutb 1990: 21)] 'It can therefore be said that Mohamed, peace be upon him, was capable of kindling among his compatriots the fire of Arab Nationalism, and could thus have united them. They would have responded gladly to his call, for they were weary of continual tribal warfare and blood feud. He might then have been able to free the Arab from the domination of Roman and Persian imperialism.' [p. 22:] 'It can be said that Mohamed was capable of starting a social movement, declaring war against the class of nobles and wealthy, and taking away their wealth and distributing it among the poor. But he did not do that....' (Abu Zaid 1992: 72–3)

Nasserism grew from a rich cultural and political heritage of secularism, modernism and pan-Arabism, and its greatest Islamist critic needed to match this impressive ideological arsenal. Much of Qutb is unoriginal—his central notions of sovereignty belonging to God are derived from Abu al A'la al Mawdudi—but his key writings are unusually compelling, sharing the energy and determined optimism of the Nasserites. The neo-fundamentalist generation, by contrast, has been up against regimes that are ideologically bankrupt and politically paralytic, which have embraced capitalism and consumerism, which have tried to use Islam to shore up perpetual autocracies, and which have been humiliated by Israel and America. It is easy for polemicists to inveigh against such bewildered and hypocritical adversaries. It is far harder to energise this moribund discourse into a positive political agenda.

The Islamist writers who followed Qutb established the terms of reference for neo-fundamentalism, although some of them warrant that label themselves. One of the most eminent is Yusuf al Qaradawi. A learned Islamist scholar, al Qaradawi argues for the repoliticisation of Islam, and the rejection of socialism, secularism and nationalism. (Al Qaradawi 1981, 1991) He has eloquently criticised 'extremist' and simplistic interpretations of Islam, stressed the legitimacy of disagreement, and proposed more flexible and subtle applications of Qur'anic principle. He has distinguished himself as a voice of moderation, for example attempting mediation in Algeria and in calling for the Taliban not to destroy the Buddhas of Bamiyan. But he holds that the misfortunes of the Middle East are attributable to the 'Western crusading spirit' and more recently he has justified suicide bombings. Ultimately, al Qaradawi's proposed solutions are formulaic. Thus his political philosophy is an attempt to reconcile the irreconcilable:

When we call for the resumption of a true Islamic lifestyle and the establishment of a truly Islamic society led by an Islamic state, we must recognize the fact that we live in a world in which human relations are interrelated and complex, ideologies are numerous, distances are shrinking and barriers are beginning to collapse. (1991: 116)

Seeking out Qur'anic justification for his every opinion, al Qaradawi resorts to rejecting 'imported solutions', espousing instead *al hall al Islami* ('the Islamic solution'). Such rejection of Westernism has become a hallmark of neo-fundamentalism. Intellectual honesty and recognition of complexity and diversity run into the limitations both of Islamist principle and Qur'anic citation and of the unmerciful realities of the Arab world. Al Qaradawi is on a slippery slope, and others have slid much further down it.

Another whose scholarship, wittingly or not, has become a charter for neo-fundamentalism is Mohamed Salim al 'Awwa. Al 'Awwa's influential book *The Political System of the Islamic State* went through many editions and revisions in the 1970s and '80s. Most of the book is a detailed critique of the failings of contemporary Muslim societies. Bassam Tibi comments:

After these preliminaries, the reader of al-'Awwa expects a clear description of the alleged Islamic system of government on which the new Islamic state is to be based. But what follows, in almost a hundred pages, is nothing but the fairly obligatory descriptive history of the formative years of Islam. The description, wrapped in modern terms, reveals conspicuously a great projection of modern legal rule into seventh-century Islam... The question of the character of the

Islamic state, which al-'Awwa's reader expects to be answered, remains open at the end of this not very engaging 422-page book. (1998: 161, 162)

In fact, the only thing we learn is the necessity of the unity of religion and the state, another hallmark of neo-fundamentalist dogma. Without much distortion, the writings of al Qaradawi and al 'Awwa can be distilled to into simplified mantras, to the effect that Islamic texts contain all the answers and the first Muslim generation is the model to be replicated. No method of intellectual exploration is encouraged, let alone taught. Hence it is unsurprising that, for rank and file Islamists, political manifestos consist of no more than a remorseless reassertion of the same simplistic formulae.

This is a template ideally suited for militant activists peddling dogma. A case in point is Taqi al Din al Nabhani, the founder of Hezb al Tahrir in 1953. His avowed aim was to establish an Islamic state on the ruins of existing regimes. He produced a detailed and exhaustive blueprint for such a state, drawing on models from Islamic history. It is a purely abstract model, and al Nabhani himself declared that he drafted it 'without paying any attention whatsoever to the sorry circumstances of Muslim societies, the conditions of other nations, or non-Islamic systems'. (Suha 1996: 40) As with al 'Awwa, political Islam is not to be judged by its relevance to solving the real problems facing Muslims, but rather Muslims are judged by their performance against the impossible standards of virtue demanded by an Islamic state. Suha Taji-Farouki notes, 'al-Nabhani wrenched out of context the institutions and practice of the historical Caliphate, construing these as timeless models of universal relevance' (p. 43).

Another neo-fundamentalist exemplar is Mohamed Abdel Salam Farag, theoretician for the group that assassinated Anwar Sadat. After the assassination, the Egyptian security forces confiscated and destroyed all the copies of Farag's pamphlet that they could find. Only ten copies survived. The pamphlet was subsequently studied by scholars including Rifat Sid Ahmed (1989) and Gilles Kepel (1993: 194 7). Farag was an electrician, self-taught in Islamism. He drew upon the writings of Taqi el Din Ibn Taimiyya, a favourite of Wahhabis and contemporary neo-fundamentalist writers. Ibn Taimiyya grappled with the question of how Muslims should react to the conquest of Muslim states by the Tartars, who then converted to Islam (at least in form) but imposed non-Islamic rule. Ibn Taimiyya resolved this with a *fatwa* that described such a state as combining elements of both *dar al Islam* and *dar al harb*. Farag concluded that in such cases Muslims were obliged to overthrow the state order, and that contemporary Egypt was precisely such a case. He rejected all incrementalist approaches to building the Islamic state, including civilian political parties and philanthropic societies, in preference for immediate violent *jihad*. He criticised those who call for study rather than action. Farag's core argument was that the Qur'an is clear about the obligation on Muslims to create an Islamic state, and because this cannot be created without fighting, *jihad* to create such a state is the duty of Muslims. Those who die without allegiance to such a state will die a *jahili* death (Rifat 1989: 136). Because this has been ignored or denied by many Muslim scholars, Farag labelled *jihad* the 'neglected duty'. He denied that there are stages of *jihad*, rather asserting that the different levels of *jihad*—the internal struggle, the struggle against the devil, and the war against infidels and hypocrites—should be conducted simultaneously. We shall return to the specifics of Farag's theory of *jihad* below.

Our final case is provided by Hassan al Turabi,[9] a subtle and accomplished scholar who has succoured neo-fundamentalism. Turabi is a uniquely accomplished Islamist theoretician with higher degrees in law and a wide familiarity with different schools of philosophy. He has advocated the rights of women and Islamist versions of democracy. Turabi increasingly uses a unique style of writing that is full of Qur'anic resonance, while rarely citing the Qur'an itself. This makes it almost impossible to translate. His is an implied argument from authority, which relies on allusion and analogy rather than deductive logic. In addition, Turabi often contradicts himself, and his writings in English have a rather different character to those in Arabic. This deliberate obscurity is a means of reconciling his considerable intellect and learning with the flawed logic of contemporary political Islam.

Turabi's theorisation of *jihad* is most clearly articulated in a series of articles written in the wake of September 11, *The Phenomenon of Political Terrorism and the Evaluation of the September Incident in America*. (al Turabi 2002) Turabi reproduces Qutb's argument that when an Islamic group has the means to overthrow by force a tyranny that stands in the way of the Islamic call, it is obliged to do so. He says that the September 11 'incident' was caused by legitimate grievances, that America's response was more severe than the attack itself, and that the operatives 'aimed at centres of military organisation and financial hegemony which are legitimate targets in wars.' He regrets only that they 'hit some thousands of innocent workers, who are not part of the army, and who are neutral in interna-

---

[9] Turabi's writings relevant to Sudan are analysed in chapter 3.

tional affairs, and some of them are of different nationalities and religions.' Although Turabi is a lawyer, and familiar with the principle of proportionality that is one of the bases of international humanitarian law, he appears more concerned with attributing the relative weight of responsibility between America and the Muslim world than in the legality of al Qa'ida's actions. Without explicitly saying so, Turabi is endorsing Usama bin Laden's depiction of his insurgency as a defensive *jihad*, responding to American aggression and occupation, which imposes an individual obligation on all Muslims to fight.

Islamic history and jurisprudence contain plentiful reference to the principles of humanity in warfare. This rich tradition has been used by the International Committee of the Red Cross in its efforts to promote respect for the laws of war. But these sources are strikingly absent from Turabi's theorising and legal work. For example, in the Sudanese military code (revised under Turabi's supervision in 1999), there is no reference at all to international humanitarian law. In his commentary on the 'September incident' cited above (al Turabi 2002), he explains that Islam is peaceable except when it is necessary to struggle for justice or resist aggression. Then there is a duty of *jihad*. He contributes no precise opinion or jurisprudence on the limits of force in *jihad*, instead simply citing more than thirty Qur'anic verses, explaining: 'The guiding Qur'anic meanings on the limits of what is right, what is permitted and what is forbidden, within the framework of violent force are to be clarified within their context.' This avoids the issue.

As a self-proclaimed liberal Islamist, Turabi should be critical of the neo-fundamentalist excess of the Afghan Taliban. But instead he is sympathetically condescending to them, implying that they are somewhat over-enthusiastic students.[10] In this same series of articles, Turabi states that the Taliban are puritans who are loyal to the aims of the *jihad* against the Soviet Union, but their poor jurisprudence did not enable them to accommodate their fellow participants in the *jihad*, and instead they drove out those they accused of being unfaithful to Islam. He argues that the Taliban were unaware that, contrary to some tribal traditions, Islam grants women the right to work, income and education, and allows for differences in opinion.[11] He also writes that they lacked the experience and expertise to reconstruct Afghanistan and deal with its refugee prob-

[10] The word *taliban* means 'students', and Turabi's political style has been one of a charismatic supervisor of students.
[11] This refers to Muslim scholars' different interpretations of Islamic sources, and not to any critique of those sources.

lem. In short, Turabi is citing Islamists' inexperience to excuse the imper-
fections of political Islam.

Contemporary neo-fundamentalism is the outcome of the dual processes of the growing conservatism of political Islam and its increasing
focus on the 'authentic' pre-modern model of the first Muslim generation. Its anti-intellectualism is made possible by the scholarship of certain
Islamist writers, including al Qaradawi, al 'Awwa and Turabi. Its ideologues are hostile to Islamist reformers (including the pioneer Salafis such
as Mohamed Abduh as well as their critics such as Fazlur Rahman) and
even hold Sayyid Qutb in suspicion as too modernist. (Kepel 2002: 220–1)
While many neo-fundamentalists are politically quiescent (Roy 1999),
their intolerance of debate and dissent leads them inexorably into the
arms of authoritarianism, either incrementally (as in Egypt) or through
militant jihadism.

Neo-fundamentalist jihads

If nationalist resistance is the first pole of contemporary jihadism, neo-
fundamentalism provides the second. The first and most defining instance
of neo-fundamentalist *jihad* is the Tanzim al Jihad group that assassinated
President Sadat in October 1981. The chief assassin was Lieutenant
Khalid al Islambuli, the theoretician was Mohamed Abdel Salam Farag,
and the assassination of Sadat was an acting-out of their understanding
of Qutb's theory of *jihad*.

Three key points about *jihad* emerge from Farag's pamphlet *The Neglected Duty*. The first, discussed above, is the imperative of immediate violent
jihad in preference to any other strategy for developing an Islamic state.
The second is the rationalisation of fighting the 'close enemy' (the Egyptian government) before the 'distant enemy' (Israel). (Rifat 1989: 141)
This is because it is worthier to fight a close enemy, because victory over
the distant enemy in the name of existing infidel rule is worthless, and
because creating an Islamic state is Allah's cause. The third is the possibility of a small group achieving their goal, just as the Prophet's outnumbered forces were victorious at Badr, with the assistance of Allah. Farag
argues that those who will establish the Islamic state are 'the believing
minority'. He writes that Islam does not gain victory by large numbers,
and 'small groups have defeated larger ones with Allah's permission', and
continues: 'The establishment of the Islamic state is the execution of
Allah's order, and we are not responsible for the consequences.' Faith and
heroism alone should suffice: indeed it is when the odds seem most hope-

less that the *mujahid* is at his greatest. Moreover, it is not necessary to wait for the right leadership before establishing the *khilafa*: the best Muslim can lead and all remaining problems can be resolved by *shura* (consultation). (Rifat 1989: 137, 146–7)

During the trial of al Islambuli and his fellow conspirators it became clear that the assassins had only the most elementary plans for seizing power and bringing about the Islamic state. (Kepel 1993: 200–2) After springing down from his truck with his small team of assassins and shooting Sadat dead, al Islambuli cried out in triumph 'I have killed Pharaoh!' It was an act of regicide in a long terrorist tradition, well planned and executed, and assisted by considerable luck. But al Islambuli had little conception of what would follow from his act of tyrannicide. There were rudimentary plans for the takeover of key government facilities, and a second branch of Tanzim al Jihad launched an uprising in Asyut Upper Egypt, over the following days, but it was localised, badly led and not coordinated with any grab for state power. At the micro-level, in both theory and practice, the organisation was extremely practical. Farag wrote of the importance of being 'clever and alert' (Rifat 1989: 141), and al Islambuli was certainly both. Beyond that was a vacuum.

The 1990s neo-fundamentalist insurrection in Egypt provides our next case. One component was the military leadership provided by veterans of the Afghan *jihad*, who had returned home after the defeat of the Soviet Union in 1989 and the subsequent failure of the Afghan *mujahidiin* to take power in Kabul. The 1990s Islamist war in Egypt was conducted by Tanzim al Jihad (the successors of Farag and Islambuli) and its larger sister and competitor, al Gama'a al Islamiyya. This insurgency began in 1991 and included assassinations of prominent government figures and secularists. Most of the violence was in Upper Egypt, where a guerrilla war was sustained against the security forces in the hills and sugar cane fields. Many Copts were murdered, and foreign tourists were attacked, culminating in the November 1997 massacre of fifty-eight foreign tourists and at least four Egyptians at Luxor. The 'Afghani' connection was evident in the leadership, styles of dress and distinctive ways of killing such as slitting throats. (Cooley 2000) Like many such atrocities, this appeared to be a gambit to radicalise the movement and derail efforts at accommodation that were proceeding in parallel. (Weaver 1999) The radicalisation gambit did not succeed. Al Gama'a al Islamiyya declared a ceasefire. The insurrection had been crushed.

An interesting aspect to this violence is its perpetrators, and specifically their declining educational standards. In the 1970s and '80s, militant

Islamists had a power base among university students and were concentrated in the cities, but by the 1990s their average age and educational standards had significantly dropped. (Ibrahim 2002: 74–5) Whereas graduates accounted for more than three-quarters of the Islamists arrested by the police in the 1981 crackdown, this had dropped to one fifth by the 1990s. (Cooley 2000: 189) The educated Islamists were instead turning towards the accommodationist strategy of the Muslim Brothers.

In Algeria, the civil war was grander in scale and atrocity, but comparable in the social base of its _mujahidiin_. The spark for the insurrection was a very real grievance: the cancellation of elections which the Front Islamique du Salut (FIS) was certain to win, drawing upon the frustrations of a generation of Algerians who had benefited little if at all from the twenty-five years of FLN rule. Initially, the militants were led by a combination of veteran 'Arab Afghans' and FIS political activists. Increasingly, a younger generation of half-educated youth and criminals took over, led by 'emirs' who obtained tangible political and economic gains from the extortion and black-marketeering in the conflict. (Martinez 2000: 100, 112) The ideological and military escalation of the _jihad_ reflected a pure Clausewitzean war logic, as the most radical and Qutbist of the Islamist jihadists, the Groupement Islamique Armé (GIA) achieved dominance with its slogan of 'no dialogue, no reconciliation, no truce'. Other militant groups, which adhered to the logic of conducting guerrilla _jihad_ as Islamist political activism by other means, were gradually squeezed. Competition among GIA 'emirs' for ascendancy contributed to the group's propensity for massacre. The murder of journalists, writers and intellectuals is a graphic instance of the killing of critique. Yet, the cycle of war, with its early cycle of escalation followed by a phase in which the army and guerrillas settled for consolidating their advantages, illustrates how even the most violent jihadism can be appropriated for localised ends. (Martinez 2000: 197–244) Luis Martinez, in his masterly analysis of the war, concludes that the GIA's logic of war made it the 'political ally of the regime'. (p. 211) There is no doubt that the extreme violence alienated the mass of the Algerian populace including most of those who had voted for the FIS in 1991 (Kepel 2002: 254–75). But we must also note that, for some important jihadist military entrepreneurs, the dead end of the radical Islamist project did not represent a failure, but rather a successful political and economic strategy of accommodating to a repressive regime and a globalising economy. The GIA's _jihad_ of terror did, ultimately, turn out to be a means of conducting politics by other means.

Al Qa'ida

The third pole of neo-fundamentalist jihadism is the globalised Salafiist *jihad* exemplified by al Qa'ida. As well as the intellectual genealogy outlined, it had one additional major theorist, the Palestinian militant Abdallah Azzam, who joined the international brigades of the Afghan resistance at an early stage, and in 1984 wrote an influential pamphlet, *Defending the Land of the Muslims is Each Man's Overriding Duty.* Drawing upon various Salafi and Islamist sources, he took Farag's argument about the obligation of *jihad* a stage further, arguing that every Muslim had an imperative duty to participate personally and contribute materially to *jihad.* He continued:

This duty shall not lapse with victory in Afghanistan, and the *jihad* will remain an individual obligation until all other lands which formerly were Muslim come back to us and Islam reigns within them once again. Before us lie Palestine, Bukhara, Lebanon, Chad, Eritrea, Somalia, the Philippines, Burma, South Yemen, Tashkent, Andalusia... (quoted in Kepel 2002: 147)

Notwithstanding rhetorical excess, this is an unusually global call to arms. However, Azzam does not overlook his national roots: 'We have not forgotten Palestine. Palestine is our beating heart.' Similarly, when Usama bin Laden issued his 'Declaration of Jihad against the Americans Occupying the Land of the Two Holy Places' in August 1996, as well as citing Azzam, Ahmed Yasin (Hamas), and Omer Abdel Rahman (al Gama'a al Islamiya), he referred to the Saudi Salafis who had criticised their government for inviting in the Americans. He used precisely the same argument as Azzam for a defensive *jihad* against the occupiers. Usama's *jihad* is also locally rooted.

In 1998, al Qa'ida enveloped a number of other jihadist organisations, notably the Egyptian Tanzim al Jihad, whose leader Ayman al Zawahiri has become a major influence. Perhaps reflecting a characteristically Egyptian state-framed world-view, Zawahiri has stressed the importance of a territorial base and preferably the control of a country for a global *jihad* to succeed.[12] (Benjamin and Simon 2002: 134)

But global Salafi jihadism *is* distinct in one major aspect, which leaves it with a rather different trajectory to its nationally-confined siblings. This

---

[12] In the wake of September 11 many writers have discounted the need for global insurgents to have such a base, arguing instead that 'network' terrorist organisations can operate without them. This is also a criticism of US policy in the 1990s which focused on state sponsors of terrorism. However, especially in view of Zawahiri's views, it remains to be seen if al Qa'ida can indeed survive without its erstwhile state sponsors.

difference is its social base, or slenderness thereof. The global Salafi jihadists have their base among a cadre of deracinated Afghan Arabs and young Muslims studying in the West. In the other insurrections described, the *mujahidiin* are both nourished and constrained by the demands and grievances of their constituencies. For many of the veterans of the Afghan *jihad*, there is no such constituency: their social base is themselves and their financier, Usama bin Laden.[13] One al Qa'ida member, arrested and interrogated in Germany in 1998, described three general types: 'people who had no success in life, had nothing in their heads... people who loved their religion but had no idea what their religion really meant... [and people with] nothing in their heads but to fight and solve all the problems in the world with battles' (quoted in Reeve 1999: 174). Al Qa'ida has been theorised as a 'network' jihadist group as opposed to a 'territorial' one (e.g. Procyshen 2001), and as an 'apocalyptic' group emerging from a 'utopian' one (Gunaratna 2002: 93), but it is probable that no theorisation of this group can capture its historical specificity.[14]

The Afghan *jihad* of the 1980s is the unique event that mobilised these Salafi *mujahidiin*, and the Gulf War and its aftermath are the context for their failure to demobilise. Among the Arab states, Egypt and Saudi Arabia were the earliest, most enthusiastic and most pivotal supporters of the Afghan resistance. Anwar Sadat provided old Soviet-supplied weaponry, training and volunteers. Mubarak was probably not unhappy that leading militants who escaped the 1981–2 crackdown fled to Peshawar and busied themselves there with fighting communism. The fact that they established international connections, and were further radicalised, and their followers were trained in commando-style military tactics, came to concern him only a decade later. Saudi Arabia provided immense finance, ideological support, and a few highly influential volunteers. It too had a policy of exporting potential troublemakers. It painstakingly constructed an Arab-Islamic consensus around the Afghan and Iran-Iraq wars that maintained its internal stability. The ending of the Afghan *jihad* in 1990 initiated a huge blow-back to the countries that had sent volunteers. As the Islamist international brigades dispersed, 'Afghanis' returned to Egypt, Algeria, Saudi Arabia and elsewhere. There were no systematic international efforts to demobilise these veterans or re-integrate them into civilian life. A recurrent story in world history is the potential of frus-

---

[13] This indeed is one meaning of the term *al qa'ida*, 'the base' or 'the constituency.'

[14] It would be an interesting exercise to analyse al Qa'ida's ideology in the light of urban millennialism, a subject that has received relatively little scholarly attention. For brief reference to a Sudanese manifestation of this, see Al-Karsany 1993: 139, 149–51.

trated ex-combatants, shunned, devalued and jobless, to start insurrections and revolutions, turn to crime and mercenarism, or simply become
social casualties. The Arab Afghans did all of these.

At precisely this point, the 1990–1 Gulf War blew apart the fragile
consensus of Arab nationalism, conservative Salafism and radical Islamism that the Saudis had laboured to maintain. The crisis created a sharp
polarity between many militant Islamists who sided with Iraq, primarily
because Saddam Hussein stood up to the Americans, and those who continued to support Saudi Arabia. (Piscatori 1991) Others condemned both
sides. Usama bin Laden offered to mobilise the Afghan veterans to
oppose Iraq, but the Saudi royal family preferred to ask the Americans.
Usama did not join the pro-Iraqi camp, but bitterly opposed the Saudi
government, and left the country for Pakistan and Sudan. Khartoum
became the repository for militant Islamists, espousing but not achieving
unity under the leadership of Hassan al Turabi (see chapter 6).

Our key point here is that whereas all other *jihads* are rooted in local
particularities, the Arab Afghans after 1990 were and are unique in that
they contained a core group that was removed from any such social base.
In fact, in important respects, Usama bin Laden's finance, employment
and philanthropy, through al Qa'ida, provided exactly such a base.

The deracinated global Salafi jihadists have carried out a series of
international terrorist spectaculars with the aim of causing mass indiscriminate death. This kind of *jihad* reflects a unique combination of skills
and ideology. The sophistication of planning and commando-type skills
are drawn from the Peshawar-based networks. The breadth of ideology
that can make it relevant to attack the United States arises from the conjuncture of Azzam's global call to *jihad* (in turn dependent on a reading of
Qutb and various neo-fundamentalist Salafis) and the agenda of Usama
bin Laden, initially focused on Saudi Arabia, which targets the Americans as infidels in the Holy Places.

With this framework, we can understand better the import of Usama
bin Laden's video-taped statements and conversations in the aftermath
of September 11. On 7 October he released a video statement to Al
Gezira, in which he said: 'Hypocrisy stood behind the leader of global
idolatry, the *hubal* of the age—namely, America and its supporters.' The
hubal was the idol that stood in the *Kaaba* until it was destroyed by the
Prophet Mohamed, thereby bringing about the age of Islam. The American presence in Saudi Arabia is thus given a profound reference from the
time of the birth of Islam. The hypocrites (*munafiqun*) were the Muslim
citizens of Medina who pretended to support the Prophet while secretly

opposing him, and by analogy, the term applies to today's rulers of Saudi Arabia and Egypt among others. (Doran 2002: 24) This was Usama bin Laden's carefully-crafted Salafist message, that a return to the original *khilafa* will be at hand following an Islamist revolution in Saudi Arabia.

Equally revealing is the thinking revealed in the video discovered by US forces and released on 8 December, in which Usama discusses the September 11 attacks on the World Trade Center with a visiting Saudi *sheikh*. The video has all the hallmarks of authenticity. Its most-quoted part indicates the careful planning that went into the operation, including the calculation of casualties and the expectation that the fire from the jet-fuel would melt the iron structure of the building.[15] Usama has run engineering companies, and he put his experience to effective use. In contrast to the sophistication of the terrorists' applied technical science, their political science discourse is rudimentary:

These young men ... made with their deeds, in New York and Washington, speeches that overshadowed all other speeches made everywhere else in the world. The speeches are understood by both Arabs and non-Arabs—even by Chinese. It has no equal the media said. Some of them said that in Holland, at one of the centres, the number of people who accepted Islam during the days that followed the operations were more than the people who accepted Islam in the last eleven years. I heard someone on Islamic radio who owns a school in America say, 'We don't have time to keep up with the demands of those who are asking about Islamic books to learn about Islam.' This event made people think [about true Islam] which benefited Islam greatly.

A mystical element in political causation is evident, reflecting a deep belief in a coming apocalypse. During the short discussion alone there are no fewer than six references to visions and dreams, plus an additional reference by Usama to an 'omen'. The visiting *sheikh* said:

Hundreds of people used to doubt you and few only would follow you until this huge event happened. Now hundreds of people are coming out to join you. I remember a vision by Shaykh Salih Al-[Shuaybi]. He said, 'There will be a great hit and people will go out by hundreds to Afghanistan.' I asked him: 'To Afghanistan?' He replied, 'Yes.' According to him, the only ones who stay behind will be the mentally impotent and the liars [hypocrites]. I remembered his saying that hundreds of people will go out to Afghanistan. He had this vision a year ago. This even discriminated between the different types of followers.

At one point, Usama claims that he had to stop his followers reporting their dreams of aircraft crashing into buildings in order to keep the oper-

---

[15] Based on the transcript broadcast on 8 December 2001.

ation secret. (It was in this context that he referred to the fact that the 'brothers who conducted the operation' didn't know anything about the precise plans until just before they boarded the planes.) Almost every other sentence of Usama's videotaped exchanges with his Saudi visitor included 'thanks to God', 'success comes from God' or similar reference to God's direct influence on human affairs. While Arabic speakers routinely use these terms as figures of speech in everyday exchanges, Usama and his 'brothers' do not use them in this commonplace metaphorical sense. Hence when the *sheikh* said 'Allah prepares for you a great reward for this work', he means it *literally*: God will intervene directly on his behalf.

There is also something missing from the exchanges: what is to happen next? There is no blueprint for revolutionary action. At one point the *sheikh* says: 'The Americans were terrified, thinking there was a coup.' But the brothers present were laughing: there wasn't a coup. This act of *jihad* was conducted for its own sake. But, at the same time, Usama and the other engineers of this act did not just seek rewards in paradise: the Islamist project aims to build the Kingdom of God in *this* world and in 'real time'. Al Qa'ida's ultimate aim of restoring the Islamic *khilafa* required either spontaneous popular uprising or divine intervention. Usama and his followers seem to have counted on both. We are again presented with the paradox of transcendental *jihad*. The global Salafi jihadists' ambition is to take and exercise political power, particularly state power, but they rely on a *deus ex machina* to deliver their victory. Islamist theory's weakest point is that it not only possesses no theory of politics, but is actively *hostile* to any such theory. Into this theoretical and practical blind spot steps the concept of *jihad* as envisioned by Qutb, and developed by Farag and Azzam, and implemented by bin Laden.

Usama bin Laden is, however, both an engineer and an experienced guerrilla strategist. He does not claim to be a philosopher. His two declarations of *jihad* against America (August 1996 and February 1998) are clear and to the point: he means what he says and says what he means, and it would be a mistake not to take his statements of intent seriously (cf. Anonymous 2002). Bin Laden's focus has been overwhelmingly on the need for a protracted war of resistance against the United States, rather than what may follow should such a war actually succeed. Moreover, he has departed from the philosophical purity of Qutb's theorisation by emphasising that his struggle is a *defensive jihad*, against the occupation of Palestine by Israel, and presence of the Americans in the Holy Places. Al Qa'ida's practice of Salafi jihadism is poorly theorised, but as a practical oppositional ideology, that is one of its strengths.

After the US missile attacks on Sudan and Afghanistan in August 1998, and also after September 11, there was a surge of popular enthusiasm for Usama bin Laden in places as diverse as northern Nigeria and Palestine. The latter simply reflected a sense that the United States, as global bully, was finally receiving its come-uppance. If we try to analyse the political philosophy of Salafi jihadism, we quickly see that it is wholly irrelevant to the struggles of ordinary Muslims for a better life, including social justice and national liberation. But its failures as a positive political project do not undermine its appeal as a banner of resistance. For its exponents, the global *jihad* is an end in itself, made meaningful by the crimes of its enemies. Success lies in escalating the fight.

The neo-fundamentalism of al Qa'ida therefore shifts between no fewer than four implicit definitions of success in *jihad*. One is achieving the Kingdom of God. A second is the personal attainment of Paradise by the martyr *mujahid*. A third is the practical achievement of political and military victory by expelling an invader from Muslim lands. The final one is the instrumentality of the struggle itself, both politically, by achieving leadership of global Islamist militancy, and transcendentally, by hastening the first two goals.

The Islamist impasse

The discussion above has highlighted the intellectual barrenness of militant neo-fundamentalist Islamism as a constructive political project for gaining and wielding power. A range of Muslim scholars has come to this conclusion, arguing instead that Islam is quite compatible with modern civil society, democracy and human rights. Abdelwahab El-Affendi is unusual among Islamists in acknowledging the failures of both practice and theory. His critique of the Sudanese experiment is frank (El-Affendi 1999). His earlier writings display a readiness to critique past and present Islamist practices for their coerciveness and utopianism. Discarding the idea of an Islamic state in favour of the 'Islamic political community' or a 'state for Muslims', he argues that freedom must be a cardinal principle: 'The original Muslim community was united first by faith and mutual solidarity, and only secondarily by coercive power. Many modern Islamists seem to seek coercive power first and faith as its derivative.' (El-Affendi 1991 b: 87) Rejecting Qutb, he advocates a democratic, free, plural Islamic community, a 'light for all humankind'. (p. 92) But this is not a liberal state with competing interest groups, rather a harmonious confederation of communities. How to get there?

One must abandon the illusions about the millennium promised by the revival of a utopian polity in which a righteous and saintly ruler will miraculously emerge to restore the long-lost age of Islam. Nor is it wise to shift our millennial hopes to the newly emerged Islamic movements, and expect that their accession to power will automatically bring an era of divine justice and saintly rule. There is simply no alternative to attaining these objectives the hard way, by doing what is needed to achieve them. (p. 93)

Unfortunately, that is all El-Affendi has to say about 'the hard way' and 'doing what is needed'. He is a perfectly good enough political scientist to critique Islamist, liberal and socialist practices, but Islamism simply does not provide him with the tools to fill in the picture of what is to be done. This is a fair reflection of the intellectual dead end of political Islam, which is also manifest in the paralysis of Egyptian political discourse.

Cairo was once the intellectual capital of the Arab world. Today, simplistic arguments, pitched at the level of international conspiracies and assaults on the integrity of the Arab personality, are the staple of Islamist writing. Meanwhile, non-Islamists have to tread carefully so as not to offend the unpredictable sensitivities of the Islamists and be accused of 'offending religion'. Fifty and a hundred years ago Islamist reformers sought to broaden their imaginative horizons, questioning conservative religious authorities such as the *ulama* of al Azhar, some of whom are even today teaching law from texts over five centuries old (Qaoud, 2000). Fazlur Rahman has described al Azhar as representing 'the late medieval body of Islamic thought with few and minor modifications' (1982: 100), and compares the institution to a 'great glacier that, although it grows huge by attracting all sorts of extraneous materials through its sheer size, slowly melts away leaving only a trail of debris'. (p. 99) By contrast, today's neo-fundamentalists are reverting to a simplistic literalism, hand-in-hand with the sheikhs of al Azhar. Oliver Roy has written of these 'new intellectuals': 'They will not be the ones to open up the ulama's corpus. The modernity they brought to the reading of Islam exhausted itself in a repetitive, uncritical and undemonstrative defense of Islam, which for them has answers to all the problems of the modern world.' (Roy 1999: 22) The modernist Islamists' idea of 'invoking religion against custom' to promote initiatives such as women's education (Hale 1997: 242) is anathema.

Moderate educated Islamists who eschew violence conduct themselves with more civility and more deference to the basic rules of argument. But our relief that they do not advocate violent *jihad* should not make us forgive their intellectual shallowness. A fine example of this, in both theory and practice, is the Egyptian historian Tariq al Bishri, who, interestingly, is a former Marxist.

The [*shari'a* and *ijtihad*] system is superior to positivist legal systems, even from the purely earthly and pragmatic angle, for it combines the dimensions of belief and of moral conduct with the social values of justice, integrity and charity, and it heals the rift between law and ethics, between the values governing social relations and the ones that steer individual conduct, between our past and our future. And in all this it gives us the feeling of belonging—to the community, to the motherland, the belief and the system. (quoted in Flores 1997: 87)

It is nicely written, but it hasn't overcome the question of how this system is to be brought into being by imperfect human beings. Al Bishri's writing is significant when we turn to examining the political role he has played. As the head of the Administrative Section of the Egyptian High Court, in 1994 he was responsible for handing down a decision that massively extended the powers of censorship of al Azhar, from merely religious affairs to responsibility for the wider moral wellbeing of the Egyptian populace. Furthermore he declared that al Azhar's decisions were binding. (Abdo 2000: 66–7) This is one among several key examples of how 'moderate' Islamism has accommodated with state power in Egypt. In this case, it gave al Azhar wide powers of censorship that it has not hesitated to use. For President Husni Mubarak, it was perfect cover for any criticisms that his government was tolerating or promoting immoral publications: anything that appeared had been approved by the *sheikhs*.

There has been no Egyptian Islamist thinker for an entire generation who comes close to matching Sayyid Qutb's learning, eloquence and vision. None has a competitor theory for how to achieve the Islamic state. Implicitly, the Islamic Trend and the *ulama* appear to hold that an incrementalist strategy of gradual Islamisation of all aspects of public life will result in the same outcome. But this is not theorised.

It is easy to mock the level of Islamist analysis in Egypt. But this vapidity does not spring from nowhere: it has taken decades to achieve. Various forms of censorship are at work. There is the censorship imposed by fear, both the threat of assassination by militant Islamists and repression by the state and the *sheikhs* of al Azhar. There is straightforward censorship of books, newspapers and conferences, which has become so routine and invasive that writers, civil servants and lecturers have thoroughly internalised it. Even the Cairo offices of some international organisations have become so terrified of free speech that they dare not be associated with any independent publication. But perhaps the most insidious form of censorship is that brought about by poor education. To explain this demands a study of Egyptian schools and universities and the values they reproduce. Naguib Mahfouz, Egypt's premier novelist, has written:

'Egypt's culture is declining fast. The state of education in our country is in crisis. Classrooms are more like warehouses to cram children in for a few hours than places of education. The arts and literature are barely taught in these institutions, which are run more like army barracks than places where cultural awareness and appreciation can be nurtured.' (quoted in Ajami 1999: 221) Egyptian higher education has been called 'the university of large numbers', but Gilles Kepel (1993: 135) questions whether the term 'university' is itself applicable:

[T]he appellation 'establishments of long-term instruction' would be a more accurate designation for institutions that provide more than half a million students with courses of study rigidly compartmentalized and offering degrees governed by an examination system that yields little to the Koranic schools in its exclusive reliance on the routine memorization of manuals.

Independent thinking is discouraged, and success relies on the slavish reproduction of the lecturer's authority. The professor will sermonise and demand rote learning from the students. In the overcrowded lecture halls it may be a challenge even to hear the lecturer's voice—a problem that can be overcome by buying the teacher's manual and memorising it for examination. Most of the best academics leave for positions in the Gulf or (especially for non-Islamists) the United States. There is a synergy between the Egyptian state's promotion of ('moderate') Islam in schools and universities and the strength of Islamic movements in the country. (Starrett 1998)

Another of our concerns here is the way in which the Egyptian education system bestows a status hierarchy upon different types of knowledge, a hierarchy which converges precisely with the values of the Islamists. At the centre of this is the prestige hierarchy in university faculties. The disciplines of pure science, engineering and medicine are elevated, while law, humanities and social science are dismissed as 'garbage faculties'. (Kepel 1993: 137) The brightest students gravitate towards the pure and applied sciences. Mechanical models for how society operates are emphasised in public discourse: the opinions of a physicist or pharmacologist will be more valued in commenting on a social problem than the expertise of a sociologist. This reproduces the Islamists' comfort with the exact sciences and mechanical engineering, and their hostility to history and social science. Qutb himself encouraged Muslims to study science, and was forthright in consigning 'philosophy, historiography, the interpretation of history, psychology (except for those observations and data that are unaffected by personal opinions of the experimenters), ethics, theology and comparative religion, and sociology (excluding statistics and observations)' to the realm of *jahiliyya*. (1990: 94)

The origins of Egypt's mass higher education value system lie in the Nasserite, secularist period, when the university model was adopted from the Soviet Union. In 1950 there were few modern universities in the country, but twenty years later almost every province had its own. Communist-style education in the 1950s and '60s was based on a faith in hard science and a mechanistic model of socio-political progress. It is both ironic and revealing that Islamism and its most hated ideological adversary should share an aversion to exploring the horizons of the socio-political imagination. The result is that the value system of even the most secularised Egyptian higher education leaves a void where it should be encouraging the exploration of socio-political cause-and-effect. It reproduces the Communists' explicit and the Islamists' implied conclusion that this void can be filled with literal social 'engineering' and divine intervention. It is unsurprising that the leading neo-fundamentalists are engineers, doctors and mechanics by training, and that their models for socio-political cause and effect are mechanistic.

There is a marked contrast between the barrenness of Islamist political thought and the creativity manifest in its organisational practice. Islamists have shown a capacity for mobilisation, discipline, patience, flexibility and social engagement that has consistently outshone the region's secularist parties and governments. Once again Egypt provides the finest example. Michael Gilsenan sums up this paradox: 'There is a feeling, to the observer, of something that is at once intensely dynamic and yet in key dimensions ossified.' (1982: 225) Since its foundation, the Society of Muslim Brothers has had different, overlapping manifestations: it has been akin to a Leninist vanguard, a Western-style liberal party, and a voluntaristic social movement (cf. Roy 1999: 46). Hassan al Banna defined his Society in these terms:

It is a Salafi 'call,' a Sunni order, Sufist sect, a political organisation, a sports society, a scientific and cultural association, an economic company, and a social idea. … By this we can see how the comprehensive meaning of Islam has acquired our idea to accommodate all the aspects of reform. (al Banna 1990)

The practice of al Banna himself served as the *de facto* model for Islamist organisation. Al Banna was a pragmatist as well as a religious visionary, who styled himself as *murshid* ('guide'). His leadership was at first based on religious authority and respect rather than command. He began his mission with thousands of face-to-face meetings with people, mostly in Upper Egypt, many of them students:

This wide network of personal relations is the source of Hassan al Banna's leadership and his hegemony over the Society. Tens of thousands of the Society's members were proud to be personal friends of al Banna, and through this friendship the *murshid* established his Society and controlled it. (al Said 1972: 47)

One of the reasons for the Muslim Brothers' rapid success was al Banna's tactics and pragmatism: he built a political party that did not label itself as such. Elements of a Leninist model of organisation were apparent in the Society's organisation from the outset. For junior members the lowest level was the Scout section (*kashafa*) and their more senior counterparts, 'travellers' or *jawala*. These were older than the scouts and played a role in leading, ensuring discipline, and shaping identity. The scouts' organisation has similarities with the youth wings of the nationalist parties and also the contemporary militarised youth sections of fascist and communist parties. (Commins 1994: 146) The basic level of membership was *musaid* or assistant Brother, followed by 'conscript' and 'working Brother'. At the top—or in the vanguard—were the 'Special Apparatus' of the Muslim Brothers, also known as *mujahidiin*. The vanguard's existence was not officially admitted, especially after it began a campaign of assassination after the Second World War. This core of the Society was organised on a cell system. Admission was based on recommendation by the Guidance Office controlled by the leadership, and unlike the lower levels, all members were men. Unlike in a Leninist system, personal virtue as recognised by the charismatic Guide was the basis for selection and promotion. The political structure was (and is) pyramidal, with ultimate control vested at the top. The Guide had a direct role in the ranking and promotion of members. On joining the neophyte took an oath of allegiance (*bay'a*) entailing absolute faith in the leadership.

This reflects the Leninist principle that the party is everything: more important than family, community and nation. But in swearing loyalty to God it takes on a wholly different aspect. In contrast to Leninist parties, for whom organisation developed into an end in itself rather than merely a means to an end, Islamist organisation has always retained its instrumental character. This is both a strength and a weakness. Islamists have never lost sight of what their organisations are *for*. They do not engage in the kinds of internal doctrinal debates and purges over organisational differences that have consistently impeded the left. But at the same time, the lack of organisational theory has been an obstruction to developing a wider movement with tactical and strategic goals. Islamist organisations have often fragmented, usually following personal disputes between their leaders. They often coordinate very poorly. However, in sharp contrast to Leninists, Islamists rarely engage in murderous internecine purges—all remain part of the wider *umma*.[16] The weak institutionalisation can also be a strength when the Islamists are in opposition, as they have been most of the time in Egypt, as it allows for flexibility and evading the repressive strictures of the state.

Also from the beginning, the Muslim Brothers developed a wider social project including a strong element of voluntarism, establishing schools and hospitals and involvement in trade and industry. By 1948 'the Society of Muslim Brothers had spread in Egypt to the extent that some researchers considered it "a state within a state".' (Haider 1996: 61) More recently, this has been described as mobilisation in the civil society sector (Sullivan and Abed-Kotob 1999), in the limited sense of voluntaristic activities displaying some autonomy from the state. There is little encouragement of dissent and free expression by the Islamist civil society organisations. The professional associations' one confrontation with the government over human rights was quickly snuffed out. (Abdo 2000: 98–9) Their main concern is delivering social and spiritual services. Egyptian Islamist networks are organised so as to escape the strict controls over civil society exercised by the government (for example Law 32 of 1964, which controls all independent organisation). Sympathetic interventions by well-placed state functionaries have also assisted the Islamists.

The strength of Islamist voluntarism was famously demonstrated by the 1992 earthquake when the slow and ineffective state response contrasted with the rapid and energetic efforts of the Islamist voluntary organisations who set up tents and distributed food, blankets and medicines to the victims. Voluntarism and a stress on providing simple, tangible material assistance has been a key strategy for gaining recruits and a stepping stone to controlling key organisations. Thus the Islamists' provision of free public transport for students to attend university classes, and subsidising Islamist-approved women's clothing, has enabled them to move from tackling a simple immediate need to gaining wider loyalties. Islamic voluntarism also has wider implications, as Islamism does not separate the charitable and political spheres of activity.

Each of these three organisational types—Leninist vanguard, civilian party and social movement—were bound together in al Banna's Society

---

[16] This tradition of internal tolerance began to break down in the late 1980s in the context of the Afghan *jihad*, and the murder of Abdalla Azzam.

and no single model supplanted the others. In addition, Islamists have also sought out a fourth organisational type, the army. With its stress on the value of absolute obedience, Islam is well suited to military structures. However, the Bedouin model of command, with an *amir* in charge of the army which is divided into four *khulafa* or banners, below which are the common soldiers, is not well suited to the demands of a contemporary military machine. Thus, Islamist governments, for example in Sudan, have retained existing secular military organisational models and only superficially Islamised them.

The Egyptian Muslim Brothers are consistently able to provide tangible solutions to micro-problems. For example, 'Islamic credit' can be an effective mechanism for helping people out of poverty, if it is honestly managed in a small community. Islamic NGOs run schools and clinics that fill the gaps of an increasingly decrepit state sector. Because only a minority of the country's 170,000 mosques could actually be administered by the Ministry of *Waqf*, the Islamists managed to take over many of the remainder. In 1992 Mubarak initiated a policy to incorporate the activists' mosques under the Ministry's control. Many Islamists merely shifted their activism elsewhere, to basement prayer rooms, while others were assimilated into the Ministry, which reciprocally absorbed their values.

The universities have been one of the Islamists' most important recruiting grounds, and by 1990, the major student unions were all dominated by the Islamic Trend. Their strategy focused on delivering simple tangible benefits, many of them aimed at women. For example they introduced and promoted segregated seating in lecture halls, helping to minimise sexual harassment. Similarly they provided minibus services, also gender segregated, for students to attend classes. To help poor female students with the problem of clothing, they helped provide cheap veils and long robes. A woman dressed in this manner could resist sexual harassment, preserve her reputation, and also save money by not having to dress in a competitive fashionable way.

The Islamists also rapidly took over the elite professional associations including the Engineers Association and the Medical Association, to be followed by the Bar and the journalists' association. One reason for the Islamists' dominance was that the older secularist elite were simply unfamiliar with the economic crisis afflicting graduates and professionals, whereas those who had experienced the major disconnect between the huge expansion in numbers of university graduates that began in the 1970s and the declining number of formal sector jobs to absorb them were personally familiar with the humiliating frustrations of being unable to find work, decent accommodation, and accumulate enough money to marry. The Islamists could mobilise this 'professional underclass' or 'lumpen elite'. (Wickham 1997)

This points to the importance of inter-generational conflicts for Islamist mobilisation. Youth are marginalised in gerontocratic political orders across Muslim Africa on both sides of the Sahara. Militant religion provides an opportunity for young people, rendered liminal in existing social and political orders, to define their identities and break free from some of the constraints imposed by their elders. In Africa, adulthood is defined less by achievement of a certain age than by assuming a social position. For men, this usually entails achieving some economic independence, for women, marriage and motherhood. With a combination of social breakdown and economic crisis, large numbers of young people, especially men, are condemned never to achieve this status, and must therefore spend most or all of their lives as 'social cadets'. (Argenti 2002) In Algeria many young people regard themselves as *kukra*, or 'cursed':

> Young adults face a relative scarcity of work and housing. Single by necessity more than choice, they know that marriage is beyond their means. Urban housing, a precondition to marriage, constitutes one of the major failures of the former regime. Thus many youth in the twenty-five to thirty age-group find themselves in an indefinite status of prolonged childhood. Entry into adult life as defined by basic changes in status—beginning a working life, leaving one's parents, and marriage—appears very precarious. (Vergès 1997: 300)

And for the younger siblings of these 'prolonged children', the incentives for study and self-betterment are reduced. In Egypt, the enduring problem of unemployment combined with the mass production of the university system means that students are prepared for a civil service that cannot offer them jobs, being imbued with a bureaucratic ethic of obedience rather than liberal or entrepreneurial values. Surveys of students confirm a depressing picture:

> The study found that 69% of the total of the sample do not expect to obtain a suitable job after graduation. 83% do not expect to get suitable housing. 88% believe that they do not stand a chance for marrying within a short period after graduation. The study also showed that 96% of the total are lying in the 'pessimist' category concerning the future. ...The feeling of deprivation coupled with the sense of injustice gives birth to anger and readiness to reject the existing system and challenge it and even to overthrow it using violence. (al Jindi 1989: 83–4)

Across the continent, new religious movements are a means of breaking out of this 'prolonged childhood'. A well-documented instance is African

Pentecostal churches, many of which are 'youth-driven in a way which is almost unimaginable in Europe', with young Africans initiating and leading churches (Ward, 1999: 235), while charismatics have been criticised for trying to 're-order society for the benefit of youth'. (Gifford, 1998: 437) Similarly it is unsurprising that Sayyid Qutb's call for a 'new Qur'anic generation' is appealing to youth, implying that his vision is achievable in the lifetime of the young. This ability to appeal to the young is one of Islamism's most enduring strengths.

Although the Egyptian Islamists have not taken state power, they have achieved an impressive ideological and practical accommodation with the regime. The synergy between state policy and neo-fundamentalism can be seen in many areas of public life including law and education. Although this has become most evident under Mubarak, its roots are much deeper. The debate between political Islam and secular liberalism was curtailed by the July 1952 coup. As in Syria and Iraq, the Arab nationalists established a secular regime, but their secularism was neither deep nor well-theorised. In the National Charter of 1962, Nasser included reference to Allah, His messages, books and messengers. Ba'athism similarly gives special place to Islam. The founder of the Ba'ath party, Michel Aflaq, was a Christian,[17] but pinpointed the special status of Islam in his book *On the Road to Ba'ath*. He famously wrote that 'Mohamed was the epitome of all the Arabs. So let all the Arabs today be Mohamed,' and described Islam as 'an eternal and perfect symbol' of the Arab spirit. (Choueiri 2000: 162) As President, Nasser was pictured every Friday praying in one of Cairo's mosques, and in 1956 he delivered his speech of resistance to Britain, France and Israel from al Azhar. While Nasser nationalised al Azhar university, he also massively expanded its role in education, publishing and broadcasting, creating an even-more powerful 'establishment Islam' in Egypt. (Gerholm 1997) Meanwhile Marxists in the region did not engage in serious debate on Islam until the Islamist movement became a threat to them in the 1980s. The left's strategy was to avoid provoking the religious sentiments of the masses, and indeed some leftist statements at that time employ similar language to the Islamists' today. Some Communists defended themselves against Islamist critiques by claiming that they were more authentic Muslims than their adversaries.[18] Their hope was that resolving social injustices would make

---

[17] After his death, the Iraqi authorities declared he had converted to Islam, claiming it was his will.

[18] The Sudanese Communist Rashid Naiel wrote a booklet along this line in the 1960s entitled *The Brothers are the Enemies of Allah, His Book and His Messenger.*

ıe Islamist movement vanish. The human rights movement has focused ɔn collective rights, with special reference to the Palestinians, partly as a means of gaining wider acceptance and finding common ground with the Islamists. Human rights activists have tried to debate calmly with the Islamists rather than provoking them with criticisms, a strategy that raises the question of where to draw the line.

The lack of democratic freedoms throughout the Nasserite era, and the heavy hand of the state, prepared ordinary Egyptians to receive a truth dictated by authority without questioning. This prolonged subjugation combined with the defeat and failure of Arab nationalist regimes to prepare the ground for political Islam. President Husni Mubarak's strategy has been to co-opt the 'moderate' Islamists and try to isolate the 'extremists', whom it has fought with repressive measures. The co-option strategy has involved seeking governmental legitimacy in religion, and hence a creeping Islamisation of Egyptian politics and society. President Mubarak is a secularist whose power base lies in the army, but a succession of compromises with the Islamists has contributed to a stifling of Egyptian cultural and intellectual life. Independent writing in Egypt has been divided between academics who write for a sophisticated minority (Professor Nasr Hamid Abu Zaid, Khalil Abdel Karim) and those who use a journalistic style to reach a wider audience, and are not afraid to provoke the Islamists (Farag Foda). Both groups have suffered.

The murder of Farag Foda, described as 'the most daring and in many ways the most eloquent opponent of political Islam in Egypt in this era' (Flores 1997: 93), on 8 June 1992 was the culmination of a campaign of censorship of secularist writings originally instigated by al Azhar and activists in the Islamic Trend. Al Gama'a al Islamiyya claimed responsibility, saying: 'Al Azhar issued the sentence and we carried out the execution.' (Abdo 2000: 68) The murder is trebly disturbing in that neo-fundamentalist jihadists carried it out; in that they clearly felt they had a warrant from Sheikh al Azhar, the highest religious authority in the Sunni Islamic world; and lastly in that it created far less outrage than one might have hoped. A comparison is apt with the execution of *Ustaz* Mahmoud Mohamed Taha in Sudan by the dictator Jaafar Nimeiri in January 1985. Even though *Ustaz* Mahmoud had little popular support and was ridiculed by the secularist establishment for his curious views on religion and custom, his execution was greeted with universal outrage. Sudanese political society concurred in describing him as a harmless old man. Intellectuals may not have agreed with his views, but Voltaire-like, they were ready to stand with him in defence of his right to air them. By contrast

Farag Foda's views, including the mockery he showered on al Azhar, were far more widely appreciated by Egyptian intellectuals. But such was the atmosphere of intellectual intimidation that most of them concurred that he had been foolish to be so outspoken.

The Egyptian government vigorously prosecuted the case and provided armed guards to other secularist intellectuals under threat, including Naguib Mahfouz. But the following year it allowed al Azhar to trump the Ministry of Culture by extending its powers of censorship. A case like Farag Foda's is much less likely now: it is much harder for such writings to find their way into print.

Another excess was the divorce decreed by the *ulama* on Dr Nasr Hamid Abu Zaid. An Islamic scholar who specialised in studying the text of the Qur'an, Abu Zaid argued that 'all interpretation is informed by contemporary socio-political and cultural factors.' (Abu Zaid 1996: 33) Lawyers from al Azhar argued that because he had criticised literal readings of the Qur'an he was apostate, and as such was not only deserving of death but could not be married to a Muslim woman. The prosecution used the hitherto-neglected principle of *hisba*, absent from the Egyptian statute books and common law, but invoked on the grounds that since 1980 the Egyptian Constitution had claimed Islam as *the* source of legislation. Judge Faruq Abd el Aleem Mursi, who had spent sixteen years in Saudi Arabia, concurred (Abdo 2000: 168–9) and handed down a verdict of guilty. Neo-fundamentalist censorship had triumphed in the university. Dr Abu Zaid and his wife Ebtehal Younes fled to the Netherlands. The government was embarrassed by the international publicity over the case. Its response was a characteristic Mubarak compromise: the following year it enacted a law that meant that only the state prosecutor and not a private individual could utilise the *shari'a* principle of *hisba* to compel an alleged apostate to divorce. For the next few years, there will be no repeat of the Abu Zaid case. But what will happen when Islamists can put enough pressure on the state to impel the state prosecutor to take up cases? Or when the state prosecutor himself is an Islamist?

In the last decade, the human rights movement has taken up the mantle of civil society and independent thought. But this too remains shackled, not just by legal restrictions on its organisational activities, but by the wider constraints on the Egyptian political imagination. One of the factors that blind Egyptian civil society to the peril of its own country's paralysis is the continuing preoccupation with Palestine and the violation of the collective rights of the Palestinians. Repeated betrayals of the Palestinian cause breed fatalism, an orientation towards conspiracy theories, and uncritical solidarity with those who oppose Israel. Fouad Ajami laments this and calls for 'the recognition that it is time for the imagination to steal away from Israel and to look at the Arab reality, to behold its own view of the kind of world the Arabs want for themselves'. (1999: 312) Unfortunately, such is the demoralisation of some liberal Arab intellectuals that in following this path they run the risk of seeing only American-style solutions to their predicament.

By 2001, Egyptian Islamists seemed to be achieving many of their goals, having gained an unprecedented control over large swathes of public life. But they were still far from their goals of an Islamic state. The reason was that they could not break the impasse established by the post-Nasserite state. Islamist activism reinforced the very structures of censorship and paralysis that deepen authoritarianism, and at the end of the day the military core of the state was ready to protect itself at the cost of all else. This became evident in the aftermath of September 11, when the government broadened its crackdown on those it deemed 'terrorists', arresting twenty-two Muslim Brothers, on the grounds that the organisation was banned. The twenty-two include professors, doctors and other professionals, detained under far-reaching anti-terrorist legislation on the grounds that their publications seemed suspicious. One investigator said, 'There was no time to read what they said, but from their titles they looked suspicious', while the head of the State Information Service explained, 'instead of bullets they are shooting concepts of extremism and deception'. (quoted by Stork 2002) In the style of *Animal Farm*, those who nurture intolerance and censorship run the risk of becoming its victims. Neither can the Islamists address Egypt's other predicaments: poverty, the need for rapid economic growth, and dependence on a strategic international alliance with the US and Israel.

A focus on Mubarak's (successful) counter-insurgency misses the crisis inherent in the stifling of Egypt's capacity for reform and creativity. The impasse is primarily a paralysis of Egypt as a nation, augmented simultaneously by the neo-fundamentalist retrogression and political-economic dependence on the West. As Fouad Ajami concludes: 'The danger here is not sudden, cataclysmic upheaval but a steady descent into deeper levels of pauperization, a lapse of the country's best into apathy and despair, Egypt falling yet again through the trap door of its history of disappointment.' (1999: 243) In Egypt and elsewhere Islamist principles and practice for organisation must be seen in the context of militarised states that consistently put *raison d'état* ahead of any other consideration, and which utilise both Islamism and Western money as tools of patrimonialism.

(cf. Tripp 1996) This paralysis reproduces an intellectually barren political imagination that in turn feeds neo-fundamentalism in both its civic and militant manifestations. Meanwhile, in their vexation, other Arab intellectuals embrace Western liberalism and American power with a similar uncritical enthusiasm. This mirror-image response—of which Fouad Ajami is an exemplar—can end up dangerously close to advocating American blueprints for the region as a solution to the failures of nationalism and Islamism.

In 1982 Michael Gilsenan concluded his study of Islam in the Arab world:

All of [the Islamist visions] represent an interrogation and a judgment on contemporary society in the name of an Eternal Truth, the ambiguities of which are invisible to the believer.... A reinvention, to be authentic and creative, must make possible an expansion of the social and cultural universe. It must never be completed nor return endlessly to earlier material in a closed, ritualistic incantation. Does the example of the ruling mullahs of Iran or of the Muslim Brothers of Egypt or Syria show this sense of creative uncompletion? I think not.... Purely rhetorical and ritualistic answers will yield nothing but a destruction of what is to be resurrected by the very people who imagine themselves to be the instruments of rebirth. Is that to be the final irony? (1982: 264)

In the following chapter, we shall see how aptly this description applies literally to Turabi's Sudan, sunk into a morass of corruption, power-hunger and violence. But it also reflects the hollow ascendancy of state-sanctioned Islamism in Egypt. Gilsenan also remarked that the Islamists' discourse of the 1970s was remarkably similar to that of the 1930s: 'There is a strong sense of a repetition of unchanged formulas, of reiteration of a message that has been frozen into immobility.' (p. 223) The same may be said after another two decades, notwithstanding the dynamism of the Islamists' activities at a community level. Is Islamism doomed to forever raise the hopes of the young and marginalised, snatching practical remedies for immediate problems, and then disappoint when it tries to engage at the level of the state or a whole society? Until there is a truly liberal Islamism, dedicated to free speech and open debate, this impasse seems inevitable.

Islamism's encounter with Sub-Saharan Africa

The main theme of the following chapters is political Islam in north-east Africa. This encounter is marked by now-familiar paradoxes, of bad theory but organisational adaptability, and effective 'small projects' but failure to achieve the 'big solution'.

In north-east Africa, political Islamism is characterised by universal aspirations but particular colourings that reflect the national origins of the specific movements. The Egyptian variant of Islamism demonstrates this well: Cairo and Egypt have long dubbed themselves 'the mother of the world'. (Ibrahim 2002: 93) Egyptian Islamism casts its argument and aspirations at a global level, and is incapable of responding to the specific requirements of African societies. It has also been constrained by Egypt's conservative state-centred Africa policy. Similarly, Salafism in Africa is coloured by its overwhelmingly Saudi sources of finance.

Historically, Islam has moved across Sudanic Africa in two waves, the first associated with conversion and the second with incorporation into orthodoxy, manifest in law and theology. The first wave has accommodated local custom (*'urf*) within local schools of Islamic law and practice, integrated by generations of local scholars and jurists to the extent that it is no longer possible to separate 'Islamic' law from custom. Sufism was the dominant form of Islam, based upon mysticism and inherited *baraka* (blessedness). Islam was closely associated with political authority, and developed legal and theological traditions that accommodated Sudanic forms of government, for example retaining non-Islamic titles for rulers, pre-Islamic symbols and rituals of authority, and non-Arab languages. The second wave of Islam is associated with promoting specific social mores alongside legal orthodoxy and Arabic. This is characteristically a struggle between Salafism and Sufism. (Westerlund and Rosander 1997) The region of the Nile Valley and the Horn of Africa has its own unique mixture of these processes, coloured by the region's geographical proximity to the Arab world. What is most striking about these processes is that they have been overwhelmingly non-violent.

Africa, both north and south of the Sahara, is little different from the rest of the Muslim world in what has been considered *jihad*. Instances include the resistance by the Moroccan Shadhiliyya order against Portuguese penetration, Amir Abdel Kader's resistance to French occupation of Algeria, and occasional campaigns of forcible conversion of non-Muslims in sub-Saharan Africa (Karrar 1992: 3, 165). In exceptional cases domestic reformist movements described themselves as *jihads*. For example, the early nineteenth-century West African *jihad* of Uthman dan Fodio 'was essentially a reform movement to purify an already semi-Islamised society rather than forcibly convert non-Muslims.' (Steed and Westerlund 1999: 59) This Mahdist jihadism was adapted by Mohamed Ahmed al Mahdi in Sudan in the 1880s, to expel the Turco-Egyptian rulers and their European mercenary generals from his land. The protracted resistance by Mohamed Abdille Hasan (the 'Mad Mullah') to the British occupation of Somalia was similar, and perhaps the last pre-modern *jihad*. However, there was no *jihad* by the Ottoman state to impose Islamic orthodoxy. In post-colonial Africa, until Sudan in the 1990s, neither did any Muslim state use *jihad* as a tool of Islamisation.

The Nile Valley Islamist project of promoting 'pure' Islam has been closely tied up with an Arab cultural orthodoxy. For Islamist theoreticians, the embrace of Islam is all-or-nothing, and demands total transformation of the individual. They mostly assume that certain values in Arab culture represent 'civilisation'. Sayyid Qutb's writings on Islam in Africa are meagre, but crystallise the dominant Islamists' viewpoint:

When Islam entered the central parts of Africa, it clothed naked human beings, civilized them, brought they out of the deep recesses of isolation, and taught them the joy of work in exploring material resources. It brought them out of the narrow circles of tribe and clan into the vast circle of the Islamic community, and out of the worship of pagan deities into the worship of the Creator of the worlds. If this is not civilization, then what is it? (1990: 89)

Similarly, the writings of contemporary Sudanese Islamists such as Hassan Makki indicate, first, a remarkable ignorance about the nature of traditional religions and cultures, and second, an assumption that they form some sort of *tabula rasa* onto which the religious and civilisational benefits of Islam can be imposed. In a revealing double error, Makki dismisses 'anthrobiology [sic]' as a 'missionary project' (1989: 67), suggesting that he has not read, or not understood, the rich social anthropological literature on his native country. His account focuses on alleged Western conspiracies and their supposed impact on the African 'personality':

The greatest tragedy caused by Western Christianity with its materialistic, commercial outlook was that it aroused expectations that could not be fulfilled regardless of circumstances. The dynamic of Western culture, with its liquor, sensational cinema and litter, spoon and fork, dress, expensive way of living and monogamy among basically staple-diet, poor, primitive and polygamous African societies, enslaved the body, corrupted the mind and created a world of confusion. The new generation faces confusion, and a crass and material form of atheism, veiled by Christian names. (p. 151)[19]

Abdelwahab El-Affendi, himself an Islamist, has criticised his colleagues' 'conception [that] presupposed that the South would act as an inert mass, waiting to be reshaped anew [by Islam and Arabism]'. (1990: 372) The Sudan government's 'civilisation project' (*al mashru' al hadhari*) is how this

---

[19] One such 'Christian' name Makki cites is 'Garang', which is a traditional Dinka name.

is manifest in policy. It has clear echoes of imperialism. In the hands of Hassan al Turabi and his acolytes, the 'civilisation project' has been conflated with both the 'comprehensive *da'wa*' and national *jihad* (see chapter 3).

The 'civilisation project' is primarily a domestic Sudanese affair, in which the governing elites draw upon the cultural resources of Egypt and the money of the Saudi Salafis and their own political imagination. Egyptian policy towards the Horn of Africa has been marked by a consistent assumption of civilisational superiority. Egyptian cultural missions have provided scholarships with the aim of educating a future Arabic-speaking elite. Islamic missionary activities have been supported.[20] The policy has never been specifically oriented towards the promotion of Islamism, but one of its unintended consequences has been to expose African Muslims to the writings of Islamists such as Qutb. Many African Islamists have sought to be educated in Cairo, especially at al Azhar.

The main thrust of Egyptian foreign policy has been resolutely realist. It has historically been preoccupied with controlling the sources of the Nile, and has sought to maintain a controlling influence in Sudan, regarding the country as a lost province detached from the motherland by the perfidious British, rather than an independent sovereign nation. This conservative approach has been Egypt's fall-back position. Briefly, under Gamal Abdel Nasser, Egypt sought to play a broader and more ideological role in Africa, coupling the African and Arab (Palestinian) liberation struggles. As Africa struggled to establish a continental organisation in the early 1960s, Nasser was active in the radical 'Casablanca Group'. Arab-Israeli competition for influence in Africa was an important theme of the period. Nasser urged African states such as Ghana to sever their ties with 'imperialist' Israel, and instead sought a broad Afro-Arab cooperation in pursuit of liberation. The aim was to create a pan-continental anti-imperialist bloc that could dominate the United Nations. Nasser's leading role in the Non-Aligned Movement, alongside Nehru and Tito, was another aspect to this. Hence Egypt supported Kwame Nkrumah's pan Africanism and was active in the Africa Liberation Committee of the Organisation of African Unity (OAU).[21] Cairo was a stopover for Che Guevara on his way to Congo in 1965. After 1967 Nasser repeatedly pointed to the parallel illegalities of the Israeli occupation of Sinai and the minority regimes in southern Africa.

---

[20] One of the reasons for the Egyptian state's tolerance of Sufism has been the importance of Sufi missionaries in spreading Islam in the Nile Valley and further afield. See Gerholm, 1997: 145.

[21] Nkrumah's wife was also Egyptian.

On winning liberation Algeria became a partner in the project of Afro-Arab political solidarity and a centre for African liberation struggles. This solidarity peaked in the early 1970s (Červenka 1977: 159–64), symbolised by the PLO being granted observer status at the OAU. PLO links with southern African liberation movements, especially South Africa's African National Congress, remain strong up to the present, and the Palestinian cause has retained resonance across the continent. As recently as the July 2002 Durban Summit, the African Union conducted a vigorous debate on Palestine and adopted a strongly pro-Palestinian resolution. But effective solidarity began to crumble after the 1973 oil price hike and its disastrous economic impact on Africa, the Libyan invasion of Chad, and Morocco's annexation of the Western Sahara. Crises including the Ethio-Somali war and the Katanga secessionist bid further divided both the African and Arab camps. Above all, the Egyptian rapprochement with Israel, and subsequently the Arab states' *de facto* acceptance of the state of Israel, reduced Arab-Israeli rivalry in Africa. This created a strategic void, filled in part by Islamist evangelism and philanthropy.

Under Mubarak, Egypt's Africa policy became more introverted and reverted to a focus on its traditional concerns in the Nile Valley and the Horn. In the 1990s Egypt found itself for the first time ever without leverage among any of the states of the Horn, and its re-engagement in Sudan was an essentially defensive process, to protect itself from destabilisation (see chapter 6). Egyptian intelligence has been hostile to any militant Egyptian Islamists taking up residence in African countries, but in other respects its policies towards Islamism have been overwhelmingly domestic.

By contrast, Saudi policy towards Africa has had the aim and effect of promoting Salafi Islamism. Unlike Egypt, Saudi Arabia has no historic engagement with Africa as an imperial power, and its fundamental national interests are not linked to an African hinterland.[22] Pilgrims from Sahelian Africa brought Wahhabist precepts back to their home countries in the nineteenth and twentieth centuries, contributing for example to a Wahhabi movement in Mali. (Brenner 1993, Hunwick 1997) One of the main thrusts of Wahhabism has been its hostility to popular Islam in Africa, which is overwhelmingly Sufi. In Nigeria, both anti-colonialism and dismay at the corruption of the modern state have contributed to a vigorous anti-Sufist movement. (Umar 1993) Saudi Arabia's active engagement in sub-Saharan Africa has been recent, and overwhelmingly

---

[22] The partial exception to this was Saudi fear of the Libya-South Yemen-Ethiopia axis that prompted modest assistance to Eritrean and Ethiopian resistance groups in the 1970s and 80s.

driven by finance. While Islamic banks handle the largest sums, funding of da'waist charities has been more influential. One of the Afro-Arab initiatives of the mid-1970s was to try to recycle some of Gulf states' petrodollars into African development, partly to offset the economic crisis triggered by the oil price increase. Institutions such as the Arab Bank for Economic Development in Africa and the Islamic Development Bank switched the axis of Arab-African relations from the radical regimes in Cairo and Algiers to the conservative and more Islamically-oriented Gulf states. Alongside Saudi Arabia, Kuwait was particularly active and generous. At the same time, Islamists 'discovered' the existence of neglected communities of African Muslims, and the first Islamic philanthropic organisations such as the Islamic African Relief Agency were founded to support them, and to promote Islam more widely.

Throughout the 1980s, Saudi Arabia tried to construct an elaborate alliance of Sunni Muslim countries and movements of all ideological shades, using its enormous wealth to buy stability, if not loyalty. One motivation for this was a rivalry with Iran, which was also active among African Muslim communities. After 1990–1, when the Gulf War represented a crisis of legitimacy for the Saudi state, it was buying off critics. In contrast to the earlier Arab-Israeli competition for the solidarity of African states, the target was the allegiance of African Muslims. This Saudi '*riyalpolitik*' was indiscriminate in its recipients. It has accommodated some Sufists (for example the Niassiyya in Sudan, Al-Karsany. 1993: 143) Many of its beneficiaries have promoted militant forms of Islamism that subsequently came into conflict with the Saudi regime itself. Some of these contradictions surfaced during the Gulf War, and more have done so since the al Qa'ida atrocities of September 11, primarily with respect to Saudi policies towards Afghanistan. On a smaller but still significant scale, Salafist largesse in Africa also ran counter to the power interests of the regime. Notably in Sudan, certain Salafi philanthropic organisations ended up abetting some of the most militant elements in a coalition between Sudanese intelligence and international neo-fundamentalist jihadists. Usama bin Laden's subversion of the Saudi channels for exporting Wahhabism led to some international Islamic NGOs being banned by the United States after September 11. (Indyk 2002) The vast and indiscriminate Saudi funding of any educational, charitable or developmental activities that could claim the Salafi label serves as an important backdrop to all the subsequent chapters in this book.

Sudan is a key intermediary in the export of Salafism through Islamic philanthropy. Uniquely among Arabic-speaking countries, in the 1970s

Sudan possessed a substantial professional class familiar with the operation of international relief and development agencies. Sudan served as a laboratory for many innovations in development and relief practice during the 1970s and '80s. (de Waal 1997a) These skilled development managers and economists not only staffed many of the international Islamist philanthropic organisations, but also contributed many ideas that influenced their policies and practices, first in Africa and subsequently more widely in the Muslim world. The first generation of Islamic NGO professionals were schooled in the world of secular relief and development, but subsequently specifically Islamic doctrines such as 'comprehensive *da'wa*' emerged.

The implications of this encounter for the Sudanese civil war's transformation into a *jihad*, and the regionalisation of the encounter between militant Islamism and its adversaries, will be examined in this book. One point however emerges clearly from the narrative and analysis. This is that the Sudanese and regional *jihads* do not neatly fit any of the three categories outlined above. To the extent that they are nationalist, they are not *jihads*. There is a neo-fundamentalist element but it is not well-rooted in local realities. The global Salafi jihadist element was transient, related to the presence of Usama bin Laden in Khartoum and the way in which Egyptian jihadist groups used Sudan as a base and Sudanese intelligence services as a vehicle.

Libya's role in the promotion of Islamism has another character again, linked to the somewhat eclectic nature of Gaddafi's Islamism, his pan-Africanism and his highly personalised relationship with certain sub-Saharan African leaders. Gaddafi's *Green Book* makes no mention of Islam, but early in his rule he promulgated a version of *shari'a*. In his interventionist policies towards sub-Saharan Africa, Gaddafi has encouraged both Islam and warfare, but never *jihad*. The organisation al Da'wa al Islamiyya was created in Libya in 1972, and Gaddafi funded many Islamic cultural and missionary projects in Africa. (Hunwick 1997: 40–1) Gaddafi's influence is also credited with the conversion to Islam of Gabon's President Albert Omar Bongo. He may perhaps be best seen as a variant of the Nasserite legacy, revealing the incomplete secularism of that political practice. (Anderson 1983) Although the ideological divides between Gaddafi, the Muslim Brothers and the Saudi Salafists are sharply drawn in the Arab world,[23] the boundaries are less clear-cut in

---

[23] Libya was the first country to issue an arrest warrant for Usama bin Laden. See Gunaratna 2002: 142.

sub-Saharan Africa, where Islamic *da'wa* creates a receptivity to neo-fundamentalism.

The Islamist impasse in the Horn of Africa takes on a different character to that in Egypt and to its manifestations elsewhere in sub-Saharan Africa. In comparison to Sufism, Islamism is a force both for modernisation and for broadening intellectual horizons, and has therefore taken hold primarily among urbanised groups. (Westerlund 1997) Islamism's association with the civilisational values of Arabism both augments and disguises the intellectual failures of neo-fundamentalism. The economic and political crises afflicting the region repeatedly provide openings for adaptable mobilisation drawing upon the religious symbolism and cultural resources of Islam. The competition with secular developmentalism and militarised revolutionary leftism has played to some of Islamism's strengths, namely its capacity for mobilising energy and resources for community development projects. Less theorised, less restricted by powerful patrimonial states, Islamists have pursued different strategies to those of their Egyptian brethren. But ultimately, in their failure to offer more than 'little solutions', north-east Africa's Islamist leaders have been reduced to raising a banner of protest and repeating the same old slogans.

3

ISLAMISM, STATE POWER AND *JIHAD* IN SUDAN

Alex de Waal and A. H. Abdel Salam

Two faces of Sudanese Islamism

On 27 April 1992 Dr Hassan al Turabi, Islamist philosopher and *éminence grise* behind the national Islamic government in Sudan, presented a lecture at the Royal Society of Arts in London on the theme of nationalism and Islam. Unfazed by the classical nudes decorating the walls and ceiling of the Society's lecture hall—and in all probability revelling in the apparent paradox of his setting—Dr Turabi eloquently presented his liberal philosophy of Islamism.

Islam, as divine word, is the eternal embodiment of truth, goodness and right. But, as message, it is addressed to man in history. To take its right course and remain in essence the same as ever, it should be aligned to those eternal principles and ideals. To take root and real form, it has to be related to the specific time context. Attachment to temporal specificity may degenerate into conservatism, conventionalism and stagnation—freezing religion in a particular past context and arresting its sustained progression in time to eternity. Excessive fidelity to immutable principle may lead to historical irrelevance and visionary abstraction from reality. The historical test for Muslims has always been to recover after every setback, seeking through the revival of faith (*iman*), the renewal of thought (*ijtihad*) and the resurgence of action (*jihad*) to salvage religion from temporal containment and ensure its progressive development, relevance and continuity in history. (al Turabi 1992: 1)

Turabi's text is interesting in its attempt to historicise Islamist practice. He also distances himself from neo-fundamentalism. His is an attempt to broaden the horizons of Islamism, to allow it to coexist, philosophically at least, with the complexities of history and the realities of political power.

71

The Sudanese community in London packed the lecture hall, both Islamists and dissident refugees, listening in polite silence. When Turabi had finished, the chairman asked for questions. A Sudanese man dressed in traditional *jellabiya* and *'imma*, sitting in the front row, caught his eye. Abdel Bagi el Rayah stood up, a few feet from Turabi. He asked to speak in Arabic: the Islamist cadres tried to shout him down, knowing Abdel Bagi and fearful of what might happen next. The chair agreed to an interpreter: exiled parliamentarian Mansur el Agab strode to the front. Abdel Bagi began his story: he was arrested, tortured, forced to lie in freezing water. His leg became gangrenous and had to be amputated. At this point, Abdel Bagi took off his wooden leg, until then concealed beneath his *jellabiya*, and thrust it in Turabi's face: 'What does your Islam have to say about this?'

The room exploded with the dissidents, refugees and exiles shouting 'fascist!' at Dr Turabi while the Sudan-government-sponsored students, embassy staff and sundry Islamists tried in turn to shout them down. After the hubbub had subsided, the chairman put the question to Turabi again. He gave a high-pitched laugh and answered: 'Islam does not permit such things.'

Turabi's lecture neatly dodged around the issue of *jihad*. This is significant, because the very same day, a group of pro-government religious leaders in El Obeid, the provincial capital of Kordofan, issued a *fatwa* in support of *jihad* in the Nuba Mountains, a province that was the site of a long running insurrection. The SPLA had mobilised support among the indigenous 'African' Nuba people, bringing the civil war into Northern Sudan. A few months earlier, in January, Lieutenant-General Abdel Karim Husseini, the Governor of Kordofan, had declared a *jihad*. A few days earlier, a large conference has convened to mobilise militias under the leadership of tribal leaders, who were bestowed with titles such as *amir al jihad*, and President Bashir was named as *imam al jihad* (African Rights 1995b: 110–11). And on the day that Turabi lectured in London, 27 April 1992, six local *ulama* met and 'issued the adduced *fatwa* to legalise the *jihad* in South Kordofan State and Southern Sudan.' (African Rights 1995b: 289–91)

The rebels in South Kordofan and Southern Sudan started their rebellion against the state and declared war against the Muslims. Their main aims are: killing the Moslems, desecrating mosques, burning and defiling the Qur'an, and raping Moslem women. In so doing, they are encouraged by the enemies of Islam and Moslems: these foes are the Zionists, the Christians and the arrogant people who provide them with provisions and arms. Therefore, an insurgent who was previously a Muslim is now an apostate; and a non-Muslim is a non-believer standing as a bulwark against the spread of Islam, and Islam has granted the freedom of killing both of them according to the following words of Allah...[1]

In short, rebellion against the Sudan government was equated with rebellion against Islam, and the Muslim members of the SPLA in the region were excommunicated. The largest offensive of the war in the Nuba Mountains was then under way, with nearly four months of continuous fighting (NAFIR 1997). Significantly, mosques in the Nuba Mountains *jihad* were desecrated by *government* troops, who covered them with graffiti (instructing the Muslims to come and pray in the government garrisons), destroying *zakat* grain and tearing up copies of the Qur'an. (African Rights 1995b: 292–5) This was not an isolated case. Government soldiers also destroyed village mosques at Mukla in Southern Blue Nile in April 1997 and Gedamayeb and Rabbasim in the Beja Hills, in that same month (Sudan Rights Programme 1998). No fewer than fourteen mosques were confirmed destroyed, damaged or looted in the Nuba Mountains between 1993 and 1997. Each one was a modest village mosque (known as *masjit*), usually with an attached Qur'anic school (*khalwa*). But nonetheless they were centres of devotion.

At a press conference in Kampala in February 1999, Sheikh Omer al Tahir, from the Beja, held up a copy of the Qur'an, partly burned in the attack on Gedamayeb, and asked, 'How can a Muslim government do this?' Imam Adam Tutu Atrun, one of the most prominent Muslim leaders in the region, commented: 'Islam does not allow Muslims to do this.'[2] For a Muslim, Sudanese or otherwise, the destruction of a mosque by an avowedly Muslim government is inexplicable.

This is a new departure for Islamism, a strain of neo-fundamentalism that is more commonly associated with the Taliban in Afghanistan. Did Turabi authorise the *jihad* and *fatwa*? Was he comfortable with it and with the subsequent attacks on mosques? We cannot tell. It certainly appears to be the antithesis of his avowed liberal Islamism, and he did not visit El Obeid during this period. There is a disconnect here. Repeatedly, when presented with evidence for gross abuses of human rights perpetrated by the Sudan government, Turabi has responded with apparent bafflement, saying that such things are not possible in an Islamic state, for example

[1] *Fatwa* issued by religious leaders, imams of mosques and Sufists of Kordofan State, 27 April 1992.
[2] Interviewed in Kauda, Nuba Mountains, 11 May 1995.

exclaiming, 'Excuse me—this is madness!' (African Rights 1995b: 276) On the other hand, since losing power he has been more frank:

Sudan's authority, culture will not develop with goodness and justice unless it is corrected by the guidance of unifying religion and the love of the country that accommodates all citizens wherever they are, north or south. In the first stages of the Salvation Revolution, these meanings prevailed with military victories through the force of *jihad*, which was directed by its God-fearing nature towards just unity and which was aiming to gather, not to fracture citizens by violence, nor to make them fear and run. The call of Islam was expanding in the South, and it was paving the way for the Muslims to gain a fair share in the hierarchy of authority. (al Turabi 2001: 8)

Turabi's Qur'anic language makes any translation both ungainly and ambiguous, but cannot obscure his recognition of the role of violence.

Most probably Turabi had no direct involvement in the El Obeid *fatwa*. The text betrays a poor level of scholarship, contrasting with the sophistication of Turabi's legalism, and reflecting its six signatories, who can be counted as second-rate provincial *ulama*. They included a former *mufti*, two *imams*, one from the army mosque in the town, and three employees of the Ministry of Religious Affairs. None were individuals of significance: all were from the province and not even the *imam* of the El Obeid grand mosque was present. In this respect, we must disagree with the elevated importance given to this *fatwa* by Yossef Bodansky[3]:

This fatwa was clearly organized and written as a universal Islamist legal document determining relations between Muslims and their neighbors in mixed societies and states without Muslim governments. The authors of this fatwa pointed to southern Sudan [sic] as the peculiar case that made them pass a sweeping and principled judgment applicable to all similar cases.... The leadership in Khartoum was not wrong, from their legal point of view, in selecting this fatwa as a guideline for the Islamist jihad strategy in such places as Kashmir, Palestine and Bosnia. (1999: 111)

In fact, the El Obeid *fatwa* was rarely cited, even in Kordofan. If Turabi's Popular Arab and Islamic Conference, which met three times in Khartoum in the early 1990s, had wanted to issue a similar judgement with universal application, they would have done it with more style, more erudition and more publicity. But Bodansky's error should not obscure our central contention: Turabi had indeed become *al faqih al askari*, the armed jurist.

---

[3] Bodansky incorrectly dates the document to 1993, in line with a translation circulating in Europe and the US in 1994.

The point we make here is not to condemn the Sudan government for its human rights abuses, nor to attack Turabi for hypocrisy. It is to ask, why did a version of Islamism that was, if not always liberal, at least consistently modernist, come to engage in such neo-fundamentalist excess? Was this a compromise arising from the necessities of wielding state power? Or is political Islam doomed to revert to such regressive manifestations, destroying the values that its advocates initially espoused?

Turabi's revolutions in Sudan

Hassan al Turabi is one of the most outstanding thinkers and practitioners of political Islam. If anyone could resolve the Islamists' impasse in both theory and practice, it is he. Turabi is credited with having revolutionised Islamist thinking, making it compatible with the rights of women, democracy and the arts, and uniting together Sunni, Shi'a and Sufi philosophies. (El-Affendi 1991a) Turabi's writings have tantalising echoes of Western social science. They are full of hints (and occasional explicit claims) that he has successfully reconciled Islamism with *liberal* modernity. For example, Turabi argued that the consensus on which the Islamic state should be ruled was not that of the *ulama*, but that of the people as a whole. Turabi's experiment is an important and instructive exercise in broadening the Islamist political imagination. But it too has been shipwrecked on the rocks of reality, in part because of its inescapable embrace of violence.

In contrast to his Egyptian counterparts, and reflecting the high status of the liberal social sciences in the University of Khartoum, Turabi, his immediate followers and his political rivals studied law, history and social anthropology. Turabi himself obtained a doctorate in law from the Sorbonne, before returning to Sudan in 1964 to lead the Islamist movement he has dominated ever since—and even after his removal from power in 1999 and subsequent arrest and house arrest, he has continued to overshadow his erstwhile students who rejected him. If there is to be a true theory of political change and power in Islamist thinking, it is most likely to be found with Turabi. And indeed Turabi also oversaw the 1989 National Salvation Revolution, the military coup that brought the Islamists to power in Khartoum.

When the Muslim Brothers founded their Sudanese branch in the 1940s, they found a very different context to Egypt. Rather than confronting monolithic state power, Sudanese Islamists faced a political system dominated by two existing Islamic sectarian parties, the Umma Party of the followers (*ansar*) of the Mahdi, and the Unionist Party (currently Democratic Unionist Party) dominated by the Khatmiyya sect and the Mirghani family. In addition, Sudan possesses multiple other Sufi sects, some of which have powerful reformist traditions. (Karrar 1992) Elements of *shari'a* were always found in Sudan's civil laws, even during colonial rule, as well as in personal law for Muslims. In a context in which public life was already enthused with popular, customary Islam, it was much more difficult for the Islamists to claim the legitimacy of resisting an oppressive secular state. In their formative period, the Sudanese Muslim Brothers' influences were reformist. Their initial debate was over whether to remain simply a branch of the Egyptian Society, or to be independent. They chose organisational independence, while sharing a common ideological heritage.

The Sudanese Islamists had no intellectual monopoly on political Islam in Sudan. Turabi faced a formidable intellectual and political competitor in the person of his brother-in-law Sadiq el Mahdi, leader of the Umma Party and aspiring Imam of the Ansar. As great grandson of the Mahdi, Sadiq commanded political and spiritual legitimacy that surpassed any that the Muslim Brothers could claim.[4] Sadiq gained a degree in politics from Oxford and wrote subtly about the history and politics of Islam. In direct challenge to the accepted wisdom of Egyptian Islamism, Sadiq claims that 'Anthropology, Orientalism, and indeed all Western study of other cultures have relatively liberated themselves from former imperial policies and become more objective.' (Al-Sadiq 1983: 231) Sadiq and Turabi have been intimate rivals for more than thirty years. As early as the 1960s, 'while the Ikhwan [Muslim Brothers] considered Sadiq a mole in the Umma, Sadiq worked with the reciprocal supposition that the Ikhwan were actually a branch of the Umma Party.' (El-Affendi 1991a: 100) Both claims have some truth: Sadiq introduced modernist Islamism to the Umma Party, while many Sudanese Muslim Brothers have retained allegiance to the sectarian parties of their families, sometimes reverting to them as they graduated from student politics.

Sadiq has consistently been a democrat, not least because his Umma Party commands the largest bloc of votes in the country. His version of Islamism is resolutely anti-secularist, advocating *shari'a* for Muslims and the unity of politics and religion. However—reflecting his comfort with electoral politics—he also elevates constitutionalism and citizenship, con-

---

[4] The transformation of militant anti-colonial Mahdism into 'neo-Mahdism' that cooperated with colonialism is an important example of quasi-modernising reformism.

cluding, 'What we are really looking for is not a reduction of religion, but an elevation of citizenship identity, and protecting it from the encroachment of any extra-citizenship considerations.' (Al-Sadiq 2000: 89) This 'constitutionalist' view asserts that the state itself cannot have a religious identity. It has interesting parallels with Imam Khomeini's successful attempts to create an institutionalisation of political power in Islamist Iran, in which constitutional order does not efface itself before the implementation of the *shari'a*. (cf. Roy 1994: 176–7)

Another competitor was Mahmoud Mohamed Taha and his Republican Brothers, who espoused a reformist ideology based on indigenous Sufi Islam, seeking legitimacy in the long history of peaceable Sufi proselytisation in Sudan (Taha 1990). While largely an elite-based movement, in some curious respects the Republicans were also conservative populists, building relations with traditional Sufi orders. *Ustaz* Taha was a pacifist, utterly opposed to ideas of violent *jihad*. A less formidable political challenge to Turabi, Taha nonetheless widened the horizons of what needed to be debated among Sudan's student activists and political elites. It is interesting to note the cautious way in which Turabi avoided a direct intellectual confrontation with *Ustaz* Taha, perhaps reflecting the fact that both of them espoused versions of Islam that would be considered eclectic by many mainstream Islamists. This encounter is a reflection of the wider problem encountered by Sudanese Islamism in its relations with the dominant Sufi traditions in Sudan (Muhammed Mahmoud 1997).

Another dimension to Sudanese Islamism is the encounter between the Arab orientation of the Muslim Brothers and an indigenous theocratic tradition in West African Islam. This dates from the time of the Sokoto Caliphate (Steed and Westerlund 1999), and had variant historic manifestations in the sultanates of Darfur and Dar Masalit in western Sudan, and recurrent Mahdist irruptions in that region (Biobaku and al Hajj 1966, Kapteijns 1985, Al-Karsany 1993). Theirs is an Islamist tradition that embraces elements of both Sufism and Wahhabism, but most importantly from the Sudanese vantage point, it is a black, 'African' tradition rather than an Arab one. It disavows the powerful centralised Sufi orders characteristic of the Nile Valley, and is the vehicle for a popular, messianic tradition. Darfur's religious traditions are closer to those of West Africa than the Nile Valley, and Sudan contains a large population of Muslim West Africans, known as Fellata and mostly Hausa and Fulani in origin. They often define themselves as 'permanent pilgrims', although many of them migrated during colonial times as labourers rather than arriving en route to Mecca. These black, non-Arab Darfurians and Fellata Muslims emerged as a significant Islamist constituency in the 1980s and '90s, and their Islamist orthodoxy was a challenge to implicit assumption of the Nile Valley Islamists that Islamism is coterminous with Arabism. To be sure, the Islamist westerners did not dispute the core cultural values of the Islamic project, including such 'Sudanese' characteristics as wearing the *jellabiya* (for men) and the *toub* (for women), while the ruling families of Fulani and Fur have commonly claimed descent from the Prophet's lineage. The populist utopianism of this 'western' tradition was poorly articulated within the more orthodox, legalistic and politically sophisticated leadership of the NIF, and as a result is hard to discern within the ideology of modern Sudanese Islamists. However, in practice the racial divide between riverain 'Arabs' and western 'blacks' proved a crucial weakness in the NIF, highlighted by the split of 1999. The critique of the 'westerners' was framed entirely in terms of the riverain elite's monopoly on power, making no reference to any Islamic precepts. The racial aspect of the encounter between 'Arab' and 'African' Islamisms remained untheorised, both in the parties' embrace and in their dissension. Indeed, Islamists *cannot* theorise this encounter, because they do not recognise any plurality in Islam or Islamism, instead insisting that in any disagreement, one party must be deviating from true Islam.

More widely, Sudan has been the locus of some of the most insightful social science in the Arab world. The overwhelming majority of it is produced by non-Islamists. Both Sudanese (Mohamed Omer Beshir, Abdel Ghaffar Mohamed Ahmed, Taisier Ali, Haider Ibrahim) and non-Sudanese (Talal Asad, from Saudi Arabia, and Ahmad al Shahi, originally from Iraq) researched and lectured in social and political sciences in Khartoum in the 1960s and '70s. Some of them, and many of their students, we will subsequently encounter among the dissidents and political opponents of the National Islamic Front. Of particular interest is the cross-over between the 'Arab' and 'African' societies in Sudan, which produced non-Arab intellectuals of distinction (Francis Deng, Sharif Harir) and some Northern thinkers with significant sensitivities to the world-views of their non-Arab brethren. Among the latter we can note Mansour Khalid, whose formulation 'noble spiritual believers' remains the most apt and sensitive constitutional characterisation of non-Christian, non-Muslim Sudanese, and Ushari Mahmoud, who identified 'Juba Arabic'— spoken as a *lingua franca* in Southern Sudan—as a distinct dialect and not merely 'Arabic spoken badly'. Sadly, not a single one of these open-minded intellectuals remains in university employment in Sudan.

Hassan al Turabi's writings reflect this generally liberal intellectual and political climate. His position appears as liberal and reformist:

Religion is based on sincere conviction and voluntary compliance. Therefore an Islamic state evolves from an Islamic society. In certain areas, progress towards an Islamic society may be frustrated by political suppression. Whenever religious energy is thus suppressed, it builds up and ultimately erupts in isolated acts of struggle or resistance which are called terrorist by those in power or revolution. In circumstances where Islam is allowed free expression, social change takes place peacefully and gradually, and the Islamic movement develops programs of Islamization before it takes over the destiny of the state because Islamic thought—like all thought—only flourishes in a social environment of freedom and public consultation (*shurah*). (al Turabi 1983: 241)

Turabi's writings tiptoe around the question of violence and *jihad*. The passage quoted above is characteristically evasive, implying that violence is the inevitable result of any attempts to thwart the progress of Islamism, while avoiding any explicit call for *jihad*. The passage is also characteristically general, concerning itself with broad historical and philosophical concerns, and saying nothing about the concrete context of Sudan. For fully twenty-eight of Turabi's thirty-eight years in politics, Sudan has been engaged in a civil war. In 1991 and 1992, the NIF government declared *jihad* against the SPLA. In the quotation that opened this chapter, Turabi simply defined *jihad* as 'resurgence of action'.

Turabi proved a master of coalition building, adapting the demands of Islamism to the Sudanese context. While the Muslim Brothers remained the core of his political mobilisation throughout, he constantly sought broader coalitions that could bring in wider Islamist groups. During the second parliamentary period in the 1960s, Hassan al Turabi was ready to enter an opposition with Sadiq el Mahdi and a range of other political forces including William Deng's Sudan African National Union—the latter never remotely an Islamist party. His was an incrementalist, compromising approach. This is perhaps the closest that any Islamist has come to a Leninist model: Turabi established his vanguard of Muslim Brothers and then built a movement around it, usually utilising the term *jabha*, 'front'. In the 1960s he headed the Islamic Charter Front. In fact, he succeeded in making the Leninist model of front-building work better than any of the Communists in Sudan.

Colonel Jaafar Nimeiri's 1969 military coup was in the Nasserite mould and the government duly cracked down on the Ansar the following year. This radicalised the Islamists who staged an uprising in 1973 and participated in a failed invasion in 1976. Nimeiri was shaken and needed a broader political base, so he sought 'National Reconciliation' with his conservative opponents. Turabi saw his chance and 1977 he took the position of Attorney General in what was still a one-party state. For six years he operated within a secular legal framework while filling the main posts in his office with Islamists. Nimeiri promulgated *shari'a* in September 1983 with the help of two lawyers who were followers of small Sufi orders, neither of them followers of Turabi, who had been moved to the position of Presidential Adviser for Foreign Affairs. One of the weaknesses of the September Laws was the poor quality of their Islamist legalism: they were not drafted by specialist Islamic lawyers at all.

In fact the 'September Laws' were in part Nimeiri's ad hoc response to an ongoing strike by judges: the mercurial President wanted to break the power of the urban opposition, among which lawyers were prominent, and play a populist card. Earlier in the year, Nimeiri attacked the judiciary, accusing it of corruption and inefficiency, and dismissed judges—including judges from the supreme court—on the grounds of 'public interest'. Among those dismissed were some suspected of corruption and others who had taken brave decisions, for example those who allowed criminal procedures to proceed against the First Vice President, Omer Mohamed al Tayeb. In protest, district and province judges offered their collective resignations and the Bar went on strike in solidarity, demanding the independence of the judiciary and the reinstatement of their dismissed colleagues, or that they be subjected to fair and proper disciplinary procedures in which they could have the opportunity to defend themselves. Nimeiri refused the judges' claims and for three months he tried unsuccessfully tried to break their strike. Instead of accepting defeat, Nimeiri's final stratagem was to introduce Islamic law—thereby instantly rendering the judges redundant.

Nimeiri turned to a former provincial judge, Annaial Abu Gurun, who had just been appointed to the newly-created position of 'judicial associate to the palace'. A Sufi and former provincial judge, Annaial said that he would be unable to draft the necessary laws unaided, and introduced a colleague, Awad Algeed—a common law lawyer, a religious man and also a Sufi. The two were assigned an office in the palace and joined by a representative of the Attorney General, Badria Suliman. These two men and one woman formed the committee that drafted the 'September Laws', in considerable haste.[5] Even though the *shari'a* had been produced

---

[5] Ironically, the laws they drafted made it a cause for investigation if two men and a women are found together in one room, without the woman being married to one of the men, and without her having a *muhrim* (responsible adult relative) present.

in a manner that smacked of incompetence, once they had been promulgated, Turabi and the Islamists defended them stoutly. Nimeiri's tactical gambit had far-reaching consequences. Among the earliest was a spate of amputations and the execution of *Ustaz* Mahmoud Mohamed Taha, leader of the Republican Brothers, in January 1985 for alleged apostasy under the *shari'a* code—Sudan's first and most infamous act of neo-fundamentalist barbarity.

Meanwhile Islamist cadres had taken key positions in government, the university and the army, and were also well placed to make best use of the oil funds flowing into Sudan from the Gulf, both from the governments there and from the Sudanese expatriates. Many Islamist institutions were established, including banks and companies, voluntary organisations, newspapers and the like. Abdelwahab El-Affendi writes:

Shortly after the NR [National Reconciliation] deal a drive to increase membership ten-fold was launched, coupled with complete decentralization within the movement to make the organization more efficient and resistant to crackdowns. Decentralization was enhanced by setting up numerous autonomous satellite organizations loosely affiliated to the group. The late seventies and early eighties saw the emergence of the Society of Women Vanguards of Renaissance, the Youth Society for Construction, the Association of Southern Muslims, the Association of Sudanese Ulama, the Islamic Da'wa (Missionary) Organization (and its off-shoot, the Islamic African Relief Agency), the Namariq Literary and Artist Society, and the Union of Muslim Literary Men, to mention only the most prominent. Although most of these groups were not directly controlled by the Ikhwan, Ikhwan could count on support from most of them in crucial moments. (1991a: 115)

Turabi's strategy was to build a power base, along the principle of *tamkiin* ('empowerment'): Nimeiri's embrace of Islamic law was an unexpected bonus. The strategy was partly designed to diffuse the Islamists' assets so that it could better evade a future clamp-down. In the event, in 1985, Turabi succeeded in jumping from Nimeiri's sinking ship just before it finally succumbed to a popular uprising, and reinvented his movement as the National Islamic Front (NIF), and in due course returned to government. Throughout this period he thrived on the failures of his secular and leftist adversaries, and on the polarisation brought about by the civil war. In 1989, his cadres mounted a military coup, pre-empting by just a few days a peace settlement between Prime Minister Sadiq el Mahdi and SPLA leader John Garang, that would have put a stop to the Islamist agenda. For much of the succeeding decade, Turabi was the controlling influence behind the military rulers, and the indubitable sheikh of the movement. He chaired the 1992 *majlis al shura* (consultative council), wrote the Constitution and subsequently emerged as head of the National Congress Party and Speaker of Parliament. In 1999 he was poised to become executive Prime Minister, reducing the President to a mere figurehead, when General Bashir abruptly and surprisingly moved against him in December that year.

Throughout this long career under so many different organisational flags of convenience, the one constant in Sudanese Islamism has been Turabi himself. At various times there have been other members of the vanguard and even seconds-in-command. But there has been no consistent politbureau or similar organisational core. Indeed, Turabi regularly recruited new younger cadres and shuffled out his senior followers. Authority in the movement has stemmed from the personal charisma of the leader himself.

The breadth of Turabi's coalitions means that it can often be difficult to pin labels upon him. His writing is flexible to the point of being self-contradictory. While he supported women's education and emancipation (in a 1973 pamphlet, written from prison), and has given the female members of his household considerable freedoms, his policies were somewhat different. The NIF embraced very conservative groups such as the Ansar al Sunna (a strict Wahhabist group) and the followers of Ali Betai (a Sufi sheikh in Eastern Sudan who pioneered self-reliant community development and Qur'anic schooling), both of which remove women from all public life.[6] A succession of decrees throughout the 1990s enforced Islamic dress on women in government offices and schools, insisted on strict segregation of the sexes in public and in schools, restricted women's travel unless accompanied by a close male relative, and in 2000 tried to ban women from working in a range of public places. Turabi's personal interest in art and literature contrasts with his acolytes' Taliban-like removal of 'un-Islamic' statues from Sudan's museums.

Turabi's ambitions were wider than Sudan. He saw the Muslim world as an integral whole and positioned Sudan as leader of radical Islam. By supporting Saddam Hussein in 1990, Turabi earned the wrath of the West, but immediately Sudan was no longer a marginal player in Arab Islamic politics. Most Muslim extremist groups converged on Khartoum, including, famously, Usama bin Laden. When the Popular Arab and Islamic Conference was formed shortly afterwards (see chapter 6) he succeeded in bringing Sunni and Shi'a Islamists together in an unprece-

---

[6] In the 1990s the NIF fell out with Ali Betai's followers and moved against them, driving many to armed opposition under the umbrella of the Beja Congress.

dented way, outflanking the conservative Organisation of the Islamic Conference and the paralytic Arab League.

If there is to be an Islamist Lenin, then it is Hassan al Turabi. As we have seen, he is a master of staying on top of the shifting coalitions of Sudanese politics. He also saw, and took, the chance to seize power and use the state for a comprehensive transformation of Sudanese society. This project did not succeed, and its failure allows us to identify the key flaws in the theory and practice of Sudanese Islamism, and its inescapable addiction to violence.

Turabi's democracy

Reflecting the Islamist theories of state power developed by Mawdudi and Qutb, Hassan al Turabi is no democrat. But he has repeatedly tried to square the circle of reconciling Islamist political theory, which is inherently absolutist, with a veneer of democracy. Turabi's written views on democracy explain how historically the prominence of the *ulama* in government arose because of the logistical difficulties of consulting the people directly to achieve consensus, *ijma*. Now, he argues, times have changed.

In [these] different circumstances other formal delegates can lawfully represent the Ummah in the process of consultation. It follows that an Islamic form of government is essentially a form of representative democracy. But this statement requires the following qualification. First an Islamic republic is not strictly speaking a direct government of and by the people; it is a government of the *shari'ah*. But, in a substantial sense, it is a popular government since the *shari'ah* represents the convictions of the people, and therefore, their direct will. (1983: 244)

What Turabi grants in one sentence he takes away, with breathtaking audacity, with scarcely a pause for breath. This is a faithful reflection of the paradox of Sayyid Qutb, who is ready to grant freedoms, but only at such a time when all obstacles to Islam's dominance have been removed, so that people will automatically but freely embrace Islam (cf. Qutb 1990: 51).

When writing in English, Turabi presents a liberal face. This is not just because he is writing for a non-Muslim audience, but also because his unique Arabic style is virtually untranslatable. When writing in Arabic, Turabi uses an innovative method, which utilises very few citations from the Qur'an and Hadith, but is enthused throughout with Qur'anic resonance and echo. Many of his most important sentences are slight rephrases of the Prophet's words, applied to contemporary contexts with considerable creativity. This is designed to give his words the air of

Qur'anic authority without needing to cite specific his sources and arguments. This method is in turn a manifestation of some of Turabi's innovations in Islamic jurisprudence, notably *istishab* ('accompanying') and *al qiyas al wasi'* ('wider analogy'). These allow the jurist to develop much more radical interpretations and applications of *shari'a*, by analysing what might have been the aims of particular injunctions. This allows the skilled jurist (i.e. Turabi) to escape from most of the restrictions that would confine, for example, the sheikhs of al Azhar.[7]

Turabi's leadership style during and after the 1989 coup indicates the contradictions that have beset his project, and his skilful justification for his opportunism. On the one hand, the coup was a highly elitist project. Only a handful of senior Islamists knew about it, and they took great pains to disguise their involvement—to the extent of sending Turabi himself to prison (where he was shunned by the other political detainees, who knew his duplicitous role only too well). This confusion was essential if Egyptian cooperation in the coup was to be obtained, and the deceit worked well enough for Cairo to speedily recognise the new government. The confusion spread into the NIF itself, which was formally disbanded, while the ruling Revolutionary Command Council (RCC) denied its Islamist colour. Senior cadres were excluded from decision-making and informed by telephone or even over the radio that they had been appointed to high positions in the government. Special 'advisers' were appointed to 'assist' governors and senior administrators, who in fact wielded greater authority than those whom they were advising. By these means, political power was highly centralised in an informal network centred on Hassan al Turabi. But on the other hand, Turabi tried to maintain a populist strand to his political mobilisation. Turabi's personal style, after his release from semi-fictional custody, was to be accessible to all Islamists. He ruled from his house, keeping an open door and listening to complainants and promising an opening-up of the regime. Ali Osman Mohamed Taha in a similar way ruled from his house, approving decisions and drafting ordinances that would then be officially promulgated by the soldiers the following day. Turabi distrusted the army and always sought to replace military rule with civilian Islamist government, occasionally shocking the generals with provocative statements about the impending dissolution of the RCC and its replacement by a civilian cabinet (for example in January 1993).

Knowing Turabi's leadership style, the military leaders on their side sought to cut him out from certain circuits of information and decision-

---

[7] We are indebted to Abdel Salam Nur el Din Hamad for this insight.

making, while he in turn tried to use his network of Islamist 'advisers' to circumvent their hierarchies. The ablest individuals became skilled at playing these networks off against each other, or at least remaining informed about their various plans, so as to position themselves accordingly.

This covert form of rule extended to the economics of the state, which was virtually bankrupt. While the NIF soldiers and businessmen plundered state assets during the privatisation drives of the early 1990s, the government itself relied on private contributions for the upkeep of essential activities, such as the expenses of key security officers. This kind of financial operation is wide open for abuse, and corruption duly entered.

For a movement whose central plank was the need for an ethical transformation of society, the degree of deception employed from the outset became a fatal contradiction. The regime started with a big lie: the denial that they were Islamists. As the Islamists exchanged recriminations in the aftermath of the 1999 split, this reality at last became public. What Turabi called 'the jurisprudence of necessity' is perhaps better labelled 'the jurisprudence of opportunism'. Turabi himself is remarkably unapologetic and frank. In a pamphlet published in June 2001, he writes:

> We thought that we have the right to fight to protect ourselves from that force of unbelief [*kufr*] until there is no more persecution [of Muslims] and religion becomes Allah's in its entirety.[8] We erected the Salvation Revolution in an ambiguous way when it first came. When it became strong, it spoke by its true name and raised its flag as the ruler. For a decade it launched a series of *jihads* to secure the Islamic project until its comprehensive rightful guidance was fulfilled. Then its characteristics were enshrined in the free constitutional legislation. (al Turabi 2001: 10)

If we turn to this Constitution for the Republic of Sudan, crafted by Turabi and adopted in 1998, the same contradictions arise between its avowed aspiration of freedom and the reality of coercion. The first problem is that all the steps of constitution building were carried out in the absence of basic freedoms and rights, including freedom of expression and association. From the night of the June coup, Sudan was ruled by constitutional orders issued by the RCC. The First Constitutional Order gave the Council all executive and legislative powers, and in the second order the RCC then delegated its powers to the Chair of the Council, General Bashir. These basic measures remained in force until 1998.

---

[8] Here, Turabi is using very Qur'anic language to give his political narrative the air of religious authority.

The 1998 Constitution has authentically Islamic components reflecting the political philosophies of Mawdudi and Qutb, but is also designed around essentially secular power structures. In important ways it is similar to secular constitutions that regulate presidential states. The Islamic nature is evident in the language used in drafting the Constitution, especially the Arabic version.[9] This raises the question of what can be an Islamic constitution that regulates the rule of Allah. According to Qutb, 'the way to establish the rule of Allah on earth is not to give some consecrated people—the priests—the authority to rule, as was the case with the rule of church, nor to appoint some spokesmen of Allah as rulers, as is the case in "theocracy". To establish Allah's rule means to enforce His laws so the final decision in all affairs be according to these laws.' (1990: 50) Article 4 of Sudan's Constitution tries to accommodate Qutb's and Mawdudi's ideas along with the democratic notions of modern constitutions, in an impossible attempt to satisfy both the political Islamism of Turabi's cadres, and the international community's demand for conformity with international standards human rights and the rule of law. This Article reads:

Supremacy in the State is for God the creator of human beings, and sovereignty is to the vicegerent people of Sudan who practice it as worship of God, bearing the trust, building up the country and spreading justice, freedom and public consultation. The Constitution and the law shall regulate the same.

As it stands, this Article does not provide any legal effect. How can anyone test that Allah is fulfilling His constitutional function, or indeed whether He is performing at all? How can the Sudanese people practice their sovereignty as worship of God?

The second section that attempts to accommodate the Islamists is Article 18 which has the title 'religiousness'. It reads:

Those in service of the State and public life shall envisage the dedication thereof for the worship of God, wherein Muslims adhere to the scripture and tradition, and all shall maintain religious motivation and give due regard to such spirit in plans, laws, policies and official business in the political, economic, social and cultural fields in order to prompt public life towards its objectives, and adjust them towards justice and uprightness to be directed towards the grace of God in the Hereafter.

Again, how is this to be effected? A speech of an Imam in a mosque can have the same effect as this article. By contrast, Article 65 can have real

---

[9] The English version is a distinctly secularised and sometimes misleading translation.

consequences on the lives of Sudanese citizens. This determines the sources of legislation as

Islamic law and the consensus of nation, by referendum. The Constitution and custom shall be the sources of legislation; and no legislation in contravention with these fundamentals shall be made; however, the legislation shall be guided by the nation's opinion, the learned opinion of scholars and thinkers, and then by decision of those in charge of public affairs.

Among the implications of this Article are some of the characteristics of *shari'a* law that are considered incompatible with human rights, such as the *hudud* punishments and the inferior status of non-Muslims.

Reflecting its origins in the absolutist thinking of Mawdudi and Qutb, Article 43 of the 1998 Constitution awards the President of the Republic almost the same powers as he enjoyed as the head of the RCC. A constitutional Islamic republic and the emergency powers appropriated by a military dictatorship provide very similar authority to the head of state. Similarly, the Constitution elides any separation between executive and legislative powers. Article 138/3 states clearly that the President is the 'leader of the executive organ and a participant in legislation'. In addition, 'the Judiciary is responsible for the performance of its duties before the President of the Republic' (Article 100) while the President has also the power to appoint the chief justice, his deputies and all other judges (Article 104/1 and 2). In fact, President Bashir has used those powers to get rid of independent judges and to appoint supporters of the regime. Similarly, Article 105 established the Constitutional Court which is appointed by the president to be the 'custodian of the Constitution'. The need for the protection of constitutional rights usually arises when the executive or the legislature abuses their powers against individuals or institutions. A body appointed by the executive cannot qualify as an independent one. The final blow against the independence of the judiciary is in Article 130, concerned with the 'Public Grievances and Corrections Board', which shall 'work at the federal level to remove grievances, assure efficiency and purity in the practice of the State and in systems, or the federal executive or administrative acts, and also to extend justice after the final decisions of the institutions of justice.'

An Islamic constitution faces the basic dilemma that an Islamic state is premised upon the virtue of its ruler and its citizens (especially the former). The premise of the award of personal freedom in Qutb's Islamist philosophy is that people will freely choose Islam, once constraints are stripped away. But these conditions do not exist in the real world. As a result of this, and also of the need to pay respects to international human rights standards, we see some contradictions running through the Constitution. The Articles concerning basic freedoms and rights include internationally recognised rights such as freedom of religion. The laws, however, do not just regulate those rights and freedoms, but rather confiscate them altogether. For example, the Penal Code of 1991 criminalises apostasy, mandating the death sentence for Muslims who change their faith. Another case is the National Security Act, which gives the director of the security organ, or any person delegated by him, the power to detain any person without charge or trial for six months. That period can be indefinite by the approval the National Security Council. Concerning freedom of association, this is governed by the law of *tawali*, legislated by Article 26 of the Constitution which guarantees freedom to organise political organisations on the condition that they abide by 'the fundamentals of the Constitution, as regulated by law'. Only those committed to the government's programme can exercise that freedom.

Turabi's rationale for a move to a constitutional order was that the Islamic movement was sufficiently well entrenched. However, he subsequently argued that the Sudanese people were not 'ready' for an Islamic state, being too preoccupied with material affairs. (al Turabi 2001) This is a characteristically Islamist mode of argument. Mohamed Salim al 'Awwa, who developed the highly influential argument that Islam was the first authentic political and legal system to be based on legitimacy and not coercion (see chapter 2), writes: 'The correct scientific method obliges us to agree upon the principle that we have to judge the people on the basis of their adherence to Islamic precepts and not the other way around: we should not judge Islam in terms of the behavior of Muslims, be they the rulers or the ruled.' (quoted in Bassam 1998: 160)

These contradictions, manifest both in both practice and in the Constitution, were not an ad hoc response to the exigencies of power. In a pamphlet published in 1987, entitled *Features of the Islamic Order*, Hassan al Turabi underlined his pragmatism. He argued that what matters is who controls the state and for what purpose, not by what means they do it. Both sympathisers and critics have identified this opportunistic tendency. El-Affendi comments: 'Turabi believes that no option should remain closed in the fight to establish an Islamic order. Being the consummate pragmatist he is, Turabi does not want to be committed... to observance of legality and peaceful transition to an Islamic order.' (1991a: 164) Turabi has participated in elections, skilfully using eccentricities in Sudan's electoral system (such as the 'graduate seats') to his advantage. He has also served two dictatorships, one of which he helped engineer, and presided

over the Islamic world's bloodiest *jihad*, in Southern Sudan and the Nuba
Mountains. In Olivier Roy's terminology, Turabi's theory is 'Islamist',
but his followers' practice is 'neo-fundamentalist' as well. Analysing
Turabi's doctrines in theory and practice, Abdel Salam Sidahmed concludes simply that for Turabi, 'An Islamic state is one governed by Islamists!' (1996: 196) We might go further: it is a state ruled by Hassan al
Turabi.

The 'Comprehensive Da'wa'

Turabi's reformist theory should dictate the progressive Islamisation of
social life and social institutions leading to the adoption of an Islamic
state by popular acclaim. In fact, the key steps to implement his vision
have been taken by the military. In 1989 the NIF faced the challenge—
familiar from the Nasserites—of using state power to enact social transformation. Over the succeeding decade they tried several variants to the
Islamisation strategy. They called it 'the civilisation project' (*al mashru' al
hadhari*), and its core ideas are most clearly manifest in the 'comprehensive
call' programme (*al da'wa al shamla*) that was at its peak in the years 1992–6,
but whose precepts informed official Islamisation policies both before
and since. There is no definition of comprehensive *da'wa*—it moulds to fit
different situations. In the Nuba Mountains, for example, it has been inte-
grally associated with *jihad*, while in much of Northern Sudan, it is a component of 'Islamic social planning'.

Alongside Turabi, the central figure in the practice of Islamic social
planning is Ali Osman Mohamed Taha, who established the Ministry of
Social Planning in order to pursue this agenda. Using the one area in
which the Islamists have achieved undeniable success, namely volunta
rism to provide education and social services, the NIF tried to put all
social policy in the hands of such organisations. According to one of its
leading theoreticians, 'Islamic social planning means a continuing revolution for the remoulding of the human being and the institutions in society
in accordance with Qur'anic guidance.' This includes, *inter alia*, 'a complete and comprehensive remoulding of the Islamic personality with a
view to making it a living, honest and conscious characterisation of
Islamic concepts, values and teachings' and 'building and reconstructing
all state institutions on principles derived from the Qur'an.' (Imam 1996)
Under Ali Osman, the Ministry of Social Planning developed the concepts of comprehensive *da'wa* and Islamic *inqilab* (literally, coup, but often
referring to total social transformation) in accordance with the NIF inter-

pretation of the *shari'a*. During Ali Osman's tenure, a Department of Da'wa was established, and the 'Comprehensive Da'wa Funds' association was formed (initially named the Social and Charitable Funds Coordination Council). The latter brought together most of the jihadist and *da'wa* organisations active in Sudan, both parastatals and NGOs. Thereafter the activities of Islamic agencies hugely expanded. They were subject to the government's relief regulations of 1992 and 1993, which, in the words of the United Nations' *OLS Review*, leaves NGOs as 'little more than an extension of the state in Northern Sudan' (Ataul Karim *et al.* 1996: 60). One of the models they adopted was the Iranian Islamic foundations or *bonyads*, which have immense autonomy from the state.

The comprehensive *da'wa* was an ambitious and complex project, involving the unification of education, proselytising, humanitarian, developmental, financial and counter-insurgency efforts. (African Rights 1997: chapter 9, de Waal 2000) The programme reached perhaps its greatest extent in Southern Blue Nile during the tenure of Ibrahim Abdel Hafiz as deputy commissioner between 1993 and 1996. The rationales for implementing the programme in this province included the fact that it had a large 'black African' population many of whom had supported SPLA incursions into the area in 1987 and 1989. Hence, 'pacification' was a priority. Visiting the provincial capital Damazin in October 1993, members of the Transitional National Assembly agreed to call it 'the Model Province' and 'beacon to guide the people of Sudan'.[10] Abdel Hafiz had been a student activist for the NIF, had worked for a prominent Islamic humanitarian organisation and had also served as a leader of the Popular Defence Forces (PDF)—his career illustrates how these functions overlap. He described the comprehensive *da'wa* as 'the consolidation of religious values in society and effecting a comprehensive departure from the [present] reality of ignorance and illiteracy and the actualisation of total interaction with the Islamic project' (quoted in Hamad 1995). On taking up his position, he brought energy to the da'waist programme. Local people were fascinated by the resources that poured in and the promises of total transformation of the area.

One of the earliest *da'wa* programmes in the region was called *mawakib al nur* (Processions of Light) and executed under Abdel Hafiz's personal supervision. It comprised Qur'anic recital and memorisation, literacy classes, military service in the PDF camps, construction of mosques, and building of schools and health centres. A community leader described

---

[10] *Al Sudan al Hadith*, 15 October 1993.

how, 'They grouped people into camps. Each village had its camp. In the camp, they brought *amirs* who gave instruction. It started at 5 a.m. with prayers, reciting the Qur'an and Islamic orientation. It included military drill. They brought NIF girls to teach the women.'[11]

A fine account of the vision of the comprehensive *da'wa* is provided by the government newspaper *Al Sudan al Hadith*, which reported on the high-level governmental visit to Damazin in October 1993. The following extract, from a Sudanese newspaper, clearly exaggerates and idealises the programme, but its language is revealing:[12]

In al Hussein ibn Ali[13] camp which we visited just after 3 a.m. in the morning, we saw them reciting the Qur'an and in the Mosque and preparing for studying after prayers. They were attired in white *jihad* garments and on them was written '*al da'wa al shamla*.' ...The women... were in Um al Mujahidaat camp in Damazin. They recite the Qur'an and study, and then hurry for military training, filled with determination and resilience.... In Bagis area we saw a small school and a Qur'anic class under a big tree. We saw a military march and the chanting of *Tahleel* [There is no god except Allah] and *Takbeer* [Allah is the greatest]. We saw sweating [hard work] in *al da'wa al shamla* camps. The whole of Damazin has turned into a cell of gratitude, administered by the Commissioner and the Peace and Development Foundation. In Suhaib al Rumi[14] camp there were groups of children who woke up early, finished marching and reading the Qur'an. They have become friends of the Peace and Development Foundation, which is taking care of them.

Ahmad Karamno [Director of the Peace and Development Foundation] says: 'We have visited areas like Fashimi which hasn't been reached by a government official for forty years. We have got acquainted with its citizens and their conditions, and it is now enjoying security and stability, and we will be seeking to direct development projects to this area... in accordance with the goals for which the Foundation was established in March 1992.' The director of the Foundation's monitoring department, Al Daw Mohamed al Mahi says...: 'The role of the Foundation is the boosting of peace efforts with significant development in support of stability, because if the citizen doesn't get development that accompanies his return to his homeland, he remains vulnerable to capitulation to the rebellion. Citizens are fleeing from areas where war is raging, and our duty is to help them find secure and stable areas.'

The Foundation has set aside an agricultural scheme for the families of the martyrs which it operates on their behalf. Damazin has more than 120 *al da'wa al shamla* camps and is getting ready at present for the graduation of more than 40,000 recruits.

---

[11] Interviewed by Alex de Waal in Jabal al Nimr, Southern Blue Nile, 1 December 1997.
[12] *Al Sudan al Hadith*, 15 October 1993, p. 5.
[13] Al Hussein ibn Ali was a grandson of the Prophet and a martyr.
[14] Suhaib al Rumi was one of the Prophet's disciples.

Evidently, the programme was closely integrated with the counter-insurgency 'pacification' of the area, resettling people displaced by the fighting of 1989–90, and training members of the PDF. The convergence with *jihad* was even more explicit in an internal NIF document for the launch of the Nuba Mountains *jihad* in January 1992. In this instance, the comprehensive *da'wa* had six main components, among which were religious indoctrination and the imposition of Islam on non-Muslims, *jihad*, resettlement of the Nuba in 'peace villages' and crackdown on all who opposed the campaign. (Salih 1995: 75, and see below)

An intrinsic element of the comprehensive *da'wa* was reforming the financial system of the state to make it consonant with Qur'anic principles. Shortly after promulgating the Islamic penal code in 1983, President Nimeiri also proposed to Islamise Sudan's revenue system. He promised that *zakat* (the tithe) and other Islamic taxes would greatly augment the treasury's income. Economists were not impressed. USAID commissioned a study that found that the projections for *zakat* income were exaggerated and fanciful: the state would quickly become bankrupt were it not for external aid. (Mayer 1985) Nimeiri was also not impressed: he dismissed the Minister of Zakat and returned to secular taxes. Islamist economists also obliquely criticised the implications of the Act, arguing that *zakat* could not replace other taxes such as the business tax, and that given Sudan's economic plight, the government would still be compelled to take measures 'incompatible with the objectives of the Islamic economic system'. (Awad 1984: 29) Economic Islamisation was dramatically slowed. Nonetheless, in the 1990s, the NIF tried to put it back on the fast track. Numerous quasi-governmental organisations were established, such as the Diwan al Zakat, the Shari'a Support Fund, the Islamic Pious Endowments organisation, and the Social Solidarity Fund (Al Takaful). For example, the Diwan al Zakat is a da'waist organisation entitled to collect *zakat* contributions: it is in effect a privatisation of tax collection. The monies it collected were distributed directly to Islamist organisations for philanthropic purposes. Its Secretary General explained:

We co-operate with the *da'wa* organisations responsible for the *da'wa* and the defence of the land and honour, like *nidaa al jihad* organisation [Call of Jihad, a philanthropic Islamic agency] and the Islamic *da'wa* Authority. We also provide funding for more than 3,000 *khalwas*.[15]

In 1992–3 the Diwan al Zakat supported the *jihad* in the South and Nuba Mountains. In 1995, it joined with the Shari'a Support Fund to

---

[15] Quoted in: *al Sudan al Hadith*, 28 April 1994, p. 6.

accelerate its activities in Blue Nile Province/State. Among its major projects were the 'Qur'anic Towns', new centres of Islamist proselytisation in the region. Seven towns were targeted, aiming 'to eradicate illiteracy, alleviate suffering and promote the spirit of piety in [these] societies'.[16] Small towns in the south of the province/state, including Kurmuk, Ulu, Chali el Fil (renamed Chali el Arab as part of the programme) and Yabus, along with Meban just over the border in neighbouring Upper Nile, experienced their first government-type presence for decades, if not ever. Volunteer cadres from the NIF, aligned with national and international da'waist agencies, visited these places, gathered the people, provided food, built schools and mosques, and taught the Qur'an. Often there were close links between these philanthropic and proselytising activities and military training and recruitment (African Rights 1997: 226–31, de Waal 2000). The Shari'a Support Fund directed resources to da'waist organisations and the PDF, the police, and public order, peace and student organisations. It also opened a *dar al tawbah* ('Repentance Centre' for prisoners) and appointed sheikhs in the state's prisons to oversee religious re-education (including obtaining *muhtadiin* or converts)—for example it paid off the fines for 500 prisoners. It sponsored the adoption of Islamic dress among women.

The *da'wa* campaigns garnered enormous coverage in the national media, and Southern Blue Nile in particular was heralded as a 'beacon' for Sudan, which had 'changed the face of the land'.[17] In neighbouring Upper Nile the Governor graciously said that 'the citizens for the first time felt there was a government' in the region when Islamic agencies operating under the Comprehensive Call began their activities.[18] It seemed as though the comprehensive *da'wa* had combined all the essential elements necessary for social transformation: resources, a coordinated comprehensive strategy, a spirit of voluntarism, and strong government backing.

Why then did the comprehensive *da'wa* abruptly vanish from Southern Blue Nile in 1996? Clearly it was far less robust than claimed by the media and government spokesmen. Advocates and detractors alike overestimated the impact of the comprehensive *da'wa*, at least in the short term.

We can surmise four principal reasons for the failure. First, the institutional capacity was just too weak. The project depended on multiple

---

[16] *Al Sudan al Hadith*, 22 April 1996, p. 5.
[17] 'A martyr lives', *Al Sudan al Hadith*, 15 October 1993.
[18] *Al Quwat al Musallaha*, 10 January 1993.

organisations enthused with voluntaristic idealism, with overlapping tasks and mandates. Too much was demanded of cadres, lines of reporting were blurred, and assessments opaque. Success was recognised and promotions were awarded on the basis of personal qualities and connections, rather than objectively-measured success. And ultimately, the entire project hinged on the charisma and organising skill of the provincial leader, Ibrahim Abdel Hafiz. As we shall see later, he simply was not skilled enough to stay on top of local ethnic politics and advance the *da'wa* at the same time.

Second, the promises of Islamic economics could not be fulfilled. Islamist micro-credit, based on the model of the Grameen Bank in Bangladesh, has high potential. But for that to be realised requires social and political stability, and a well-run institution. None of these factors were present in Sudan, especially in marginal rural areas such as Southern Blue Nile. At a higher level of operations, Islamic banks do not have a good record of stability, tending to finance their high rates of return from speculative and sometimes illegal activities. In Sudan, Egypt and elsewhere, they have been beset by scandals and collapses. Islamic commercial enterprises, like much of Sudan's capitalist class, relied on import-export deals and environmentally-damaging agricultural practices. Lastly, as pointed out by Sudan's foremost Islamist economist, Professor Mohamed Hashim Awad as early as 1984, an Islamic revenue system just does not add up for a country like Sudan. (Awad 1984) Moreover, in the mid-1990s, Sudan's economic crisis was at its nadir, and no amount of personal piety could wish away the state's financial crisis. Furthermore, for the da'waist companies and philanthropic organisations in Southern Blue Nile, an additional problem was their reliance on external funds including those provided by Usama bin Laden, who was obliged to leave Sudan in 1996 for Afghanistan. It appears that the government quietly confiscated most of his assets, leaving the front-line activities in places such as Southern Blue Nile bereft. Other Gulf-based philanthropists were also unreliable. Finally, financial accountability was very poor and the *da'wa*-ist organisations often abused their tax privileges, for example by importing vehicles without having to pay excise duty, and then re-selling them at a profit. By 1997, the Ministries of Finance and Commerce were openly criticising the da'waist organisations' abuse of their status and accusing them of corruption.

A third reason for the failure was that the targets of the programme were not as enthusiastic as its proponents believed. Those who advocated the comprehensive *da'wa*, and indeed the 'civilisation project' as a whole, had unerring faith in Islam's capacity for total social and personal trans-formation. The writings of Hassan Makki (1989) and other Islamists betray a marked lack of sensitivity to the non-Arab societies of Sudan. The Islamists share with other extremists the belief that conversion re-quires a total rejection of the past. There is no room for gradual change, but rather an insistence that those who convert to Islam should be trans-formed totally and should reject their former cultures and even their fam-ilies. The 'civilisation project' need not negotiate: its benefits are self-evident. Six years on, Sudanese Islamists admit that the comprehensive *da'wa* was unpopular among local people, who asked why a corrupt and ineffective government was trying to teach them about virtue and social transformation. Resources provided by the government and the da'waist agencies were received and utilised, but with a deep scepticism. People ate the food, listened politely, but then went their own way.

The final and most immediate reason for failure was that the compre-hensive *da'wa* became entrapped in local ethnic politics. For a start, it antagonised local people, for whom popular Islam was perfectly compati-ble with traditional beliefs. A local community leader described Ibrahim Abdel Hafiz's confrontation with the Ingessena:

His activities concentrated on Islamisation, especially of the Ingessena. *Al da'wa al shamla* provided generators and supplies. But they were against the culture of the people. Not just the culture of the Ingessena but even others too. For example Ibrahim Abdel Hafiz wanted to ban the musical instrument the *waza'*. He said it should be abolished, it was a sign of laziness. The Ingessena breed pigs, and Ibrahim Abdel Hafiz insisted that they should all be killed. He accused them of paganism. In fact the Ingessena also have dolls made of wood, statues [*tamasiil*] that they bring out at harvest time. He accused them of worshipping them as idols and said they should be destroyed. He also stood against the *kujurs* [traditional priests].[19]

Sulaf el Din Ahmed, a Islamist economist who has since become head of Sudan's Humanitarian Affairs Commission, had long proposed winning pig-keepers away from this practice by offering them incentives such as Islamic micro-credit. (African Rights 1997: 220) In fact, the NIF cadres had neither the patience nor the sensitivity for this kind of approach, and their methods of encouragement consisted of slaughtering pigs and, where possible, forcibly relocating villagers into 'peace camps'.

It is interesting to contrast this distinctively neo-fundamentalist ap-proach with that of Malik Agar, the commander of the SPLA forces that

---

[19] Interviewed by Alex de Waal in Jabal al Nimr, Southern Blue Nile, 1 December 1997.

entered the province in 1996. Commander Malik is a Muslim Ingessena who interrupted the research for his doctoral thesis on the indigenous languages of the province in order to join the SPLA. His mentor in the Movement was the Nuba leader, Yousif Kuwa Mekki, a former school-teacher and cultural activist who, as a university student, had founded a Nuba organisation called Komolo ('youth' in the Miri Nuba language), and who, as Governor of the SPLA-controlled areas of the Nuba Moun-tains from 1989 until shortly before his death from cancer in 2001, pre-sided over a revival of traditional popular culture in the region. Until 1991, SPLA radio's popular cultural programmes were in the hands of a Nuba folklorist, Mohamed Haroun Kafi. The Ingessena, like the Nuba, were not ready to submit to such blunt cultural assimilation, and resisted by force of arms.

Equally significant in the ethnic politics of the region was the way in which the comprehensive *da'wa* created an ethnic conflict between the Funj and Fellata communities. Shortly after taking power, the NIF had enacted a law that offered Sudanese citizenship to any Muslim who met residence requirements. This rectified the long-standing anomaly whereby West Africans who came to Sudan as labourers and pilgrims in the colo-nial period, known collectively as Fellata, were denied citizenship, and often exploited as a result. It also cemented support for the NIF among this constituency, which already had Islamist leanings. Some of the most vigorous Islamists, such as Ibrahim Abdel Hafiz, were eager to utilise the Fellata in the vanguard of the comprehensive *da'wa*. But the local Funj and Ingessena peoples of Southern Blue Nile saw the issue in terms of ethnic power. One *'omda* (middle-ranking administrative chief) who had joined the opposition explained:

Under the cover of *al da'wa al shamla*, they organised the Fellata, claiming they were better Muslims. They confiscated land and gave it to the Fellata. This is one of the main reasons why people went to the opposition. For example the Jandel [agricultural] scheme, which was created by the NIF after it took power. Most of the land on this scheme is cultivated by the Fellata. All the workers are Fellata. The government said that it is necessary to invest in the land and for that reason the Fellata must be brought. Jandel created a lot of problems for us, that we did not have with the [longer-established] Takamul scheme.[20]

In passing, we should note that the Jandel scheme was financed by a com-pany owned by Usama bin Laden, who was resident in Sudan at the time. It was also used as a training camp for the PDF (and, according to local

---

[20] Interviewed by Alex de Waal in al Mahal, Southern Blue Nile, 30 November 1997.

reports, foreigners as well). The nexus of commercial agriculture, military training and *al da'wa al shamla* again recurs in the mid-1990s in Sudan.

Along with land and labour, the problem was competition for local political authority. Ibrahim Abdel Hafiz planned to create a *nazirate* for the Fellata, so that they could have their own semi-autonomous tribal authority. This brought opposition from the Funj, who had the sole *nazirate* in the province at the time. Funj leaders formed a delegation to the provincial headquarters in Damazin and wrote to the President. In January 1995 a delegation of between ten and thirteen of these Funj leaders was arrested in Roseires and imprisoned. The local authorities crushed the dissent, but they could not contain the incipient ethnic strife. When the SPLA crossed the Ethiopian border and captured Yabus, in the southern tip of Blue Nile, in February 1996, and the Sudan Alliance Forces began raids north of the Blue Nile river, there was an immediate focus for local discontent. Later in 1996, after the province was changed to a state in accordance with the new federal constitution, Abdel Hafiz was removed, and the comprehensive *da'wa* activities in the area ceased.

What does this demonstrate? To start with, the NIF's ineptitude at local politics in Southern Blue Nile does not refute Olivier Roy's thesis that for Islamists 'the sociological reality of differentiation... is perfectly mastered as a tactic, but ignored as a concept'. (Roy 1994: 201) Rather, it shows the limits of tactical adroitness: it is useful when building a power base in opposition, but is simply not enough when in government. Their approach is capable of manipulating the differences but incapable of solving the problems. This was demonstrated across the entire territory of Sudan.

Holding the reins of state power, the Sudanese Islamists remained enthralled by the myth of the unity of the *umma*, and failed to recognise the fatal absence of any theory of social conflict, ethnicity or class. Hassan Makki, for example, attributes the civil war to conspiracy, and sees 'the invisible hand of the Church behind the mutiny scene and mutiny culture'. (1989: 7) According to his analysis, ethnic and religious divisions are the result of the 'sinister motives' of the West, specifically 'Mission and secular discourse extremism. For the last thirty years (since 1955) Sudan has witnessed a militant brand of secular discourse. It became the norm for such discourse to express itself by raising arms, involvement in guerrilla activities against the right of Islamic culture to exist in the South and to dominate in the North' (1989: 5). He also condemns 'anthro-biologists' (*sic*).

When the Islamist discourse shifts from polemic to policymaking, its tone changes utterly. Islamist social planning is imbued with essentialist conceptions of humanity and society, above all a simplified conception of the homogeneous *umma* or community of believers. Characteristically, Turabi wants to have it both ways, attempting to reconcile the particular with the universal ideal:

[A] Muslim should relate progressively to household, neighbourhood, fatherland or country, and to Dar-ul-Islam (the Muslim commonwealth), and beyond to the whole world. Each cycle of socio-geographic association deserves regard, compassion, devotion and solidarity, but should not eclipse the full scope of ever-wider horizons of human associations. Regard for the general association may take moral precedence; but the immediate is never totally forsaken as autonomous unit or overlooked as a distinct factor of the general. Although a Muslim is imbued with a sense of universal human brotherhood and is inspired by a world-wide missionary urge, he proceeds from the practical and the immediate to the ideal and the general. The Prophet of Islam declared that he was an apostle unto mankind, but began his mission with his immediate clan and tribe in Mecca, to extend it gradually beyond all limits of people or place. (al Turabi 1992: 2)

Insofar as Turabi has a sociology, it conflates objective description with normative idealism. His philosophising does not help a politician or administrator at all when confronted with the real challenges of social planning and managing ethnic relations. Abdelwahab El-Affendi similarly recognises difference, but does not theorise it. He defines the Muslim polity as 'a decentralized pluralistic association based primarily on choice rather than on coercion.... a free association of mutually co-operating communities'. (El-Affendi 1991b: 96) Moreover, these communities are non-territorial, and free from 'interest-group' politics.

The NIF simply lacks any strategy for reconciling political or ethnic plurality, other than tactical manipulation. Unsurprisingly, at a national level, Islamism became a hostage to Arab racism and ethnic politics. This was evident in 1988 when two NIF parliamentarians from Darfur defected from the party, accusing its leadership of Arab racism. They joined the Democratic Unionist Party. Subsequently Daud Bolad, a former NIF stalwart from his student days and NIF coordinator in Darfur in 1985, leapt even further and joined the SPLA. He accused the NIF of Arabism (Salih 2000: 75–6). In one of the least successful military operations of the war, Bolad was despatched at the head of a small SPLA force into Darfur in December 1991 to foment an insurrection there. This was a gamble comparable to Che Guevara's fatal *foco*-ist adventure into Bolivia, as there had been very little political planning beforehand. When it came to consummating his strategy of military attrition, the SPLA leader seemed to suffer from the same blind spot as the Islamists, and depend upon a spontaneous popular uprising. It did not happen. Bolad's force was dispersed and defeated. Most of them walked for months through Chad, the Central African Republic and Zaire to return to safety, while Bolad himself was captured along with his notebooks. In an extraordinary twist, the Governor of Darfur and his jailor and interrogator was his former bodyguard from student days, Colonel Tayeb Ibrahim, known as *sikha*, 'iron bar', for his skill in wielding this instrument at student demonstrations. Bolad was never seen again, and his network in the region was quietly but ruthlessly dismantled.[21]

But the ethnic politics of the NIF is more complex than the simple identification of Islamism with Arabism. As we have seen, Ibrahim Abdel Hafiz in Southern Blue Nile favoured the Fellata, who originate from West Africa. Across Sudan, it is the rural minorities—such as the Fur, Masalit and Berti of Darfur, the Baggara Arabs of Kordofan and Darfur, and the Beja of the East—who are the most devout in their everyday lives. They also have the strongest history of militant Mahdism. Some, such as the Beja of Hamush Koreb, are more conservative than the NIF, notably with regard to the status of women. Following the defeat of Bolad's SPLA incursion, Governor Tayeb Ibrahim played on the religiosity of the Fur and took lessons in the Fur language, partly motivated by the fear that violent repression would generate the very insurgency he was trying to repress, as had happened earlier in Kordofan. However, Arab neo-fundamentalists commonly regard some of these rural groups' practices as 'un-Islamic' and part of the programme of Islamic social planning was to cure what the da'waist agency al Ithar al Khairiya (Altruism or Purity) called 'social cavities', by, for example, sponsoring mass circumcision ceremonies among uncircumcised Beja.[22] Many Beja themselves were driven to take up arms against the government, citing the government's repression of their form of Islam. Devout neo-fundamentalists from the Beja and other non-Arab groups reject the NIF assaults as racist. Neo-fundamentalism being so poorly theorised, such differences cannot be reconciled. When Sudan's Islamist movement split in 1999/2000 it did so in part along ethnic lines, with many of the 'westerners' staying with Turabi and the riverain Arab elite group aligning with President Bashir.

---

[21] Had the operation been launched a few years earlier, it might have met with more success. In 1987–9 there was a civil war in Darfur, largely between Arab and Fur militias, which was settled by a peace conference initiated by the Sadiq el Mahdi government and concluded by the incoming RCC.

[22] *Al Inqaz al Watani*, 13 February 1996, p. 6.

Jihad's dead end

In Islamist-ruled Sudan, *jihad* is not an abstraction. The country is at war. *Jihad* was in fact an integral part of the comprehensive *da'wa* programme. While the ideology of the comprehensive *da'wa* has faded, *jihad* has not been revoked, and the language of *jihad* still recurs when the President and other senior figures address their cadres. It is worth studying the popular discourse and practice of the Sudanese *jihad*, because even should it be officially abandoned, its legacy will live on. For this discussion, our main focus will be on the Nuba Mountains.

The Nuba Mountains *jihad*, as described at the opening of this chapter, is an instance of following the neo-fundamentalist logic of *takfir* (excommunication) to its conclusion. It is a step beyond the al Gama'a al Islamiyya murdering Copts simply because of their faith and the Taliban blowing up Buddhist statues.[23] The Sudan government has been evidently uncomfortable with its own *jihad*. Most of Hassan al Turabi's writings scrupulously avoid the issue of the civil war. In his English writings, the closest he comes to justifying violence is when he sees it as the inevitable result 'whenever religious energy is suppressed'. (Turabi 1983: 241) Similarly, Sudan government official statements tend to play down the combat element of *jihad*, preferring to focus on, for example, 'transforming *jihad* from the "*jihad* through the gun" to another *jihad* in the field on investment through training and equipment of *mujahadiin* for the reconstruction of the land.'[24]

But war has its own logic. The protracted war and associated economic and political crises have intensified the government's Islamism. The culmination of this was the declaration of *jihad*, reconstructed to take on the most literalist meanings.

The reconstruction of the concept of *jihad* in the NIF's narrative is illustrated by the so-called wedding of the martyrs (*urs al shaheed*). Members of the PDF refuse to marry in the expectation of marrying in paradise; that is after they become martyrs. They reject marrying earthly women, *huur al-dunia* (dark-eyed virgins of the earth), in their eagerment to marry *huur al jinana* (dark-eyed virgins of paradise). Families are expected to treat the death of their loved ones in the *jihad* with jubilation, and should not mourn, since death is *urs al shaheed* (the wedding of the martyrs) which should be celebrated. (Salih 1998: 76)

---

[23] There is a long history of Sunni intolerance towards Shi'ism, including Wahhabis destroying Shi'a mosques in Saudi Arabia, with the sanction of the highest authorities, in the aftermath of the Gulf War. Intra-Sunni intolerance of this kind is highly unusual.
[24] Quoted in *Al Sudan al Hadith*, 19 December 1992, p. 11.

Turabi undoubtedly encouraged these ceremonies, which were very traumatic and unpopular among the bereaved families. The government was never sufficiently confident to declare the women who opposed the *urs al shaheed* (or indeed conscription for *jihad* itself) as apostates, and merely beat them up in the time-honoured manner of repressive states.

The pure 'Islamic' model of an army has a simplified, flat command structure with an *amir*, four *rayat* or 'banners', and a mass of *mujahidiin*. None of the Sudanese generals in power would have seriously considered surrendering their secular hierarchy for this battle formation. Turabi recognised this also. Military Islamisation went no further than giving Islamic titles to existing ranks, the mobilisation of tens of thousands of young *mujahidiin*, either as volunteers or forced conscripts, and measures to ensure the political loyalty and ideological fervour of all ranks.

Unfortunately for these young Sudanese, their commanders often took short cuts on good planning, logistical support, technical prowess and strategic command, hoping that righteous fervour would compensate. It did not work out that way. Mass assaults by *mujahidiin*, however zealous, proved very costly in terms of human lives and material. Battle-hardened SPLA troops were confident when they confronted the *mujahidiin* columns, knowing that the latter were inexperienced, and also knowing that as well as killing and wounding many, they could capture stocks of arms and ammunition. For example, in the attack on Tullishi mountain between February and May 1992, SPLA soldiers even relaxed their guard duty, because the *mujahidiin* 'would give us a warning of their attacks by their shouts of "Allahu Akbar!" The trenches were so close that we could hear the shouts and make ourselves ready when they attacked.' (NAFIR 1997: 7) It was one of the most sustained and ferocious battles of the entire war, with day-and-night bombardment of the mountain, followed by massed infantry attacks. Iranian advisers participated, according to the SPLA troops who overran their forward headquarters and killed two of them. But the *jihad* ground to a halt when the forces failed to take Tullishi mountain. At the same time, the regional authorities instituted a policy of forced displacement, aiming to relocate the entire Nuba population away from the hills, and encouraged a policy of mass rape by their troops. It didn't succeed. In May they finally declared they had captured Tullishi mountain and withdrew: the SPLA forces still in control there were relieved and amused.

The official status of the Kordofan *jihad* is deeply ambiguous. As mentioned at the top of this chapter, its theological underpinning was amateurish. It was primarily the initiative of two men: the Governor of

Kordofan, Lieutenant-General Sayed Abdel Karim al Husseini, and his notably zealous Commissioner for South Kordofan, Abdel Wahab Abdel Rahman Ali. Most of the troops were PLDF recruited locally, with the leaders of Arab tribes bribed with Toyota landcruisers and the title of *amir al jihad*. Yet it involved repeated air-strikes, which required authorisation on a day-to-day basis from the General Headquarters in Khartoum, and the use of technology unprecedented in the Sudanese war such as flares to direct night-time bombardments. It even involved the front-line deployment of foreign military advisers.[25] The Vice President, General Zubeir Mohamed Salih attended the April 1992 conference in El Obeid, and after it had concluded, President Bashir himself came to receive the title *imam al jihad*. (African Rights 1995b: 108–9) But even while Khartoum provided this high-level backing, the Vice President was trying to remove Abdel Wahab Abdel Rahman and put in place a rival officer, Mohamed el Tayeb Fadl, as Commissioner of South Kordofan, with a mandate to negotiate a ceasefire with the SPLA. Most probably, Husseini's declaration of *jihad* in January 1992 had as much to do with trying to trump his rivals and critics in the government and army as with mobilising against the SPLA.

The Kordofan *jihad* was the locus of an acrimonious power struggle. After negotiating a ceasefire with the SPLA at Bilenya, Mohamed el Tayeb was removed when Abdel Wahab Abdel Rahman engineered his (brief) detention. In the few weeks of his return to Kadugli Abdel Wahab sabotaged this agreement, which involved a ceasefire and free movement of civilians (who were suffering severe food shortages). Subsequently he was dismissed again and a new civilian Commissioner was brought in. Throughout this period, while the military intelligence in Kadugli was fervently in support of extreme measures, including eliminating large numbers of educated Nuba, the army relied on Nuba soldiers and NCOs for many of its troops, and as stories of the excesses of the *jihad* spread, there was an upsurge in discontent within the ranks. In April 1992 more than 100 Nuba army officers and policemen were arrested, accused of planning a 'racial coup'. Meanwhile, the forced relocation of Nuba villagers to North Kordofan, where they were simply dumped, starving and often naked, on the outskirts of towns, created an outcry in Northern Sudan. Until then, the war had been largely invisible, but when the citizens of towns such as El Obeid and Bara rushed to aid the wretched displaced Nuba—and were stopped from doing so by the security services—

[25] They were withdrawn after the capture and execution of the two by the SPLA.

its excesses became common knowledge. There were diplomatic protests from Western embassies and even the UN became concerned. The Nuba *jihad* had run into unconquerable obstacles: SPLA resistance, infighting within the government institutions, and now popular sentiment among Northern Sudanese.

Had it continued along the lines dictated by its architects, the Kordofan *jihad* would have become genocidal. The logic of war dictated a return to more conventional approaches. The *jihad* was not formerly abandoned, but its methods were modified. It became a nasty counterinsurgency, using Nuba conscripts to fight against their brethren in the SPLA, and occasionally reverting to the language of *jihad* in order to mobilise re-cruits and demonise the enemy. The degree of fervour and atrocity ap-pears to have depended on the character of the commander in question, and whether they had personal vendettas against particular communities or individuals. Some army and PDF units continued to destroy mosques as late as 1998.

Several other aspects of ideological escalation in the jihadist phase of the war deserve attention. One is forced conscription. The army and PDF needed more people, and conscription among the townspeople of the North was deeply unpopular. Instead the focus was shifted to margin-alised areas and displaced people including street children (African Rights 1995a). A number of training camps were established at which youth and children were drilled and trained for military service. Pro-longed forced conscription has its limits: it generates popular opposition and unwilling troops. Secondly, the language of *jihad* was adopted by sun-dry militias, notably the *murahaliin* of western Sudan, whose raids into the South were responsible for numerous atrocities including forced abduc-tion and enslavement.

The final element is the utilisation of Salafi philanthropic da'waist organisations, mainly funded from Saudi Arabia, for military training, resource mobilisation and orientation of recruits to the army and PDF. A number of these philanthropic organisations have been marked by weak systems for approving and monitoring programmes, and sometimes poor financial accountability as well. Their headquarters, let alone their patrons, may be oblivious to what is implemented on the ground in their name. Reports back may consist of bland endorsements of charitable works and accounts of enthusiastic embrace of Islam—much in the line of the newspaper accounts of the comprehensive *da'wa* cited above. Meanwhile, officers in the field may have entered into very close cooperation with their military and security counterparts. A couple of testimonies from the

Nuba Mountains indicate how their activities are seen locally. Because of the sensitivities involved, informants and the identities of the agencies are concealed. The first testimony is provided by a medical assistant.

When the army goes on operations, it relies on the support of the Islamic agencies. In October 1995, when the army was planning an operation to Kauda, they held a meeting in Abu Jibeha at the building of the Commission. The civil authorities and the Islamic agencies were there. Everyone was asked to contribute for the operation. [Agency X] and [agency Y] were present. They made their contributions, including money and food. [Agency X] also contributed fuel.'[26]

The second testimony is from a former resident of Kadugli:

'In Kadugli my office was adjacent to the office of [an Islamic agency], so I am well-informed about their activities. They first came to Kadugli in February 1993. They have a range of activities. They have devout Muslim women who give lessons in Islamic religion. They make video cassettes of Islamic teaching which they show to the public.

But the most important work of [the agency] is with the forces of the Sudan Government, including the Popular Defence Forces, the *mujahidiin*, the army, the military intelligence and the Popular Police.

[The agency] were working secretly. In their office, you will find a table and a chair, but you will not see their true work. But I have close knowledge of what they really are doing.

At the end of each month, all the members of the PDF in Kadugli will go to the [the agency], and receive 15,000 Sudanese pounds and one sack of sorghum [90 kilos]. This is also the case for the *mujahidiin*.

All the staff of [the agency], up to the director in Kadugli, have been trained as *mujahidiin*. They all have their arms. The director is [A]; her husband [B] is a captain in internal security. Every evening, most of the employees of [the agency] will gather at the office of General Security.

[The agency] assists the Popular Police force [*Shorta al Sha'abiya*]. They provide them with their uniforms with special insignia, and other equipment. The Popular Police have posts around the different parts of Kadugli. Their job is to ensure respect for Islamic law, to prevent people from drinking, and to patrol at night. The members of the Popular Police receive salaries from the government and rations from [the agency]. They are given sorghum, lentils, fresh dates, oil, onions, salt, beans and soap by [the agency].

[The agency] works in several peace camps administered by the government and PDF, including Murtah, Um Sirdiba and al Atmur. They distribute rations to the people. Their aim is that everyone should become Muslims.

[The agency] supports the Government chief Kafi Tayara el Bedin. Kafi Tayara is the senior government chief in South Kordofan. He is responsible for recruiting to the PDF, organizing the administration and carrying out govern-

---

[26] Sworn affidavit, Kauda, 22 May 1997.

ment policies. He is very faithful to the National Islamic Front. [The agency] gives each Amir [senior government chief] supplies. Each week they are given fuel for their work. Also, Kafi Tayara has a private security force estimated at more than one hundred armed men, and a private prison. [The agency] supports this.

[The agency] provides the army, PDF and other government forces with food and medicine. In public meetings in Kadugli town, it calls for contributions to support military operations. For example, in the military operation to Keiga el Khel in 1993, they provided food to the armed forces. It also made a camp near the site of the operations and took nurses there to treat the wounded. At that time, all staff members of [the agency] were carrying arms.

Another [agency] programme is called *shelafa fi ahal*. This means that when soldiers go on operations, the agency takes care of their families, providing them with necessities. At the same time they transport supplies to the front.

During Ramadan, [the agency] prepares breakfast in Kadugli town and calls people by megaphone to share it. They do this every day. After eating, people are shown videos about *mujahidiin* and *jihad* to encourage them to join and support it. At the time of *Eid*, [the agency] provides a ram to the families of leaders of the NIF, PDF and *mujahidiin*.'[27]

This illustrates, at a local level, the high degree of inter-dependence of the party, government, military and da'waist agencies. In a small town with just a handful of individuals running these different institutions, all of whom share the same social background and political orientation, and who socialise together, such cooperation is unsurprising. This was a marriage of convenience, and of no little deception. The Sudanese army, security and PDF simply needed the resources. This did not make for efficiency or effectiveness. It had its limits at local, national and international levels. Locally, the involvement of the da'waist agencies in the war simply deepened local people's cynicism. Nationally, the nexus between their activities, their commercial offshoots, and certain extra-budgetary security services became a threat to the army General Headquarters' control. Mismanagement and corruption also took a toll. And internationally, allegations of links with international terrorism became an embarrassment. After the assassination attempt against President Hosni Mubarak in 1995, Salafi agencies came under scrutiny. The Ethiopian government expelled several because of their employees' alleged involvement in the plot. Hence some scaled back. Meanwhile, they found operations in Bosnia and Afghanistan more attractive. After 1999, the Salafi and da'waist involvement in *jihad* was further complicated by the Bashir-Turabi split, as most of the cadres and leadership of these agencies were sympathetic to Turabi.

[27] Sworn affidavit, Mirawi, 3 June 1997.

The demise of the *jihad* does not however entail the end of the government's war efforts. In the 1990s, the government embarked upon an ambitious long-scale programme of upgrading Sudan's military capability. This has been conducted largely in secret, and has included the expansion of the staff college and the construction of military industries which will, in time, produce sophisticated weaponry. At first funded through international Islamist networks (including Usama bin Laden), this is now supported by oil revenues. Although the ideological fervour of the *jihad* may have been diluted, the war-making capacity of the state remains considerable.

Ultimately the 1990s *jihad* relied on deceit. The reality of the war and the brutalities of the suppression of dissent led to the thorough discrediting of the moral values that the NIF claimed to uphold. While the killing of enemies of Islam can be justified, the torture carried out in the security services' 'ghost houses' and rape of women and men can never have any ethical excuse.[28] The *jihad* has not led to the moral purification of the country and the *mujahidiin*: on the contrary, Sudan has seen the extreme degree of prostitution, corruption, and moral degradation. Finally, the split within the ruling party and the publication of accusations has made this picture indisputable even among the Islamists themselves.

It is evident that the war in Sudan cannot be won. The SPLA has proven that the people of Southern Sudan, the Nuba Mountains and Southern Blue Nile cannot be ruled against their will. The *jihad* has simply failed, and the increasing level of armaments possessed by the government cannot deliver a victory. The only solutions are peaceful agreement with power-sharing of some kind, or a partition of the country. But even within a truncated 'Northern' Sudan, the jihadist project has reached a dead end. The Sudanese experience of the 1990s has shown that violence cannot resolve the fundamental theoretical problems of political Islam. *Jihad* cannot fill the void.

What next for the Sudanese Islamists?

Throughout the 1990s divisions between Hassan al Turabi and Omer al Bashir were rumoured. Some held the Islamist-army split to be funda-

---

[28] In an exceptional case, one detained army officer alleged that he had been raped in detention. The public humiliation associated with such an admission indicates that it is very likely to be true. The failure of the government to investigate this, a clear case of immorality under the *shari'a*, is a clear example of the failure of the Islamic state to achieve the ethical standards to which it claimed to aspire.

mental, while others dismissed it as a clever NIF ruse to keep their adversaries off guard. In retrospect, it is clear that the split was real, but the two sides had effective means of mediating their differences for a long period. The divide surfaced in 1993, when Turabi tried to accelerate the dissolution of the RCC and the formation of a civilian cabinet and transitional national assembly (which came about in October). It was evident again in the debate over the 1996 elections, and finally culminated in the showdown of 1999–2000. There were many components to the division. Turabi's adventurism had led the Sudan government into deep trouble with its neighbours and had led to dangerous international isolation (notably following his support for Iraq in 1990).

Turabi's ideal was not just an Islamic government but an Islamic opposition as well, a concept soon to be formulated in the concept of *tawali*, a neologism that is best translated as 'succession' or 'the way ahead'. By 1996, Turabi maintained that the time had come for a move towards an Islamist democracy: he believed that his revolution had built a sufficiently strong constituency that he could win elections. In addition he felt that the generals had become too deeply entrenched in power and too pragmatic to be serious about moving decisively towards an Islamic state. His strategy was to bypass their decision-making structures by going to the Islamist grassroots, where his support was strongest. And indeed, for several years, the limited liberalisation pursued by Turabi served him very well.

The military officers and senior ministers were less convinced: they feared that if Bashir were to run against Sadiq el Mahdi in a free election, the latter might well win. Hence they insisted that the 1996 elections be organised without the legalisation of any political parties, and Bashir duly won. Turabi continued to mobilise his cadres, and took the position of Speaker of the National Assembly. From this vantage point he sought to appeal to the cadres of the single party, the National Congress, and to the regions (states under Sudan's new federal Constitution). During 1999 Turabi gathered more power into his hands, proposing the creation of the post of executive Prime Minister and directly-elected state governors. Had they been implemented, this would have amounted to a constitutional coup that awarded executive power to Turabi and reduced the President to little more than a figurehead. By September, it seemed that Turabi had won on all counts: his people were in most key positions, and as the Assembly had gradually passed all his proposals, the moment for a counter-strike appeared to have passed. But, at the eleventh hour, Bashir struck back. On 12 December 1999 he imposed a State of Emergency, suspended the National Assembly and stripped Turabi of his powers. It was not a coup. Senior Islamists including Ali Osman remained in place, Turabi stayed at liberty and there was a flurry of mediation efforts.

Turabi kept his options open. His first steps were strictly legal: he challenged Bashir in court. On 9 March 2000 the Constitutional Court rejected Turabi's petition against the dissolution of the National Assembly. Although the Constitution contained no article empowering the President to act in this way, and many that provided for the reverse, the Constitutional Court decided that it had no jurisdiction over such 'political' matters. This affirmed the ascendancy of the executive and the lack of any judicial independence, and it made a mockery of the rule of law. For Turabi it was ironic: when he had drafted the Constitution he had not envisaged these absolute powers being used against himself, and his entire project was premised on the personal virtue of the head of state.[29]

The split fatally undermined the legitimacy of the Islamist project in Sudan. The two camps accused each other of corruption and criminality, and produced evidence in support of their claims. Turabi accused Bashir of being a dictator, accompanied by a group obsessed with power and wealth, destroying the fundamentals of the Islamic project, dismantling its power structures and corrupting its political and economic assets, abetted by foreign infidels. (al Turabi 2001: 10) Turabi's followers called on the army no longer to fight, and contemptuously described the war as the '*jihad* of oil'. The Islamists' main argument, that they were a political movement based on ethics, was contradicted by their open recognition of what Sudanese had known for a decade or more: that they had engaged in corruption, torture and deceit. The slogan 'Islam is the solution' sounded hollow, and the failures could not be blamed on just one part of the regime.

The division took on a regional and ethnic character. Turabi's followers included many from the west of Sudan, who pointed out the way in which state power has been monopolised by the riverain elite, including almost all of Bashir's camp. A *Black Book* was published detailing this, and—remarkably—even mentioning the name of Daud Bolad as a 'martyr'.[30] Perhaps the most telling part of this crisis was the fact that it was

[29] An interesting parallel is the detention and prosecution of Anwar Ibrahim in Malaysia, in 1998. Having brought personal conduct into the heart of political discourse, Ibrahim was unable to offer the defence of privacy when he was accused of sodomy. See Kepel 2002: 96–8.

[30] The *Black Book* was written by some of Turabi's followers, who subsequently took an independent line.

entirely self-inflicted. Islamists had become accustomed to blaming their defeats on external conspiracies, but in this case there could be no denying that the disaster was entirely home-grown. The dispute was purely and simply over power, and the cynicism with which both parties pursued the conflict undermined any claims to moral virtue. (El-Affendi 1999)

The confrontation came to a head in May 2000, when was Turabi removed as Secretary General of the National Congress Party and although he was formally confined to his house, he was able to appear in public with armed guards and challenge Bashir. There was speculation that he would declare *jihad* against Bashir and even launch a coup. It did not happen. Turabi's project of a quasi-democratic Islamic state had been halted. The question was, what would take its place? In recognition of the strength of Turabi's following, and the unwillingness of the government to provoke a potential civil war among the Islamists, Turabi's followers were permitted to organise a legal opposition party, the Popular National Congress. The National Congress itself struggled to reassert itself, but time and executive power were on its side. Being able to dispense patronage, it won itself wider support, especially in the rural areas. At the end of 2000, Bashir won presidential elections.

What is next for the Sudanese Islamists, still in power in Khartoum but seemingly incapable of using that power for anything other than staying in office? Sudan needs a political imagination that replaces the 'civilisation project' (*al mashru' al hadhari*) with a 'civil project' (*al mashru' al medani*) (Abdel Salam and de Waal 2000, Ajawin and de Waal 2002). But do the Islamists have what is needed to make this adjustment? Or will the Islamist impasse remain, theoretically resolved but in practice destroyed by reversion to violence?

The Sudanese Islamist project has the dilemma of four options, all of them unworkable. The first is to move towards a broad-based Islamist coalition, embracing the sectarian-based Umma Party and DUP. This would entail the current government losing most or all of its power. First, government jobs would have to be shared out, and many of the current ministers would lose office. Second, the sectarians' demand for electoral democracy would reveal the narrowness of the National Congress Party's base. The sectarian parties, despite their internal problems, would probably win a plurality of votes. Without executive power, the NCP would probably evaporate, much as Nimeiri's Sudan Socialist Union did in 1985. This scenario might also entail a form of constitutionalism that would supplant *shari'a* as the ultimate source of national authority. The Umma and DUP would also most probably insist on a peace settlement with the

SPLA, further diluting the Islamist power base in government. It would create an atmosphere in which the flourishing of civil society cannot be avoided, as occurred in the mid-1980s.

A second option is a variant of this: to focus on a re-Islamisation of society, or the creation of an 'Islamic civil society'. This appears to be Turabi's strategy. Turabi took a bold and perhaps foolish step when he concluded an agreement with the SPLA in February 2001 (endorsed a year later). He was roundly condemned by his former comrades for having sold out to the enemy, and this also provided the pretext for the arrest and detention of Turabi himself and numerous senior members of his group. But the Memorandum of Understanding with the SPLA also indicates an interesting longer-term strategy. This is a recognition of the futility of trying to establish an Islamic state without having first established an Islamic society. The attempt to impose Islamisation by force having evidently failed, Turabi appears to be embracing an accommodation with Sudan's non-Muslims and Muslim non-Arabs, as the basis for re-energising the Islamist movement from below. The argument is that Islamist rulers will win their argument by force of example; their personal piety will inspire others. He seeks theoretical justification for this by returning to the Medina verses of the Qur'an as a source of inspiration, rather than the *shari'a*, and arguing that the Qur'an contains no model of an Islamic state.

But Sudan's experience with political Islam militates against this strategy succeeding. One element is the legacy of Turabi's own years in government, which are not easily forgotten by Sudanese. Turabi's disavowal of violence carries little credibility. His claim that when the Islamists adhere to violence they become incapable of promoting their call may be correct, but it is open to the rejoinder, when did the Islamists *ever* reject violence? Even before they were in government, Sudanese Islamists were practitioners of violence, at school and university. Their demonstrations were notable for well-orchestrated violence, and one of the ways of training cadres they employed was to make them quarrel with drunkards and alleged apostates. Moreover, in his post-September 11 writings he has clearly justified the use of violence against the centres of American power. (al Turabi 2002)

The imprint of the NIF's decade-long Islamist experiment will endure in Sudanese political and cultural life. The Islamist movement will not collapse if its leaders are removed from power. But how its endurance will translate into political programmes is another question. Turabi is characteristically optimistic about the depth of support for an Islamist programme, but the extent of popular Islamist consciousness may simply be a product of the lack of a coherent alternative political programme, and the NIF's success in blackmailing Muslim politicians into accepting its discourse. Turabi has not left a politician or thinker of stature to inherit his mantle, and he is testing the limits of his own credibility through his opportunism. His critics will contend that the *de facto* definition of an Islamic state in Sudan has simply become one that is ruled by Turabi himself.

The third option, which seems to be favoured by the generals and NIF cadres who ousted Turabi from power, is to use Islam as a cover for what would be a pragmatic military or dominant party regime, as in Egypt. Possibly, such a government would be willing to share power with the SPLA, but at the cost of thwarting the pressure for democracy in the country. Such a government would, like Nimeiri in the early 1980s, rely almost entirely on its security apparatus and its power of patronage to keep the opposition alternately intimidated and co-opted. The expanding secret military industries and the still-growing security apparatus indicate that Omer al Bashir and his colleagues consider this their preferred option. Oil revenues make this more possible, but international intolerance of dictatorships makes it more difficult. Moreover, such a government would face relentless opposition from the Islamist movement itself, not only Hassan al Turabi but other extremists as well. However, this is the most likely option. Many Sudanese, especially those from the dominant commercial-officer class, have adopted the outward signs of Islamism, but are in fact utilising their alignment with the regime in an opportunistic way. Meanwhile, many erstwhile Islamists are themselves using their access to state power as its own reward rather than as a means to promote an Islamist agenda.

This brings us to the fourth and final option, which would be to regress to a neo-fundamentalist agenda, Taliban-style. The jihadist project has incubated violent neo-fundamentalism in Sudan, which may be a fringe phenomenon at present, but may yet become incorporated into the mainstream. Recent years have seen incidents of extremist violence uncontrolled by the state, for example two attacks against Ansar al Sunna mosques (the second blamed on Takfir wa al Hijra), shooting in Usama bin Laden's house, and the killing of the singer Khujali Osman. These are another indication that violence has become ingrained in the Islamist project. Moreover, there are rural constituencies that might be ready to embrace neo-fundamentalism, if they are sufficiently rewarded. Should Sudan adopt the neo-fundamentalist course, it could only lead to isolation, reversing the government's recent successes in achieving international respectability, and hence to continual war.

Exhausted by war, with many of their cadres dead, and enticed by the possibility of self-enrichment through oil exports, Sudan's ruling Islamists are concerned simply with staying in power. None of Turabi's disciples has the potential to succeed him as theoretician, revolutionary, or *sheikh* of the Islamist movement. The most perspicacious say openly that the experiment has failed, others proceed by paying lip service to their now-empty ideals. But meanwhile Sudan's political and economic problems persist, young Sudanese are as frustrated as ever, new students graduate having read Qutb and Turabi, and the currency of *jihad*, though debased, has yet to be discarded.

Implications

Sudan, with its multi-ethnic, multi-religious communities and its cultural diversity and strong democratic traditions, was arguably the least suitable place for the Islamists to begin their project of capturing state power. But the structural weakness of the Sudanese middle class and the defeat of the left in the 1970s, combined with the polarisation brought about by war, made it possible for Hassan al Turabi's genius to engineer an Islamist revolution. That revolution has now failed, both practically and theoretically.

Islamism in Sudan is in an impasse. It cannot move forward: it is not equipped with the political imagination or state practice to make sense of the modern world, or to run a state. Islamism's appeal ultimately relies on what cannot be explained: an ethical transformation among human beings or the direct intervention of the Almighty. Rarely in the modern world can radical political philosophers such as Sayyid Qutb and Hassan al Turabi have been so influential in shaping the thoughts and actions of generations of activists. Turabi is perhaps unique in having lived to see his project come to its logical peak of wielding power, and then fail. The failure of Islamism in Sudan is ultimately his: it is a philosophy with deceptive promise and fatal weakness.

Jihad cannot be dismissed as just a deviant offshoot of Islamism in Sudan. This and the previous chapter have shown how, for both theoretical and contingent historical reasons, violence has become an integral part of the Islamist conceptual vocabulary. As the Sudanese NIF has discovered, the Kingdom of God is not at hand. Those tasked with fighting a war and keeping state institutions functioning cannot rely on divine intervention to help them out. The Islamist project in Sudan, once its adherents had taken power, was inherently flawed. *Jihad* was tried as a way out of the conundrum but it too failed, and both the attempt and the failure witnessed neo-fundamentalist excesses quite incompatible with modernising Islamism as well as human rights. Those contradictions ultimately surfaced in the 1999 split between Turabi on one hand and President Bashir and Ali Osman on the other, with the managing director dismissing the mullah-in-chief. But the Sudanese state still cannot achieve stability, as it remains publicly committed to an Islamist neo-fundamentalism that promises more than it can deliver. Can the 'constitutional Islam' offered by Sadiq el Mahdi offer a way out? Sudanese Islamism may yet win a reprieve through this opening on the horizon of its political imagination, but that too is weighted down with the failures of its proponent, who has held office and failed to deliver. Any solution for the Islamists will involve paying a heavy price, in terms of abandoning their dream of an Islamic state, and by the Islamists in power today losing office. Sudanese can live as Muslims only in the absence of an Islamic state.

4

ISLAMIC POLITICAL DYNAMICS IN THE SOMALI CIVIL WAR
BEFORE AND AFTER SEPTEMBER 11[1]

Roland Marchal

Political developments in post-colonial Somalia were closely linked with the Cold War. International interest in Somalia was shaped by a regional and global assessment of threats and claims made by the two international camps, more than it was by the realities on the ground. The eruption of the civil war in Mogadishu in late 1990 went largely unnoticed, since the world was on the eve of the second Gulf War. When international intervention was launched to save the victims of starvation in December 1992, Somalia's crisis was not considered on its own merits but rather as a test case of a new way to build an international coalition, framed by the discussions within the UN Security Council.

Again, after 11 September 2001, Somalia has become the focus of renewed international interest, not because of its unresolved crisis but, this time, because this country is described as a safe haven for all kinds of terrorist groups, including al Qa'ida led by Usama bin Laden. On 26 September 2001 a Somali Islamist organisation, al Itihaad al Islaami, was put on the US authorities' blacklist. On 7 November the accounts of the most important Somali company, al Barakaat, were frozen and some of its

[1] This paper is based on fieldwork undertaken in difficult conditions from 1991 until 2001 and contacts with Somali actors mostly in Southern Somalia, though a few comments on the situation elsewhere in Somalia, in what is called today Somaliland (formerly North-Western Somalia) and Puntland (North-Eastern Somalia), are made. A first version of this paper was presented at a symposium on Islam in Africa: 'A Global, Cultural and Historical Perspective', Binghampton University, 19–21 April 2001.

staff arrested on the allegation that this company was channelling huge amounts of money to al Itihaad and al Qa'ida.

This chapter does not intend to discuss the long history of Islam in Somalia, which has been extensively addressed by a number of writers (Lewis 1998, Trimingham, 1965, Samatar 1992, Hersi 1977, Mukhtar 1995, Helander 1999). It is concerned with the development and growth of Islamic political or quasi-political trends during the civil war, and discusses aspects of the new situation created by the events of September 11 and the US reaction to them.

Somalia has a long intimacy with Islam. But the social structures and organisations in the country, including the low level of urbanisation, the co-existence of pastoral production systems in a large part of the country and agriculture in the inter-riverine area, and clanship have shaped a form of Islam distinct from that in other countries in the Horn of Africa. Furthermore, from 1969 to 1990 the Siyaad Barre regime was hostile to any public political assertions of Islamic agendas. But the dictatorship could not freeze globalisation, nor prevent its impact. It tried to repress the growing opposition formed by new religious trends, though the latter were not strong enough to provide any effective political alternative. The subsequent period of the civil war could be described as the confluence of different dynamics, the result of which has yet to be assessed fully. First of all, Somalia became a place where Islamic charities developed their activities in competition with traditional Western NGOs. Although there is no way to measure their political impact as such, these charities have acquired a significant influence in the social realm and specifically among the urban youth. Secondly, despite the utterly pessimistic perception of a country at war, business developed in Somalia in an extraordinary way and Mogadishu has become a free port for the whole region, where goods are brought from Saudi Arabia, Yemen and Dubai and then re-exported to Kenya, Ethiopia and even Uganda. The Gulf business class has been a source of inspiration for many emerging Somali traders who often became more religious, even militantly so, in order to build the trust necessary to get access to their counterparts on the eastern side of the Red Sea. Thirdly, other dynamics are present, which may be more related to the context of violence as will be described below. All these changes have occurred in parallel with the development of political Islam. After ten years of civil war, though the strength of these movements is still debatable, it is clear that they seem influential enough to play a role in the resolution of the Somali crisis.

In the first section some new features and changes of Islamic practices are described as they took shape before the civil war and played, directly or indirectly, a crucial role in the way new Islamic groupings were created. The second section provides some insights into the re-Islamisation of public life during the first years of the civil war. A third section considers the way Islamic Courts were set up in Mogadishu, first from 1994 up to 1997 in its northern part and then, after their collapse, in south Mogadishu starting in mid-1999 and continuing up to the present. The fourth section discusses the way political groupings have had to reshape their strategy to win and keep a popular basis throughout the period since the end of the international intervention in Somalia. A last section discusses the case of al Barakaat.

The Siyaad Barre regime facing globalisation

Although Islam developed in Somalia from the ninth century and 99 per cent of the population are Muslims (Nelson 1982: 105), there are many differences in social practices within the country that should be considered. The former British colony of Somaliland (north-western Somalia), being the closest to Arabia, has more cultural bonds with Arab culture than other parts of the country. This is reflected by the fact that women's public life is less developed than in the South and that up to now, fewer girls are sent to school than in the South. However, other reasons may also play a role: for instance the urbanisation process has not been as significant in Somaliland as in the South, while the influence of the state has been weaker. The pastoral way of life, which is the main mode of production in Somaliland, does not encourage schooling and the reluctance to send children to school was certainly reinforced by the impact of the indirect rule practised by British colonisers who, for budgetary reasons, tried to minimise any disruptions to Somaliland's social fabric.

The former Italian Somalia underwent a very different experience since coastal civilisation developed more and was influenced by travellers from Islamic countries like Persia, Yemen, Oman and the Zanzibar Sultanate (Cassanelli 1975). It is worth emphasising here that *zawiyas* (*jamaca* in Somali) developed in the nineteenth century alongside older *tariqas*. A good portion included agricultural settlements and recruited members from marginalised groups within Somali society, a feature that would be of great importance in the civil war. While there is a historiography of the proto-nationalist upheaval led by Mahamed Abdille Hasan (in Somali, Maxamed Cabdulle Xasan) (Abdi 1992, Jardine 1923, Touval 1964), much less emphasis has been given to the main trend of Somali *tariqas*. There groups were mostly politically neutral and reluctant to get involved in party politics after 1949, with the exception of the traditional opposition to any moves on education that was interpreted as running a risk of Christianisation.

Religious belief was, of course, very strong but integrated especially in agricultural areas with other beliefs like rainmaking (*roobdoon*), *saar* (spirit cult) (Lewis 1986) and witchcraft whose history is linked to the various communities that had settled in the area, being Persian, Arab or African (especially slaves during the Zanzibar period).[2]

In July 1960 the former British and Italian colonies merged. Until the military coup of October 1969 Somalia was ruled by civilian governments, and political life, though not fully democratic, was at least semi-competitive. Two political issues were under Islamic scrutiny: the elections and the contentious debate on the writing of the Somali language.

Although at the end of the elections there were only very few parties besides the hegemonic Somali Youth League,[3] the process was much more tumultuous: just before the elections, in order to get elected, candidates were shifting their allegiance and creating new political bodies for a few weeks as a way to mobilise support among their sub-clans or communities (Castagno 1964, Lewis 1988). In 1969, more than sixty such parties emerged before the elections but only five stayed, since many of the MPs elected on behalf of new organisations quickly joined the main parties once again. The role of religious leaders was not specific in the sense that everyone was campaigning among his kinsmen and it would be difficult to claim that any Islamic trend was represented in the Parliament, though some MPs were known to be more religious than others. There was also an ongoing debate about which alphabet should be used to write the Somali language: different systems were proposed but a unifying factor for the religious scholars was to choose the Arabic one, since it was that of the Holy Qur'an and would have eased religious teaching. (Laitin 1977)[4] This debate, nevertheless, was not a clear cut-contradiction between secular and religious oriented people since no-one was pushing either a secularist or Islamic agenda.

---

[2] For an excellent illustration, see the description of the Bardheere *jihad* provided by Lee Cassanelli (1982).

[3] Despite the fact that among the thirteen founding members in 1947, there were at least two important religious figures, Abdulhader Sekhawe Din and Haji Mahamed Hussein, the SYL was a quite secular organisation and its name reflected the opposition to 'old-fashioned' leaders, either traditional or religious.

[4] One illustration of such a trend could be Ibrahim Hashi Mahamud, whose book *Somali in the Quranic script* was published in 1963.

Changes began when the military took power in October 1969. General Mahamed Siyaad Barre became President and gave room to a cluster of young intellectuals trained in Western universities who were appointed to key positions of the state apparatus. Outside the country, emphasis has been put on the 'scientific socialism' officially adopted by the regime in 1970 and the subsequent modernisation agenda of the government. Inside Somalia, things were initially less clear, mostly because Siyaad was extremely popular and religious practices were not directly obstructed. Nevertheless, social cohesion was weakening since various forms of political mobilisation were undermining the traditional gender division of labour (Samatar 1988). The decision in 1972, after lengthy debate, that the Latin alphabet should be used to write Somali was a further blow to Islamism. But the key move occurred in 1975 when a new Family Code, in many aspects quite close to the secular Tunisian one, provoked radical opposition from religious circles. Ten *ulama* who openly condemned the new law were executed in January 1975, and the government orchestrated a campaign against all those 'religiously backward-oriented' people who were siding against 'progress'. (Adam 1995) Some religious people who were already concerned by the growth of cooperation with the communist countries thought that the military regime was eventually leading Somali society towards atheism.

Nevertheless, the most crucial factor was not located in the political debates, though they were triggering a new Islamic consciousness. Somalia was no longer the isolated country it had been. In February 1974 Somalia became a member of the Arab League, mostly in order to get increased international aid and diplomatic support against Ethiopia in its irredentist claim to Somali unity. Through grants and scholarships, this decision helped to increase the number of students trained in foreign religious institutions, not only in the still-quiet Sudan but also in al Azhar and in Saudi Arabia, where new Islamic trends were developing. This dynamic was not reversed by the alignment with the West after the Somali army was defeated in the Ogaden war in 1977–8. On the contrary, Islamism was invigorated in this period. The Iranian revolution in 1979 and its impact on the Arab countries fostered the development of political Islam throughout the region. In the 1980s this alignment was strengthened through the fact that the United Arab Emirates (and specifically Dubai) became an important trading partner, though to a lesser extent than Saudi Arabia or Italy. Flights connected the two countries twice a week and the movement of people from Somalia to the Gulf States increased (even though for many migrants, the motivation was ultimately to reach Western countries).

There is very little information on modern Islamist groupings during the Siyaad Barre regime. Before the end of the 1980s there seemed to be various groups, mostly underground, which may have had a notional influence. For instance, we can note a few organisations including Wahdat Shabab al Islami (Islamic Youth Unity, known in Somali as Waxda) or Jama'at Ahlal Islami (Society of Islamic people) and its offspring, Jam'at Islah (in Somali Islaax, the Reform Group). However, nothing of what is quoted below (Aqli 1993) has been cross-checked and the Somalis with whom the author discussed those groups were not inclined to believe that they had any deep impact.

Waxda was established in August 1969 in Hargeysa, the capital of the former British colony. It was an Islamic institution whose teaching referred increasingly to Sayyid Qutb, Mawdudi, Nadawi and other new Islamist thinkers. When the secularist trend became prominent in the regime, they went underground and started publishing leaflets against the 'socialist' state. In 1978, in the aftermath of the defeat in Ogaden, dozens of members were arrested and jailed in Southern Somalia. Those who escaped jail rallied UFO, a self-help organisation made up of local intellectuals who were also imprisoned in 1983 (Africa Watch 1990). After the national Somali army destroyed most of Hargeysa and Burco in 1988, Waxda started again in the refugee camps in Ethiopia and supported the Somali National Movement (SNM) (Compagnon 1990) that was leading the struggle against the regime in Somaliland. After 1991, when Somaliland declared again its independence, this group became deeply involved in educational institutions, keeping close links with Kuwait.

Jama'at Ahlal Islami, known in Somali as Ahli, was founded by Sheykh Mahamed Moallim after he received his religious degrees from al Azhar. This important figure of Somali Islam was Qadiri and initiated *tafsir* at the Abdilqaader Mosque in Mogadishu with modern references and a wish to address contemporary issues. After the *ulama* became openly critical of the regime in 1975, many followers were arrested and Ahli disbanded completely. Some members who escaped to Saudi Arabia set up a new group under the leadership of Sheykh Mohamed Ahmed Garyare that became known as Jama'at Islah (in Somali Jamaca Islaax). This group was the first and only one to get acquainted with the international organisation of the Muslim Brothers.

Other groups arose in Mogadishu, as they did in other Arab countries. Takfir wa al Hijra already had a few followers. By 1980 a new group of former religious students of Saudi institutions established a group called

Salafi characterised by a strong adhesion to Wahhabism. All those groups seem to have tried without success to unify, although a new organisation, Hezbe Itihaad al Islaami, was created in Mogadishu.

As mentioned before, to the best of the author's knowledge there is no hard evidence of the influence—even sometimes of the existence—of those groups. But that does not mean that the Islamic trend was not growing among the urban youth. Many young religious people were meeting in certain mosques. Official allegations that Islamic militants killed the Roman Catholic Bishop of Mogadishu, Salvatore Colombo, in July 1989 are dubious (Simons 1995: chapter 7), but show that they were also seen as a potential problem by the dictatorship. Nevertheless, in the absence of documented research, one has to be careful and not take claims for granted. In particular, as in other Muslim countries, it is debatable whether what has been described as a re-Islamisation process was the result of those militant organisations or whether it was the complex conjunction of internal social dynamics and external factors brought in by the unwilling acceptance of globalisation by the Somali dictatorship.

Globalisation was indeed a problem, which was very reluctantly addressed by the ruling elite. Actually, for most of the duration of the dictatorship, books and foreign newspapers were not allowed in Somalia. With hindsight one may say that this prohibition helped to give religious literature an undisputed status, while hampering the development of other political ideologies, especially liberal ones. Because of the repressive nature of the regime, many cadres and intellectuals were put in jail in the 1980s and, like their predecessors, were denied any reading material except for the Qur'an and *tafsir* books. Somalis used to illustrate that situation by quoting as an example the fate of Mohamed Abshir Muse, who was chief of police in 1969 but resigned before the elections, as he wanted to oppose the massive corruption in the electoral process. At that time, he was known as a man appreciating the joys of life. After Siyaad Barre's coup, he was kept isolated in jail for years with a Qur'an as his only moral support and came out as a dedicated Wahhabi.

Nevertheless, Islamism did not appear as an alternative to the regime. As mentioned above, its organisations were not strong enough and could not effectively appeal to large sections of the population, especially the rural communities and nomads who had a very different understanding of Islam and politics. As the framework for political activities became increasingly clan-based, militant Islamic militants had little to offer. Armed opposition—first in north-eastern Somalia (the Somali Salvation Democratic Front, SSDF, set up in 1979 [see Markakis 1987]), then in the north-west (SNM) and later in the south (United Somali Congress, USC (see Compagnon 1990))—was based, or came to be later, on an alliance of clans fighting a regime which was itself seen as an alliance of Daarood clans.[5] Although this vision encapsulates as much propaganda as reality, it had a tremendous mobilising influence, especially in the nomadic areas where clanship is at the core of all relationships and where the bulk of the fighters were recruited. Despite the creation, in the very last months of the regime, of different Islamic opposition groupings, they were in no way able to play a significant role in the upheaval in the capital city. They just reflected the same trend of shifting allegiances and fissions that clan-based armed organisations had already witnessed.

To summarise, Siyaad Barre to a certain extent wanted to implement a project of modernisation through authoritarianism but failed for many reasons: the defeat by Ethiopia and the collapse of Somali irredentist nationalism; the lack of success in dealing with his opposition without entering into a military confrontation; and his inability to understand the changing period of the late 1980s where the Cold War was no longer enough to justify international support to a predatory elite. Although political Islam was not marginal in the 1980s, it could not get support from large portions of the youth and urban population. The reasons are linked not only to the social fabric of the Somali society (clanship) but to other factors as well: for example, its leading figures were considered too young, lacking the moral authority of clan elders, and their propaganda was seen as too alien to Somali society. Arab civilisation was, of course, intimately linked to this political trend but Arab States (Saudi Arabia, United Arab Emirates) were also seen as misbehaving in front of the Somalis and arming the government against its own population.

Managing chaos: 1991-?

The period between January 1991 and December 1992 was undoubtedly the pivotal moment of the civil war in the south of Somalia. After December 1992 there were many other outbreaks of fighting in Mogadishu and elsewhere in the south, hundreds of people were murdered but never did the killings reach the level of the period before the international intervention. Although we cannot elaborate on this dimension here, this aspect has to be borne in mind.

---

[5] All Somali clans belong to a confederation of clan families such as Daarood, Hawiye, Isaaq, Dir, Raxanweyn. Non ethnically Somalis are Arabs, Gibil Cad (white skin) and Bantus.

To a large extent the first upheaval in the capital city in late December 1990 was an event unplanned by the opposition and took the form of a popular uprising against the dictatorship and the clans that were rightly or wrongly associated with it. It started on 30 December 1990 and lasted till 26 January 1991, culminating in an ambiguous conclusion: Siyaad Barre and his followers abandoned the capital city in good order and went to Kismaayo. But the capital city was far from under control despite the (much-contested) election of Ali Mahdi Mahamed as new President of Somalia on 28 January by a cluster of Hawiye politicians. Militias from various Hawiye clans were lurking around, plundering and exterminating loosely identified supporters of the old regime (actually any Daaroods). No leader was able to put them in camps or to keep a grip on them: this was a consequence of both the lack of any real organisation among the opposition and the increasingly open struggle for power among its leadership, between General Mahamed Faarah Aydiid and Ali Mahdi. (Marchal and Messiant 1997)

Security in Mogadishu deteriorated to the lowest level, even for people who belonged to the most heavily armed Hawiye sub-clans. Many analysts have said that the state had collapsed whereas in fact things were much worse. Although parts of the national army were still functioning (and allied with Siyaad Barre), old traditional bonds among the urban population collapsed, armed youth were flooding the capital city and one could witness the violent outbreak of all kinds of social and economic contradictions within the population. Many Hawiye males were potential fighters and those who had a job before did not return to their workplace but were waiting for a very unclear future position. The situation in Kismaayo where troops faithful to Siyaad Barre were stationed was at first better, but the implosion occurred within the following year for reasons which are not so different from those mentioned in the case of Mogadishu.

After several clashes in Mogadishu in the spring and summer of 1991, a major war started in November 1991 and lasted until March 1992. In the spring of 1991 and 1992, while a fragile lull reigned in the capital city, the Hawiye USC attacked or counter-attacked the remnants of Siyaad Barre's forces that were trying to defeat their internally-divided Hawiye opponents. While attention here is focused on Mogadishu and Kismaayo, one should keep in mind that low intensity fighting was the norm in Central Region and in the inter-riverine area where it created the conditions for the destructive starvation of 1992. (de Waal 1997a)

People in Mogadishu and maybe elsewhere had to cope with this difficult period in an atmosphere of extreme insecurity. Moving around could be a dangerous exercise since bandits were on the loose: one could be killed for nothing, a shirt, a clock, or just clan identity itself. The risks were, of course, much higher for people who were from unarmed or weaker clans, but this feeling of insecurity was spreading everywhere and affected the whole of society. Such a situation gave room for new forms of behaviour.

For instance, many young urban people took refuge in the mosques to avoid the fighting and thereby came into contact with more militant figures who were not part of what they described as a clan-war among Muslims. This was notably the case for people who were not from the Hawiye clan: a good number of Daarood tried to save their lives this way. It is difficult to know whether they were successful since different mosques were attacked and looted, as clan paranoia reached its peak. Other changes also occurred, some of which reflected religious sensibilities. For instance, Western clothes were no longer worn by women who instead preferred the traditional *dirrha*, and increasingly even unmarried women wore the *shaash* to cover their hair and neck. As always in Somalia, this should not be explained only by religion: Western clothing was associated by the *mooryaan*[6] with wealth and it was most inappropriate to send this signal. Since insecurity was high, especially during battles in town as the author witnessed, people were reading the Qur'an and praying more regularly than before the upheaval: they had to be ready to die and were searching for at least some relief in the face of this havoc. Religion was also instrumental to provide a certain security. The *mooryaan* disliked religious people but feared them in the sense that attacking them could provoke a bad reaction from God. So, in the end, in a situation perceived as highly anomic, identification with Islam became a means to seek security: both in one's identity and in the face of a ruthless society.

Nevertheless, secularist attitudes did not disappear overnight. In comparison with Somaliland and Puntland, the mixing of the sexes in public spaces was not an issue in Mogadishu. Women were not restricted in public life. To a large extent, this issue remains outside the influence of most Islamic radicals. Fasting throughout Ramadan was also not so common: in 1991 and 1992, restaurants were opened at midday downtown and many believers were not fasting every day of the month. This situation changed radically during the international intervention, in 1993 and in the following years: it then became difficult to find a normal restaurant

---

[6] '*Mooryaan*' was one of the Somali terms used to describe the fighters and, from 1992 onwards, the bandits, alongside '*dayday*' or '*jiri*'. See Marchal (1993).

(i.e. one not functioning for *gaal*, that is foreigners, or more precisely, '*kafir*') to be open throughout the fasting hours of the day.

What about the Islamic groups? Despite the fact that many were set up at the dawn of the upheaval in Mogadishu, they were neither so active nor visible in the hardest period of the fight. One may believe that, if still in existence, they were keeping a very low profile and were completely outnumbered by other factions that had recruited the nomadic youth through clan appeal. But leaders were not indifferent to religious resources. For instance, Ali Mahdi, as soon as he was elected in a dubious manner in January 1991, requested women to go back to the home, citing religious justification. However he was not an Islamist, on the contrary he is known as Qadiri and this use of religion was mostly tactical. Later on, in March 1991, one of his deputies, Hussein Haji Bod, tried to establish an Islamic militia group made up of people from various Hawiye clans whose aim was to arrest the thugs and implement *shari'a*. This attempt failed completely in a matter of two or three days: the *mooryaan* were not keen to see their friends caught to suffer *hudud* punishments![7]

Mogadishu as always was the arena of confusion and a delicate balance of forces. In late 1992 there were at least seven organisations whose influences were anything but marginal. The first was Ahle Sunna wa Jama'a. This looe organisation gathered prominent figures of traditional Islam in the South, the *tariqas*, especially from the Qadiriyya and Ahmadiyya. The group was set up with the support of General Aydiid in order to counter the influence of the most radical trends and to protest against the fact that foreign Islamic NGOs were working with those Salafi groups and not with people appointed by the General. Its constituency was potentially large, since it controlled a good number of mosques, but at the same time it was not in a position to attract either the youth or intellectuals. Later on this group got enough funding to rent 'technicals' (pick-up trucks mounted with heavy guns) and, from time to time, visit Lower Shabelle (the region at the southern flank of Mogadishu) and other places to campaign against the 'young Westernised *sheykhs*' as they were called by traditional religious leaders. But their real strength was not really expressed through such means. Local pilgrimages, *mawlid* commemorations and *dhikr* and *saar* ceremonies were once again widely practised from 1993, an indication of their influence among the rural population as well as in urban areas, but lay people were not discriminating in a situa-

---

[7] There was also another dimension linked to the competition between Ali Mahdi and Mohamed Faarah Aydiid.

tion characterised by a great scarcity of resources. They could attend the *daw'a* organised by an Islamic group to get some food or free medicine without changing their allegiance to the *tariqa*.

A second group was Ansar-e Sunna, a Wahhabi organisation. It was made up of traders and returnees who had close connections within Saudi Arabia. Its strength was mostly among the traders, most notably because of its access to aid provided by Saudi institutions such as the Saudi Red Crescent. For instance, it used to pay up to US$50 to a family whose female members were dressed the way it wanted. Despite its financial means it could not be very influential since women were too involved in public life or, at least, in the economic realm. In addition, its rules were also opposing the way of life of the numerous people from the countryside who migrated to the capital city, either as displaced people or having followed their sons and husbands who were fighting with one of the Mogadishu factions. This group was also competing with other groups that were more flexible.

A third group, Al Majma al Islam, was set up a few weeks after Siyaad Barre left Mogadishu and tried to play the role of a Supreme Islamic Council, a gathering of *ulama* and Islamic scholars who pretended to be the true representative of all Muslims within Somalia. Its success and influence were short-lived and it played no major role in the country or in the capital city afterwards. To a certain extent, its failure reflects problems faced by many other groupings, not only parts of 'civil society' (if any existed in such circumstances) but also of the political arena: the fact that many people were influential as individuals did not lead to an increase in influence by them as a group because of the lack of organisation and divisive issues of clanship.

In 1992 al Itihaad al Islaami became the most visible group and was also the most radical. First of all it was the only one that armed itself and established organisational rules to differentiate between sympathisers and full members and thereby exercise effective organisational discipline, including keeping the confidentiality of its internal discussions. Its strategy of taking power by violence was one major point of difference with the others. There is also another striking difference: it was recruiting urban and semi-educated youth while other armed groups were giving priority to nomads. To a large extent it is the only group that set up a national or at least regional strategy and tried to organised its activities all over Somalia and in the Ethiopian Ogaden. Since very little is known on its internal coordination and membership, it is difficult to describe the conditions in which it developed. What is sure is that it obtained support and training from Sudan and invited 'Afghans' to help establish training centres for its new members. Since some of its cadres were senior officers from the former national army, it had informants in all factions and was seen by them in a very ambivalent way. At certain times, it was instrumental in challenging a contested leader or weakening his political discourse but, despite all its connections, al Itihaad was never accepted among the factions because this would have allowed it to monopolise the Islamic reference.

Another group, al Tabliq, could be described as a quasi-opposite organisation. As in Djibouti, this group is known only for its quietist proselytism: groups of Tabliq members have been touring the countryside and teaching religion to the local communities. This group is not known to conduct military activity. It has some members who are prominent business people in Bakaarah, the main Mogadishu market, but critics argued that commercial operations with big Pakistani merchants might have been the key explanation. No evidence is currently available to certify such claims.

A last group should be mentioned at this point, though the list may not be complete. This is al Islaah, which has no direct connections with the group of the same name set up in the 1980s. Al Islaah was at first an Islamic NGO operating at the interface between Somalis and international Islamic NGOs (mostly from the Gulf States and especially Kuwait). Recruitment targeted a range of constituencies. There were a fair number of former supporters of al Itihaad who thought that military means would not be able to enforce the Islamic state they wished and that a more protracted strategy of building a social hegemony was required. There were some more moderate intellectuals who found a job in the NGO projects and who were also advocating a softer approach, at least in the short term. At the very beginning activities were very modest and the projects that were implemented demonstrated a real social commitment. They included schools, mother-and-child health units, and so on. Later on, al Islaah developed a strong basis inside Bakaarah market in South Mogadishu. Most of its members here were middle-rank traders and wholesalers. In the long run, this organisation may appear as one of the very few successful NGOs in Mogadishu throughout the civil war. Thanks to the external support it received, it was able to build a network through different groups of the population and may today control most of the schooling institutions in the capital city. Al Islaah reflects quite well the ambiguity of those groups. It contributes in an important way to the development of an Islamic trend, and opposes the presence of any Western institutions in certain fields like education. Its newspaper from time to time has a quite militant tone, but no leaders have ever been involved in military activity and some may appear as relatively open and moderate on certain social issues. Al Islaah was certainly one of the most influential kingmakers in the Arta conference, which was held in Djibouti from May to late August 2000 and which resulted in the formation of the Transitional National Government (TNG).

It is difficult to go very deep into a discussion on the ideology of these Islamists. Most of those new groups appear to have the same Islamic references, which include Sayyid Qutb, Mawdudi and Hassan al Banna. Therefore there are no clear-cut doctrinal or ideological boundaries between them and sympathisers may shift from one group to the other, notably from al Itihaad to al Islaah and vice versa. Religious education is not so impressive in Somalia for lay people, as compared for instance to Sudan. What helps to explain the number of those groups are the many differences they have on mundane issues, like ablution, age of marriage and so on. Rituals more than ideology have been the bone of contention.

The real issue at stake is the context in which those members and sympathisers have been recruited, and the access those groups allow to symbolic or economic resources. Many traders, especially those new to the business, became members since, rightly or wrongly, they thought that they could get better access to Gulf markets, and easily get visas, loans and contracts with foreign Islamic NGOs. The fact that al Islaah and al Itihaad were managing orphanages, schools and health centres means that those organisations were able to employ people and recruit educated staff who had no future in the context of the civil war and whose predicament was appealing. Many of their followers had, at one stage or another, supported the factions but could not accept the way the leaders were using their support for selfish ambitions.

Since Mogadishu was too unstable and violent, and any armed Islamic group could be seen as a direct competitor to the other more important factions (and therefore be crushed), in late 1991 Islamic militias under the umbrella of al Itihaad removed themselves to the major coastal cities in the South: Kismaayo first, then Baraawe and Merka and even Boosaaso in Puntland. The strategy was to take over the ports and get resources from them to fund other activities, at first military reinforcement and then other socially-oriented projects including control of mosques, schools and the like. Their justification was that the other factions were unable to manage any public infrastructure since there was no command structure, and that disagreements and incidents were therefore the norm not the exception. These Islamic militias used to settle in a place through the patronage of a local member of their group belonging to the powerful clan of the area: though they were adamant that clanship was a 'sickness', they knew how to use it for their best interests. Nevertheless, it is also true that the port in Kismaayo was managed in a smoother way than before they had control over it. But economic interests could not be kept away from the 'normal' militias and their leaders indefinitely. When General Aydiid counter-attacked Siyaad Barre's forces in the spring of 1991 and his forces reached Kismaayo, Islamic militias who were managing the port argued that they were neutral in the fight and wanted to keep control of it. However, that was not allowed by the clan factions and a bloody battle ensued. The vast majority of the Islamic militia was drawn from the Daarood clans and, clearly, General Aydiid's supporters were expecting significant revenues from the port. As rightly forecast by al Itihaad, the latter could not manage the port. The remnants of al Itihaad then escaped to Gedo region and built their stronghold around the town of Luuq and Buulo Haawa, which they controlled up to the Ethiopian military intervention in August 1996.

In Kismaayo, a military confrontation determined the fate of the Islamic group. In other places, the scenario was different. In Baraawe, al Itihaad took over but could not get support from the population, as was, to a certain extent, the case in Kismaayo. This could be explained in different ways. First, Baraawe has a long tradition as a religious city for *tariqas* and local religious people saw the newcomers as the same kind of invaders and outsiders as the more secular and disruptive factions. *Tariqas* were getting support from General Aydiid who was concerned then by the growing influence of fundamentalists. Moreover, the main clans of the area, though they at first wanted to be neutral, rallied under Aydiid's umbrella. Although this Islamic group had to leave when Aydiid's forces went through Baraawe to reach Kismaayo, they were, in a sense, already defeated by the adverse reaction of the population. USC militias then settled and for a long time there was no possibility of coming back. In Merka, things went better for the Islamists since they stayed there without political challenge. However, in January 1993 US-led intervention forces were due to arrive in the town and al Itihaad preferred to leave without a fight.

In Boosaaso the situation was more complex and reflected a process that needs to be analysed since it was repeated in other regions of Somalia, notably in Gedo. North-eastern Somalia is populated mostly by Harti clans, whose biggest sub-clan is the Majeerteen, which divides itself in many sub-clans one, the Mahamuud Saleban being the most numerous.

People from the Boosaaso area are mostly from small sub-clans and though those groups are numerically small, their economic power is crucial. This economic elite chose to support al Itihaad to show their lack of trust in the major clans whose aim at that time was to reclaim power and wage war. In that sense, these militants became, willingly or unwillingly, part of clan politics in the region. The support they gained was more of a means to oppose certain clans and clan leaders than to push towards any kind of Islamic reform. Significantly enough, al Itihaad was attacked just a few months later, in the summer 1992, by militias led by the most secularist leader of the north-eastern region, Colonel Abdullahi Yuusuf Ahmed, who had begun to receive support from Ethiopia.

A similar logic applied in Gedo region. Here, clashes between the Somali National Front (SNF), the faction claiming to represent the dominant Mareehaan clan of the region, and al Itihaad reflected to a large extent the division between *guri* and *galti*, i.e. indigenous people against the newcomers from Mogadishu and Galgadud (in the Central Region) who were from different sections of the same Mareehaan clan. As in all other areas where al Itihaad has been present for a while, there was an identification between the organisation and the individual leaders who provided local 'anchorage' for it. Between 1993 and 1996 the key leaders of al Itihaad in Gedo were from Reer Ahmed (with one Eli Dheere from Buulo Hawa), a Mareehaan sub-clan only based in Gedo. Despite the presence of many other Mareehaan and Daarood in the area, local people were inclined to support al Itihaad as a way to show their dislike of 'allogenous' Mareehaan who were leading the SNF and were controlling the access to international assistance in the Gedo region. For other local indigenous people such as the Gobweyn farmers, this period was also their first relative normality after the wars and starvation of the preceding years.

The international intervention from December 1992 to March 1995 was a very ambivalent event for the growth of such groups. On one side, Western aid was flooding the country to fund projects that fitted its frameworks. Internationally-sponsored projects included co-education, an emphasis on women's income-generating activities and similar staple activities for development NGOs. These goals were undoubtedly achieved more in rhetoric than in practice, but such discourses were mobilised by opponents of those Islamic groups, especially by women activists, who got more autonomy than ever to pursue their agendas. On the other side, there was a clear though undeclared confrontation, even before the manhunt against General Aydiid from June to October 1993 (which was supported by a good portion of Mogadishu's residents, especially in the north of the capital).[8] Many groups saw Somali nationalism and xenophobia as a political resource to get access to the political arena or to open the doors to Islamic aid. It was easy for the fundamentalists or traditionalist Islamic leaders to make loud statements opposing Christianisation through education, prostitution of women and so on. All these fears were recurrent in the political discourse even under Siyaad Barre who wanted to limit as much as possible contacts between foreigners and local people, but they were put in a new context, a competition between Western or Christian ideas and the Islamic Somali identity. This competition was not only between Islamist Somalis and Western NGOs, it was also between Western NGOs and foreign Islamic NGOs that mobilised themselves to supply more aid, to start more projects and to fight what they identified as Christianity. One may expect that some Somalis were emphasising these fears and exploiting this rivalry in order to get more resources, a logic that was at the core of Somali attitudes towards foreign powers throughout the Cold War.

It should therefore come as no surprise that all those Somali Islamist groups developed more during the international intervention than beforehand. But other dimensions played a major role as well. For instance, as mentioned above, in 1991 and 1992, clan hatred and violent competition were the norms. After 1992, this was much less the case: life, once more, had value and people started to be concerned not only with politics (a strange concept in such a setting) but with their livelihoods and by their future. Many Islamic NGOs proved that they had the capacity to deliver and succeeded in obtaining dedicated people to act as their counterparts. They also tapped new sources of funds. By contrast, Western NGOs had to cope with their past legacy in the country and the common reality that their funds were embezzled or diverted. But one should be careful in making this argument: Islamic NGOs also had to cope with thugs and crooks, and many had poor systems for accounting for their funds. And in the event, most of the major international Islamic agencies scaled back or left Somalia before the end of the UN intervention. By 1994 the Balkans became a more attractive place as for them, as well as for Western charities. Nevertheless, since those NGOs and their Somali counterparts were the main humanitarian presence in Mogadishu after

[8] As far as clan is concerned, UN and US military could not get support from the Mudullod (whose Abgaal is the main sub-clan) and they tried to build a 'third force' with Murosade and Hawadle clans. This does not mean that many Mudullod individuals did support or even provided intelligence to the UN in the manhunt.

1995 (though at a much lower level), they were able to build a real constituency among the population. One may certainly speak about patronage, dependency and lack of alternatives, but one must recognise that Western NGOs had only a symbolic presence and impact on the urban situation in the capital city.

At the same time, all those organisations were facing problems. We must be aware of a particular feature of Somali culture in the context of the civil war. As soon as an organisation becomes powerful, it is thereafter referred to as a clan organisation and thereby 'belongs' to the clan of its leader. Whether or not an individual is a 'clanist', social life and interaction are closely linked to clan identity. Relatives visit one, and one cannot escape those family relationships and the obligations they entail. Potentially controversial discussions take place very often only in a homogeneous context. As mentioned, new-born Islamists have not managed to transcend these clan loyalties. For instance, when the 'war' against Aydiid started in June 1993, Islamists divided among themselves. Some who were mostly related to General Aydiid's clan wanted to get involved and fight alongside the faction leader against the 'Americans'. The others were reluctant since, in the previous period, General Aydiid was seen as a major threat for them. Splits occurred then and subsequently took a long time to be repaired, since people had died and no-one wanted to lose face. The same dilemmas occurred later on when al Itihaad had its base in Luuq and, for a while, supported the Rahanweyn Resistance Army in Bay and Bakool against Aydiid's faction. Many Islamists thought that such an involvement was unwise since it was not 'their' war. Therefore, one should not be surprised that, in some Islamist organisations, leadership has been collective, while in others, including al Itihaad, the names of leaders are not known, or different individuals are cited as leaders depending on whom you talk to.

To a large extent, when Southern Somalia witnessed the departure of the last UN contingents, the balance in favour of Islamic groups was positive. The Western world had failed to solve the Somali crisis. Western aid reached a very low level and diplomatic disinterest was the norm. Politically, the Islamist Somali groups were not strong enough to offer an alternative to the factions. Nevertheless, some of them had been able to develop a social influence in the towns, and build a real constituency. They were working consistently with the youth, women and traders, and were becoming more flexible on certain issues, making a difference between members who should comply with their strict regulations and sympathisers who were adapting themselves to the new situation. Certainly, as reflected in Gedo region after 1994, one of their main aims was to get rid of any Western presence and use a *de facto* monopoly to reduce any opposition. One should take note of the problems faced by certain local NGOs (those that were effective ones, not those operating as a business or in a predatory way) that tried to set up educational institutions or women's groups. As soon as co-education was introduced, opposition was raised, incidents created and pressures put on the local staff. In this sense, the violent context in which all those groups were set up was still defining their options and strategies.

The Islamic Courts experiment

The establishment of Islamic Courts in Mogadishu constitutes an interesting case that allows us to assess the contradictions any Islamic agenda may face in the current situation in Somalia. For the purpose of the analysis, one may consider the first attempt made in North Mogadishu and then consider the situation after mid-1999 in the southern part of the capital city till the Arta conference.

As explained earlier in this chapter, although urbanisation was not clan-based, after March 1992 Mogadishu became divided into two parts. North Mogadishu (known after its major area, Karaan)—except the Huriwaa or Pastificio area—was under the control of Ali Mahdi Mahamed while South Mogadishu, excluding Medina, was under the control of General Mahamed Faarah Aydiid. 'Control' actually is not the best word to describe the situation since none of these leaders was able to set up any administration or establish even some institutions. The reality was that no armed group hostile to one leader could operate in the area he was nominally controlling. The clan context, however, was very different.

In North Mogadishu the major part of the population was Abgaal and associated clans (under the name of Mudullod). A majority of the population inhabited Mogadishu before the civil war and Abgaal territory was adjacent to that part of town. It had many implications for security. Banditry was not framed by nomadic ethos but mostly by delinquency and petty criminality. In the southern part of the capital city, all major clans were represented and there were also many newcomers from the bush, which means that banditry was organised eventually through nomadic ways.

At the beginning of 1994 Ali Mahdi was facing huge difficulties within his own Mudullod clan. He had not been able to win the war against General Aydiid in 1992, was not a major player during the international intervention despite the manhunt against Aydiid, and opposed the Hiraab peace agreement, a popular agreement struck by opponents of both faction leaders to ease the relationship between the two parts of the town in January 1994. While the UN gave political emphasis to General Aydiid in the search for a 'national solution', thieves were becoming more active in North Mogadishu and Ali Mahdi was blamed for the deterioration in security. The decision to set up Islamic Courts was taken in this context by a weakened leader facing increasing challenges from his own faction.

Although politicians were far from enthusiastic, the general population welcomed the idea and Islamic Courts started recruiting militias and judges with popular support. The officials were religious leaders but none of them were known fundamentalists. People were impressed by the fact that these militias, whatever past they had, stopped chewing *qaat* and harassing civilians. The implementation of the *shari'a* became a motto. And, in the following months, *hudud* punishments were enforced in the most serious cases. For a few years, security in North Mogadishu reached a quasi-normal level that the population had not enjoyed since the late 1980s. For several years, it became rare to see people moving with weapons in Karaan: even foreigners like the author could move at night and activity continued past twilight.

Islamic groups and especially al Itihaad, who had most of their offices in the southern part of the capital city, opened branches in North Mogadishu and also became involved in the Courts. Since they had been defeated several times, they opted for a more subtle and indirect strategy. Some of their cadres began organising the militias, while others were lobbying for a stricter implementation of what they believed to be *shari'a*. Things were moving very smoothly for them since the charismatic leader of the Courts, Sheykh Ali Dheere, was moving closer to their views and openly advocating an extension of the Courts' mandate.

But one should never believe that political developments could be linear in Mogadishu. The Islamic Courts also achieved legitimacy because General Aydiid was seen as an overall threat for the Abgaal, his power in South Mogadishu a humiliation. When General Aydiid died in early August 1996, all major players in North Mogadishu reassessed the situation.

First, politicians and traders were increasingly concerned by the power of the Islamic Courts: the latter had taken over the Eel Mahan port—the main Mogadishu port had been closed from October 1995—and set up a taxation system, which was hardly acceptable for them. Their monopoly of coercion meant that they should, sooner or later, be rewarded by political positions, which was also a bone of contention. Their strength also gave them control of part of the Middle Shabelle and allowed them to raise taxes there as well. In a nutshell, they had ceased to be a tool and had become competitors.

At a clan level there were also tensions linked to different issues. The first was the *de facto* dominance of the judges belonging to a certain sub-clan. Critics accused them of working for their sub-clan and not the entire Mudullod clan. The second issue was that most of the thieves who were arrested belonged either to non-Abgaal clans (therefore weaker in the territory controlled by the Islamic Courts) or to other sub-sections of the Abgaal than that of the judges. The gulf between the Courts and their opponents became even wider when Muuse Suudi Alayow, another political figure from the same sub-clan as Sheykh Ali Dheere, who was operating in Medina, decided to campaign in Karaan as well.

In November 1997 the situation deteriorated very quickly. The elders of the Mudullod clan decided to curb the power of the Courts and humiliated their leader who thought that a hard-line attitude could reverse the situation. He was wrong, since several major fights divided the Courts' militias who split along sub-clan lines. When this event occurred, it became clear that the militias were still unconvinced about the use of *shari'a*. Even Sheykh Ali Dheere, who by then was seen as very close to the fundamentalists, made speeches to raise support from his own sub-clan against Ali Mahdi and his supporters. In February 1998 the Islamic Courts ceased to operate in North Mogadishu and the division among the Abgaal became a paramount security constraint. North Mogadishu became unsafe, as was South Mogadishu for years.

The Islamic groups supporting the Courts lost an opportunity because they moved too fast and misinterpreted the enduring ambivalence of lay people towards the young fighters. Many who are seen as delinquents are also available to fight for the clan in case of need. There is no alternative to this duality except a real lasting political settlement in Mogadishu and indeed in Somalia as a whole. The economic and political elites have not yet accepted that they have to pay for an autonomous administration (whether Islamic or not), which has to enforce rules for everybody (Marchal 2000).

To a certain extent the implementation of Islamic Courts in South Mogadishu took all of this into account, in that the Islamists have been part of the process from the beginning. As mentioned above, the clan composition of South Mogadishu is more heterogeneous than in the north of the capital. Nomadic customs are stronger since there are many newcomers from the Central Region. For years the late General Aydiid opposed any move to set up Islamic Courts, though some of his followers were advocating them: he would not accept that any structure could be even slightly independent from his grip. After his death things were frozen for a while but started moving because of the situation on the ground.

Several areas near Bakaarah market had become dangerous to the point that business was deeply affected. In other places (downtown in the oldest area) and near the former Military Club, groups of thugs were operating at all hours and disrupting the life of all inhabitants. All these areas were clan-homogeneous in the sense that a majority of the residents belonged to the same powerful clan and that the others had no say. Some religious figures (and, among those, one leading member of the Ahmadiyya and some big business people) decided to set up clan-based Islamic Courts.[9] These Courts employed judges and militias who belonged to the same sub-clan and their authority was, in principle, limited to their kinsmen. It was, therefore, quite a curious interpretation of Islam, but this limitation was not a problem in the first period since the Courts' activities were focusing on specific areas where they had legitimacy. These first successes changed the shape of order in South Mogadishu and opened roads for collaboration between the various Courts.

One should also emphasise that those Courts were established at a time the factional order (one may say disorder) was clearly demonstrating its inability to address the problems of the people. Despite an agreement signed in Cairo in December 1997, little was actually done in Mogadishu to implement at least the first part of the deal. The so-called Benaadir Administration painfully established in the spring and summer of 1998 met with incredulity from the business class and the lay population and eventually collapsed.

If the population was ready for an alternative solution, the Islamic Courts as set up were not yet able to fulfil their expectations. There were different steps to be taken, in which the Islamic groups, especially al Islaah and al Itihaad, played a crucial role. The first one was to clear all obstacles within the sub-clans in which the Courts were recruiting. It was not an easy task: a number of attempts had already been made which had collapsed through the lack of participation of sub-sub-clans or of certain figures. These grievances needed to be accommodated with positions, employment and sometimes money. In the case of the Murosade, this

---

[9] There were five Islamic Courts linked to Murosade clan and to three sections of Haber Gidir, Ayr, Duduble, Salebaan. It should be emphasised that those Courts had no authority at all over the sub-clan Saad of Hussein Aydiid and Osman Ato.

result had not yet been reached owing to the strongest opposition of Mahamed Qanyere Afrah who claims to be the leader of the clan. The second difficulty was over cooperation between the Courts. This was desperately needed to allow the Courts to operate not only in very delimited areas but in most parts of South Mogadishu. Islamic groups in addition to al Islaah, al Itihaad and business people led the move. Again, one should underline the difficulties since all the sub-clans involved had a record of incidents, unbalanced decisions, rivalries and ambitions that ordinarily make any deals very fragile. And problems were still there although they were carefully managed by a coordination of the Courts.[10] The third additional move was to organise mixed platoons to secure certain areas: this could still be a problem since, during a fight, Islamic Courts' militias might line up their kinsmen against another section of the Islamic Courts. If there is an incident between two clans, then one may expect cooperation between Islamic Courts based on these two clans to be tense for a while.

Despite some achievements, the Courts in South Mogadishu faced at least two limitations. One was that they could fight or arrest people but they could not judge them. After the failure in North Mogadishu, religious leaders thought that it would be too reckless to apply the Islamic law while they had still so many problems in controlling their own militias. Therefore, thieves, when arrested, were kept in jail for a while and then released. Occasionally, killers arrested on the spot were killed: that could be seen as an endorsement of the *shari'a* but also as a decision in line with the customary law (*heer*), deeply respected by rural people. The other main difficulty was that Aydiid's sub-clan was still refusing to set up its own Courts while other Courts had no authority on people belonging to that sub-clan.

Funding the Courts was a paramount problem. Again the failure in North Mogadishu was taken into account. At first, there was no real attempt to raise taxes from truck drivers or business people. Contributions were given voluntarily by those wishing to do so. One can see it as philanthropy but one can also notice that these Courts were working, first of all, to ease security near the main market places and to clear any roadblocks affecting trade. To a certain extent, protection money was paid another way and traders understood quite well that they were saving money paying for them. When the Courts became too militant, as was

---

[10] For instance, relations between militias belonging to the Salebaan and Murosade Islamic Courts were often tense, owing to the course of the war between them in 1991–2.

the case in June 2000 in Merka,[11] key business people withheld their contributions for a week and the message was clearly understood by the
Courts, who cooled down and changed their local representative.

The behaviour of the militias was another problem. Of course, they
received religious training and were under the authority of religious figures, who had a history of honesty. Nevertheless, extortion still occurred,
as the author witnessed. One could not expect them to change overnight
since some of their cadres were less-than-dedicated, and occasionally became greedy.

In spite of real achievements, many religious leaders involved in the
Courts saw the limitations of their work. Government was needed! And it
is clear that when the Djibouti President announced to the General
Assembly of the United Nations in September 1999 that he wanted to
take the lead in solving the Somali crisis, the al Islaah leadership decided
to get involved: its chairman, a leading Muslim intellectual, had already
given up his position to become involved in Mogadishu politics supporting the group led by Abdiqassem Salad Hassan. It was time for the whole
organisation to back his candidate.

Many Somalis in Mogadishu put their hope in the Arta Conference
held in Djibouti from May to late August 2000. This conference claimed
to represent fairly all clans of Somalia and civil society, and to establish a
government for Somalia. While there is no point in discussing all the
claims and counter-claims here, it is worth making a few remarks on the
role taken by these Islamic movements in this process.

As always, a Somali gathering such as the Arta Conference was full of
confusion, misunderstandings and unexpressed ambitions. Nevertheless
the Arta Conference was eventually structured by a few groups as well as
the Djibouti President, who had his own agenda and wanted to see some
of his Somali friends play a major role in any government established by
the Conference. Among them, al Islaah was certainly the most organised
and was able to play an influential role using the Islamic Courts on one
the hand, and mobilising a cluster of big business people on the other. Its
influence could be measured by the number of parliamentarians who
sympathise with its ideas. Around one-quarter of the Parliament is in one
way or another linked to this trend. This tentative figure just shows the
relative advantage of an organised group in front of individuals cam-

---

[11] A hand-grenade was thrown into the compound of an international NGO, and a festival
planned for the day of the African Child was banned under the pretext that women were
performing pornographic dances (i.e. traditional dances in a normal vocabulary).

paigning only for their own sake. For its part, al Itihaad also has a dozen members of the Parliament.

Nevertheless, it would be wrong to assume that the Transitional National Government (TNG) set up in Arta has a clear Islamic agenda. Despite numerous allegations coming from the factions opposed to the TNG, its President and the Prime Ministers (Ali Khalif Galeyr and Hassan Abshir Faraah) are not known Islamists. Very few ministers in the cabinets are known to be inclined to support fundamentalism. Since the TNG was—or became—more a way to share the pie than to build a decent administration, things were more complex and confused. The overriding TNG priority was to get international recognition and financial support from Western countries and institutions. Arab states (such as the UAE, Yemen, Egypt and Saudi Arabia) were very helpful but they would not provide much apart from strong diplomatic support. This does not mean that the Islamic groups gave up their own agendas, rather that time was needed. Despite some hesitations expressed by hard-liners, the Islamic Courts constituted the bulk of the new police and armed forces. Although their cadres were not always at the forefront, they were in charge.

Ethiopia was the most concerned by these developments. Its army intervened for the first time in August 1996 and destroyed Islamist bases in Luuq and Buulo Haawa. In the fighting, nationals from several Arab countries were killed. Ethiopia has repeatedly intervened since. From that date its policy has been to secure a buffer zone through alliances with dubious leaders lately organised in the Somali Reconciliation and Rehabilitation Council (SRRC). In 1998 the stakes were raised following the outbreak of the Ethio-Eritrean war. As part of its military strategy, the Eritrean government assisted insurgent groups in Ethiopia such as the Oromo Liberation Front (OLF) and Ogaden National Liberation Front (ONLF), using supply lines through Somalia. Although the assistance was limited, controlling the border through military cooperation with the Rahanweyn Resistance Army and other 'friendly' forces became an Ethiopian priority, backed by a demonstrated readiness to commit Ethiopia's armed forces deep into Somali territory.

Al Itihaad could not stand militarily against the Ethiopians, despite popular outrage throughout Somalia against the incursions. After 1996, al Itihaad scaled back its strategy of developing an independent military base, in favour of working within Somali political and clan structures such as the Islamic Courts and the institutions established by the TNG.

The Ethiopian Prime Minister Meles Zenawi reluctantly attended the end of the Arta Conference. Despite claims made by the factions opposed to the conference who were stressing the role Islamic groups or figures were playing in and around the TNG, he reached an agreement in November 2000 with the newly-appointed President to curb the logistical support insurgent groups, including the OLF, the ONLF and al Itihaad, were getting from Mogadishu and give room to his Somali allies from Somaliland and Puntland. This agreement did not work and the confrontation between Ethiopia and the TNG became a new dimension in the Somali crisis. Ethiopia's next step was to isolate the TNG diplomatically, and in February 2001 a high-level military delegation visited Khartoum and persuaded Sudan to cut back its diplomatic efforts on behalf of the TNG. Throughout the Arta Conference and its aftermath, Sudan's position was somewhat ambiguous: it supported the TNG in international fora but also worked with the opposition, which formed the SRRC in early 2001. The Ethiopians, still fully mobilised in the aftermath of the Eritrean war, which had been concluded militarily in Ethiopia's favour in June 2000, indicated their readiness to intervene militarily up to Mogadishu, if they still faced what they considered a serious threat from any insurgent forces based in Somalia. This strategy seemed to work.

The post-September 11 era

The fact that al Itihaad was targeted by the US government after September 11 came as no surprise to many observers. First, al Itihaad undertook terrorist actions in Ethiopia from mid-1995 and provided logistical support for 'Afghans'. Moreover, there is evidence that those who carried out the attacks on the US embassies in Nairobi and Dar es Salaam in August 1998 received logistical support from Islamic groups and charities based in Gedo. It is not unlikely that contacts existed between al Itihaad and al Qa'ida, mostly through Khartoum and Dubai.

Nevertheless, it is debatable to closely associate this Somali group with al Qa'ida. Throughout the last five years, al Itihaad's political agenda has been focused on Ethiopia more than Somalia. As analysed previously, its strategy in Somalia was no longer to attempt to get control of a territory but to work within the communities and the clans and win support for its Islamic agenda. One certainly can raise questions and concerns about how it has shaped the attitudes of the younger generation and the way its understanding of Islam is going to reshape the urban social fabric of Somalia. But al Itihaad had never spelled out an international terrorist agenda, except solidarity with other radical Islamic groupings. Its involvement in Ethiopia is linked to the history of the past twenty years, including the fact that many Ethiopian Somalis found refuge in Somalia and later played a role to connect Somali armed factions with Ethiopian insurgent movements, such as the OLF and ONLF. Its influence in Ethiopia has yet to be independently assessed since the Ethiopian regime has a vested interest in describing its opposition as Islamist or terrorist-driven (Medhane 2002). Moreover, Usama bin Laden claimed that his supporters were deeply involved in the 3 October 1993 battle in Mogadishu in which the American forces suffered eighteen fatalities and were forced to withdraw. Some US writers supported this claim (Bodansky 1999) but hard evidence has been lacking. Though some Islamists were siding with General Aydiid, others were neutral and, as analysed elsewhere (Bowden 1999),[12] the Delta commandos had underestimated the mobilisation of Aydiid's clan after the killing of its elders in July 1993 by American helicopters bombing the house where they were meeting.

Nevertheless, the US government targeted not only this armed organisation but also a prominent Somali company, actually a holding company called al Barakaat, which was put on the list of organisations funding terrorist activities on 7 November 2001, its assets being frozen and some of its staff placed under arrest. Al Barakaat's history provides a good entry point to understand some dimensions of the new Somali economy as well as the ambiguous role Islam (more than political Islam) has played in reshaping part of the business class throughout the civil war.

Somalia's economy has been characterised for at least the two last decades by a huge influx of remittances (Jamal 1988, Aboagye 1988). There have been over the years, before and after the beginning of the civil war, attempts to assess the amount of money which is remitted yearly. No satisfactory answer is available. An educated guess would be around US$300 million annually for the last decade. Al Barakaat is one of the leading Somali money-transfer companies and by and large the most important in Southern Somalia. Its activities became noticeable in 1992, and by 1994 it was seen as the most efficient in Mogadishu and indeed the region. At the end of 1994 al Barakaat became the main shareholder of a telecommunications company, Betelco, which started operations in the capital city. A few years later, associated companies were set up in Somaliland (1997) and in Puntland (1999). In 2000 Betelco, in association with the other telecommunication companies operating in

---

[12] Bowden's book is a fairly accurate description of the context of the fight, based on extensive interviews with Somalis and American officials. There is no mention of a significant role played by the fundamentalists as compared to Aydiid's supporters. My own personal fieldwork confirms this thesis.

Mogadishu, started an internet service provider in southern Somalia, which was also closed by the US government. A few months before this al Barakaat had also become involved in a soda factory, which was to produce drinks under a Pepsi-Cola license. Because of legal problems, however, this factory has only been able to manufacture mineral water for local consumption in the capital city.

Although no clear information is available regarding the ownership of the money-transfer company,[13] al Barakaat correctly claims that Betelco belongs to a large group of shareholders, many currently residing overseas. It is known that some of them do not share any kind of Islamic agenda. Al Barakaat operates in this sector as do other companies: local investors guarantee the safety of the investment, the majority of which they paid for, and they get a share of the branch's profits. Betelco uses AT&T services as international carrier, selects the equipment which is bought by the branches and provides the technical expertise as required. The same rule applies for the internet company and the water factory. The chief executive of al Barakaat was employed in the 1970s and early 1980s at Citibank in Jeddah or Riyadh. He was then hired by one of the richest traders of Mogadishu, the late Hashi Weliye, to manage his money-transfer operations in Jeddah, as many big traders were already involved in that sector even before the outbreak of the civil war.

According to many Somalis, al Barakaat's management certainly has a peculiar understanding of Islam. As do other companies, it has employed kinsmen of the managers (that is a condition for getting clan protection, if any threat occurs) and religious people from all clans. This religious commitment should be contextualised. In the civil war situation in Somalia, its means that people are deeply honest and not wholly linked to their clan affiliation. It is important since feuds might prevent normal operations in remitting money. In this sense al Barakaat operates as many other companies do, especially in the money transfer sector. But al Barakaat was specific in its association, in the sense that Salafi Islam was promoted within the company. It can be argued that that Salafi Islam was neither a Somali feature nor the most tolerant one (no women were employed by al Barakaat, nor were women among the shareholders of any company established by al Barakaat). Nevertheless, one must recognise that this form of Islam has been widely practised on the other side of the Red Sea without creating any US or international concerns.

---

[13] According to the *Wall Street Journal*, the main shareholder of the money transfer company is an Islamic banking conglomerate, Dallah al Baraka Group chaired by Sheykh Saleh Kamel, which is also currently under investigation. See Dorsey (2002).

Al Barakaat is also known to have been funding many Islamic NGO projects in Benaadir region (especially schools, both regular and Qur'anic). Politically al Barakaat adopted the same attitude as the other big companies with respect to the factions: it provided telephone lines and at a later stage provided mobile phones to their leadership.[14] Nevertheless, it was clear that there was no sympathy for them. No hard evidence of any links between al Barakaat and al Itihaad is available to the author. When a staff member of al Barakaat was involved in an incident against an international NGO in Merka, a mission was sent from Mogadishu to investigate the case: as a result, the staff member was sent back to headquarters (but not fired).

Al Barakaat also played a significant role in funding the Islamic Courts in South Mogadishu, as did many business people who are not known to be deeply religious. Despite the plethora of articles written by journalists, one should emphasise again that those Islamic Courts were not by nature fundamentalist, though key figures of radical Islamic groupings played an important role in coordinating them. During 2000 al Barakaat was on good terms with the TNG and its then Prime Minister, Ali Khalif Galeyr. However, after an argument at the beginning of 2001, the TNG started using another company, headquartered in Hargeysa. After the US decision, the TNG set up a committee to investigate the case. While attending a meeting at the Security Council, the foreign minister of the TNG urged the lifting of the ban on the Somali company.[15]

One may try to list some of the effects of the US decision on the Somali economy, especially in southern Somalia. First, al Barakaat not only transferred money but also kept deposits for Mogadishu traders who feared robbery. Many small and middle rank traders have therefore lost most of their capital and are now excluded from the market. Many who put their money in the company, so as to pay to have their houses built, are also facing problems. Many traders were using al Barakaat to send their money to Dubai, Djibouti or Yemen: that money is also lost to them. The US decision has far-reaching implications beyond remittances.

The US government has remarked that other companies can take over in the sector since al Barakaat was only one among many. Nevertheless, the whole remittance system is based on trust, and many people fear that the US decision could be extended to other companies. Many of those

---

[14] When Hussein Aydiid stated linking al Barakaat to al Itihaad and al Qa'ida, business people in Mogadishu pointed out that he was in debt to the tune of more than US$ 40,000 with the company.
[15] Ayamaaha website, 13 March 2002.

companies had some of their staff members arrested in Kenya, Djibouti, Pakistan and maybe elsewhere. Somalis in the diaspora may feel reluctant to send money while risks seem high. Al Barakaat was so efficient because of its large network of branches, not only in the main cities of southern Somalia (other companies have branches, maybe not as many as al Barakaat, but could deliver), but also in the countryside where people are most affected by the inadequate rains and hyper-inflation. No other company will be able to build a similar network in a short time. This is going to be a major problem for the rural population. Although the number of households getting remittances is much less than in town, the impact of remittances there is greater, as will be the loss. Other companies, though keen to broaden their scope, fear that they will be targeted by the United States. Many people, rightly or wrongly, believe that al Barakaat got into trouble because it was the most prominent in that sector, where legality is notional (agents overseas have no license, transfers are not properly documented and so on). Moreover, those companies will not employ al Barakaat staff, either overseas or inside Somalia, since they believe, again rightly or wrongly, that the US government could see their new employers as fulfilling the same political agenda. This fear is going to delay the establishment of new global networks. The building of such a global network needs fresh cash to be kept by local branches so that people may get their money quickly without waiting for the amount to be actually transferred to Dubai and cash sent to the branch in Somalia. There is doubt that potential investors would want to take such a risk at this time, given the possibility of a US military intervention.

US government officials are right in thinking that the market will create alternatives to al Barakaat. But this process would take months at a time when the economic situation in Somalia is gloomy as a result of the inadequate rains and the effects of hyper-inflation created by massive quantities of fake banknotes put into circulation throughout the last year by traders close or not to the TNG.

Concerning the telecommunication sector, all telecommunications companies have been investing most of their profits throughout the last few years. This allowed their networks to expand to minor urban centres and to sections of the countryside. This is going to be frozen for some time since they are all short of cash and will be hard put to meet their needs in Mogadishu. These two networks are going to be overloaded for some time, which will make communications with the Somali region and the outside world more difficult and costly. This will also have a negative (though not dramatic) effect on the remittance economy. The huge expansion of al Barakaat's grid in Mogadishu helped lower protection costs for those companies. Although al Barakaat security is still operating for the time being, the other companies fear that they will have to cope alone with the new situation. This will mean the employment of more guards and the diversion of money from needed investments.

As discussed, in recent years Mogadishu has witnessed the growth of Islamic charities providing social services to the population and international connections for business people. Al Barakaat was certainly one of the actors in that realm since it was funding, among other projects, a significant number of schools and orphanages in Mogadishu and Afgooye. One may question the curriculum and the kind of Islam that was taught to children but these projects were also, in important ways, offering an alternative to social exclusion and absolute poverty for families with no other options. The freezing of al Barakaat assets outside Somalia meant that its contributions to those kinds of projects were immediately cut. This did not lead to an improvement of the situation on the ground. Since people continue fear a US military strike or intervention, any evidence which could link those schools to the Arab world has been removed. But this was a very superficial response and does not provide a significant reassessment of the content of these projects. If the schools close, no one can guarantee that the children will not end up in the streets. An alternative has yet to be proposed.

As events unfold, different dynamics may affect security in Mogadishu. There are other factors as well linked to the overall political situation, but two are directly related to the US decision on al Barakaat. They represent the worst-case scenarios. Nevertheless, they should be considered. The first one is the impoverishment of the population and the fact that theft and banditry may develop as a consequence. As mentioned above, many small traders are now out of the market, some are former militiamen and might go back to those activities; remittances may not arrive as easily as before and this will generate grievances and tensions; projects may close and youth find ways of surviving in the streets. Of course, the likelihood of deterioration in security can be linked equally to the overall environment. The second aspect is linked to the future of al Barakaat staff and especially of its numerous militias. As already experienced by the Islamic Courts, unpaid militias may quickly forget their religious orientation and revert to predatory behaviour. They will be more inclined to do so since they will have the feeling that they are paying the price of allegations or arbitrary decisions made by faraway people. Such militias are not going to be recruited by other companies for clan reasons and therefore will have to struggle for a living. This is going to dramatically affect the situation in the capital city and elsewhere.

To a large extent the fact that the Somali situation is again being reshaped by the aftermath of September 11 demonstrates that Somalia is embedded in global economic and political relations. The lack of state and the civil war provide dimensions to that reality. Does that mean that this tragic event could provide a new opportunity besides the pressures on Islamic radical groups?

The extensive definition of 'terrorism' used by the US government allows targeting groups and movements that may not have any democratic agenda. In this sense, certainly, it offers some relief for Somalis who support a more liberal agenda. Nevertheless, international pressure and engagement should meet some basic requirements if it is to be regarded as legitimate, and therefore be effective. First, decisions have to be justified and evidence produced. For the time being, only allegations have been circulating. If this situation continues, Somalis will see the US focus as merely revenge for what happened in 1993. The ban on al Barakaat has harmed the general population and is not regarded as justifiable. Moreover, the American security-focused approach does not fit well with Somali politics: many of the current most enthusiastic Somali supporters of the United States have no liberal—not to mention democratic—agenda and have been allied with Islamists in the past. They are trying to build an international constituency by endorsing US mottoes, not by working internally to create decent conditions for a peace settlement that would marginalise the radical groups. Internationally, we are seeing another attempt to get a quick fix using the regional organisation, IGAD, as a means to avoid a thorough reappraisal of the Somali crisis and of its possible solutions.*

The renewed US interest in Somalia, persisting rumours of military action by American forces and the subsequent lack of motivation to address the Somali issue in Washington may also create some unintended results. Beyond the bitterness of a population victim to questionable decisions in faraway places, the radical Islamic groups may build on a new legitimacy since they will appear as having successfully resisted another American offensive, just as General Aydiid did after 3 October 1993. In this case, directly or indirectly, political Islam may again be at the forefront of Somali politics.

* The ban on al Barakaat was lifted in late 2002.

5

ISLAMIC N.G.O.s IN AFRICA
THE PROMISE AND PERIL OF ISLAMIC VOLUNTARISM

M. A. Mohamed Salih

This chapter seeks to situate Islamic NGOs in Africa in the specifically Islamic tradition of voluntarism, to illustrate and explain their varied manifestations and to examine their wider social and political impact. Some of these NGOs provide relief and humanitarian assistance to poor communities during emergencies, natural disasters (prolonged drought and floods), famine and epidemics. Others are engaged in long-term development activities, including community development, agriculture, water, health and education in the least-developed Muslim countries. Some Islamic NGOs are involved in *da'wa* (i.e. Islamic call, an equivalent to Christian evangelism), conversion to Islam as well as publishing, broadcasting and disseminating Islamic teaching and values. In short, they are as varied as secular or Christian NGOs. However, Islamic NGOs distinguish themselves from other NGOs by the fact that voluntarism is a religious duty in Islam, and those NGOs which profess an Islamic identity claim also to advance a Muslim way of life and expand the Islamic *umma* (community) world-wide. As there is no distinction between ethics and law in Islam, there is also no distinction between NGOs' social, economic, political and religious functions.

This chapter examines the varieties of ways in which Islamic NGOs have left their imprints in the African continent, arguing that some of these NGOs have been used as a vehicle for spreading political Islam at an accelerated rate, combining propagating the faith with providing material rewards among the disenfranchised Muslim poor. In common with Western-style NGOs, Islamic NGOs have gained a considerable outreach and became part of the global NGO movement, with all its promises and setbacks. On the one hand Islamic NGOs comprise a modernising force operating in the field of development, while on the other they agitate for an exclusive Muslim community (*umma*). Hence they embody two contradictory discourses, one that reinforces global/universal values and the other that asserts the specificity of Islam. Some Muslim NGOs seek to solve this contradiction by being cronies of militant Muslim groups, including an emergent tide of indigenous African Islamic fundamentalism.

Voluntarism in Islam

A simple definition of Islamic NGOs is that they are voluntary (national, regional or transnational as well as community-based) organisations for which Islam is an important inspiration to do good and also an identity marker that distinguishes them from NGOs with similar orientation and objectives, but which lack such an Islamic identity. Islamic NGOs comprise communities of interest with diverse motives and objectives, including social, political and economic interests. They share a common foundation in the basic principles of Islamic law and ethics, a foundation which is manifest both in their religious orientation and in the specific manner in which they obtain and dispense their resources. As with other key determinants of practice in Islamic societies, the basic principles are to be found in the Qur'an and *Sunnah*.

Because there is no separation between ethics and law in Islam, there is also no separation between economic and humanitarian principles. Both derive legitimacy from Islamic sources of law. (Edge 1996) These sources of law are of two types. Primary sources are the Qur'an and the *Sunnah* (the Prophet Mohamed's pronouncements and acts). Secondary sources include: *ijma* (consensus), *qiyas* (reaching a legal decision on the basis of evidence, precedent or analogy in which a common reason, or an effective cause, is applicable), *ijtihad* (exerting the sum total of one's ability to uncover God's rulings on issues from their sources such as Qur'an, *Sunnah* and *ijma*) and *masalaha* (congruency or reconciliation).

According to Islamic primary sources, humanitarianism is an integral part of Islamic alms or *zakat* (the third of the five pillars of Islam). As part of an elaborate welfare system, *zakat* is considered by most Muslims as the cardinal Islamic principle of humanitarianism and solidarity. Moreover, because of the integration of economic and social life in Islam, the distinction between Islamic humanitarianism and altruism does not exist.

The basic Islamic texts are specific about how the duty of alms giving is to be realised. The resource base of voluntary activities in Islam include, first, *zakat* (Islamic tithe); second, *kharaj* (land tax); third, *sadaqat id al fitr* (an equivalent to a poll tax, which every Muslim must pay, except the absolutely poor, and which is given on the conclusion of Ramadan); fourth, *waqf* (pious endowments); fifth, gifts and donations; sixth, voluntary services (for education, defence, etc.); and lastly, obligatory family support. A Muslim is therefore obliged by religious duty to do good, which is considered an act of faith, an issue with far-reaching implications for what I call the promise and peril of Islamic voluntarism.

Zakat is a realisation of Muslim social welfare and the duty of Muslims to care for the poor and the needy. *Zakat* is collected from a number of items that constitute personal wealth. These include cash in hand, in the bank or on loan to others, in any currency, and also the resale value of bonds, securities and shares. According to Hanafi *fiqh*, *zakat* must be paid on the value of all jewellery (gold and silver) as well as other forms of gold and silver held by a person. *Zakat* is levied from owners of property held for sale at a profit, including any rental income. Saving is also subject to *zakat*. Traded goods and profits from business are also *zakat*-able, after debt repayment. The family home is not included within *zakat*-able items, along with a stipulated number of livestock and a stipulated quantity of crops, including grain, fruits and pulses. Also, *zakat* is not payable on certain capital investments such as buildings, furniture and equipment, which are not traded as part of the business. Also items acquired for everyday use, such as clothes, furniture, decoration, family car etc., are not *zakat*-able.

According to Islamic humanitarian principles, eight categories of people are identified as rightful recipients of welfare benefits under *zakat*. The Qur'an states: 'Zakat is for the poor, and the needy and those who are employed to administer and collect it, new converts, and for those who are in bondage, and in debt and service of the cause of Allah, and for the wayfarers, a duty ordained by Allah, and Allah is the All-Knowing, the Wise.' (Surat Al-Tauba: 60) Rephrased in Arabic terminology, the eight categories of *zakat* obligations are as follows:

(1) *Fughara*, to those living in absolute poverty, without possessions, income or means of livelihood;
(2) *Al Masakin*, to support those who cannot meet all their basic needs;
(3) *Al Amiliyn Aliha*, to *zakat* collectors;
(4) *Al Muallaf Ghulubahum*, to persuade those sympathetic to or expected to convert to Islam;

(5) *Fi Al Riqab*, to free from servitude or slavery;

(6) *Al Gharmin*, to relieve excessive debt or borrowing incurred in the process of meeting basic needs;

(7) *Fi Sabillillah*, to fight a religious cause or the cause of God and

(8) *Ibnu Al Sabil*, to support those stranded on a journey, without means to meet their basic needs.

In addition to *zakat* there are at least four other sources that can be tapped directly by the poor or the state for the generation of more revenue. These are as follows. First, *kharaj* is a form of compulsory tax collected by the state during disaster, economic crisis or large-scale emergency. *Kharaj* is also collected when *zakat* is not sufficient to meet all the needs of the poor. It is a form of taxation administered by *bait al mal* (treasury) and is imposed by the state on the wealthy sectors of the population. In addition to supporting the social welfare of those drastically affected by calamities, *kharaj* can also be used for the rehabilitation of public services such as health, education, transport, public buildings etc.

Second, *zakat ul fitr* is paid at the end of Ramadan. In the recorded sayings of the Prophet Mohamed, Ibn Abbas narrated that *zakat ul fitr* is compulsory on every Muslim. Like *zakat*, it purifies the soul and provides sustenance to the hungry. The recipients of *zakat ul fitr* are more precise than the eight categories of recipient of *zakat*. *Zakat ul fitr* is paid locally to the poor. In recent years and in some wealthy oil-exporting Muslim countries such as Saudi Arabia and the Gulf states, *zakat ul fitr* is paid into the accounts of transnational Islamic charity organisations. *Zakat ul fitr* is then distributed among the Muslim poor in the least-developed Muslim countries, utilising worldwide networks of client organisations.

Third, *sadaqat* refers to any act of charity, which according to Islam is a solemn indicator of virtuous Muslim selflessness. It demonstrates Muslims' submission to God and concern for fellow human beings. The Qur'an states: 'You shall not attain righteousness unless you spend on others that which you love, and whatever you spend verily Allah has knowledge of it.' (3: 92) *Zakat* and *kharaj* can be paid to Muslims or *ahlu al kitab* (believers in the holy books, i.e. the Bible and the Talmud, namely Christian and Jews, respectively). In essence, social welfare in Islam is a duty to be observed by the wealthy and a right to be received by the disadvantaged or those who cannot meet their basic needs.

At a wider level of synthesis, the principles of Islamic humanitarianism are integrated into economic policy. This is outlined by Taleghani (1982: 25), who argues that, while Islam has preference for private ownership of property, it employs *zakat* against unlimited freedom of appropriation.

The main objective of *zakat* and other sources of revenue (as described above) is to execute the state's responsibility as the guardian of the public good and to promote the welfare of the poor. According to Taleghani (1982: 25–9), in Islam economic and humanitarian principles become one and the same.

In an ideal Islamic system, private ownership of the means of production is designed to avoid unlimited freedom of private ownership that leads to unbridled capitalism, while also preventing public ownership that would result in the total denial of the individual's right to ownership. Property ties and economic relationships are bound up with patterns of thought and with human sentiments and instincts; the social milieu reflects the totality of these ties. Labour is the source of the right of ownership, except in the case of slaves. But persons who are not able to work, or whose labour is insufficient to meet their needs, must not be condemned to destitution. The poor and socially handicapped have rights of recompense for past labour or as progenitors and guardians of a future potential. The right of ownership and distribution of products made from natural resources is based on the right to disposition and distribution in order to ensure that the earth and all its natural resources belong to everyone. The state, as the guardian and the representative of the general welfare, has the right of supervision and distribution. The sources of the finance of the Muslim city-state (Medina) included *zakat, kharaj,* bounty and donations (*sadaqat*) paid by wealthy Muslims.

Islam encompasses elaborate rules and regulations dealing with credit and lending principles, inheritance, sharing of common resources (water, land and energy) and others. These are ultimately bound by strict religious rules and regulations, which govern Muslim economic behaviour.

Among the main differences between Islamic and secular approaches to welfare is that, first, Islamic economic policy revolves around *zakat* and social welfare rather than social welfare revolving around economic policy. In addition, *zakat* payment is not only a religious duty bound by religious beliefs entwined with the theory of 'good' and the theory of 'right', but also a religious duty to be observed with the best of intentions (*niyah*). Putting it simply, paying *zakat* with bad *niyah*, for example doubt, anger or just to get the *zakat* collector off one's back, will eventually call into question the truthfulness of the faith of the payer.

This model of welfare economics runs into serious difficulties, arising from its central assumption of the importance of personal virtue, and the precision with which it specifies revenue sources and the targets of its dispensation. Applying these detailed directives in a complex modern society is rather more difficult than in Arabian city-states at the time of the Prophet.

Kuran (1986: 135) laments the limited scope of 'Islamic' economics:

The central feature of the Islamic economic system is that individuals are guided in their economic decisions by a set of behaviour, norms, ostensibly derived from the Qur'an and the Sunna. Two other features stand out: zakat, a tax considered the basis of Islamic fiscal policy, and second, the prohibition of interest, viewed as the centrepiece of Islamic monetary policy. All Islamic economists consider this trio—the norms, zakat, and zero interest—the pillars of the economic system. If zakat can be understood to mean poor-due, it then becomes obvious that Islamic economics is a social welfare economics and not a comprehensive economic theory.

Seen within the perspective of the designs of political Islam, the state is the only authority rightfully entitled to collect *zakat*, depositing it in the *bait al mal* (Islamic treasury) and using it to address specific social problems. (Edge 1996) If social security and solidarity are catered for by *zakat*, then *zakat* becomes an important political tool and a focus for ideological claims.

Al Qaradawi (1981: 72) makes the point that 'the declaration of the poor due along with prayers in the Holy Qur'an and in the *sunnah*, is an enough testimony for the deep and strong relation that exists between the two'. However, this 'deep and strong relation' between *zakat* and its associated welfare provision and the fundamentals of Islam has not been sufficient to provide for effective revenue and welfare systems for modern states. *Zakat* resembles the Western concept of taxation, but is not equivalent to it, and the revenue it yields can by no means support the multitude of obligations and varied activities and responsibilities expected of a modern state. In response to this, most modern Muslim states have introduced *zakat* as an obligatory but supplementary source of revenue, to address among other things the question of poverty alleviation and to augment solidarity among its supporters.

Al Qaradawi (1982: 79–80) outlines three major factors on which the Muslim *ulama* based their consensus on *zakat*. The first is that the payment of poor-due is obligatory so that the poor and the needy can be helped adequately and be enabled to devote themselves to the worship of God. Second, the payment of poor-due cleanses Muslims from their sins and dirt. It creates in them righteousness and piety, kindness and mercy by eradicating the spirit of greed and lust. Thereby a wealth-obsessed and selfish heart turns into a generous one that meets the rights of others squarely and sincerely. This has been contained in the Command of

God: 'Take alms of their wealth, wherewith thou mayst purify them and mayst make them grow, and pray for them. Lo thy prayer is an assuagement of them. Allah is Healer, Knower.' (9: 130) Third, 'God has showered a blessing on the rich by granting them wealth, and has elevated their status with surplus wealth. As they lead a happy life, it behoves them that they should pay the poor-due and be grateful to God for granting them such bounty.'

Although *zakat* is supposed to be the main source of revenue for the Islamic state, it is clear that *zakat* alone cannot alleviate poverty or cater for the magnitude of needs created by the modern state. Taxation other than *zakat* must become the main source of revenue. Because of the political implications of instituting *zakat* as a source of state revenue, many states, including those with Muslim minorities, have used *zakat* as a supplementary source to revenue generated through taxes. However, once a state pronounces itself Muslim or opts for the introduction of Islamic *shari'a* law, *zakat* becomes a focus of social, religious, economic and political interest, without being the mainstay of the economy.

At the absence of an Islamic state, Islamic NGOs and voluntary groups commonly undertake the theoretical role of the state by laying claims on *zakat* and its distribution among the poor, albeit in a modern NGO setting. *Zakat* in many states with a majority Muslim population has been distributed through an elaborate voluntary system rather than its accumulation in a centralised *bait al mal* under state control. In this context Islamic NGOs can bring together the totality of Islamic ethics, law, politics and economics in a completely modern form of caring for disenfranchised Muslim communities and individuals. The possibility of using this approach as a valuable political resource has proved attractive to some Islamic NGOs and their political sponsors.

However, the picture of a complementary division of labour between state and voluntary sector is a simplification. The relationship is fraught with political tensions. We should bear in mind that Islamic NGOs are diverse and range from the politically militant to the simply benevolent. On the one hand Islamic NGOs have acquired the organisational capacity and structure of modern secular NGOs, while on the other hand they lay claim to a religious role inspired by the intimate association between religion, politics and economic welfare in puritan Islam. However, the assertion that Islam is a holistic way of life in which there is no separation between religion and politics makes it difficult for any Islamic NGO to deny its potential or actual political role—witting or unwitting—as active contributor to one version or another of political Islam.

Evolution of Islamic NGOs within the African NGO movement

The emergence of Islamic NGOs, in the strict modern definition of the concept, is recent. It dates back to the colonial period and was to a large extent a reaction to Christian missionary activities and the latter's capacity to combine religious, educational, health and social activities. Although the colonial authority tolerated Sufi orders and treated them as communities of quiescent a-political believers, their attitude towards associations organised by educated elites under an Islamic banner was not one of encouragement, to say the least. Moreover, secular professional and ethnic urban associations were encouraged and were largely used by educated Africans to lobby for the improvement of the social conditions in their home areas. At a latter stage these associations became nuclei for most of Africa's modern political parties that led the agitation for independence.

Elsewhere I have described (Salih 1999) how, in independent Africa, NGOs have developed through four phases. First, the 1960s and '70s were a period characterised by the transformation of community-based organisations and urban associations into 'modern' urban charity and local voluntary development organisations. The establishment of these associations was an extension of some of the urban associations established during the colonial period. In fact, there has been a great deal of continuity between modern and traditional grassroots community-based organisations, although the latter are larger in number and more widespread than modern NGOs. In this respect Schneider (1988: 85) was correct to observe: 'But once dialogue with outside parties and foreign NGO partners become necessary—within a given aid or development project for example—such groups tend to assume the appearance, name and behaviour of NGOs.'

Not all African states have tolerated the emergence of independent voluntary associations, operating outside the state sanctioned domains, particularly in development, which was for long a state monopoly. In severely divided African societies, the state perceived the emergence of NGOs as a negation of the state-centred development model hailed as the foundation stone of nation-building project. Religious voluntary associations were particularly targeted because of the state's recent memory of mosque and church agitation for independence, potentially a challenge to an effort bent on building a nation-state premised on the one-language, one-supra-state model. Furthermore, with memories of Islamic *jihad* against colonial rule and the potential role of religion as a destabilising factor, most African states were intolerant towards religious dissent. Some

African states feared that such voluntary associations might develop into organised political opposition. The state therefore resisted the formation of NGOs with an iron fist. Some states denounced NGOs and their leaders as traitors, parochial, watchdogs for foreign powers and a threat to national security. (Salih 1999)

Later, by the 1970s and '80s, African NGOs began to expand rapidly under the influence of foreign NGOs and to a large extent as a result of recurrent droughts and civil wars, in countries such as Angola, Chad, Ethiopia, Mozambique, Sudan, Somalia and Uganda. The 1980s were dubbed the decade of the Africa crisis. This phase was characterised by new features. First, there was an increase in foreign NGO activities, particularly in relief and rehabilitation in war-torn countries. Second, there was an increasing acceptance of foreign agencies, including Islamic NGOs, by some African states, which began to value their contributions to public services (relief, health and education) as they alleviated pressure on heavily curtailed national expenditure. The Afro-Arab dialogue, which began during this period, was augmented by the new-found power of the Islamic world, particularly the oil-rich Arab countries' influence through petro-dollars. (Kunibert and Mohamed Salih 1992) The first among the Islamic NGOs which began to penetrate the African scene included the Islamic African Relief Agency and a myriad of Islamic banks supportive of Islamic co-operatives and private or collateral investment.

Third, the late 1980s and 1990s were characterised by the formation and emergence of African NGOs independent of the state, and the proliferation of national, sub-regional and regional African NGOs, with organisational structures similar to foreign NGOs and increasing co-operation and dialogue among and within foreign and African NGOs. Foreign NGOs had by then realised that they could no longer ignore the significant role of local grassroots and intermediary organisations in development. (Salih 1999: chapter 8) This was also a period of great political transformation exemplified by popular struggles for democracy and the rule of law following the collapse of one party states and military regimes in most African countries. The creation of a people's space for political and economic participation meant that NGOs, both secular and religious, foresaw the opening of new opportunities not only for development work but also for engaging the state. As this chapter will show, Islamic NGOs were not an exception to this trend.

Fourth, the 1990s were dominated by consolidation and refinement of African NGOs' operational capacity, including the development of mechanisms for monitoring and evaluation, with an increasing call for accountability, transparency and professionalism. The late 1990s were characterised by transnational and intra-regional cooperation as well as partnership between diverse NGOs, both religious and secular. All these developments have occurred with the main objective of rethinking the NGOs' mission, mode of operation and future development. As a result of almost two decades of existence and development interventions, there is now an increasing awareness of the role of NGOs in society, an increasing variety and multiplicity of NGOs' activities and a more active and engaged NGO community at all levels: local, national, regional and transnational.

In this context, the rise of Muslim, Christian and secular NGOs in Africa is driven by at least three major crises. There is the African crisis, which refers mainly to the economic crisis and its social ramifications. There is a livelihood crisis emanating from civil war, drought and famine aggravated by the economic crisis. And thirdly there is a governance crisis, including economic mismanagement, corruption, abuse of power and disrespect for human and civic rights by military and one-party authoritarian states. However, it is impossible to disentangle these crises which are mutually reinforcing and impact on each other in many ways.

The range of activities in which Islamic NGOs are engaged illustrates that they are either responding to the African crisis or taking advantage of it, or both. The politics and economics of Islamic voluntarism inspire the specificity of Islamic NGOs in their response to the Africa crisis. This particular aspect of Islamic humanitarianism gives Islamic NGOs a peculiar role relative to their secular counterparts. An example is Sudan, where the state was determined to use all measures to promote a comprehensive programme of Islamisation, and used the urgent need for relief, development and service provision as a vehicle for this agenda. In 1990, the National Islamic Front (NIF) government in Sudan initiated two new policy directives aimed at supporting the work of national Islamic NGOs. These policy directives were first, *al Tamkin* (empowerment of Muslim minorities in regions that are dominated by Christian or traditional believers such as Southern Sudan and the Nuba Mountains). The second was *al Takaful* (social solidarity) whereby part of *zakat* is distributed among Islamic NGOs which in turn redistribute alms among the Muslim poor. Similarly the revenue generated from state controlled *Waqf* (privately donated property endowed for a charitable purpose in perpetuity) was distributed among Muslim NGOs, which in turn distributed it among poor Muslims or those who would potentially become Muslims.

The emergence of Islamic NGOs in Africa cannot be isolated from the factors which contributed to the emergence of secular NGOs in general, i.e. the economic, governance and livelihood crises. However, Muslim NGOs have stretched their concern with these crises further, by superimposing on the African crisis the need for replacing the failure of Western development model(s) with an Islamic 'civilising project'. Since most governments in the Muslim world have adopted a Western-style political system, it is natural that such concerns mostly grew outside the state sector, a sector considered by the Islamic movement as a manifestation of Western decadence. Elsewhere, Islamic NGOs have co-operated with regimes that declared themselves Islamic (Sudan, Mauritania, Libya etc.). They have operated independently in countries with minority Muslim populations (Ethiopia, Kenya, Mozambique, South Africa, Uganda and Sierra Leone, among others).

The magnitude of the presence of Islamic NGOs in Africa is shown in Table 5.1 below, which illustrates an impressive expansion relative to the pre-1970s situation. Generally this observation is consistent with the evo-

Table 5.1 GROWTH OF AFRICAN ISLAMIC NGOs, 1980–2000[1]

	1980			2000		
	No. of NGOs	*No. of Islamic NGOs*	*%*	*No. of NGOs*	*No. of Islamic NGOs*	*%*
Benin	23	3	13.0	144	31	21.5
Burkina Faso	56	9	16.0	171	29	16.9
Cameroon	42	9	21.4	89	17	19.1
Central African Republic	12	0	–	57	9	15.8
Chad	29	5	17.2	68	23	33.8
Ethiopia	23	0	13.2	150	13	8.7
The Gambia	17	2	11.8	81	17	21.0
Kenya	57	8	14.0	268	23	8.6
Mozambique	14	2	14.3	154	19	12.3
Mali	33	5	15.1	74	21	28.3
Niger	13	3	23.1	69	29	42.0
Nigeria	1,350	54	4.1	4,028	523	13.0
Senegal	50	19	38.0	112	35	31.2
Sierra Leone	65	3	4.0	80	9	11.2
Sudan	19	5	26.3	71	29	40.8
Tanzania	17	3	17.6	147	27	18.4
Uganda	34	8	23.5	133	37	27.8
Total	1,854	138	–	5,896	891	–

[1] Sources: NGOs and Voluntary Organisations Registry of the countries cited; ECA, 1996 *Source Book of African People's Organisations*, 2 vols. Public Administration, Human Resources and Social Development Division, Economic Commission for Africa, Addis Ababa.

lution of the African NGO movement. It has also come about because most Islamic NGOs operating at the national level are supported by trans-national NGOs, both Muslim and non-Muslim. Some national Muslim NGOs have engaged in collaborative projects with a wide range of bilateral and multilateral agencies.

The table also reveals that the total number of NGOs operating in Africa has increased from 1,854 in 1980 to 5,896 in 2000: they have grown three-fold (about 310%). In 1980, Islamic NGOs represented about 7.4% of the total NGOs operating in Africa, while in 2000 they represented 15.1%. Islamic NGOs, both African and non-African, have grown from 138 in 1980 to 891 in 2000: they grew more than six times (about 640%) between 1980 and 2000, i.e. twice as fast as secular and religious NGOs put together.

Because the growth of Africa's NGOs sector occurred at the onset of the democratisation process during the late 1980s and early 1990s, it is safe to argue that their expansion is the result of the emergence of a reformed post-colonial state. The newly-acquired freedom of organisation has granted greater possibilities for the emergence of different interest associations, including Islamic NGOs.

Furthermore, the proliferation of Islamic NGOs could be viewed as part of the Muslim world's search for alternative development approaches embedded in the Islamic movement's negation of Westernisation.[2] It can therefore be argued that the core values ushered in by the emergence of Islamic NGOs are inseparable from the factors that contributed to what is known as the Islamic resurgence, succinctly depicted by Esposito (1998: 165) as follows:

(1) Islam is a total and comprehensive way of life. Religion is integral to politics, law, and society.
(2) The failure of Muslim societies is due to their departure from the straight path of Islam and their following a Western secular path, with its secular, materialistic ideologies and values.
(3) The renewal of society requires a return to Islam, an Islamic religio-political and social reformation or revolution, that draws its inspiration from the Qur'an and from the first great Islamic movement led by the Prophet Mohamed.
(4) To restore God's rule and inaugurate a true Islamic social order, secular-inspired Western codes must be replaced by Islamic law, which is the only acceptable blueprint for Muslim society.

[2] For more on this theme see Roff 1987, Watt 1988, Choueiri 1990, Marty and Scott 1994, Marty and Scot 1995, Jansen 1997, Esposito 1998, among others.

(5) Although the Westernisation of society is condemned, modernisation as such is not. Science and technology are accepted, but they are subordinated to Islamic belief and values in order to guard against the Westernisation and secularisation of Muslim society.

The process of Islamisation, or more accurately re-Islamisation, requires organisations or associations of dedicated and trained Muslims, who by their example and activities are willing to struggle (*jihad*) against corruption and social justice. Islamic NGOs are a leading model of how this process can come about. Not all Islamic NGOs adhere to such a comprehensive blueprint, but those established to spread Islamic values and teaching as well as conversion of non-Muslims into Islam (see the case of the World Islamic Call Society below) are largely motivated by such objectives. Others use Islam as a reminder of the failure of Western-style development, while others abuse Islam and exploit the lure of religion to access financial resources. They aim particularly at the funds made available by transnational Islamic organisations and financial institutions such as the Organisation of the Islamic Conference (OIC) and the Islamic Development Bank among others.

The Tawhid Islamic Association (Uganda) is a case in point. A brief overview of its activities allows us to identify how many Islamic NGOs function. The Tawhid Islamic Association was registered on 26 February 1988 under Ugandan law, and is located in Kinsenyi, a sub-county of Kampala. The main objectives of the association are as follows: first, to undertake the responsibility of preaching, propagating and spreading the Islamic call (*da'wa*); second, to construct, and develop mosques, schools, orphanage centres, and clinics for the purpose of establishing strong Islamic institutions; and third, to improve, promote and develop the religious, social and economic welfare of the Islamic community in East Africa. Since its inception, the association has implemented projects, including the Tawhid Islamic Centre, which consists of a mosque with the capacity of two thousand persons at a time, and nine Islamic primary schools. The association also constructed twenty mosques, sunk seven boreholes and sponsored over eighty orphanages in different parts of Uganda.

Since 1999 the Tawhid Islamic Association has expanded its education activities and built new schools to meet the objective of providing educational opportunities for Muslim children in general and especially the poor. In view of this, the association prioritised the following steps as its immediate plan: (1) expansion of primary schools, (2) building a new secondary school so that Muslim children need not enrol in Christian missionary secondary schools, and (3) income-generating activities in order to cover some running costs.

There are two other Tawhid Associations in Sudan and Tanzania. However, my research is not categorical in determining whether these three Tawhid Islamic Associations and their business interests are connected with Tawhid Uganda. Nonetheless, the three Associations are engaged in similar activities and one of Tawhid's objectives is to 'to improve, promote and develop the religious, social and economic welfare of the Islamic community in East Africa'. Nonetheless, Tawhid could be seen as a moderate business-minded association and makes good use of its funds by investing the income generated from its business activities in targeted charitable activities.

In short, the case of the Tawhid Islamic Association represents the dominant trend and type of the activities undertaken by Islamic NGOs operating at the national level. Other Islamic NGOs are engaged primarily in relief. Their strategy and effectiveness depend largely on the political environment and the receptivity of the government in place. For instance, in Sudan, Kenya, Mauritania, Mali, Niger, Somalia, Tanzania and Uganda, Islamic NGOs have built on the existing Muslim base and popular Islam (religious sects, orders) to advance their activities. In other cases, African states are so overwhelmed by the economic and social problems that this crisis has generated that they are not in a position to object to any material support provided by Islamic NGOs.

In summary, African Islamic NGOs are active in conventional NGO fields such as development, education, women, child care; community health, environment, water, sanitation, shelter; legal assistance, advocacy, networking; relief, famine and food distribution in emergency operations. As I will explain latter in relation to transnational Islamic NGOs, they have also acquired skills in conversion to Islam and Islamic evangelism. Islamic brotherhoods have gone a long way in tapping this resourceful phenomenon.

Muslim Brotherhoods and Islamic NGOs

In the introductory section of this chapter, I mentioned gifts, donations and the provision of education as religious obligations which capable Muslims are expected to fulfil. Educating young Muslims about their religion is one of the oldest voluntary activities in which Muslim *ulama*, religious sects and concerned Muslims have been engaged. By and large, Islam was spread through the combined effort of *jihad* followed by

Muslim *ulama* and religious sects, which spread Islam voluntarily. Voluntarism continued to be the principal modality for Islamic education and proselytisation until the twentieth century. It is only during the closing decade of colonial rule that the study of Islam became part of official national curricula, a trend that continued into independence. Even after independence Qur'anic schools continued to expand, at times not welcomed by the mostly secular state-sponsored education establishment. Meanwhile, where education has been treated as a legitimate and encouraged domain for Islamic voluntarism, Qur'anic schools became important institutional frameworks for integrating gifts and donations, which are equally important parts of obligatory voluntarism.

The first case I detail here illustrates the relationship between some militant Islamic sects, brotherhoods and NGOs and the spread of religious violence in northern Nigeria. The main objective of these militant groups is to convert the states where they have emerged into Muslim states: short of that, their aim is to install Islamic *shari'a* law at least in the northern states of Nigeria. Most important among Islamic brotherhoods in northern Nigeria are: Jamaatu Nasril Islam, the Zak Zaky Shi'ite Muslim fundamentalist movement, the Ansarul Din, the Ahmadiyya, and the Jamatul Muslemeen Council. These Muslim brotherhoods and sects build their creed on the determination to advance Islam and ensure the application of *shari'a* as a Muslim way of life. Almost all incidents of religious violence have involved one or more of these militant Islamic groups. These movements receive generous support from Egyptian Brotherhood organisations and Saudi- and European-based Islamic NGOs, with various connections, particularly to American Muslims. Nigerian Islamic brotherhoods have developed sophisticated networks for fundraising activists, with frequent visits to Saudi Arabia, the United States and Europe where they maintain contacts with transnational Islamic foundations.

Prominent Islamic religious personalities such as the Sultan of Sokoto and the Emir of Kano still hold political sway across northern Nigeria, with a large number of chiefs and millions of followers behind them. They are not militant, but their legitimacy rests on Islam. Hence they have consistently been sympathetic to some forms of political Islam, while simultaneously being vulnerable to political challenges founded on militant Islam.

One of the most renowned and militant Muslim activists and scholars was the late Shaikh Abubakar Gumi of Kaduna. He founded and led Jamaat Izalat al bidi' wa Iqamat al Sunna, a militant anti-Sufi movement dedicated to the eradication of innovations. Shaikh Gumi condemned Sufi orders as heretical and un-Islamic, and opposed them by using the

Federal Radio Corporation of Nigeria (FRCN Kaduna), two newspapers (*New Nigerian* and *Gaskiya ta fi Kwabo*) and recorded cassettes of his teachings. Kukah (1993: 218) observed that, by 1978, 'some of his pupils had penetrated the main political institutions like the army, the media, the universities and the business world in the country, bolstering his base within and outside Nigeria'. With his contacts in high places, including President Shagari, Shaikh Gumi had developed an aura of influence around himself which gave Jamaat Izalat al bidi' wa Iqamat al Sunna legitimacy and acceptance. However, Shaikh Gumi found himself under immense pressure from Nigeria's traditional Muslim establishment such as Jamaatu Nasril Islam (JNI) and its supporters in the leadership of political parties in northern Nigeria. (Kukah and Falola 1996) The ferocity with which the religious-political alliance of the northern establishment attacked Shaikh Gumi was regarded with scepticism by many Nigerians who understood that his teachings might go beyond religion to the advocacy of an alternative political order. No matter what Shaikh Gumi's political religious teaching and political manoeuvring might have entailed, it reveals that the Muslim movement in northern Nigeria is far from unified, but in fact divided and beset by ideological as well as material differences. It is notable that Shaikh Gumi was supported by the Saudi Islamic Relief Association.

Meanwhile, Saudi philanthropists also supported Shaikh Gumi's establishment rivals, such as the Sultan of Sokoto. (Umar 1993: 162) The rapport that the Sultan established with the Saudis yielded donations for the promotion of Islam in Nigeria. He had little problem persuading the Saudis that donations to the cause of Islam in Nigeria would not be used for promoting Sufism. This was important given the Saudi Wahhabi antagonism to Islamic Sufi orders, which abhor the idea that a Muslim country could be ruled by a king. Thus we see transnational Islamic philanthropy simultaneously supporting two ideologically conflicting forms of political Islam.

Much has been written about brotherhoods and NGOs in Egypt, and this chapter will not revisit this case. However, it is appropriate to emphasise Sullivan's (1994: 215) observation that private Islamic associations in Egypt are evident up and down the Nile, in villages and large cities. They range from small organisations of five people or so, operating out of satellite villages, to large societies (even corporations) employing scores of health care professionals, educators and clerical staff in middle class suburbs of Cairo. In general, these Islamic private voluntary organisations are part and parcel of the *jamiyyad khayyria*, or charitable associations, which are registered by the Ministry of Social Affairs.

Islamic voluntarism has not always been put to good use and has in some circumstances been used to the detriment of devout disciples. The case of the Ansar and the Khatmiyya sects in the Sudan is instructive. During the 1940s Sayyid Abdel Rahman al Mahdi (the leader of the Ansar) and Sayyid Ali al Mirghani (the leader of the Khatmiyya) were able to make considerable investments in the agricultural and industrial sectors. (Abdel Rahim 1969) Sayyid Abdel Rahman relied on his father's nineteenth century ideological creed: the *ratib* (book of prayers) and *manshurat* (proclamations). Shabab al Ansar (the Ansar Youth), armed with the *ratib* and the *manshurat*, constituted a paramilitary organisation in the tradition of Islamic *jihad*. (Warburg 1978: 21–24) Sayyid Abdel Rahman reconstructed *gezira* Aba, where his father had begun his rebellion against Turco-Egyptian rule in 1881. Together with the Mahdi's tomb in Omdurman, Aba Island became a destination for *muhajirin*, holy pilgrimage. Shabab al Ansar provided labour and a contingent of political support. (p. 41) Likewise, the Khatmiyya sect, under the leadership of Sayyid Ali al Mirghani, created Shabab al Khatmiyya and encouraged pilgrims to visit his father's tomb in Kassala town in Eastern Sudan, who provided labour as well as investing in the industrial sector, particularly in perfumes (known as Bint al Sudan or 'Sudan Girl').

Unfortunately, these religious sects were (and are) parasitic and never invested in religious education, let alone secular education. Their disciples remained committed to the mystique of the leadership rather than voluntarism to improve their lot. However, with the general spread of education and political awareness, some younger followers of the sects began to search for more dynamic manifestations of political Islam. In this context, the linked expansion of African Islamic NGOs and brotherhoods is not a coincidence. Muslim brotherhood organisations are dynamic and are capable of exploiting modern institutional and organisational frameworks and adapting them to their needs. The evidence available suggests that, far from being backward looking and exclusivist, Islamic brotherhoods selectively integrate their activities within the wider global NGO movement, thus expanding their following and outreach and proving attractive to the wider aspirations of young Muslims. The following section illustrates how Islamic voluntary associations and NGOs have been able to expand their activities from Qur'anic schools to Islamic universities, showing their capacity to reinvent Islamic structures by adapting Western education models and putting them to the service of their grand objectives of establishing a universal *umma* and responding to the African crisis in the realm of ethics and values.

From Qur'anic schools to Islamic universities

The presence of a large benevolent sector operating outside or within the state structure is not new in the Islamised parts of Africa. In most of pre-colonial Africa, Muslim *ulama* of various religious denominations, sects and Sufi orders created around them disciples often attached to the tomb of the order's founder. In most cases *ulama* maintained a certain degree of aloofness from the state and depended on local communities that were generously provided the necessities of life. (Trimingham 1959) The *ulama*, religious sects and Sufi orders have depended on voluntary work carried out by the disciples or the seekers of healing and *baraka* (blessing). In some cases they have accumulated sufficient funds to care for the poor in the host community, while in others they have invested the surplus in modern sector (agriculture, transport, trade, etc.).

Most Qur'anic schools (*madaris*, sing. *madrasa*) were established by *ulama* with the prime intent of preserving and expanding the teachings of the founders of the Sufi order or sects to which they belong. Some Qur'anic schools were established by disciplines of Sufi orders or close to the tomb of a founder of a religious sect. Others have been established as part of the mosques' duty to the surrounding Muslim community and are often supported by an Imam (religious leader) or a religious teacher. Such Qur'anic schools were widespread throughout Muslim Africa, with varying degrees of density and social significance. These schools were often single-teacher institutions. They were found in both rural and urban areas. Children are taught citation of the Qur'an, the Prophet Mohamed's teachings (*hadith*), grammar (*nahu*), and ethics (*akhlaq*). Many of these have developed gradually through community, private or government support into Islamic schools. These include schools in Swahili-speaking East Africa and also in Sudan, Eritrea, Senegal, Sierra Leone, Mali, Mauritania, Niger and Nigeria, among others.

In Nigeria, Kamal ud-Din (student of the Muslim cleric Shaikh Muhammad al-Labib Taju l-Adab) founded the Adabiyya Muslim Society in 1943 among the Yoruba with a primary school in Ilorin integrating Islamic and Western education. (Reichmuth 1993: 186–7) The school operated within the wider rubric of the Ansar al-Islam Society, the new name for the Adabiyya Muslim Society. Many of the teachers and the graduates of Ansar al-Islam Society Schools found their way to Egypt and other Muslim countries for further education, many more held high positions as civil servants and the administration of the education establishment in northern Nigeria. The influence of the graduates of these Islamic schools on the political development of Nigeria cannot be underestimated. (Mohamed Salih 2001) The trend has continued. Since the 1970s, a considerable number of Islamic schools have been established in metropolitan Kano by businessmen, *ulama*, Islamic organisations and the government. (Barkindo 1993: 102–3) The Kano Foundation, Shaikh Isa Waziri, Shaikh Aminu Deen, Malam Hassan Sufi and Shaikh Nasir Kabara began a frenzy of Islamic school building. This mode of operation continues until today, therefore giving impetus to the emergence of a large number of Islamic schools and associated social and political trends.

Muslim schooling in Mali is another example (Brenner 2000). Brenner laments that, in 1982, the Malian Council of Ministers decided that the Education ministry should assume responsibility for the *madaris*. It was recommended that the *madaris* conform to the new regulations concerning their operation. The religious orientation of the schools would be respected, although they would also be required to teach the full secular curriculum of the state primary schools. Although Mali has not yet established an Islamic University, it is well known that memories of Timbuktu, the first Islamic university in sub-Saharan Africa still echo with strong emotional resonance. With the state recognition of Islamic schools, it probably will not be long before there is a call for reviving the past glory of Timbuktu's Islamic University.

In Eastern Africa, according to Sperling's (1993) work, the founders of the Shamsiya Kibarani *madaris* in the Kenya and Tanzania coast, a network of forty Islamic schools, have been conscious of the role such schools could play in the future of Eastern Africa's development and polity. In 1973 Shaikh Muhammad Ali Mwanboga established a network of Qur'anic schools in East Africa in order to spread education among Muslim communities of the Swahili-speaking coast. Shaikh Muhammad Ali Mwanboga had never hidden his interest in contributing to the establishment of a Muslim state. The aim of that state is envisaged as to foster Islamic education and teaching to produce moral citizens in order to replace the corrupt secular government officials of the day. The network is also seen as a counter-Christian crusade and it is intended to halt what its founders commonly perceive as attempts by the state to ensure the dominance of decadent Western values.

In sum, Islamic schools are common in Muslim countries, albeit with different structures, funding sources and modalities and organisational principles. One of the major changes that has influenced such Islamic schools is the increasing influence of foreign Islamic NGOs, operating at Africa-wide or national levels. (Sperling 1993) Donor support includes upgrading of school structures and materials, importing of Islamic teachers from other parts of the same country or abroad, payment of subsidy and provision of food. In addition to their contribution to religious education, most foreign-supported Islamic schools have some ties to activists with political leanings to Islamic political parties and organisations.

The Young Muslim Association (YMA) of Kenya provides an excellent illustration of the new Islamic schools and their role in influencing society by repackaging the old-style Qur'anic schools. The YMA is a Kenyan-registered Muslim charity. Started after independence in 1964, its aims were to look after the well-being of the Muslim community in Kenya. By 1968 it had started one of its major projects, the Garissa Muslim Children's Home, catering for Muslim orphans from all over Kenya. In 1969 the Garissa Muslim Children's Home was established with two main objectives: to provide relief to the Muslims inhabiting northern Kenya, and to counteract the activities of the Catholic Church, established much earlier and actively pursuing its own activities among the youth of the area. According to the YMA, while the apparent motive of the Catholic intervention was to be relief and charity work, the subtle yet real motive was to convert Somali Muslims to Christianity. A fact-finding mission sent to Garissa in 1969 recommended that a child-care facility be established to care for Muslim children.

The second range of activities in which the YMA is involved is education, such as the Young Muslim Primary School (Garissa), with 800 students, both boys and girls. While the infrastructure (building, teaching materials, etc.) is provided by the YMA, the government of Kenya provides the teachers and obliges the school to teach the Kenyan primary school curriculum. However, in addition to the national curriculum, the school provides an Islamic environment, including the observance of Islamic values, prayers, fasting and extra-curricular Islamic lessons. The YMA pays the salaries of Islamic education teachers in support of Islamic *madaris* and Qur'anic education (Garissa Young Muslim Nursery School, Nakuru and Nyahururu Islamic Centres) and grants a limited number of bursaries to bright Muslim students from poor families to attend university and college education in Kenya. The Islamic call (*da'wa*) branch of the YMA is the most controversial, particularly its role in conversion (known to the YMA leadership as reversion, i.e. to revert Christian Somalis to Islam). 'Revertees' are taught the basics of Islam at various centres in order to equip them with the foundations of Islamic faith.

Africa's governance crisis mentioned above has, in a sense, delivered believers to a domain of religious morality and ethical values as an antithesis to a corrupt state. Opting out of the state institutions did not stop at primary and secondary education, whose graduates cannot influence the highly-educated state operators. Promoting Islam at a higher political level required greater ambition. In response to this, creating an Islamic University education became an obvious option. Islamic business, banks, engineering, import-export and benevolent organisations feel comfortable with the graduates of these universities. On their part, such universities devote their curricula to instilling in their students a strong orientation towards the study and application of Islamic ethics and moral standards.

This ambition reached its zenith in Sudan. The University of Holy Qur'an and Islamic Sciences, Omdurman, was established in 1990, a year after the military coup of 1989. The University comprises two previously-existing institutions, namely the Holy Qur'an College, established in 1981 and the Omdur'man Higher Institute, established in 1983. The new institution's mission is to contribute to the intellectual, scientific, economic, social and cultural development, with particular reference to the following:

(1) Affirming and authenticating the identity of the nation.
(2) Teaching all sciences of the Holy Qur'an and the Prophetic *Sunnah* as well as Arabic language and all Islamic and social sciences.
(3) Studying Islamic heritage and enriching the life of Sudanese society through Arab and Islamic civilisation.
(4) Carrying out scientific research on issues affecting society through the medium of the Islamic intellectual concepts which correspond to the current issues of the world and interact with the environment.
(5) Co-operating with universities and institutions of higher education in the country and other countries in the world.
(6) Contributing effectively in qualifying various sectors of the society to assume their role in discharging the tasks and duties of the Islamic state.
(7) Educating students and awarding them academic degrees.

In order to achieve its objectives, the University of Holy Qur'an and Islamic Sciences established four faculties and a female students' centre. These are as follows: Faculty of the Holy Qur'an; Faculty of *Shari'a*; Faculty of Arabic Language; Faculty of *Da'wa* and Information; Graduates' College and Female Students' Centre. The extra-mural activities of the university include the Holy Qur'an Institute, considered the University's window to society, which organises activities through open courses, Holy Qur'an recital diplomas and Islamic studies; model Qur'anic schools and specialised training courses in the various domains of knowledge; the

National Institute for Qualifying Holy Qur'an Memorisers; a Research and Preachers' Training Institute; an Arabic Language Teaching Institute; a Holy Qur'an Research Centre; the Institute of Qur'anic methodology; and the Al-Nilein *Da'wa* Centre. Unlike other universities, the University of the Holy Qur'an and Islamic Sciences encourages independent learning and self-study through a network of ten regional University Centres and libraries located throughout the country. It also has its own printing facility devoted largely to the printing and free distribution of copies of the Qur'an. In fact there is little difference between the activities of the University of Holy Qur'an and Islamic Sciences in spreading Islam through *da'wa* and Muslim NGOs such as the Tawhid Islamic Association (already discussed above) or the International Islamic Call Society (to be discussed in the following section). Saudi Arabia shoulders the bulk of the financing of the University.

The second case I present here is Mbale Islamic University, Uganda, which differs from the state-sponsored University of Holy Qur'an and Islamic Sciences in important ways. Mbale Islamic University was established in 1990 and consists of four faculties, Arts, Business Studies and Public Administration, Education, Islamic Studies and Arabic Language. The University became a member of the League of Islamic Universities and therefore qualified for funding from the OIC at the latter's eighth session held in Tehran in December 1997. This is part of a pattern. Mbale Islamic University was also officially recommended for endorsement and funding by the Islamic Commission for Economic, Cultural and Social Affairs (ISCECSA) which works very closely with the OIC. Most of the funding came from Saudi Arabia, which also established two mosques through the establishment of a *waqf* (pious endowment) for the University. Meanwhile, other donors for Mbale Islamic University include the Islamic Solidarity Fund, the International Islamic *Da'wa* Society (Libya) and the Islamic Committee of the International Crescent, among others. ISCECSA is represented on the university's governing board. In the context of a secular state, suspicious of Islamic extremism, Mbale Islamic University has sought to promote its agenda through keeping a low political profile.

The education, philosophy and objectives are not different from those of the University of Holy Qur'an and Islamic Sciences in Sudan. However, the main difference is that the Mbale Islamic University is not politically charged in the same way as its Sudanese sister, which was established during a period of heightened Islamic fundamentalism under state direction.

In short, the development from Qur'anic schools to Islamic Universities is an important part of a modern Islamic voluntarism responding to the myriad crises confronting African states and society. It also added complexity to the socio-political environment within which they operate, often giving the impression that they could succeed where secular governments failed. Rather than solving the governance crises, Islamic educational establishments put forward their own alternative governance model, which is at odds with African aspirations and more tolerant way of life.

Transnational Muslim organisations

In addition to NGOs operating at the national and regional levels, there are also seven major transnational Islamic foundations and societies operating throughout the world, with significant financial and human resources. These transnational Muslim NGOs are engaged in diverse activities ranging from activism, conversion, evangelism and development activities throughout the Muslim world. Instead of going through all of these organisations, we examine the cases of the International Islamic Relief Organisation and the Islamic Call Society.

Table 2 below shows a sample of transnational NGOs and their countries of operation in Africa. The table is not exhaustive and has excluded some smaller NGOs. The table shows that these Islamic NGOs originated outside sub-Saharan Africa, notably in Britain, the United States and Arab Muslim countries (Saudi Arabia, Kuwait, Libya and Egypt). They mostly concentrate in countries with large Muslim populations (Sudan, Nigeria, Kenya, Morocco, Somalia, Tanzania, Uganda and Senegal, among others), while some are more interested in minority Muslim populations in countries where Christianity is dominant (Burundi, Democratic Republic of Congo, South Africa, Sierra Leone, Malawi, Mozambique).

Some transnational Islamic NGOs have joint global NGO networks and have created partnership with the UN system and other secular and religious transnational NGOs. The variety of networks and partnership arrangements in which they are involved offers them the opportunity to connect with global NGO trends, problems, evaluation and monitoring methodologies, lobbying and advocacy. The following case studies illustrate this.

First, we consider the case of the International Islamic Relief Organisation (IIRO) which is concerned with three major development areas: health, education, and relief. The IIRO and a few of its African and other development activities are then introduced. What is presented as the pre-dominantly secular orientation of IIRO is then contrasted with the proactive role of the Islamic Call Society in the spread of Islam and conversion of non-Muslims.

According to its publications, IIRO seeks to serve the victims of natural disasters and wars: orphans, refugees and the displaced, all over the world. Relief work is conducted on purely humanitarian grounds, without any distinction on the basis of ethnic, linguistic or religious considerations. IIRO has, however, discovered that more than 80% of the refugees and victims of wars and disasters are Muslims. Some IIRO relief programmes are therefore directed towards the provision of medical, educational and social support for those in desperate need of them. IIRO also encourages entrepreneurs. It sponsors viable economic projects and small businesses that can help the victims to find employment, earn a living and thereby lead a productive and fruitful life again. To fulfil these objectives, the IIRO has established a wide network of national and international contacts with various Islamic and non-Islamic relief organisations, institutions and individuals. It has developed an excellent working relationship with organisations such as the office of the United Nations High Commissioner for Refugees (UNHCR), the Federation of Red Cross and Red Crescent Societies, the International Organisation of Migration, the Norwegian Refugee Council, the Federation of African Voluntary Development Organisations (FAVDO), Oxfam, the Refugee Study Programme at Oxford University, the Save the Children Fund, the International NGO Working Group on Women Refugees, and many others.

Recently, IIRO has joined the International Council for Voluntary Agencies and become a member of its executive committee. It has joined the Economic and Social Council of the United Nations (ECOSOC) in a consultative role, and the Conference of Non-Government Organisations. IIRO is chairing the General Committee for Relief, which comprises of more than fifty international Arab and Muslim relief organisations.

Since 1989, IIRO has been engaged in emergency relief operations in Afghanistan, Bangladesh, Sri Lanka, the Philippines, Indonesia, Egypt, Morocco and Kyrgyzstan, through provision of tents and relief items. It also assisted the victims of armed conflicts in Somalia, Rwanda and Burundi through provision of tents, clothes, food items and other relief items, including educational and medical services. IIRO is also active among the Tuareg refugees in Mali and Mauritania were it provided food, medical supplies, sanitary services, education, vocational training and orphanage care.

Table 5.2 MAJOR TRANSNATIONAL ISLAMIC N.G.O.S AND
COUNTRIES OF OPERATION[3]

Transnational Islamic NGOs	*African Countries*
ISRA (Denmark)	Chad, Kenya, Mali, Senegal, Sudan and South Africa
The Islamic African Relief Agency (IARA), (USA)	Chad, Ethiopia, Kenya, Mali, Nigeria, Senegal, Somalia, Somaliland, Sudan, Tanzania, Uganda
Muslim World League (Saudi Arabia)*	Burkina Faso, Burundi, Comoros, Congo, Ethiopia, Gabon, Kenya, Mali, Mauritania, Mauritius, Mozambique, Niger, Nigeria, Senegal, Sierra Leone. Somalia, South Africa, Sudan, Tanzania, Uganda
World Islamic Call Society (Libya)*	Burkina Faso, Democratic Republic of Congo, Egypt, Guinea, Libya, Malawi, Morocco, Senegal, Sierra Leone, South Africa, Sudan, Uganda
World Assembly of Muslim Youth (WAMY) (Saudi Arabia)*	Africa is served through the Sudan office
League of Islamic Universities (Saudi Arabia)*	Egypt, Kenya, Sudan, Uganda
Organisation of the Islamic Conference (Iran)*	Burkina Faso, Burundi, Comoros, Congo, Ethiopia, Gabon, Kenya, Mali, Mauritania, Mauritius, Mozambique, Niger, Nigeria, Senegal, Sierra Leone. Somalia, South Africa, Sudan, Tanzania, Uganda
International Islamic Council for Da'wa and Relief (Egypt)*	Burkina Faso, Democratic Republic of Congo, Egypt, Guinea, Libya, Malawi, Morocco, Senegal, Sierra Leone, South Africa, Sudan, Uganda
International Muslim Relief Network (USA)	Somalia, Sudan
International Islamic Charitable Foundation (Kuwait)*	Chad, Ethiopia, Kenya, Mali, Mauritania, Niger, Nigeria, Senegal, Somalia, Somaliland, Sudan, Tanzania, Uganda
International Islamic Relief Organisation (Saudi Arabia)*	Burkina Faso, Egypt, The Gambia, Malawi, Mauritania, Morocco, Senegal, Somalia, Sudan, Uganda
Ibrahim Bin Abdul Aziz al Ibrahim Foundation (Saudi Arabia)	Kenya, Somalia, Sudan

[3] Source: personal communications and various internal annual reports.

Table 5.2 continued

Human Concern International (Canada)	Benin, Eritrea, Somalia and Sudan
Mercy International (USA)	Ethiopia, Kenya, Somalia, Sudan
Horn of Africa Relief Agency (HARA), (Kenya)	Djibouti, Kenya, Somalia, Sudan
Islamic Relief Worldwide (USA)	Egypt, Ghana, Sudan
Al Haramain Islamic Foundation (Saudi Arabia)	Kenya, Somalia, Sudan, Tanzania Uganda.
Islamic Relief Worldwide	Mali, Sudan
Al Tawhid Foundation (Uganda)	Sudan, Tanzania, Uganda
World Ahlubait Islamic League (UK)	Tanzania (with strong business interests in the UK, USA, Canada, Finland, Sweden, Tanzania, United Arab Emirates, India and Pakistan)

* Note: These are inter-governmental organisations, which provide considerable material and ideological support to national and transnational Islamic NGOs.

The IIRO's Department of Urgent Relief and Refugees (DURR) has
established relationships with many NGOs and international organisations that are working in the emergency fields, for the purpose of generat-
ing the required resources for their mutual operations. It co-ordinates,
with other humanitarian and international organisations, humanitarian
projects for the benefit of the victims of disasters. IIRO co-operative
operations includes partnership with UNHCR in acting as an implementing agency of the UNHCR in Tanzania among Rwandan and
Burundian refugees.

The IIRO seems to put its network and membership of international
organisations to work. For instance, it co-operated with MSF Holland in
the field of medical services, with the World Food Programme (WFP) to
distribute food to the poor and refugees in Tanzania, Mozambique, and
Sierra Leone, with UNICEF to install drinking water projects in Iraqi
Kurdistan. It worked jointly with the Islamic Development Bank, which
supports some of its programmes to assist Muslims in desperate need. In
Sierra Leone, it co-operated with the National Committee for Rehabilitation and co-ordinated the efforts of NGOs and government to help the
displaced peoples who had fled from the civil war.

Thus, it is clear that in most respects, the IIRO's activities, structure,
mode of operation and development programmes are not different from
those of secular transnational NGOs. However, there are three major differences: first, it has an emphasis on working in Muslim countries and
among poor Muslims, particularly in the least-developed Muslim coun-

tries; second, it has a Muslim staff committed to its objectives and third, it has a focus on support to education, particularly within the formal education curriculum, sponsoring teachers and students and publishing. It must also be noted that after the August 1998 terrorist bombings in East Africa, the IIRO was one of four Islamic charities accused by the Kenyan authorities and the FBI of being implicated in al Qa'ida's activities. This allegation points to a fundamental weakness in Saudi-based Islamic philanthropy.

In contrast to the IIRO, the World Islamic Call Society (WICS) has developed three main areas of intervention which portray an explicit religious and political agenda. One is Society *Da'wa* and Islamic Centres, the second conferences, institutional support and relief, and the last is research, information and publication. A synopsis of some of the activities of the WICS is given below. By its very nature, the WICS is a religious organisation committed to the spread of Islam and the creation of a universal Islamic *umma* as its ultimate goal. One of the main objectives of Islamic *Da'wa* centres is to introduce Islam and disseminate Islamic culture and conversion. It is also active in printing translations of the Qur'an as well as religious and cultural books into local languages.

Newly-converted Muslims are provided with material assistance and Islamic publications in their own language to assist them in learning more about the faith. Educational and professional courses to teach them skills and to help them integrate into their new societies are organised for the new Muslims in Chad, Southern Sudan, Mali, Ghana, Nigeria, Uganda, Benin and The Gambia. Another objective is to counteract the spread of Christianity in Africa. An example of this is a project called 'Countering the Christianisation Efforts', with a seminar held on Christianisation (February 1997) in Sudan in co-operation with the African International University. The seminar was entitled 'Christianisation and Colonialist Penetration', with the main aim of exposing the methods allegedly used by Christian evangelists in their efforts to weaken Islam and destroy the Muslim character, and thereby subvert those plans.

On the side of publication and propaganda, World Islamic Call Society activities include Qur'an printing, recording and translation. More than 1,215,000 copies of the Qur'an have been printed in various sizes and distributed in various parts of the world. Special WICS editions of the translations of the Qur'an in French and English were also published, with 10,000 copies in each language produced and distributed.

Globally, the WICS has co-operated with UNESCO to develop a number of projects. Most prominent among these projects are the 'Individual and Society in Islam' compilation which was published in English.

The second volume is the Great Islamic Encyclopaedia financed and supervised by the WICS, also in co-operation with UNESCO, under the title 'Diverse Aspects of Islamic Culture'. The volume was previously published in French and has recently been published in Arabic. It also co-operates with ISESCO in the field of spreading the Arabic language and Islamic culture. This also includes co-operation in the fields of education, culture and science and is jointly implemented in the Sahel belt countries. Since 1998, WICS has vowed to combine its Call activities with food and medical convoys sent to poor Islamic countries (Niger, Nigeria, Mali, Chad, Sierra Leone and Guinea). Each convoy includes a number of physicians and nurses in support of this effort as well as for religious teaching.

Not all transnational Islamic voluntary organisations are supported by inter-governmental organisations as indicated in Table 5.2. Some rich Muslims from oil-rich countries such as Saudi Arabia and Kuwait have established their own transnational NGOs which are engaged in activities similar to those of inter-governmental organisations. However, Table 5.2 reveals that the majority of Muslim transnational voluntary organisations are private, while a few are connected with specific Muslim sects or orders (Shi'a, Ismaili, Ahmadiyya, Qadiriyya, etc). Some transnational Islamic NGOs such as the Aga Khan Foundation began as Islamic sect-specific orders, but at a later stage declared themselves non-denominational organisations. The Aga Khan Foundation is one such organisation that was originally closely tied to the Ismaili Muslim community, but gradually developed into a global foundation, with projects throughout the world including Africa. This is elaborated below.

The Aga Khan Foundation is one of the most prominent religious foundations in the African continent despite the fact that it portrays itself as a non-denominational organisation. It has its roots in the Fatimid caliphate, as the first major Shi'a state in North Africa (Tunisia) during the 9th century. As a result of migratory movements and mission activities in its history, the Ismaili community has come to settle in a wide swathe of countries across the globe. Its traditions fall within four broad geographic and ethnographic groups: Central Asian, Persian, Arab and South Asian, all of them united by their allegiance to their present, 49th hereditary Imam, Prince Karim Aga Khan. Ismaili settlements in Africa primarily comprise Ismailis of Indian sub-continental origins, while recent settlements in the West comprise Ismailis from all the above nationalities and traditions.

In 1905 the Aga Khan ordained the first Ismaili Constitution for the social governance of the community in East Africa. The new administration for the Community's affairs was organised into a hierarchy of councils at the local, national, and regional levels. The constitution also set out rules in such matters as marriage, divorce and inheritance, guidelines for mutual co-operation and support among Ismailis, and their interface with other communities. The modern Ismaili history began in 1948 when the 46th Imam, Aga Hasan Ali Shah, emigrated to India and settled in Bombay, where he established his headquarters, and became known as Aga Khan I. He was followed by Aga Khan II who lived only for four years after assuming the Imamite. At the time of his accession, Imam Sultan Mahomed Shah, Aga Khan III, was under eight years old, and when he reached the age of nine, Queen Victoria bestowed upon Aga Khan III the title of His Highness.

Following the Second World War and the difficulties East African and other developing countries had to face, the Aga Khan Foundation's main objective was to secure the social welfare and economic well-being of the Ismaili community. In 1945, the Aga Khan Ismaili Community created the East African Muslim Welfare Society (EAMWS). By the 1950s EAMWS was already engaged in an effort to train businessmen, agriculturalists and professionals. This process has continued, albeit with new emphasis on developing modern institutions for social and economic development in the Indian sub-continent and East Africa. The Aga Khan Foundation is also the arm of the Ismaili school of jurisprudence. Although described as an institution concerned with Indian and Pakistani Muslim affairs, a number of indigenous East African Muslims have benefited from the foundation's charitable work and activities.

Today the Aga Khan Foundation defines itself as a non-denominational, international development agency. Its mission is to develop and promote creative solutions to problems that impede social development, primarily in Asia and East Africa. Established as a private, non-profit foundation under Swiss law, it has branches and independent affiliates in twelve countries. It is a modern vehicle for traditional philanthropy of the Ismaili Muslim community under the leadership of the Aga Khan. Although the Aga Khan Foundation denies any political role in East Africa, the Ismaili community is well-represented on individual bases by politicians who have a religious leaning towards the Ismailia order.

Islamic NGOs after the East African bombings and September 11

The transnational political role of Islamic NGOs was highlighted in the aftermath of the August 1998 bombing of the US embassies in Nairobi,

Kenya, and Dar es Salaam, Tanzania, in which more than 250 people were killed and 5,000 others injured. The incidents were blamed on the terrorist network run by Usama bin Laden, then living in Afghanistan. Five Islamic NGOs were banned and a team of Kenyan police and US Federal Bureau of Investigation (FBI) agents raided the offices of one of them, Mercy International, a few days later. The other four—the Al-Haramain Foundation, Help African People, the IIRO and Ibrahim Bin Abdul Aziz Al Ibrahim Foundation—were raided by Kenya's law enforcement officers. According to the NGO Co-ordinating Board's Director, John Etemesi, the organisations 'had been found to be working against the interests of Kenyans in terms of security'.

The bombing was condemned by Muslims, and notably by the three East African Supreme National Islamic Councils of Tanzania (Baka-wata), Uganda (NAAM), and Kenya (SUPKEM). Known for their varying roles to promote Muslim interests at the national level, the leaders of the Supreme Islamic Councils were quick to defend the non-violent nature of Islam.[4] But Muslims, Muslim leaders and Muslim NGOs throughout the world also protested against the banning of the five Muslim NGOs in Kenya and the rapid and indiscriminate way in which the Kenyan government appeared to accuse all Muslims of complicity in the atrocity. It was reported that while addressing the mourners in Nairobi at the bomb site, Kenyan President Daniel arap Moi said that those behind the bombing 'could not have been Christians'. These remarks were widely publicised and instantly drew criticism from Muslim leaders who claimed that their religion was being wrongly associated with violence. Sheikh Ahmad Khalif, head of the Supreme Council of Kenyan Muslims, commented that 'Islam like any other religion does not support the killing of innocent people for whatever reason'. The reaction of West African Muslim NGOs was also swift. Baraham Diop, President of the Senegal Federation of Ulama stressed that Islam is a religion of peace, tolerance and dialogue and is against any violence and any form of terrorism, whatever its objective. Sani Aladji, the Chair of the Yaounde Chapter of Cameroon's opposition Social Democratic Front noted that 'generally Islam advocates negotiation and compromise'.

The US retaliation, in the form of cruise missile attacks on Sudan and Afghanistan, drew rapid response from Islamic activists and NGOs. For example, in Lome, Togo, Islamic groups threatened to retaliate against

[4] For more on the historical antecedence of these Muslim councils see Constantin 1995.

the raids by targeting US installations. Muslims found themselves in the familiar position of condemning both an atrocity carried out by their co-religionists and the American response to it.

Before the East African bombing had subsided to the background of global terror attacks, the world was shocked by the September 11 attacks on New York and Washington. A pattern of abuse of Islamic NGOs by terror networks began to emerge but with a more global profile. This cemented the suspicion that some terrorist groups might have used Islamic NGOs as front organisations. Globally, the condemnation of September 11 by moderate transnational Muslim NGOs was immediate. The Non-Governmental Expert Group on the Implementation of the Action Plan for the Preservation of the Rights of Muslim Communities and Minorities in the OIC Member States, meeting in Sofia, Bulgaria, on 12–14 September 2001 stated that,

We utterly condemn what are apparently vicious and cowardly acts of terrorism against innocent civilians. We express our deepest sorrow for Americans that were injured and killed. We offer our condolence to all victims of this cowardly terrorist attack. There is no cause that justifies this type of an immoral and inhumane act that has affected so many innocent American lives. We support all efforts to investigate and immediately capture the evil persons responsible for these immoral and cowardly acts.

The Islamic Society of North America, the Islamic Organisation of Latin America, the Islamic *Da'wa* Center of Latin America, the European Islamic Conference, the Cultural Practice Strategy in the West, and the European Federation of Islamic Academies signed the statement. However, beyond this show of support the American peoples and condemnation of the September 11 terrorist attacks, the picture is diverse and showed different sentiments in different parts of the Muslim world. On the whole, African Muslim NGOs' responses to September 11 were mixed. For instance even Sheikh Muhammad Kakeeto, leader of the radical Islamic Tablikh sect in Kampala, declared that, 'killing innocent people is against the Koran'. He continued, 'Americans should not make a mistake of attacking anyone without getting proper information. It should not be an-eye-for-an-eye approach'. Unsurprisingly, when the United States began its bombing of Afghanistan, sentiment shifted. The *Cape Times* quoted the Secretary General of the South African as he offered support to Muslims who want to defend Afghanistan 'by force if necessary', and encouraged volunteers to join the fight: 'We have since the start of the war against Afghanistan, made it clear that we reject the

US-led military onslaught on what we believe is an Islamic country and support the right of Muslims all over the world to align themselves with the jihad.'[5]

In all cases, responses to September 11 were refracted through local political agendas. In northern Nigeria, where Islam was already a focus for political struggles over power at state level, responses were polarised. On 14 September, the Islamic Youth Organisation in Gusau, the capital of Zamfara State organised anti-American rallies and clashed with the police. The same day, thousands of Somali supporters of al Itihaad al Islami, a militant Islamist group, did the same, brandishing Kalashnikov guns and pictures of Usama bin Laden.[6]

Besides the apparent discursive narratives, the September 11 events brought Islamic NGOs under the scrutiny of the war against terrorism. The alleged infrastructure of bin Laden's al Qa'ida and other terrorist organisations was described in the American media, and it included a number of prominent Islamic philanthropic organisations. Given their role in Africa, this led investigators to follow the trail to where Islamic NGOs were operating in the continent, and led commentators to assume that wealthy Islamic voluntary organisations could buy the loyalty of poor Africans. The English weekly edition of *Al-Ahram* in Egypt lamented. 'The list of 22 most wanted terrorists released two weeks ago by the US State Department included twelve Africans. These are seven Egyptians, two Kenyans, one Tanzanian, one Libyan and one Comorian, testimony to the fact that Islamic fundamentalism is no longer the sole purview of Middle Eastern or North African states, but exists in much of sub-Saharan Africa as well.'[7] There was also rampant speculation that Usama bin Laden and other terrorist organisations might be seeking haven in poor least-developed African Muslim countries, such as Somalia.

Of particular relevance to Africa is the current debate on the triangular relationship between Islamic banks, business interests and Islamic NGOs. There are two particularly complicated cases involving suspicion of links to Islamic terrorist groups being investigated after September 11. The first is that of Sudan Al Shamal Islamic Bank, which acknowledged that bin Laden held three accounts at the bank, but claims that he was never a shareholder.[8] Al Shamal Bank maintained accounts with a num-

[5] Quoted in Hashim Aidi, 'Islamic Fundamentalism is Gaining Ground in Africa', in *Africana Daily*, 24 October 2001.
[6] A commentary by Gamal Nkrumah, *Al-Ahram Weekly*, 27 September 2001.
[7] *Africana Daily*, 24 October 2001.
[8] Al Shamali Bank statement dated 13 October 2001.

ber of Western banks including Crédit Lyonnais, France's third largest bank. Second, two international Islamic relief organisations were accused. One of them, Mercy International (registered in Switzerland), had already been decertified by the Kenyan authorities after the East African bombing 1998. The second is the Muwafaq Foundation, a Saudi-funded Islamic relief organisation which was registered in Jersey, in the British Channel Islands, and which had also been a target of suspicion by the FBI in 1998. Although no evidence was cited against it, the assets of a money launder for Islamic extremists linked to Muwafaq was named as terrorist supporter.[9] Although no evidence has been found to directly implicate these Islamic voluntary organisations in either the 1998 or 2001 atrocities, the FBI interest in their activities and those related to them might tarnish not only their image, but also the image of similar Islamic voluntary organisations.

The reaction of Islamic NGOs to September 11 and the US retaliation illustrates four points. First, it confirms our assertion that the majority of these NGOs operate within the parameters of Islamic voluntarism. This voluntarism treats Islam as an all-embracing faith in which there is no distinction between the provision of social welfare, economics and politics. However, Islamic NGOs are diverse and some of them are much closer to this fundamental position than others. Second, transnational Islamic NGOs could be used as political instruments to further the interests of particular Islamic group or groups. Because their operations are not purely philanthropic, some of them wield substantial economic power and therefore have developed economic interests that could only be served through a global network of support. Third, seemingly non-political groups such as schools and Sufi orders have been increasingly lured by the expansion of Islamic NGO activities and financial resources they command. It is therefore natural that their reaction to the terrorist attacks in the United States and to the East African bombings was based on defending a religious faith and identity rather than judging the facts behind the events. Finally, the global solidarity between Islamic NGOs is derived from the specificity of the contribution Muslim NGOs make towards creating a universal Muslim *umma*.

Conclusion

The growth and proliferation of Islamic NGOs is a response to the multi-faceted crisis afflicting Africa and the need for wide-ranging responses.

[9] *Guardian Unlimited*, 23 September 2001.

Islamic agencies differ from their secular and mainstream Christian counterparts in deriving their philosophy—or at least a substantial part of it—from the basic precepts of the Islamic faith. This allows them to situate their practical activities within a wider social and moral framework, which offers to their adherents the promise of finding a comprehensive ethical response to the African crisis.

Extremist Islam has often found 'popular Islam' corruptible, and an easy prey. This can be explained by the subtleties of Islam in its benign form, hence its fragility in the face of the overt rhetoric of the jihadists (old and new) and the rewards of the material world. The unifying ideology in both is less the mystique of Islam than its advocacy of a universal religion, which finds the possibility of expanding the *umma* in the modern globalising world. Here again expanding the *umma* implies both the secular and the profane, that is, expanding the *umma*'s global outreach with all its economic and political rewards, on the one hand, and expanding the faith or the ideological reproductive force that makes the *umma* unique and appear to be alive. The pragmatism of extremist Islam (in which all is justified as long as it is for sake of God) provides a vehicle for other aims, in which Islam is used as an instrument of domination.

The case of the IIRO presents us with the paradox that one of the most conventional and 'secular' of Islamic NGOs should be implicated by the FBI as a funding conduit for terrorist activities. This brings the contradictions of Islamic NGOs sharply into focus. Any organisation based in Saudi Arabia is subject to the conflicting pressures of Salafi philanthropy and the excess of money available in that country. The overlap between *da'wa* and *jihad* combines with the Islamist premise of the goodwill of the individual philanthropist to create a situation in which extremists can easily utilise Islamic NGOs. Conflicts of interest arise that can be resolved only by open debate, freedom of information, and effective regulatory and supervisory mechanisms. None of these preconditions exist in Saudi Arabia. Thus even if an Islamic NGO located there seeks to be professional and independent, it is vulnerable to being infiltrated by groups such as al Qa'ida. More explicitly da'waist organisations such as Muwafaq al Khairiya and Al Birr al Dawliya (both blacklisted by the United States after September 11) are even more vulnerable to this kind of subversion. The implication of this observation is that if Islamic philanthropic organisations seek to become truly professionalised, they need to submit to the kinds of professional standards and codes of conduct that are increasingly demanded of Western NGOs and private sector companies. Should they take this route, then they will lose much of their specifically Islamic character.

More widely, the greatest attraction of Islamic voluntarism is also proving its greatest weakness. Islam, interpreted as social and political system, is a totalising project. Subsuming charity within a project of social justice is a very attractive proposition. But it is one that is inherently incompatible with modern concepts of 'civil society', which stress the autonomy, diversity and creative pluralism of social organisation. By subscribing to Islamist philosophies, Islamic NGOs are vulnerable to the fundamentalist argument from authority, namely that what is demanded by a fundamentalist reading of the Holy Books is a religious requirement, and thus both an ethical and a legal imperative. International Islamic NGOs that have religious, social and financial roots in Saudi Salafism are especially susceptible to this argument. Moreover, a state that claims to be Islamic will of necessity seek an identity of goals and methods with these philanthropic organisations. The consequence is that these organisations are inexorably drawn, as if by force of gravity, towards fundamentalist agendas, starkly implying the proliferation of violence, stifling the democratic process and monopolising areas of economic activity.

Thus the dividing line becomes blurred between Islamic NGOs using secular strategies to realise their religious objectives and Islamic NGOs that premise their activities on religious claims to universal values. Voluntarism in pursuit of a better world, whether religious or secular, has global appeal as an alternative to mainstream development. In the circumstances it is unsurprising that an underlying current in both secular and religious Islamic NGOs is their adherence to a paradigm linking the trio of justice, right and the public good. In the case of secular NGOs, this trio of humanistic values is usually treated as separate domains of intervention, giving rise to NGOs that specialise in human rights, social service and development respectively. While Islamic NGOs operate within an integrated framework, most of their domains of actions are not specifically 'Islamic', nor do they require religious credentials to justify their pursuance. Moderate, popular and militant Islam each prescribes notions of justice, rights and the public good, each with different strategies. It is the fundamentalists, however, who have the intellectual and physical power to enforce their interpretations on their more nuanced co-religionists, both through threat of *takfir* and through the lure of funds and a universal vision, and deriving their credence from Africa's poverty and underdevelopment. Thus international Islamic NGOs run the risk of falling into the trap of Islamic militancy.

Here lie the perils and not the promise of Islamic NGOs and the dangers that they may pose to African societies. Some Islamic NGOs in

Africa may signify the emergence of highly centralised Muslim communities hostile to all values that are intrinsically African, including pluralism, tolerance and diversity of faith beyond the Islamic *umma*. In essence, such Islamic NGOs are overtly or covertly trying to superimpose on African reality an alien and militant package of values.

6

THE POLITICS OF DESTABILISATION
IN THE HORN, 1989–2001

Alex de Waal

This chapter seeks to tell some parts of the story of the Islamist international and its adversaries in the Horn of Africa in the period between the Islamist coup in Khartoum in June 1989 and the advent of the Bush administration in 2001. This period was marked by some dramatic swings in regional and international alignments, and was punctuated by acts of terrorism, retribution and clandestine subversion. An abiding theme is that the politics of *jihad* is local, rooted in the grievances and strategies of specific groups or individuals.

Three major themes recur. The first is a consistent tension throughout the 1990s between 'realist' and the 'Islamist' doctrines of foreign affairs in Khartoum. On the whole, the military officers who held formal executive offices of state were pragmatists who did not want to expose Sudan to the dangers of an adventurist foreign policy, while the leadership of the NIF under Hassan al Turabi was in favour of an ideologically driven, regionally aggressive policy. At times the two converged, while at other times only one was dominant. At key points during the decade, Khartoum was quite literally speaking with two voices, and a reading of the direction of Sudanese policy on key issues such as terrorism simply depended on whom one believed. On the other hand, there was a real convergence of interest between the parties on key issues, notably holding on to state power.

A second theme is a Metternichean *Realpolitik* by states, with Egypt and Ethiopia in particular resolutely identifying their state interests and pursuing them. Sudan's regional adversaries were also engaged in covert action intermittently aimed at containing or removing the government in

Khartoum. Briefly, in 1996–7 the 'new leaders' in Eritrea, Ethiopia, Uganda and Rwanda formed an axis that looked as though it would reshape half the African continent. Thirdly, US policy proved to be slow and inept—but it was also unlucky. Shortly after a coherent policy emerged in Washington, predicated on the axis of governments in power from Asmara to Kigali and their semi-covert wars against Sudan and Zaire-Congo, that axis collapsed, leaving US policy stranded without the means to achieve its aims.

Our task is complicated by the fact that much of the history remains chronicled solely in the archives of security agencies—and in the heads of security officers, some now deceased or otherwise unwilling or unable to talk. All accounts of the politics of the region, including this one, are built upon information calibrated according to different levels of security clearance. Much information is in the public realm, but many of the key episodes are still shrouded in secrecy. Some of those involved in policy-making keep their distance from public discourse, silencing their critics by claiming they are privy to insider knowledge that gives their still-unwritten accounts an indisputable authority. This chapter tries to probe some of those domains of secret history, but can only be regarded as a first cut: the participants themselves must be challenged to recount their stories and write their memoirs. In doing so, it neglects the roles of some of the post-1991 insurrectionary forces in Eritrea and Ethiopia. Because rebels seek publicity, their stories tend to be better told than those of their secrecy-loving adversaries in state security institutions. This account places more emphasis on the decisions of state apparatuses in the region.

The key problematics emerged in the first months after the 1989 coup. Once the National Islamic Front (NIF) had seized power in Khartoum, its Islamist project was never purely domestic. This was as much by necessity as by design. The dictates of statecraft in north-east Africa in the 1990s, as in previous decades, have demanded engagement with the affairs of neighbours. As Brigadier Omer al Bashir launched his coup, he knew that Egyptian endorsement (deceitfully obtained) was crucial, and that Sudan was already embroiled in civil wars in Chad and Ethiopia/Eritrea, while thousands of Ugandan troops were fighting on Sudanese territory. In reaction, Sudan became a hub for the export of militant Islamism, bringing it into undeclared war with its most important neighbours and ultimately confrontation with the United States.

A central question is, what was the nature of the military-Islamist coalition that governed Sudan in the 1990s? It does not appear to have been government by cabinet, or personal rule. Rather, Khartoum was

marked by a plurality of power centres, particularly when it came to foreign policy and security. General Bashir and his immediate circle marked
one power centre, Hassan al Turabi and his circle another. Some key
figures, such as Colonel Ibrahim Shams el Din, appeared to have the
authority to operate independently without reference to anyone else. An
individual with a senior position in Sudan's bureaucracy or diplomatic
corps needed to develop a fine sense of who was who with respect to any
particular policy or programme.

This approach was in turn made both possible and necessary by the
basic deception at the heart of the June coup. In order to gain respectability (especially in Egypt and Saudi Arabia), the role of Hassan al Turabi
had to be concealed. Without holding any official position, Turabi was
trying to rule Sudan in the same highly personal way that he had built the
Islamist movement, by holding court, listening to his acolytes, and encouraging them to go off and use their initiative. Subsequently, Bashir
and his circle have emphasised the divisions between them and Turabi
that existed from the earliest days of the coup. These divisions certainly
existed, but the government has clear interests in exaggerating them—
the governance of *da'wa* and *jihad* was more complex than many would
like to admit.

1989–90: surviving amid a regional conflict

In the days after Brigadier Omer al Bashir's seizure of power on the night
of 30 June 1989, most observers were confused about the identity of the
putchists. Some Sudanese, nothing that the putsch pre-empted the
planned meeting between Prime Minister Sadiq el Mahdi and SPLA
leader John Garang by just four days, suspected the hand of the NIF. But
Hassan al Turabi had been jailed along with other parliamentarians and
the NIF had been banned along with other political parties. And Bashir
made statements that he would accelerate the peace process, talking to
Garang 'soldier to soldier'. In a hasty gesture it quickly regretted, the
Egyptian government rushed to support Bashir. On one point Sudanese
and outsiders were unanimous: this was the most poorly-organised coup
to have succeeded in Sudan's long, often tragic, sometimes comic, history
of military attempts to take state power. The power base of the new
regime seemed narrow, its senior members gauche and ill-prepared.
Bashir accused the previous government of failing to support the army to
fight the war, but his initial steps did not seem likely to stiffen the military's resolve: he dismissed all officers more senior to him and promoted

himself to the rank of lieutenant-general. Many speculated that, as soon as the rainy season was over, the SPLA would launch an offensive and bring the government to its knees. And this is very nearly what happened.

In June 1989 the civil war was already deeply regionalised, and governments in the region were not only hostile to an assertively Islamist regime in Khartoum, but ready and willing to do something about it.

The war had been regionalised from its very outset. When the Bor mutineers fled to Ethiopia in May 1983, they rapidly received support from the government of Colonel Mengistu Haile Mariam, in the form of training camps, arms, intelligence and radio facilities. The camps in Gambella, south-western Ethiopia, were closed societies completely run by the SPLA and supported by Ethiopian security. (African Rights 1997: 62–84) Mengistu's support came at a high price. He intervened directly in the leadership of the SPLA, insisting that his chosen candidate for leader should be loyal to him, sympathetic to his socialist ideology, and above all, opposed to Southern secessionism. Ethiopian support for the SPLA was clearly a response to the way in which the Eritrean People's Liberation Front (EPLF) and Ethiopian opposition movements used Sudanese territory as their rear bases. In addition, the SPLA fought inside Ethiopia against the Oromo Liberation Front (OLF), in effect acting as an additional Ethiopian army division. (Africa Watch 1991: 325–7) At key moments, Ethiopia had provided logistical support to SPLA operations, for example the incursion into Southern Blue Nile ('Kurmuk I') in 1987. While it had stationed military advisers with the SPLA, Ethiopia had never sent its own forces across the border in substantial numbers.

Uganda was also engaged in the Sudanese war. When the National Resistance Army (NRA) of Yoweri Museveni captured Kampala in January 1986, the remnants of its enemy, the Uganda National Liberation Army (UNLA) fled northwards towards their provincial power base. Their leadership regrouped in Juba, from where they posed a serious threat to the new Ugandan government. Khartoum rightly feared the implications of the long-standing personal and political relationship between Yoweri Museveni and John Garang, and assisted the UNLA. In May 1987 four brigades of the Ugandan army, totalling 14,000 men commanded by General Fred Rwigyema, entered Sudan and fought the Sudanese armed forces alongside the SPLA. The Ugandans provided artillery and infantry support, transport and helicopters (both gunships and transport) to the SPLA as it sought to surround Juba. The forces remained into 1989, when they began to withdraw. The incursion had achieved its objectives, with the SPLA in control of most of Equatoria and threatening Juba. At that time the NRA was at the peak of its strength and morale, and some of the Ugandan officers urged the SPLA command to capture Juba. Had they tried, they might well have succeeded. But Museveni's government was young and needed to gain international respectability, and the NRA firebrands were restrained. Moreover, Museveni believed that the SPLA should build up its movement through popular mobilisation and a long struggle, rather than having victory delivered to it on a plate. Hence, Uganda replaced its combat troops with military advisers. They helped tighten the noose around Juba in January 1990, and the city looked deeply vulnerable. In October that year, Kampala's fall-back option of resuming direct military intervention was decisively undermined when the cream of the officers who had fought in Sudan slipped away to invade Rwanda.

Sudan was also embroiled in the Chadian civil war, though this turned out to be of lesser consequence for Sudanese politics. For some years, a combination of local political rivalries in Darfur and intervention by Libya, some with the tacit support of Prime Minister Sadiq el Mahdi, had led to intermittent intense fighting between Chadian factions in western Sudan. At the time of the coup, a peace conference was underway in the Darfur regional capital, El Fasher, which was moving towards a settlement of the local conflict. The new regime backed this process, and also discreetly supported the Chadian rebel group headed by Idris Deby that launched a lightning offensive from Sudanese territory and captured Ndjamena in December 1990. Thereafter, Sudan was confident of a friendly government in Chad. However, had either Darfurian or Chadian politics taken a different turn, the RCC could have found itself with a hostile neighbour ready to offer support to the SPLA on its far-western flank.

The most important linkage was with Ethiopia. The mutual cross-border subversion of the 1980s took on a completely different quality in the last weeks of 1989. In essence, the Ethiopian and Sudanese wars became entangled to the extent that only one regime could survive.

In 1989 the SPLA was fighting a conventional war, and its aim was total military victory. The new regime in Khartoum was weak. With the support of Uganda and Ethiopia the SPLA leadership was confident. Had the Ugandans and Ethiopians coordinated in the field, they might have prevailed, but each was intent on its own interests. Only the SPLA's Commander-in-Chief, John Garang, had the overall picture, and it appears that he planned offensives in Southern Blue Nile ('Kurmuk II') and on Juba. 'Kurmuk II' became decisive.

The background to this offensive was the escalation of the war in Eritrea and Tigray. In March 1988 the EPLF scored a spectacular victory at Afabet, prompting Mengistu to make a hasty peace with Somalia (with which it had been formally at war since 1977), so as to re-deploy forces from the Ogaden to the northern front. Despite this, the Ethiopian army continued to lose ground consistently. Ethiopian intelligence obtained information, correctly, that the EPLF was preparing to attack the port of Massawa. Mengistu feared, also correctly, that the loss of Massawa would be a prelude to the ultimate surrender of all his forces in Eritrea. This time, Mengistu decided that the weakest link in his enemies' coalition was Sudan.

The October 1989 'Kurmuk II' operation consisted of SPLA troops, but backed by an unprecedented level of Ethiopian artillery support. Ethiopian forces themselves were poised to cross in support of a major SPLA offensive aimed at capturing Damazin, the provincial capital and also site of the dam that provides water for the Gezira and electricity for Khartoum. If Damazin were captured, the new government in Sudan would fall. Two years previously, in 'Kurmuk I', the Sudanese army had taken just 42 days to mobilise sufficient funds and forces to recapture Kurmuk from the SPLA. Sadiq el Mahdi had toured Arab capitals appealing for funds, with considerable success. This time, Khartoum faced a less favourable international climate, after Egypt had discovered its error and while Western countries were queuing up to condemn the military junta for imprisoning all elected politicians plus many trade unionists, journalists, lawyers and others. In addition, owing to the post-coup dismissals, the army did not have the same military competence on call. The SPLA was well-armed and confident—in fact, it was over-confident. (Lam Akol 2001. 141 6) The regime faced its worst military crisis.

What averted disaster was a counter-offensive by a crack commando brigade of the EPLF, the very same force that had been prepared for the attack on Massawa. During the previous ten years, the EPLF had occasionally sent advisers and trainers to other fronts in Ethiopia, but this was an unprecedented operation: an entire elite brigade launching a mechanised assault from Sudanese territory, in close coordination with the Sudanese army. (The other force involved was the OLF.) In stage one of the operation, the SPLA was pushed out of Kurmuk by Sudanese government forces. In stage two, launched in the New Year, the EPLF attacked across the border. The SPLA was routed on the border and then its headquarters at Asosa was captured, virtually intact. It seems that

SPLA forces were caught unprepared. Asosa was also a refugee camp, and this marked the beginning of the long march of the Uduk people, who were the main inhabitants of the camp. In fact the SPLA suffered its worst defeat to date, losing a substantial proportion of its heavy weapons, which the EPLF handed over to the Sudanese army. The Ethiopian garrison was also defeated and dispersed. EPLF forces went deep inside western Ethiopia as far as Begi and Dembi Dolo. They took with them a small OLF contingent that was inserted there—officially this was announced as the 'Asosa operation' of the OLF—and after just seven days, withdrew. Mengistu was taken completely off guard—he compared the situation to a football game with the ball being passed from one wing to another. He hastily redeployed troops to Wollega.

The EPLF brigade had done its job and redeployed back in Eritrea. Less than a month later it was among the forces that opened fire on the Massawa front, taking the Ethiopians by surprise again. Massawa was captured and Mengistu's fate was sealed.

The fact that the EPLF was involved on such a scale and at such a critical moment should alert us that there were high stakes in this confrontation. The full story remains untold. However, there is a credible explanation for the course of events. This is that 'Kurmuk II' was accompanied by a message from Mengistu to Bashir. This offered the Sudanese government a simple choice: either it should cut off support to the EPLF (and the Ethiopian fronts), or the SPLA, with Ethiopian assistance, would capture Damazin and the Roseires Dam, and the SPLA would thereby come to power in Khartoum. According to this account, Bashir's deputy, General Zubeir Mohamed Saleh, called the EPLF to say they could do nothing—the game was up. The EPLF sent its head of intelligence, Petros Solomon, to assess the situation. He flew to Damazin with Zubeir. His assessment was that a joint Sudanese-EPLF attack could save the day. Accordingly, the elite EPLF brigade was secretly trucked to Damazin and did its work.

Whatever transpired in the days after 'Kurmuk II', it is certain that the Bashir government returned the favour by providing greater facilities to the EPLF and also the EPRDF. Access to Sudan was important for the rebel fronts: this was their route for obtaining relief supplies and fuel (some of the latter provided by the Sudanese). It was also their means of access to the international community. During February-May 1991, the EPLF and EPRDF decisively routed the Ethiopian army and brought the war to an end. Sudan had secured its entire eastern border. Overwhelmingly, this victory was due to the long hard struggle of the EPLF and

EPRDF: even had Mengistu's Kurmuk gambit succeeded, he could only have delayed the collapse of his government and not reversed the tide of the war. But for the Sudanese generals, they felt they had tasted vicarious victory. Exaggerating their own role, they attributed the EPLF-EPRDF triumph to their own small and belated engagement.

The aftermath of the Asosa operation marked the beginnings of serious dissent from within the inner core of the SPLA. Commander Kerubino Kuanyin had earlier written a memo to John Garang arguing that the SPLA was making a strategic error in allying itself so closely with the Ethiopians. (He argued for much greater self-reliance and adherence to the tenets of revolutionary warfare as taught by the Cubans.) Kerubino's critique had already landed him in detention. The Asosa disaster should have caused Garang to reconsider the wisdom of his close alignment with Mengistu. It did not: Mengistu continued to praise Garang for his 'loyalty' and Garang did not flinch from sticking by his failing friend. When the Ethiopian army collapsed in April-May 1991, the SPLA continued fighting against the victorious EPRDF for a further three months, losing many soldiers in the process, and evacuating its rear bases and refugee camps in Ethiopia's Gambella province. That military and political disaster paved the way for the 'Nasir Group' led by Riek Machar and Lam Akol to announce its coup against Garang, that succeeded only in splitting the SPLA and sparking devastating internecine warfare.

On the other hand, the SPLA leader John Garang was fully aware how he had been very close indeed to an outright military victory courtesy of Ethiopian intervention. (He was to come similarly close in 1997.) This realisation has informed his strategic calculations ever since: victory is something that can be snatched at any moment, given the right conditions and the necessary international backing.

Our main concern here is the impact of these events on power relations *within* the Khartoum government. After the June coup the Sudan government was a coalition between ideologues (Hassan al Turabi, Ali Osman Mohamed Taha) and military officers (Generals Bashir and Zubeir) with some bridging both categories (Colonel Ibrahim Shams el Din). The ideologues always had an agenda of exporting radical Islam to the neighbouring states and beyond; the military officers were mostly hostile to this because of the obvious security implications of antagonising neighbouring countries. But after 'Kurmuk-Asosa', the military officers realised that a regionally offensive strategy could be an integral part of defending the security of their revolution. Their regime, and the Islamist project in Sudan, would never be safe unless their revolution could also be exported to their neighbours, or threats from their neighbours could at the minimum be neutralised. Before turning to the question of who was running Sudan's foreign and security policies, and to what purpose, we must turn to another pivotal episode that occurred when the Bashir regime was barely a year old.

Raising the stakes: the Gulf War and after

Successive governments in Khartoum had followed the principle that, whatever their true interests and real motives, they should not offend Egypt and Saudi Arabia in any serious way, and certainly never offend them both at once. The NIF had implicitly adopted the same policy, despite its discomfort with Egyptian crackdowns on the Muslim Brothers. Iraq's invasion of Kuwait on 2 August 1990 caught the government in a dilemma. The following day, Sudan's Foreign Minister abstained from the Arab League motion to condemn the invasion.[1] The government was divided. President Bashir and the executive all concurred that they should fall into line with the Egyptian-Saudi line, and on 10 August Sudan supported the Arab League resolution to send troops to defend Saudi Arabia, albeit with reservations.[2] King Fahd reportedly offered Sudan several hundred million dollars for joining the anti-Iraq coalition.

Then Hassan al Turabi openly declared his support for Saddam Hussein. It was flagrantly contrary to every tenet of Sudanese national interest, and the Foreign Minister and others in the government were appalled. Saddam, a lifelong secularist who had violently repressed his domestic Islamists and had fought a long and bloody war against Iran, was an unlikely hero for the Islamists.[3] Why did Turabi do it? Probably, he thought that Iraq would win the war, and that there would be popular Islamist insurrections across the Arab world, including in Saudi Arabia, Egypt and Algeria. And indeed, Turabi read the popular mood well. The Gulf War shattered the façade of Sunni Muslim-Arab unity that had

---

[1] Jordan, Mauritania, Yemen and the PLO also abstained, and Libya walked out of the meeting.

[2] Libya and the PLO supported Iraq, Algeria and Yemen abstained, and Jordan and Mauritania also supported the resolution but with reservations.

[3] Sudanese-Iraqi relations were complex. In April 1990 the Sudan government broke a coup by pro-Iraqi Ba'athist army officers, executing 28 of them, and creating immense bitterness. The Sudanese Ba'athists were divided by Turabi's pro-Iraq stand in August. In 1988, an Iraqi Shi'a leader had been assassinated in Khartoum, probably by the Iraqis, while attending a NIF conference, and the Sudan government had failed to condemn Iraq. This created problems between Khartoum and Teheran and the Iraqi Islamists.

been maintained with such difficulty and expense by the Saudis and Egyptians over the previous decade. Militant Islam appeared ascendant across the region. The Afghan *mujahidiin* had just driven the Soviet army out of their country, and the Arab 'Afghan' brigades were beginning to disperse across the Middle East and North Africa. The Islamists were mobilising in Egypt and preparing to take control of most universities and professional associations; in Algeria they were shortly to gain a majority of the popular vote; in Jordan they had already won 34 of the 80 seats in the House of Representatives; and in Palestine the *intifada* was growing in strength with Hamas challenging the PLO for mass allegiance. Many Islamists trooped to Baghdad, and Saddam embraced them, also putting *'Allahu Akbar'* on the national flag.[4] Iraq hosted a 'Popular Islamic Conference' to challenge the Saudi-controlled Organisation of the Islamic Conference (OIC), which met in Baghdad on the eve of Operation Desert Storm and called for a *jihad* against the West and its forces in Arabia.[5] But the Islamist embrace of Saddam was beset by contradictions (Piscatori 1991). Most Egyptian Islamist leaders, including Sheikh Omer Abdel Rahman were notable in failing to add their voices to the call for *jihad* (he said that those on both sides should be killed), while some of their followers saw the conflict as between Islam and America, representing the great Satan. (Auda 1991) As with all other Islamic movements, national strategies dictated the response. For the Arab and Muslim 'street', Saddam was suddenly a hero because he stood up the Americans, spoke out on behalf of the Palestinians, and spoke some frank words about the Gulf monarchies, especially Saudi Arabia. As the American troops arrived in Saudi Arabia and the war began, Islamist support for Iraq hardened. The Islamist alliance with Baghdad showed that, as a resistance ideology, the Islamist movement was ready to make opportunistic alliances. But it also illuminated the movement's fundamental weaknesses: it had no charismatic leader with truly international stature, and its component parties were all mired in local politics.

Incurring the wrath of the United States and Europe, and suffering 'international isolation' did not worry Sudan's Islamists. Abdelwahab El-Affendi, noting how Iran, Iraq, Libya and Afghanistan are regarded in the West as international 'troublemakers', wrote at the time: 'The phenomenon of "disruptive Islam" indicates that the international order

---

[4] Arabic is renowned for its calligraphy. But the lettering on the Iraqi flag is a mundane scrawl.

[5] Sheikh Bin Baz, Saudi Arabia's leading *mufti* called, with some discomfort, for a *jihad* against Iraq, labouring to explain that non-Muslims could also join this *jihad*.

now in its death throes was established and stabilized in the absence of Muslim influence.' (1991b: 59) Had that international order really been in its 'death throes', and had there been Islamist revolutions across the Arab world, Turabi would have been congratulated for his courage and vision, instead of being criticised for his impetuousness.

By siding with the 'troublemakers', Turabi created a decade-long crisis in Khartoum. He must have known that he would precipitate a rapid cutback in international assistance, and that thereafter the United States and major foreign donors would be unforgiving, so that Sudan would face its deepening debt crisis alone. The ensuing financial crisis was massive: total aid receipts, which had averaged about $1 billion in the mid-1980s and were still over $500 million per annum in 1991, fell to just $136 million in 1997, of which only $15 million was received directly by the government. (Ajawin and de Waal 2002: 45–7) The Gulf crisis also entailed the exodus from Iraq of tens of thousands of Sudanese migrant workers, and a fear that the Saudis would retaliate by either expelling Sudanese or blocking their remittances back home—Sudan's single largest source of foreign currency. The crisis also coincided with a severe drought, and panic buying of food led directly to a food price hike of unprecedented proportions and a nationwide famine. (de Waal 1997: 100–1) Turabi may even have expected military action against Sudan (which was rumoured, then and since, to have allowed its territory to be used for storing Iraqi missiles and chemical weapons).

Turabi also invoked the hostility of Egypt. Unexpectedly, the Islamist government in Khartoum liberated Sudan from Egypt's shadow. For the first time in its short history as an independent state, Sudan was openly contradicting Egyptian policies and interests.

Turabi was appealing to the masses. As so often with Islamist thinkers, his internationalism combines an astute if general critique of the existing order with an ambitious call for a new moral order:

The most-far reaching prejudice to Muslim unity was the introduction of the national state, entailing the inculcation of nationalist ideology and the establishment of different states, each with rigid borders, sovereign authority, separate public order and paramount national interest. That was totally alien to the Islamic tradition of one international community with open frontiers, homogenous order, limited political authorities, and relative particular interest…

Like the national state, these inter-national schemes [such as the Arab League] failed to serve any meaningful cause for the Muslim member-societies or to satisfy their yearning for unity…. But perhaps the highest disenchantment was that the Organization of the Islamic Conference, a professedly Islamic association, turned out to be politically impotent and totally unrepresentative of the true spirit of community that animates the Muslim people. (al Turabi 1992: 6, 8)

Turabi was trying to turn Islam's lack of a theory of nationalism to his advantage, by pretending that it had a theory of internationalism—or to be precise, international revolution. In the era of the Prophet, Islam moved directly from being the religious order of a city state (Medina) to being an ideology of imperial conquest.[6] Similarly, having achieved state power, Turabi duly mobilised his cadres to set up alternative structures for internationalist Islamism. In 1990 Sudan abolished visa requirements for nationals of Arab countries, and opened its borders to a wide range of Islamic extremist forces, including Usama bin Laden, who left Saudi Arabia when the King preferred to retain American troops rather than Usama's preferred option of mobilising the international *mujahidiin*. The following year, Turabi established the Popular Arab and Islamic Conference (PAIC) as a radical alternative to the Arab League and OIC. This was an immediate inheritor of the Iraqi-sponsored Popular Islamic Conference. It brought together the Iranians, the Iraqis and the Salafi jihadists in one hall, and for its first meeting also included secular groups like George Habbash's Popular Front for the Liberation of Palestine. Turabi aspired to unite all the disparate Islamist and Arab movements, but did not succeed. The PAIC was initially headed by Turabi himself, but when he was temporarily incapacitated by a Sudanese karate expert in a Canadian airport,[7] it was taken over by Mustafa Ismail, a future Foreign Minister. There were some spin-off organisation and conferences, including the 'World Islamic Organisation for Human Rights' and the 'Islam in Africa Organisation'. Even though the PAIC was manifestly anti-Saudi, this did not hinder the flow of funds from Salafi philanthropic organisations to some of these offshoots. By December 1993 Turabi was back in charge, hosting an even larger gathering of Arab and Islamic organisations, including some secularist ones, plus representatives from Albania and Bosnia. Turabi himself had been involved in mediating between the PLO and Hamas, and also in Algeria and Afghanistan, in all cases without success. The PAIC meetings were also somewhat chaotic and only achieved consensus at the highest level of generality. But Turabi's activism was bringing him unprecedented prominence. *Middle East Contemporary Survey* commented: 'One way or another, there could be no doubt that Turabi put on the best show in the world of Islamic activism. Whether or

---

[6] This insight is owed to Mohamed Mahmoud.

[7] Hashim Badr el Din's defence that he was acting in self-defence won him an acquittal, as neither Turabi nor the Sudanese government were ready to testify in court.

not he actually gave that world a sense of direction seemed less certain.'[8] At the third meeting of the PAIC in March-April 1995, eighty different delegations attended, ranging from Chechnya to Louis Farrakhan's Nation of Islam, and the conference called for the replacement of the Universal Declaration of Human Rights. But, despite Turabi's claims that the meeting represented 'the first expression in the world of the honor of Arabism and the current Muslim awakening', the PAIC's dream of establishing a 'single pan-Islamic authority' was no more than rhetoric.[9] The divisions among the Islamists were on show for all to see, and barely three months later, the attempted assassination of Husni Mubarak killed off even this rhetorical unity. The fourth PAIC, scheduled for 1996, was postponed indefinitely.

During this period, militant Islamist organisations converged on Khartoum, including Tanzim al Jihad, al Gama'a al Islamiyya, Islamic Jihad (Palestine), Abu Nidal, Hezbollah and Hamas. In August 1993 the US listed Sudan as a state sponsor of terrorism, specifically because of the presence of the Egyptian, Lebanese and Palestinian organisations. Usama bin Laden and his al Qa'ida network did not figure high among American concerns at the time: indeed Usama was primarily known as a businessman, employer and philanthropist. Sudan was contradicting the basic tenets of its Arab policy, by persisting in estranging Saudi Arabia and Egypt. In December 1992, after Saudi Arabia had stripped Usama bin Laden of his citizenship, it implicitly accused Sudan of destabilising it by sheltering him. After Usama was implicated in the 13 November 1995 truck bomb in Riyadh, it stepped up the pressure, and may have been involved in the armed attack on Usama's house in Khartoum shortly afterwards (Reeve 1999: 183–4). Egypt was similarly unhappy over the hospitality given to Egyptian militants. The question of just how deep the Sudanese involvement in these terrorist attacks went remains controversial. But there seems no doubt that senior security officers and politicians were facilitating terrorist activities, and the label of 'state sponsor of terrorism' was well-warranted. Turabi went so far as to label the assassins as *mujahidiin*, and those who died as *shuhada* (martyrs).

While making a grab for leadership of international militant Islamism, Turabi was also, more parochially, making a bid to stay as leader of the Sudanese Islamists. The semi-clandestine role he had played in the months after the coup was not to his liking, and he feared that he might yet be upstaged by the generals who had taken power. Had President Bashir

[8] *Middle East Contemporary Survey*, 1993, p. 146.
[9] *Middle East Contemporary Survey*, 1994, p. 107.

aligned himself with Cairo and Riyadh, he might have become a clone of Husni Mubarak, nodding in the direction of Islam while repressing the Islamists, with the support of both Egypt and Saudi Arabia. And Sudanese history had a compelling precedent for a military ruler who had turned on his erstwhile ideological mentors—Jaafar Nimeiri had crushed the Communists in 1971.

Sudan weathered Desert Storm and its fallout. Turabi's gamble was a debacle, but not a total disaster. The Saudis did not stop remittances or expel Sudanese workers. During this entire period Saudi-based philanthropic agencies operated in Sudan and channelled millions of dollars to a range of activities, some of them bordering on support for the military. International Islamists funded Sudan's military industries (al Turabi 2001: 8).[10] This diversity of sources of income facilitated the peculiar form of Islamist governance that developed in the early 1990s, based on the comprehensive *da'wa* (see chapter 3). Da'waist governance was decentralised, marked by nexuses of resource flows between philanthropic agencies, security agencies, and commercial companies and banks. There were many rackets established to pursue special agendas. For example, a da'waist philanthropic agency might import vehicles tax free, use some for its own purposes, and then sell others at immense profit in order to set up a company or to finance an extra-budgetary security organisation linked to an international militant group. Leading civilians in the regime could utilise the Islamic agencies to establish their own independent security apparatus, bypassing the established security organs. For example, the agency Amn al Ijabi ('the constructive security') operated in this manner, beyond the purview of other security institutions, in the mid-1990s. In other cases, companies or da'waist organisations would be granted concessions to run commercial farms or import-export businesses, and in return would help fund training of the Popular Defence Forces. Some leading security officers were engaged in special projects such as supporting the Ugandan Lord's Resistance Army or Eritrean Islamist organisations,[11] and would persuade an Islamist philanthropic organisation to assist. The

[10] Sudan's Military Economic Board was established in 1982. It was formally dismantled on World Bank insistence shortly thereafter, but not all the military-owned companies were dissolved (de Waal 1994). Military industrial cooperation with Iraq began in the 1980s and continued throughout the 1990s, including the period of Usama bin Laden's involvement. Allegations of the manufacture, storage and use of chemical weapons have been made throughout most of this period.

[11] Eritrean People's Conference/Islamic Jihad and Eritrean Islamic Salvation Movement/ el Ekhlas.

Islamist finance itself was also dispersed and often outside any state purview, with key individuals handling investments in different parts of the world and thereby building unassailable power bases. Among these are Abdel Rahim Hamdi, Osman al Mudawwi and Awad al Jaz. Al Qa'ida itself was a characteristic combination of commerce, philanthropy and jihadism. Usama bin Laden invested heavily in legitimate businesses such as gum arabic. He built roads that combined strategic import with economic benefit and helped establish Sudan's nascent military-industrial complex. Usama also provided employment for veterans of the Afghan *jihad* and their families, who would otherwise have dispersed. He facilitated the training, planning and financial activities of militant organisations encamped in Sudan.

The stakes were raised again by the American military intervention in Somalia, which had regional consequences unforeseen by both its architects and its detractors.[12] Operation Restore Hope was launched in December 1992 with the stated aim of making the country safe for the delivery of international relief. But for the radical Islamists and the Sudan government, the intervention was interpreted as a bid for US control of north-east Africa, and a precursor to a 'humanitarian' military intervention in Sudan. Some Western relief agencies were indeed calling for the latter, primarily because of the humanitarian consequences of interfactional fighting in the South. The intervention spurred greater interest in Somalia and its neighbours (especially Kenya) by both Sudan and al Qa'ida. It looked to them as though, having defeated Iraq, the United States was turning its attention to the Horn of Africa. Subsequently, Usama bin Laden has claimed a major role in the battles in Mogadishu that forced the US withdrawal. The only evidence in support of this is the statements of al Qa'ida itself: none of those who were present at the time including the Somali militia leaders, who are usually extremely frank about their military activities and coalitions, have reported a significant presence of non-Somalis. Most likely, al Qa'ida would have liked to have become involved but did not have sufficient time to do more than recon-

---

[12] The violently inconclusive end to the Siyaad Barre regime in January 1991 was in part an unforeseen outcome of the Gulf War. The final battle in Mogadishu coincided with the coalition offensive against Iraq, and thus garnered no diplomatic attention, other than a US warship diverted to the Indian Ocean, which despatched helicopters to evacuate the few remaining diplomatic personnel. In a nice irony, one of those evacuated was the Sudanese ambassador and his wife, who gave birth to a baby on board the American ship. By contrast, the imminent fall of the Mengistu regime in Ethiopia just three months later was the focus of major diplomatic efforts, which facilitated the rapid recognition and consolidation of the new EPRDF government.

naissance. The significance of the episode was psychological: the American withdrawal was seen as a landmark in Muslims' capacity for defeating the superpower's agenda. It was a minor reprise for the miscalculation and defeat over Iraq, and it emboldened Khartoum and its guests.

Regional jihadism and response

Sudanese regional policy during the period 1990s can be interpreted in one of several ways. It can be seen in a linear fashion: as a policy of regional aggression based on promoting political Islam, which ended up antagonising all its major neighbours by 1995, and thereby induced a concerted response that would have brought the regime down in 1998 or 1999, had it not been for the decision of the Eritrean and Ethiopian leaders to engage in a war between themselves. It can also be seen as an internal power struggle between a 'realist' doctrine of foreign and security policy, and an 'Islamist' school. This section will suggest that it was a combination of both. The story is complex and key episodes will be omitted here, including the intimate relationship between the regional war and the various peace negotiations.

The linear story of over-reach has much validity: by 1993–4 Sudan was strong both on the civil war battlefield and in the region, though isolated internationally. Four years later the regime was on the point of being overthrown. Why did General Bashir and his more pragmatic or 'realist' colleagues engage in a policy that brought about a predictable response that was so nearly fatal? Partly it appears to have been poor judgement: seeing themselves as sponsors of the EPLF and EPRDF victories in Eritrea and Ethiopia (as well as Idris Deby's in Chad), they thought that they could pull off the same trick again, this time with an Islamist hue. The humbling of America in Mogadishu fed their hubris. Partly it appears to have been that they did not have the requisite control: senior Islamist officers were operating autonomously, or running specialised intelligence agencies that kept an eye on the army itself. And there is the ever-likely explanation that they were just poorly informed.

Uganda was Sudan's first and most constant adversary, and also became the pivot of the regional strategy to confront Sudan and Zaire-Congo. It is also a clear example of how regional jihadism was built upon local grievances.

After 1990 Uganda remained hostile to Sudan, but Museveni had missed his chance of installing the SPLA in Juba. Museveni's argument, based on his experience in Uganda and his intellectual heritage from

Frelimo, was that the SPLA should build its capacity in a protracted struggle.[13] Ugandan soldiers advised the SPLA, but excepting some hot pursuit operations, the Ugandan People's Defence Force (UPDF) was not committed inside Sudan territory. In the early 1990s the UPDF's capacity was also diminishing. Economic constraints and donor pressure led to a downsizing of the army from over 100,000 to about 40,000 men; and it was also becoming less efficient and more corrupt with officers engaging in trading in gold, timber and army material and funds. Some of the ablest officers had joined the Rwandese Patriotic Front (RPF), while HIV and AIDS also severely depleted the ranks of experienced soldiers. With the SPLA also massively weakened after the 1991 split, the Sudan government saw an opportunity to turn the tables on Uganda, not merely defending its southern border but taking the war to Uganda itself.

The Lord's Resistance Army (LRA) in northern Uganda was Khartoum's first tool. The LRA phenomenon has been widely discussed, and will not be detailed here. The LRA began as a syncretist cult arising from the extreme demoralisation of Acholi society, alongside the political failure of the Museveni regime to include the Acholi in the political and economic reconstruction of Uganda. The forces that became the LRA emerged in 1987 from the ruins of its predecessor, Alice Lakwena's Holy Spirit Movement. The name LRA was adopted in 1992, and it established close links with the Sudan government two years later. The LRA differs from most of the movements sponsored by Khartoum in that it has no connection to militant Islam other than opportunistic alliance with the Sudan government, implemented through military intelligence and certain da'waist organisations with offices in Juba. For the following seven years, the LRA relied heavily on Sudan's support.

The Allied Democratic Forces (ADF) in Uganda is a much less well-studied phenomenon. It arose in part from an authentically Islamist movement in Uganda, the Tablik youth movement, and as such warrants closer attention. The Tablik movement has roots in the Tablighi Jamaat, founded in India in the 1920s and based in Pakistan from the 1960s. The parent Tabligh organisation has been historically focused on education, proselytisation and the improvement of personal morality, rather than engagement in politics. (Kepel 2002: 44–5) In Uganda, it quietly built up a wide following, especially among young people, and became a network that could subsequently be used to mobilise and recruit militants. A range

---

[13] Not all of his commanders agreed, especially after the SPLA's failure to complete its capture of Juba in 1992.

of factors contributed to the feeling of marginalisation and exclusion among Uganda's Muslim youth, including discontent among Muslims following the reappropriation of property confiscated by Idi Amin when the Asians were expelled, and a perception that the Museveni regime had failed to incorporate respected Muslim leaders in powerful positions. Another factor was a division within the Muslim community over the appointment of the Mufti of Kampala. Two different factions, one pro-Iran and the other pro-Pakistan (rooted in the Tabligh), contested for the position, taking the case to court. In March 1991, the decision was announced in favour of the pro-Iranian candidate, an announcement that coincided precisely with President Museveni's departure to visit Iran. This sparked immediate discontent among the losing pro-Pakistan group. A group of 450 Tablik students took over a mosque and killed four policemen. They were overcome, detained and taken to Luzira prison, which then became the recruiting ground for their movement.

The dispute over the position of the Mufti has to be seen as a conflict over the resources that flow from control of the position. The Mufti dispenses charity and scholarships, and the faction that loses out needs to seek these material rewards from elsewhere. In the context it was natural for them to turn to radical Islam. Hassan al Turabi had visited Uganda in 1986 and helped establish philanthropic organisations in the country, as well as providing a network that linked the Tablik students to Pakistan and the opportunities for scholarships that existed there.

As so often, detention radicalised an incipient Islamist movement. When the Tablik prisoners were released in 1993, they had forged the radical core of a movement, which immediately moved to western Uganda, where they established a camp at Buseruka. They began guerrilla raids the following year, attacking in the western Rift Valley. A counterattack by the UPDF overran the base, where they found Islamist literature, and also evidence that some of their teachers had been trained in Sudan and one each in Pakistan and Afghanistan. The UPDF concluded that it was committed to *jihad* and had a clear strategy of destabilising Uganda. Forty members of the Tablik escaped to Zaire where they established another camp, and began to receive military assistance from Sudan.

According to Uganda, throughout this period, the Tablik movement had links with the Sudanese embassy in Kampala, which was a conduit for funds and contacts with the wider Islamic movement. The extent of Sudanese links with the Tablik and the LRA prompted Uganda to sever diplomatic ties with Sudan in April 1995. It also reportedly had links with Usama bin Laden. Abu Ubaida al Banshiri, a member of Tanzim al Jihad who was heading al Qa'ida's project of creating a multi-ethnic Islamist army, set up a cell in Nairobi in 1993 (partly in response to the US intervention in Somalia) and married a Kenyan woman (Benjamin and Simon 2002: 121). He visited Uganda in May 1996, where he drowned in a ferry accident in Lake Victoria.

The ADF itself formed in 1996, and from the outset had Khartoum's sponsorship. Military intelligence in Juba supported a training camp for the ADF, and together with a da'waist agency, providing logistics, arms and food. Zaire's President Mobutu Sese Seko was happy to cooperate with this, envisaging the ADF as a counter-force to the imminent Ugandan-Rwandese offensive against the former Rwandese army and genocidal forces in encamped in eastern Zaire. Other members of the ADF included the National Army for the Liberation of Uganda (NALU, a leftover of the Ruwenzuru resistance movement in western Uganda), and other remnants including some former Idi Amin loyalists led by Moses Ali (who were flown from Juba to the ADF's base in Zaire), plus the West Nile Bank Front and the Uganda National Rescue Front. The NALU was the key additional partner: it had local legitimacy and the remains of an infrastructure in the Ruwenzori Mountains. The LRA was not part of the ADF, but the two shared the same rear base in Juba and enjoyed similar backing from Sudanese intelligence.

The ADF fighters were reportedly zealous and courageous. Ugandan officers who fought against it say that the troops were brave in combat but strategically inept. They remark on its lack of trained commanders. Their operations included guerrilla raids and a series of terrorist attacks in Uganda's main towns. Forty-three bomb explosions, killing 62 people in Kampala and Jinja and injuring 262, were attributed to the ADF.[14]

The ADF's first serious attack into Uganda was staged at Kasese in November 1996. By this time the conflict had again become a regional war. To appreciate the regional significance of the ADF, and subsequent events, we must first turn to Eritrea and Ethiopia and their escalating confrontation with Sudan, which reached its peak during 1995–7.

When the EPLF defeated the Ethiopian army and took power in Asmara in May 1991, it was not the sole political or military representative of the Eritrean nationalist movement, though it was by far the most powerful. At the time there were a number of other Eritrean factions, most of them drawing on a Muslim lowland constituency, which were

---

[14] See Yoweri Museveni, 'Fighting Terrorism in a Dependent State', *The New Vision*, 24 September 2001.

almost wholly squeezed out of the EPLF-dominated political process. Some of these factions, such as the Eritrean Liberation Front-Revolutionary Command and Eritrea Jihad, had enjoyed close links with Sudanese intelligence over the years. In fact, shortly after the June coup in Khartoum, the Sudanese Islamists had armed some of the more Islamist-oriented Eritrean factions, but soon discovered that they only had the capacity to harass the EPLF and not the Ethiopian government. On a couple of occasions, the ELF and Eritrea Jihad were using Sudanese-supplied landmines and other weapons to destroy trucks carrying Sudanese supplies destined for the EPLF. Realism dictated that Khartoum focus its support on the EPLF, especially after the latter's Asosa Operation. From about 1990–2 security cooperation between Sudan and the EPLF was extremely good. President Isseyas even employed Sudanese security officers.

After liberation, discontent resurfaced in the Eritrean lowlands. The EPLF failed to make serious headway among the lowland communities. It did not provide political space for their leaders, and most of those who joined the government and party were quickly relegated to marginal positions. Meanwhile, the fragmentation of command and the over-confidence of Sudanese foreign policy decision-making meant that the policy of supporting Islamist organisations was resurrected. From 1993 onwards, a low-level insurrection in the Eritrean lowlands gathered pace. Among the guerrillas were Islamists, including Arab 'Afghans'.

President Isseyas Afewerki reacted rapidly and decisively. In January 1994 he condemned Khartoum, and thereafter announced that the Sudan government would be overthrown within a year. Eritrea began training SPLA forces in Southern Sudan almost immediately, while also training the guerrillas of the Beja Congress in eastern Sudan, followed by the creation of SPLA's 'New Sudan Brigade'. Eritrea's strategy was political as well as military: it brought together the SPLA and Sudan's northern opposition parties to create an expanded and potentially effective National Democratic Alliance (NDA), with military forces. In an act of calculated insult, the Eritrean President cut off diplomatic relations with Sudan and handed over the Sudanese embassy in Asmara to the NDA. The political efforts culminated in June 1995 with the Asmara conference which brought together all the parties to the NDA, which adopted a common political programme. It was a triumph for Eritrea.

From 1990 to 1995 Khartoum was the favoured destination for a host of international Islamic militants. There were several training camps, for example at Soba, where Illich Ramirez Sanchez, *alias* 'Carlos the Jackal' *alias* 'Sheikh Hussein', and other specialists in terrorist methods were stationed. In September 1994 a number of the operatives were dispersed throughout the region, under various covers including Sudan Airways and Islamic philanthropic agencies. After June 1995 substantial parts of the network were exposed, and the militants sought other means. For example, there was a somewhat clumsy plan to murder President Isseyas, to be carried out by a single assassin, Nasr el Din Abu Khairayat. He was intercepted and gave an account of the covert network.

By 1996 western Eritrea was becoming increasingly dangerous, with landmines laid on roads and other guerrilla attacks. Movement was possible only by armed convoy. A series of offensives in January-March 1997, led by SPLA forces but using the Beja Congress for local intelligence, and backed up by the Eritrean Defence Force, resulted in the border becoming sealed against infiltration from Sudan. The Sudan government counter-attacked in April, but much improved security had been attained in western Eritrea.

Asmara's stance must also be seen in the context of the EPLF leadership's bid for a regional role. President Isseyas saw himself as the most effective political-military leader in the region, and recognised a natural ally in Rwanda's Paul Kagame. In 1996–7 Eritrea became deeply involved in Rwanda's Zaire campaign and subsequent political and diplomatic attempts to reconstitute the Democratic Republic of Congo.

Ethiopia was slower to move towards confrontation with Sudan than either Uganda or Eritrea, but when it did move, its role was potentially decisive. The events surrounding the EPRDF victory in May 1991 provide an important background to what subsequently happened. The EPRDF campaign that overran most of central Ethiopia and culminated in the occupation of Addis Ababa was supported by the EPLF, and utilised Sudanese-supplied fuel. One of Sudan's major aims was to dislodge the SPLA, hoping that withdrawal of Ethiopian support would lead the movement to collapse. The EPRDF was happy to receive Sudanese backing, but cautious about getting too involved in the Sudanese civil war. However, repeated attempts to open a dialogue between the EPRDF and the SPLA, with the aim of securing protection for the Sudanese refugees in their camps in Gambella, all foundered on the refusal of the SPLA leader to contemplate the fall of the Dergue and the need to talk to its adversaries. John Garang was loyal to Mengistu Haile Mariam to a fault. In fact he was more loyal than most of Mengistu's own officers, who surrendered in May 1991, while the SPLA fought on in Gambella for a further two months, suffering heavy losses in its battles with the advancing

EPRDF. The fact that some Mengistu stalwarts fled to Southern Sudan and took refuge with the SPLA and even made some half-hearted attempts to invade Ethiopia from SPLA-controlled territory did not help mend fences. In 1992 the EPRDF allowed the Sudanese army to use Ethiopian territory to attack the SPLA—in fact it even provided an advance guard to secure the first kilometre of Sudanese territory.

As with Eritrea, security cooperation was extremely good. Ethiopian dissidents in Sudan were in danger of being detained and shipped to Ethiopia. Sudan established a consular office in Gambella, which also served as an intelligence office for keeping tabs on the SPLA, and investigating the potential for Islamist mobilisation in southern Ethiopia.

Ethiopian calculation of its national security interest has been consistently been conventionally realist, under successive regimes of contrasting ideological colour. Once it had secured itself in power, the foreign policy of the EPRDF government assumed many continuities with its predecessor's regime. The Ethiopian calculation is that the strategic threat to the country is presented by Egypt, whose politics have been structured around its desire to control the headwaters of the Nile, and which has therefore sought to isolate Ethiopia and prevent an alliance of the states in the Horn from emerging to challenge its subregional hegemony. Ethiopia has also consistently sought to prevent militant Islam from getting control of any state in the Horn. Ethiopia was therefore concerned about the possible threat of a militant Islamic government in Khartoum, even before the Bashir regime became actively engaged in destabilising Ethiopia. The first Ethiopian contacts with the SPLA were opened in 1993: the leadership decided that the collapse of the SPLA (which then seemed a distinct possibility) would not be in Ethiopia's interest. The first covert military advice to the SPLA was set in train. However, the two military officers sent to assess the capacity of the SPLA returned with a very discouraging report. They were impressed with the courage of the troops but dismayed by the poor command and control. Professionally, the Ethiopian military was reluctant to become involved with the SPLA. Politically, the need for a counter-balance to the dominance of the NIF prevailed. In 1994 a small-scale training programme was begun, starting with the basics: the preparation of training manuals for NCOs. Meanwhile, Eritrea was pressuring Ethiopia to upgrade its operations against Khartoum.

Also in 1993 Sudan asked the IGAD (Inter-governmental Authority on Development) countries to take over the mediation in the civil war from the Nigerian-led effort, which had not succeeded. Bashir's calculation was that with Ethiopia and Eritrea friendly and Kenya neutral, IGAD would be a sympathetic forum. Ethiopia and Eritrea took the lead in drafting the IGAD Declaration of Principles (DoP), which contained the declaration that religion and the state should be separate and that Southern Sudan was entitled to self-determination. This was a much more balanced DoP than the Sudan government was expecting, and the Khartoum delegation promptly walked out of the peace talks when it was tabled in May 1994. The lukewarm pursuit of peace through IGAD was the chief non-military plank of the strategy of what became known as the 'front-line states'.

As with Eritrea and Uganda, however, it was the Sudanese Islamists' assertive export of their revolution that was the main factor driving the breakdown in relations. Khartoum fostered ties with a number of existing groups, most of them founded during the multi-ethnic guerrilla struggles against the Dergue. Some already had Islamist leanings, in others they encouraged Islamism, with varying degrees of success. Among these groups were the Oromo Liberation Front (OLF), the Islamic Front for the Liberation of Oromia, the Ogaden National Liberation Front (ONLF), the Beni Shangul Liberation Front and al Itihaad al Islami. With the partial exception of the last, each of these was an organisation that had emerged during the 1970s and '80s, primarily in resistance to the Dergue, and which articulated local or (in the terminology of revolutionary Ethiopia) 'national' grievances.

The OLF was by far the most significant of these. It developed from Oromo nationalist movements in the 1960s and '70s, crystallising as an organisation in 1974. In important respects the OLF was a diverse organisation, whose central committee was poorly coordinated and unable to exercise control over its political and military wings. Some of its membership overlapped with the All-Ethiopia Socialist Movement (MEISON), which was co-opted and later destroyed by the Dergue. Most of the Front opted for guerrilla struggle and in the late 1970s and early 1980s it controlled substantial swathes of territory in south-eastern Ethiopia. (Africa Watch 1991: 82–94) It gained significant support from the Somali government. In 1981 it opened a front in western Ethiopia from bases in Sudan, where it operated in territory with both Muslim and Christian Oromos. While the OLF ideology is secular nationalism—it seeks an independent Oromia or at the minimum much stronger Oromo representation in government—regional and religious factors have at times divided its leadership. Oromo nationalism has at times identified Islam as a mobilising factor, and some of its members have had Islamist leanings.

In 1991–2 the OLF joined the EPRDF-led Transitional Government of Ethiopia, but then walked out accusing the government of rigging elections. (Leenco 1999) It engaged in armed insurrection, mostly in eastern Ethiopia, in 1992–5 but was largely defeated by Ethiopian government forces. Thereafter, some OLF forces resorted to terrorism, planting bombs in Addis Ababa hotels and restaurants, while others regrouped in Sudan and Somalia. In the case of Sudan, an OLF contingent was supported by the Sudan government in the mid-1990s, before being disbanded under pressure from the Ethiopian government. In the case of Somalia, OLF alliances with other rebel groups (ONLF, al Itihaad al Islami) and subsequently support from Eritrea kept its military activities alive, though small-scale.

The Islamic Front for the Liberation of Oromia (IFLO) was founded by Sheikh Jarra in 1985 as a breakaway faction of the OLF. It also received assistance from Somalia and at some moments in the late 1980s was reported to be conducting more military operations than the OLF. The 'Islamic' in its title is primarily opportunistic: it proved a useful means of obtaining financial support from Saudi Arabia and the Gulf states. The ONLF is founded among the Ogaden clan of Ethiopia's Somali population, a group that sees itself as consistently repressed by central governments in Ethiopia. It has no specific Islamist leanings, but at times in the late 1990s came to rely on al Itihaad al Islami for financial assistance. The Beni Shangul Liberation Front was an insubstantial group founded in the 1980s and based in the lowland area of Ethiopia bordering Sudan. Most of its leaders were Sudanese-educated.

For all groups with grievances against the Ethiopian government, Sudan was a natural place to look for support. The Horn had a well-established tradition whereby 'my enemy's enemy is my friend', and groups of any ideological inclination ready to oppose Addis Ababa were ready to seek assistance from Khartoum. In the years 1993–5, when Sudan's foreign policy was highly ideologically coloured, an 'Islamic' label was all that was required to gain that assistance, and thereafter, any insurgent group was entertained. The face they presented to Khartoum was likely to be very different to that they presented to their supporters: to the former they would exaggerate their constituency and their military prowess, and emphasise their Islam, while to the latter they would play on local grievances and aspirations.

The Ethiopian government regarded these threats as containable, at least until 1995. One reason for this was that senior members of the EPRDF remained on close terms with their counterparts in the NIF and the Sudanese security services. They were confident that Khartoum would not cross the line from tolerating troublemakers into active destabilisation. Addis Ababa had a sense that support for terrorism was not state policy in Khartoum, or at least that those supporting it would be marginalised over time. Events such as the handover of Carlos the Jackal to France in 1994 seemed to indicate the basic pragmatism of the Sudan government.

This changed abruptly with the attempted assassination of Husni Mubarak as he attended an OAU summit in Addis Ababa in June 1995. The assassination was an al Gama'a al Islamiyya operation conducted with the support of al Qa'ida and certain key individuals in the Sudanese apparatus. It appears that the high-ranking Sudanese officials facilitated the assassination by bypassing the established security agencies, using personal networks for planning and da'waist agencies as cover. Some of the key generals and security officers were completely in the dark, and indeed had given their personal assurances to their Ethiopian counterparts that the OAU summit would pass off without incident.

Ethiopia was shocked by the assassination attempt and felt humiliated. The strategy of relying on one faction in Khartoum to keep control of another had failed spectacularly. Thereafter, Khartoum would no longer be given the benefit of any doubt: it had to prove that it was not sponsoring terrorism. Ethiopia decided that it could not distinguish between different components of the government: all were to be held equally responsible. President Bashir took some steps to remove or marginalise the most prominent individuals widely suspected of being involved in the assassination attempt, but there was no internal purge, let alone a palace coup. To the contrary, the policy of regional confrontation escalated. Some significant terrorist operations—such as the despatch of Nasr el Din Abu Khaiyarat to Eritrea, the escalation of bombings in Uganda and Ethiopia, and two aircraft hijackings (to Egypt and Eritrea)—were carried out after June 1995.

Ethiopia stepped up its military engagement with Sudan. Its first operation was undertaken to prevent the defeat of the SPLA in Equatoria. This, the Parajok operation of October 1995, was jointly planned and implemented by Eritrean, Ethiopian and Ugandan forces under the command of a senior Ethiopian officer. The training of SPLA forces in Ethiopia was resumed, with more than ten battalions trained and despatched to various fronts. In February 1996 the SPLA and Ethiopian military jointly occupied Yabus at the very southern tip of Southern Blue Nile, and destroyed a Sudanese airborne counter-offensive. The strategic plan was to expand northwards to occupy Southern Blue Nile, open a land corridor across to South Kordofan, and thereby create a new front line some 1,000 km. north of Equatoria. This would have cut the Sudan government's supply lines into the South and also prevented the development of the oilfields. Unfortunately it also involved cutting a deal with Lam Akol, who controlled the intermediate territory in Upper Nile, and the SPLA leadership baulked at this and halted the operation in November 1996. The Ethiopians also invited smaller contingents of the Umma Party, Democratic Unionist Party and Sudan Alliance Forces (SAF) to open bases in western Ethiopia, just north of the Blue Nile, and the SAF established a small 'liberated area' in Menza in 1997.

The most imminent threat to Ethiopia's security was from the eastern, Somali frontier. In July 1996 there was an assassination attempt against the Minister of Transport and Communications, Abdel Majid Hussein. The minister was struck down by six bullets stepping out of his office in Addis Ababa in August 1996, and was very fortunate to survive. Two of his bodyguards died. It was widely believed that al Itihaad al Islami, with its connections to ONLF and OLF, was responsible. Among the guerrilla forces active in Ethiopia in the 1990s, al Itihaad is a special case, and it is described in more detail below and in Chapter 4. For the purposes of this narrative, it is important to note that Ethiopia's response to the threat posed by al Itihaad was to despatch its forces across the border into Gedo region of Somalia, attacking al Itihaad's bases in Dolo and Luuq in August 1996. Partly for that reason, and partly because heavy rainfall made military operations difficult, its engagement in Sudan was limited during the summer of 1996. Meanwhile, a more ambitious war plan was being put together by the Eritrea-to-Rwanda axis of the 'front-line states', a group sometimes dubbed the 'new leaders'.

Over the previous two years, since the Rwandese Patriotic Front (RPF) had taken power in Kigali in the wake of the genocide of the Rwandese Tutsis and moderate Hutus, General Paul Kagame had joined the emergent club of the front-line states. A common threat from Sudan had already brought Uganda into coalition with Eritrea and Ethiopia; they were now joined by Rwanda. The former Rwandese army and Interahamwe militia were not only threatening Rwanda, but Uganda also. The emergence of the ADF in Zairean territory, sponsored by Sudan, indicated that Uganda and Rwanda were threatened by an axis of Khartoum-Kinshasa-Goma (the latter being the headquarters of the former Rwandese *génocidaires*). The leaders of the front-line states shared a common set of enemies and were joint inheritors of a tradition of armed liberation struggle. Ethiopia dispatched forces to the UN contingent in Rwanda, and both Eritrea and Ethiopia began training the Rwandese Patriotic Army, now the country's national army.

The axis of front-line states became a close operational coalition following a meeting in Kampala in October 1996, attended by the chiefs of staff of the four countries, senior security officers and Paul Kagame himself. Out of that arose a grand strategy, at once for pre-empting the Khartoum-Kinshasa-Goma axis and for promoting the common political agendas of the Asmara-to-Kigali axis of states. Subsequently, this was seen as a US-backed conspiracy, but in reality the United States came late to a coalition forged from common interest and force of circumstance.

The depth and coordination of this coalition are of interest, as are the differences among its members. The military and political operations that were implemented in the ensuing year combined both strategic aggression and improvisation. Let us turn to an overview of the military operations that ensued. These marked the turning point in the regional war, putting the Asmara-to-Kigali access on the strategic offensive.

The first priority was the Rwandese *génocidaires*' camps in Kivu, eastern Zaire. The second priority was raising the military pressure on Sudan as part of a longer-term aim of imposing a new government in Khartoum. The latter aim was overtaken, in part, by the decision to take the Kivu operation up to Kinshasa itself. The Kivu operation began in October 1996 and escalated with the attack on the base of the former Rwandese army at Mugunga in November. The RPF was in the lead, with a company of Eritrean commandos in support. It appears that the Rwandese requested Eritrean rather than Ethiopian assistance because they suspected, correctly, that Eritrea would be more ready to take the war to another level. Following its early successes, Rwanda decided to take the war beyond Kivu and to overrun the whole of Zaire. And indeed Eritrea played a significant military and political role in putting Laurent Kabila in power in Kinshasa. Meanwhile, in an augury for some of the splits that would later rend the coalition, Rwanda criticised Uganda for its lack of zeal in the Zairean operation.[15]

Uganda's involvement was across its own borders to the west and north. This requires us to pick up the story of the ADF, whose first serious attack on Uganda was staged on 13 November 1996, the same day that

---

[15] This criticism has some ironies as many of the Rwandese commanders were formerly officers in the NRA, and at least one senior officer in the RPF who led one of the brigades that captured Kinshasa was purely Ugandan.

the Rwandese troops crossed the border to attack Mugunga. Clearly, this timing was not just fortuitous. The Ugandan army responded by invading Zaire, where it remained up till 2003. Meanwhile, it also played a supporting role in an offensive into Sudanese territory, alongside SPLA forces and under Ethiopian command, and using Ethiopian mechanised forces and heavy weapons. The first target of this operation was Yei, in central Equatoria, and the rationale for the attack and its timing was to place Ugandan forces in a strategic position to cut off a planned Sudanese army advance into Zairean territory.[16] Sudan had openly threatened to invade in December 1996, and had bombed the Ugandan border garrison at Moyo in September. This had given Museveni the pretext he needed for issuing a counter-threat to invade Sudan. Thereafter, most Ugandan operations were targeted at airfields in north-eastern Zaire/ Democratic Republic of Congo, with the aim of preventing Sudanese flights bringing supplies to the ADF. For two years the ADF continued to pose a serious threat in western Uganda, but by 1999 it was facing defeat.[17]

Hence the SPLA capture of Yei in February 1997 must be seen primarily as an operation to protect the flanks of the alliance thrust into Zaire. There was much speculation at the time that the SPLA would continue and capture Juba, and indeed John Garang made the somewhat premature statement that the war was now 'over'. As will be evident, the alliance's objective was not Juba at all: had they intended to capture the city they would probably have sent a force up the east bank of the Nile as well. Moreover, the Ethiopians considered that the time was not yet ripe for the SPLA to capture the city, while the Ugandans calculated that the casualties would be too great.

By this time the Ethiopians had already launched a joint military operation in Sudan alongside the SPLA. This was a swift incursion into Southern Blue Nile by a mechanised force that captured Kurmuk and Geissan in a single day, and so panicked the Sudanese army that it began to evacuate Damazin. Had the force commander wanted to occupy the town he could have done it. John Garang called the BBC from the area

---

[16] The Yei operation does not appear to have been a major part of the initial plan of action, but was decided upon later when Prime Minister Meles Zenawi visited Uganda, meeting with President Museveni in Gulu.

[17] After the outbreak of the second Congo war in 1998, Sudan became directly involved with a brigade in the DRC itself, as well as persuading Libya to finance and deploy a Chadian brigade. These forces fought on the side of the Kabila government, clashing with Ugandan forces, most notably at Businga in February 1999. Later in that year, both Sudan and Chad withdrew their forces.

and announced the total success of 'Operation Black Fox'. As with Yei, the Ethiopians were happy to have him take the credit. They had sent a message to Khartoum. The SPLA remained in control of the area.

Shortly afterwards, the Sudan government removed the OLF from the area and invited Ethiopian security to inspect the evacuated bases. The operations were also a challenge to Bashir to adopt a policy of good neighbourliness, and to agree to resume peace negotiations. This military pressure undoubtedly provoked the concessions that the Sudan government made during 1997. First it signed the Khartoum Agreement with the SSIM of Riek Machar in March, in which it agreed to self-determination for Southern Sudan including a referendum on unity or secession (a formula repeated shortly afterwards in the Fashoda Agreement with the SPLA-United of Lam Akol). Second, it returned to the IGAD forum, signing the Declaration of Principles (although, it later said, as an agenda for discussion rather than a blueprint for a settlement). The military pressure probably also hastened the split between Bashir and Turabi, although that was not one of its aims. Meanwhile Sadiq el Mahdi escaped from Khartoum to Asmara in March 1997.

Further to the north, there were joint military operations in eastern Sudan by NDA forces (the majority of them the SPLA's 'New Sudan Brigade') supported by Eritrean advisers and a surprisingly small number of Eritrean troops. There was some puzzlement at why the NDA with Eritrean support did not try to capture Kassala or even the small town of Tokar. Possibly the Eritrean army was unenthusiastic about fighting in Sudan. Alternatively, the leadership may have been preoccupied with advancing on Kinshasa. Lastly, the Eritreans were well aware that capturing a major northern Sudanese city such as Kassala would either provoke the fall of the Sudan government or bring other Arab countries into the war, and they were not ready for either. Although Eritrea was more aggressive in its rhetoric than Ethiopia, it was also politically wedded to the NDA (having sponsored the 1995 Asmara Conference) and was not ready to precipitate the downfall of the Sudan government until the NDA was ready to take over—which it clearly was not.

Khartoum protested that it had been invaded by Ethiopia and Eritrea. Such was Sudan's international isolation, and such was US complicity in the alliance's activities that its complaints were dismissed out of hand. Bashir had no international forum in which to argue his case.

Hence, in the early months of 1997 the front-line states had Khartoum by the throat. They let the opportunity pass: they believed time was on their side. The military situation was well under control, with more forces being trained. Sudan was in financial meltdown. The main challenge was creating political unity in the Sudanese opposition, while the next round of offensives was planned, which would have consolidated the SPLA's control over virtually the whole of Southern Sudan. The wisdom of allowing the opposition to mature rather than having victory handed to it on a plate seemed to be vindicated by the erratic behaviour of Laurent Kabila following his elevation to the presidency in May 1997.

Sudan's escape from isolation, 1998–2001

On 12 May 1998 the entire political landscape in the Horn changed when Ethiopia and Eritrea went to war over the disputed border area of Badme, a piece of rocky territory scarcely big enough to serve as a cemetery for the tens of thousands of young people who were killed on both sides over the following twenty-six months of intermittent slaughter. The war was a political gift for which Khartoum could never have dreamed. Hassan al Turabi was jubilant, saying that Allah had intervened and the weapons supplied by the Americans to Ethiopia and Eritrea were now being used by these countries against each other.[18] The two governments separately sought rapprochement with Khartoum. Ethiopia, which had never broken off diplomatic relations, and which had always continued some security dialogue, upgraded its relations first. It did so cautiously, still allowing the SPLA forces in Blue Nile to use its territory as a base for supplies, and even putting its own forces on standby to intervene in support of the SPLA in March 1999. But Ethiopia quickly withdrew its support from the Northern Sudanese dissident forces which had bases in Ethiopia. The most significant of these was the SAF, whose close alignment with the Eritrean leadership caused suspicion in Addis Ababa. Ethiopia closed the SAF's facilities and later ordered it to leave; in late 2000 it intervened militarily against the SAF in Menza and imprisoned some of its members.

Sudan's success in building its oil pipeline and exporting its first oil in August 1999 also had implications for Ethiopia. One reason was that the Ethiopian region of Gambella is an extension of the same oil-bearing geological formation as Southern Sudan. There is oil under Gambella, but it is only commercially viable to pump it out through Sudan—build-

---

[18] It was also a personal testament to the prescience of the Sudanese ambassador to Addis Ababa, Osman Sayyed, who had long warned the Ethiopian government that President Isseyas was unpredictable and might attack it, 'closing the circle', having already sent his troops into Djibouti, Yemen and Sudan in his seven years as president.

ing a separate pipeline would be disproportionately expensive. Another reason is that Ethiopia's cash flow was severely squeezed during the war, a problem worsened by the high price of fuel on world markets and the high fuel consumption of the army. In May 2000 Sudanese fuel assisted the Ethiopian army's decisive offensive against Eritrea.

Eritrea re-established relations with Sudan, though more slowly and with less clarity. For a while it seemed as though President Isseyas was ready to fight both Ethiopia and Sudan at the same time. But the need for a friendly western neighbour while he faced the immediate and over-whelming threat of Ethiopia meant that relations were normalised. The first chance occurred in the context of a peace proposal arising from the second NDA Congress in Massawa, Eritrea, in September 2000. Although the peace plan died a rapid death, contacts between Asmara and Khartoum intensified. Subsequently, the Sudanese embassy was returned to the Sudanese government, roads were opened, and NDA military activities scaled back (with a few notable exceptions such as the November 2000 attack on Kassala).

The IGAD peace process had been one arm of the Ethio-Eritrean strategy on Sudan. As the military pressure mounted, the Sudan government was more and more ready to negotiate within the IGAD process and accept the IGAD Declaration of Principles as the outline of a settlement. Khartoum saw, with some justification, that a peace deal of this kind would be little more than a negotiated surrender of its principles, leaving it with a share in power as compensation for abandoning its political programme and ideology. Though there was no secretariat or negotiating procedure, the IGAD process did have serious political weight behind it, and had Khartoum and the SPLA agreed that the time was ripe for negotiation, the interest and leverage were there for bringing about an agreement. After May 1998 the IGAD peace process simultaneously became more politically even-handed and lost its momentum. In 1999, at the instigation of both the member states and foreign donors, the IGAD Sudan Peace Secretariat was set up in Nairobi under Kenyan control. The preferred language to describe this was 'revitalised', but in fact the new procedure was almost completely paralysed. The US government, which could have pushed the peace process forward more vigorously, preferred to support the front-line states with a low-key approach.

The Ethio-Eritrean war had two other major implications for the narrative of militant Islamism in the Horn. One is the intensification of the conflict between Ethiopia and Somalia, focused on al Itihaad al Islami, and the second is the reassertion of the role of Egypt. In both cases, we see *Realpolitik* taking precedence over ideology.

In 1996 al Itihaad was a significant insurgent force, capable of mounting small-scale but deadly operations in Ethiopia. It had financial and military links to international Islamic militants including, it is probable, al Qa'ida. The Ethiopian military's attack on Luuq destroyed what appeared to be an international training camp for militants. The defence of the town was organised by a small group of non-Somalis, displaying considerable military skill. Eighteen 'white' men—probably Arabs or Pakistanis—were known to have been killed, plus others who were drowned in the Jubba river. Thereafter, al Itihaad's insurgent strategy was to align itself with other groups, notably the ONLF, while keeping a low profile for itself. It no longer maintained permanent camps, with the exception of a presence at Ras Komboni at the southernmost tip of Somalia. Its continuing presence in Somalia was rendered easier by the continuing presence of Ethiopian troops, which were dispatched across the border on several occasions, and took a long-term role in training the Rahanweyn Resistance Army based in the Bay region. This enabled al Itihaad to carve out the political territory of Somali nationalism for itself. In addition, the clumsy Ethiopian handling of a peace gesture by Ogaden elders in 1997 closed the door on a possible reconciliation with the key constituency of Ethiopian Somalis. Feeling humiliated by Addis Ababa, many Ethiopian Ogadenis supported the ONLF and took arms, funds and the Qur'an from al Itihaad.

The Ethiopian strategy at this time was one of containment. But after May 1998 Somalia became a proxy battleground in the war with Eritrea, and Ethiopia's approach was not to take any chances, and instead always to intervene forcefully. Shortly after the war began, the Eritrean government began providing training and arms to OLF units based in Somalia.[19] Several thousand OLF fighters were trained in Eritrea itself and then transported to Somalia. There they shared plans and facilities with the ONLF, and thus al Itihaad. Small units of the OLF and ONLF regularly penetrated into Ethiopia, where they were usually detected and attacked by the Ethiopian army. Meanwhile, the Ethiopians supported 'friendly' factions in Somalia and made it clear that they were ready to use their own troops to intervene, if necessary going right up to Mogadishu itself. To the extent that militant Islamists were sustained in Somalia during this period, and were active in destabilising Ethiopia, it was largely a by-product of the Ethio-Eritrean war. During the conflict, Ethiopian troops also crossed the Kenyan border in pursuit of OLF forces.

[19] Ethiopia for its part was also supporting armed opposition against the Eritrean government.

Sudan supported Islamist groups in Somalia, and along with Djibouti led the way in recognising the Transitional National Government (TNG) in Mogadishu. But it did so with a close eye on its national interest, anxious not to antagonise Ethiopia. Khartoum was fearful that after the Ethio-Eritrean war was over Ethiopia might resume its earlier Sudan policy. In February 2001, three months after the Ethiopian-Eritrean peace agreement was signed in Algiers, Khartoum quickly backed off from support for the TNG. It seems probable that Addis Ababa insisted that Somalia lay primarily within its sphere of influence.

The Egyptian role in the politics of destabilisation in the Horn is curiously lacking in energy. This may appear puzzling given the fact that radical Egyptian Islamists were based in Sudan from 1990 onwards and that one of these groups tried to assassinate the Egyptian President a few years later. In fact it was quite consistent with Egyptian state policy. Cairo treated the security threat from the Islamists based in Sudan as precisely that—a security threat. Hence its policies were an extension of its domestic strategy of dealing with militant Islam solely as a security problem. In parallel, President Mubarak accommodated the wider Islamist agenda, both in Egypt and in Sudan. Meanwhile Cairo's policy towards the Horn of Africa stayed locked in traditional *Realpolitik*, which meant it would follow a kind of 'dual containment' aimed at both Sudan and the Asmara-Addis-Kampala axis. From 1990 until 1998 Egypt found itself in the historically unprecedented situation of having no real influence in any of the countries of the Horn: Sudan was led by radical Islamists, the Ethio-Eritrean axis was implicitly hostile, and the 1992–3 intervention in Somalia had failed. Egypt had no means of responding to this potentially strategic threat to its interests. It was not ready to support the Sudanese opposition—it hosted many NDA leaders but provided them with no political backing to speak of (and occasionally rendered some of them *persona non grata*), and did not contemplate supporting the guerrilla struggle of the Beja, whose territory abuts Egypt.

Historically Egypt regards Sudan as a 'lost territory' rather than as a foreign country. Egyptians have boasted that no government has come to power in Khartoum without their assent. Indeed this is the way in which Egypt exerts its influence: through the army and security forces. The Islamisation of the armed forces after 1989, and the dispersal of security authority among different agencies, made it far more difficult for Egypt to use its traditional means of making and unmaking governments.[20]

[20] Nonetheless, Mubarak threatened to overthrow Bashir after June 1995.

Throughout the mid-1990s the Egyptian government was engaged in a fierce struggle with its militant Islamist enemies, notably al Gama'a al Islamiyya and Tanzim al Jihad. Assassinations of senior government officials and the murder of the secularist writer Farag Foda marked the early stages of this campaign, and the mass murder of tourists at Luxor on 17 November 1997 marked its last and biggest atrocity. In the intervening years there was a guerrilla insurrection in the mountains and irrigated fields of upper Egypt, with the security forces taking ruthless measures against the militants. At least 1,200 were killed. Cairo often blamed Sudan for sponsoring the insurgents, and more than 200 were detained in July 1995; in January 1996 six were sentenced to death, accused of having smuggled weapons from Sudan with intent to carry out terrorist attacks, and duly executed in July. From August 1994 onwards Egypt began moving its forces into disputed Halaib area on the Red Sea Coast. Initially it sealed the border, and then used its ability to occupy Halaib as a means of punishing Khartoum, and ultimately it annexed the territory.

If Cairo was fearful of radical Islam in Sudan, it was also worried by the front-line states, which controlled the sources of the Nile—a question of national survival for Egypt. Egyptian policies towards its southern neighbours are dominated by the hydro-politics of the Nile Valley. Approximately three-quarters of the Nile waters originate in Ethiopia, but Egypt is entitled by the 1959 Nile Waters Agreement to utilise 55.5 cubic km. of water, about two thirds of the river's total flow. By the late 1980s Egypt was exceeding its quota, and its demand continued to grow, driven by an expanding population and ambitious land reclamation projects. Under the 1959 agreement, upstream states can only utilise water with the prior agreement of Cairo. However, Ethiopia never signed, and Egypt has been fearful of Ethiopia using the Nile waters for its own development, or becoming the hub of a coalition of states that control the river's headwaters. At worst, this has been a kind of zero-sum game, aimed at keeping Ethiopia weak by supporting its neighbours' efforts at destabilising it. At best, it has been a policy of go-slow cooperation. Thus the Asmara-to-Kampala axis was bad enough: its saving grace was that it was in conflict with Khartoum. Had the axis gained the controlling influence in Khartoum, the basic premise of Egypt's *Realpolitik* would have been stood on its head.

Egypt was trapped, and its response was to focus on neutralising the threat posed by its own radical Islamists who had taken up residence in Sudan. Using the UN Security Council sanctions, imposed after the assassination attempt against Mubarak, Egypt pursued this. Co-operating with

Saudi Arabia and the United States, it ensured that the most prominent foreign militants were identified and expelled from Sudan. Usama bin Laden was the most famous of these, leaving in May 1996, but many others also departed for Afghanistan. Cairo was reverting to its traditional policy of cooperating with Sudanese security. Egypt also made clear its hostility to Hassan al Turabi, but it had no means of effectively intervening in Sudan's domestic politics. When Turabi was removed in December 1999, Egypt welcomed and supported the move, but it was essentially an internal struggle resolved internally.

The Ethio-Eritrean war created an opening for Egypt. It exploited it, like a python that squeezes each time its victim exhales. Initially, it cynically tried a game of divide-and-rule in the Horn, hinting at sympathies for Eritrea. However, its major role was to take advantage of the way in which Sudan was released from its IGAD trap. The spark for this was Sadiq el Mahdi's request to the Libyan government that it open a channel for communication between the NDA and the Sudan government.[21] When the Libyans did this in August 1999, the Egyptians joined them and soon became the senior partner. This Joint Libyan-Egyptian Initiative for Reconciliation in Sudan (to give it the title it most commonly uses for itself) focused on political reconciliation among the Northern political parties and objected to the principle of self-determination for Southern Sudan. But it has not been institutionalised or formalised. It issued a nine-point statement in 2001, but has not been pushed consistently or energetically. Its main role has been to stake out the Egyptian position that no agreement should be reached over Sudan without the consent of Egypt.

Egypt's policy towards Sudan since 1989 has reflected Egypt's own ambivalence towards political Islam. While fighting the violent manifestations of Islamism, Husni Mubarak has allowed Islamists to set the tone for the political climate in the country. While Sudan presented a clear and present security danger to Egypt, Egypt was resolutely hostile—even though it may not have had the means to respond decisively. Once key individuals had been removed from Sudan, such as the leading militants of al Gama'a al Islamiyya, Cairo had no problem with a government in Khartoum that imposed *shari'a* law, promoted *da'wa* and even fought a civil war in the South in the name of Islam.

---

[21] The NDA was excluded from the IGAD process, initially for the historical reason that it had no real presence when IGAD was established in 1993–4, and subsequently because of objections from Khartoum, which was using every means to slow down the process. Later, the IGAD Sudan Peace Secretariat also objected on the curious grounds that it would 'complicate' the peace process.

US policies: searching for coherence

The final piece of the story of regional conflict and destabilisation is the role of the United States. During the 1990s the sole military action in Khartoum was a missile attack by the US government, in which the al Shifa pharmaceutical factory was destroyed. Especially in the aftermath of this attack, US policy towards Sudan excited a great deal of controversy and no little posturing. This, the final section of this chapter, tries to place the US policy within the framework set by the structure of Sudanese jihadism, the roles of the front-line states, and the unrelenting logic of events.

In confronting the United States at the time of the Gulf War, Hassan al Turabi expected a contest in which his adversary would be resolute and cunning, but the Islamists would ultimately prevail. He was wrong on both counts. US policy towards Sudan during the Clinton Administration was ineffectual, but ultimately prevailed in its minimum agenda simply because US power is so great.

United States policy evolved over the decade. The United States had been frustrated with the weakness of the Sadiq el Mahdi government, to the extent of even hinting that it would welcome a coup.[22] After the coup, various sanctions automatically came into force, on account of the overthrow of an elected government and human rights abuses. But dialogue was maintained, with a peace plan floated in early 1990. Khartoum's support for Iraq in the Gulf War caused a cutback in embassy staff and accelerated an already decreasing level of aid. The execution of Sudanese employees of USAID in Juba in July 1992 contributed to a strong Congressional resolution on human rights. A major US concern was humanitarian access in Southern Sudan, with various plans floated including safe havens for civilians. Support for the SPLA was not seriously entertained because at this time the movement was engaged in a particularly bloody phase of its internecine strife. Meanwhile the convergence of a range of radical Islamists on Khartoum rang alarm bells in the FBI and the CIA and among the State Department's counter-terrorists.

By 1995, not one but two policies had crystallised. One was a framework for pursuing America's regional concerns. This was founded on supporting the 'front-line states' of Eritrea, Ethiopia and Uganda, in their effort to contain Sudanese destabilisation while simultaneously seek-

---

[22] Colin Campbell and Deborah Scroggins, 'Officials: US May Welcome Coup in Sudan; Military Rulers Might Improve Famine Relief,' *Atlanta Journal and Constitution*, 27 January 1989.

ing a peace settlement through IGAD. The regional specialists at the State Department and National Security Council (NSC) recognised their common interests with the front-line states, agreed in principle with their approach, and recognised the effectiveness of pursuing a regionally-based solution. This policy moved into gear in 1996.

Meanwhile, the Counter-Terrorism Bureau of the State Department and other related agencies had fixed upon a parallel policy with another overriding priority: ending Sudan's hospitality to terrorists. The United States placed Sudan on its list of state sponsors of terrorism in 1993, when the investigation trail into the World Trade Center bombing led to Khartoum. However, US counter-terrorists appear to have found Khartoum to be a useful spot for keeping tabs on Islamic militants, and where necessary keeping contacts with them. Sheikh Omer Abdel Rahman, the Egyptian leader of al Gama'a al Islamiyya who was subsequently convicted of seditious conspiracy to wage a war of urban terrorism against the United States (i.e. 'inspiring' the 1993 World Trade Center bombing), was given the last of his many US visas in Khartoum in 1990. One of the persistent gripes of some American career diplomats is that the closure of their embassy in Khartoum in February 1996 deprived them of excellent sources of information on Islamic militants. Khartoum was particularly important as an intelligence source because of the failure of Saudi Arabia to cooperate with the CIA and FBI investigations into terrorist attacks on US bases in Saudi Arabia, and the absence of any US presence in Afghanistan. The counter-terrorist policy superficially converged with the regional policy in that both were hostile to Khartoum. But getting the two to fit properly was more difficult. Each had different priorities, and the different policymaking units worked largely in mutual isolation.

Although the two policies were in place before the end of the first Clinton Administration, a passionate anti-Khartoum stand became closely identified with the second Clinton Administration, and especially three individuals: Susan Rice (Assistant Secretary of State for Africa from 1996), Gayle Smith (National Security Adviser for Africa from 1998) and John Prendergast (deputising for the other two in different capacities). This troika was undoubtedly influential, and has since become the focus for a somewhat acrimonious debate in Washington policy circles. Without doubt, Susan Rice nursed a personal animosity towards Khartoum that stood in the way of making nuanced judgements and led her to take some provocative actions, such as her visit to SPLA-controlled Southern Sudan in her last weeks in office. This discussion tries to focus on the context and constraints of the policymaking and implementation, which can at least provide a context for assessing whether the Administration's strategy was visionary but unlucky, or intrinsically flawed, or did indeed achieve its core goals.

Initially, US policy was focused on enthusiasm for the new governments in Eritrea, Ethiopia and Uganda, and support for their programmes of regenerating their countries. Backing for their attempts to find a solution to the Sudanese conflict through IGAD naturally followed from this. It was a pro-Ethiopia and Eritrea policy, not an anti-Sudan one (enthusiasm for Uganda was both slower to come and more mixed). This first step, of supporting these so-called 'front-line states', was the critical one. The Administration also became charged with a sense of moral outrage at the 1994 genocide in Rwanda and guilt that the United States had stood by and let this crime be committed, an episode that also evoked memories of its failure to come to the aid of the Eritrean and Tigrayan peoples in the famine of a decade earlier.[23] Supporting governments that are bringing their countries back from the brink of disaster is a generally laudable policy and few begrudged the slack that was cut for these regimes in the early 1990s. Criticising and sanctioning Sudan for its human rights abuses was also unobjectionable, and the moralism that this represented had already become a feature of US policy in Africa in the elder Bush Administration.[24] But this policy began to enter murkier waters when the Sudanese civil war, in parallel with the aftermath of the Rwandese genocide, evolved into the regional conflict outlined above, and Washington's favoured governments took a lead in actively intervening to bring down the Khartoum and Kinshasa regimes. The United States had moved from moralising to actively taking sides.

In designing their strategy for Sudan, the leaders in Asmara, Addis Ababa and Kampala drew from their own experiences of successful guerrilla struggle. They supposed that an alliance of like-minded guerrilla forces could liberate Khartoum and transform the political landscape. But they were also realistic about the frailties of the NDA and the weaknesses of the SPLA, and saw the need to intervene directly them-

---

[23] For Gayle Smith, the 1984–5 famine was a formative episode. It is significant also that Presidential Decision Directive 25, the Administration's misconceived lesson-learning from the Somali debacle, was a principal reason for the refusal to intervene to prevent the 1994 Rwanda genocide. The author of PDD 25 was Susan Rice.

[24] Virtually the first act of Secretary of State James Baker on assuming his position in January 1989 was to call for Sudan to make humanitarian assistance available to the South. Ambassador Melissa Wells in Mozambique was active in pursuit of peace and Ambassador Smith Hempstone in Kenya was outspoken in support of democracy.

selves. And herein lies the key to understanding Washington's policy, as initially conceived. The US Administration was similarly unimpressed by the capacity of the Sudanese opposition, so that its intermediaries were the front-line states themselves, and not the SPLA. After July 1994, the RPF government in Kigali joined the club, and by 1996 Rwandese concerns were taking equal rank with its partners'. Though Washington was neither the architect nor the lead player in the emergent 'grand plan' of the expanded axis of front-line states, it was in the informational loop. In late 1996, it gave a green light to the military interventions and expected the region's governments to deliver. In Zaire/D R Congo, the axis members went further than Washington expected. In Sudan, the irruption of the Ethio-Eritrean war in May 1998 unseated the Administration's strategy.

At the same time—November 1996—the United States announced that it would provide $20 million worth of surplus military supplies to Eritrea, Ethiopia and Uganda. The SPLA and NDA received nothing, but this did not dampen the popular impression (assiduously cultivated by Khartoum) that America was arming the opposition. In July 1997 the United States promised assistance to the opposition-held areas, and in November imposed bilateral sanctions on trade with Sudan. The policy moved to a higher level with a meeting between Madeleine Albright and John Garang and NDA leaders in Uganda on 10 December 1997. America's intentions were made clear in a statement attributed to a senior member of the Administration, speaking anonymously: 'This meeting is a demonstration of support for a [future] regime that will not let Khartoum become a viper's nest for terrorist activities.'[25] The policy was crystallised in the President's visit to Uganda in March 1998. President Isseyas' refusal to attend the regional leaders' summit with Clinton in Entebbe was an augury that all was not well within the coalition, but the following month Clinton 'dropped by' to greet Isseyas when the latter was visiting the State Department in Washington.

No comparable consensus was achieved on Zaire/D R Congo. While some members of the Administration implicitly supported Kagame's Kivu operation, others feared for its consequences. The Americans were in fact stampeded by the French and Canadian governments and a vocal chorus of relief agencies into support for an international intervention force in eastern Zaire in November 1996, but this momentum was overtaken by events when the Rwandese forces overran the *génocidaires*' bases much more quickly than expected and about 600,000 displaced Rwandese

---

[25] 'Quote of the Day,' *The Washington Post*, 11 December 1997, p. A30.

promptly returned home. As the Rwandese-led offensive rapidly overran Zaire, US policymakers were similarly running to catch up with events, and the support they extended to Laurent Kabila was in recognition of a *fait accompli*.[26]

In this context we can turn to the controversial issue of the extent to which Khartoum was ready to cooperate with US counter-terrorist efforts. The most striking incident occurred in March 1996, following a request from the US ambassador, Tim Carney, to the Sudanese government that it should expel Usama bin Laden. Usama's name had first appeared on the list of suspected terrorists in Sudan in 1993, but it had only risen to prominence after the Riyadh truck bomb in November 1995. On 3 March, General El Fathi Erwa (then serving in Khartoum, subsequently Sudanese ambassador to the UN) met with Carney and David Shinn (head of East Africa at the State Department) and reportedly made an offer to hand over Usama bin Laden to the Americans. More contacts followed.[27] However, the State Department and NSC did not consider the 'offer' real—indeed senior members have denied any knowledge of it. (Benjamin and Simon 2002: 246–7) Moreover, the Americans did not have enough evidence to secure a conviction and instead they reportedly proposed that Usama be returned to Saudi Arabia, where the process of dealing with the militant might be more expedited (i.e. King Fahd might have him beheaded). The Saudis had their domestic reasons for not wanting to receive Usama back home: he was too much of a threat. In May, Sudan withdrew its 'offer' and instead Usama departed for Afghanistan with several planeloads of militants, to assist the Taliban to prepare for their final assault on Kabul. It appears that the Sudan Government and its senior officials helped themselves to many of his assets left behind.

In retrospect, taking Usama into US custody would have been justifiable. Even keeping Usama in Sudan might have limited his scope for terrorist action, and left him exposed to surveillance and even extradition at a future date. (It would also have allowed him to maintain and expand his business empire.) Was the great opportunity for preventing September 11

---

[26] One reason for the speed of the offensive was precisely the fear that the US would intervene to halt it, because of strategic or commercial interests. The Eritreans' own experience of presenting the US with a military *fait accompli*, when in May 1991 they compelled the US to reverse its long-standing opposition to Eritrean independence, was also influential in this strategy.

[27] See: Barton Gellman, 'U.S. was Foiled Multiple Times in Efforts to Capture Bin Laden or Have Him Killed,' *Washington Post*, 3 October 2001; David Rose, 'The Osama Files', *Vanity Fair*, January 2002.

missed? This episode raises many questions, most of which cannot be answered.

First, it is important to note that the Sudanese 'offer' could not have been made in wholly good faith. Even if el Fatih Erwa, a non-Islamist career security officer with a history of being close to the CIA,[28] had wanted to hand over Usama, it is virtually certain that more powerful Islamists would have blocked him. At the time, Turabi was bitterly critical of what he saw as a betrayal. The handover of Carlos to France in 1994 is not an indicator of good faith by Khartoum: Carlos was not an Islamist and had no political constituency, he brought no money, and France had a powerful inducement on offer, in the form of satellite images of Southern Sudan. Usama's case was different on all counts—especially the last, as the United States was not going to make any moves towards normalising relations until Khartoum had delivered major progress towards ending its sponsorship of terrorism. Most probably, the Khartoum hardliners knew any such offer would be rejected by both Washington and Riyadh, and allowed the talks to proceed while Usama made other plans.

Second, an exclusive focus on Usama bin Laden overlooks the context of US policy at the time. The Administration's regional policy had a broader agenda, which included seeking a solution to the war through IGAD, stopping threats against US personnel in Khartoum, and promoting human rights and humanitarian access in Southern Sudan.[29] However, it was the Counter-Terrorism Bureau that would have handled any such offer, not the regional specialists in the State Department and NSC. Here we must note that Washington also had a broader *counter-terrorist* agenda, namely ending state sponsorship of terrorism by Sudan. In 1996, Usama bin Laden was one of many prominent terrorists hosted or supported by Sudan, and Washington's strategic concern was to end Khartoum's hospitality for them all, to 'drain the swamp'. Only in exceptional cases was the United States concerned with a single individual—as France was with Carlos—and Usama did not yet fit this bill. Washington's counter-terrorists worked closely with Egypt, which had its own list of named individuals that it wanted expelled—and Usama was not on this list.

---

[28] He was a major operator in the 1984–5 'Operation Moses' that extracted Ethiopian Falasha Jews to Israel through Sudan, and was later a key interlocutor between the General Bashir and the EPLF and EPRDF.

[29] The incident also highlights the different approaches of Egypt and the Asmara-Addis-Kampala axis. The Egyptians wanted individuals expelled from Sudan, the regional axis wanted a broader settlement to the Sudanese problem. The offer came just as the Clinton Administration's second-term team was taking up its posts and deciding on its strategy.

Subsequent to this, the Administration reportedly spurned Khartoum's offers to share intelligence including its files on international terrorists. In April 1997 and again in February 1998, the Sudan government wrote offering the FBI access to data in its possession, using intermediaries.[30] According to Carney, they were rebuffed. Others in the Administration claim that they responded but Khartoum failed to deliver anything. Khartoum wanted some deliverables up front, which Washington would not provide. The situation improved only in 2000, when both parties managed to clarify their positions. The United States was, for the first time, able to coordinate its regional and counter-terrorist policies and offer a framework for how it would respond to Sudanese cooperation. In Khartoum, Bashir deposed Turabi in December 1999, and over the next fifteen months gradually gained more freedom of action, cemented by the jailing of his rival in February 2001. Even more importantly, fifteen senior Islamist military officers, including the pivotal figure of Ibrahim Shams el Din, died when their plane crashed in Upper Nile on 4 April 2001. Only in May 2000 did the United States send its first counter-terrorist experts to Sudan, and then their brief was to investigate whether Sudan was maintaining terrorist training camps, not to examine the Sudanese security agencies' extensive files on al Qa'ida and other terrorist organisations. Sudanese cooperation was hampered by a profound scepticism about whether its opening would be reciprocated. There was simply no mutual trust, and progress was still painfully slow. Khartoum's envoys were full of charm and promise, but the practical outcomes were meagre. Only in the spring of 2001 did cooperation accelerate, as the incoming Bush Administration began a review of Sudan policy. The first US eyes passed over Khartoum's dossiers in the autumn of 2001, and were reportedly impressed by what they found.

Another important decision was to close down the US embassy in Khartoum in February 1996. This was initially mooted in response to threats against the staff there, subsequently shown to have been exaggerated, and followed through because of the Administration's determination to take a strong stand against Sudan. Carney opposed this decision. In retrospect, this was a muddled decision that yielded no benefits, and contributed to real risks.

Another question is: did America actually have the technical capacity to process the information even if it had been provided? Here we should note the critiques of Gerecht (2001) and Baer (2002), which focus on the

---

[30] See David Rose, 'The Osama Files', *Vanity Fair,* January 2002, pp. 70–1.

poor quality of intelligence gathering and processing, including the short-age of Arabic speakers in the US intelligence services. Two incidents indi-cate that disinterest and lack of capacity might have been a constraint. First, when the Ethiopians overran the al Itihaad al Islami base at Luuq in Somalia in August 1996, they captured a trove of documents which they handed over to the Americans. These are reported to have lain un-translated for more than a year. Second, US officials were uninterested in terrorist-related information available from the numerous Sudanese security officers who had defected to the opposition. One of these, who had extensive information about international terrorist networks approached the Americans in 1997, and was rebuffed. The low level of tradecraft in US government institutions will recur as a factor that undermined the Administration's policies. Instead of seeking a scapegoat among policy-makers, perhaps we should seek it in the systemic failures of institutions.

If the aftermath of September 11, obtaining any scrap of information on al Qa'ida became a strategic national priority for the US, and the Clinton Africa team's decisions have been portrayed as the administra-tion's biggest blunder, supposedly committed because key members of the team were viscerally hostile to Khartoum. Could the relationship have been handled more productively? Undoubtedly, yes. It is possible that keeping the embassy open and following up proactively on the offers of opening the files would have yielded key pieces of evidence that could have prevented the August 1998 embassy bombings and even the Septem-ber 11 atrocity. This would have required a more coordinated approach between the regional bureau and the counter-terrorists, to provide Khar-toum with a roadmap towards normalisation. It would have required a less partisan approach by the Assistant Secretary of State for Africa.[31] But it would probably also have needed a more united regime in Sudan in which individuals such as Turabi and Shams el Din could not block coop-eration.

From the viewpoint of 1997, however, the wider US plan for Sudan was on track, courtesy of the active engagement of the axis of front-line states. Having invested time, energy and political capital in reaching a high-level consensus in Washington, Clinton's Africa team was not going to abandon it so quickly even when it was undermined by the Ethio-Eritrean war. But from May 1998 US policy towards Sudan was like a stagecoach missing two of its four horses, and the two most powerful ones

---

[31] Susan Rice and her defenders have also pointed out that some of her accusers are not independent, having taking contracts for the Sudan Government. 'J'accuse', *Elle*, May 2002.

to boot. Its moral and political ambition was now incommensurate with its capacity to deliver. Logically, it should have reconsidered, and invested more energy in the IGAD peace process.

Events, again, intervened. In retaliation for the August 1998 bombings of its embassies in east Africa, the Americans fired cruise missiles and destroyed the al Shifa pharmaceutical factory in Khartoum, alleging it was owned by Usama and was manufacturing chemical weapons. A small circle of senior figures in the Administration took the decision: the regional specialists were not involved. Former NSC officials defend the decision resolutely. (Benjamin and Simon 2002: 351 ff) The key piece of evidence was a soil sample that contained traces of a precursor to the deadly chemical agent VX. This piece of evidence cannot be explained away: something was going on. There is additional circumstantial evidence that Sudan possessed chemical weapons, and well-informed Sudanese security officers concur that they were manufactured in another facility at Hilat Koko, and stored in a military base south of the city. Some have surmised that there could have been cross-contamination of soil near al Shifa by engineers moving between it and other sites such as Hilat Koko. The attack on al Shifa was so precise that only one watchman died and minor damage was inflicted on a nearby biscuit factory. But al Shifa was also, almost certainly, an innocent pharmaceutical factory.[32]

The al Shifa attack raises a number of questions. One set relates to decision-making in Washington. Very few individuals took the decision to strike and made the choice of target. The rationale was wholly within the ambit of counter-terrorism, with little regard to the impact of the US strategy for Sudan and the Horn. By not consulting the regional specialists, the inner circle missed the chance of considering facts relevant to the strike and its likely consequences. Another set of issues, not considered here, concerns the political symbolism of the strike, which was interpreted by many pundits in the 'wag the dog' context. Since September 11 fewer Americans are ready to repeat the allegation that President Clinton merely wanted to distract attention from the Monica Lewinsky scandal. A third issue is the way in which a decision, taken for counter-terrorist reasons, nailed the Administration's colours to the mast: there was now no turning back from the regional policy of confrontation with Khartoum, despite the changing regional realities.

[32] Vernon Loeb, 'A Dirty Business: Because of a cupful of soil, the U.S. flattened this Sudanese factory. Now one of the world's most respected labs, and some of Washington's most expensive lawyers, say Salah Idris wasn't making nerve gas for terrorists, just iboprofen for headaches.' *Washington Post*, 25 July 1999, p. F1.

Technologically 'smart' but politically dumb, the attack turned out to be a major propaganda win for the Sudan government. Among other things, Khartoum now had a card to play at the UN Security Council: demands for an independent inquiry into the attack and compensation. The attack also marks the beginning of the cult of Usama bin Laden, with Pakistani families naming their boys 'Usama' and the production of Usama posters and t-shirts, and more militant jihadists uniting under al Qa'ida's banner (Reeve 1999: 203–4). But the strike also terrified Khartoum. It probably accelerated the opening of the dialogue on counter-terrorism.

After May 1998, reliant on the Sudanese opposition, to a lesser extent the Ugandans, and the United States' own institutions (State Department and USAID), the policy of confrontation with Khartoum was never likely to succeed in its maximum aim of installing a broad-based democratic government. The institutions just could not deliver. The timing was poor, because the State Department was cutting back on its staffing and resources devoted to Africa, and in early 1996 had evacuated all its embassy staff from Khartoum. But even considering the reduced capacity available, the policy was implemented neither smoothly nor effectively: tradecraft was bad. Three examples will suffice.

First, the diplomatic leg of US regional policy—support for the IGAD peace process—remained lame. Rather than taking a leading role, the United States, through its Special Envoy Congressman Harry Johnston, fell in behind the half-hearted efforts of the IGAD countries. It stayed this way until Bush's Special Envoy, Senator Jack Danforth, was appointed in September 2001.

Another example is the State Department's promise of $10 million to support the NDA. This promise was first made in the wake of President Clinton's July 1997 statement on Sudan and a visit by senior officials to Asmara, Addis Ababa and eastern Sudan. President Bashir seized on this and travelled to Qatar, returning with a matching $10 million cheque (and indeed more). But it took until February 2002 for the contract for the first $1 million to be provided to the NDA, and the conditions written into the contract were so onerous that some NDA officials questioned whether it was worthwhile signing up.

A third case is the Sudan Transitional Assistance and Relief (STAR) programme, which was also first floated in June 1997, initially as a means of providing assistance to areas outside Operation Lifeline Sudan, such as the NDA-controlled areas of eastern Sudan and the SPLA-held areas of the Nuba Mountains, as well as providing development assistance to areas in which the SPLA had consolidated its control (O'Toole, Salinas and D'Silva 1999). Envisaged as a rapid and flexible modality for circumventing the problems of the UN-led Operation Lifeline Sudan, STAR quickly became captured by a USAID bureaucracy with its own interests and procedures, and which ended up confounding the higher policy objectives. Some of the middle ranking USAID bureaucrats tasked with putting these ideas into practice were themselves 'captured' by the SPLA and became its uncritical advocates, others were simply incompetent, some were both. It was only in September 2000 that the first assistance began to flow to the Beja areas of eastern Sudan.[33] USAID and its contractor, the International Rescue Committee, then had to begin relearning lessons that had been learned four years earlier when the first cross-border assistance from Eritrea had begun. Unfortunately, in the three years since the idea of STAR had first been envisaged, most of the NDA-controlled territory had been lost to the government, and the Beja Relief Organisation had become demoralised. The case of Menza, an area of Blue Nile controlled by the Sudan Alliance Forces, is even worse. In some respects Menza was a 'model' case of a 'liberated area', with a functioning indigenous relief agency providing micro-credit, a human rights society and a women's co-operative. But despite repeated appeals from the agencies working in this area, STAR staff refused even to recognise the existence of Menza, let alone to plan for relief. SAF and its humanitarian wing, Amal Trust, struggled on but lost most of their territory in 1999 and finally the last forces there surrendered in early 2001, never having received so much as an aspirin from STAR.

The overwhelming focus of STAR was Southern Sudan. Mandated as a mechanism for promoting better administration and civil society, its impact was predictably contrary. It established a joint committee with the SPLA, the Development Assistance Technical Team, that handed a *de facto* veto over its funding practices to the SPLA. America was taking the unprecedented step of treating a rebel movement like a government, except that most aid to government is conditional on a number of demands concerning democracy and human rights. No such conditionality was required of the SPLA, which was thereby encouraged to take a harsh line with international NGOs, insisting on them signing a Memorandum of Understanding that ceded much of their autonomy. STAR allowed the SPLA to set up its own dependent 'civil society' organisations, while undermining the nascent independent ones that had been tentatively emerging. At the outset, USAID recognised the absence of a functioning

---

[33] In a wonderfully-misleading acronym, this programme was called 'SOAR'.

legal system as a major gap in the governance of the SPLA-held areas. In deference to the SPLA, the judiciary programme was treated just like an administrative capacity-building project. STAR and its subcontractor, the British NGO Christian Aid, found themselves supporting a curious programme of so-called 'para-legals'. Nowhere else in the world would US funds have been allowed to support a judicial system that had no pretence to independence and whose chief justice was an appointee of the 'minister of the interior'. When its story is documented, STAR will stand as a textbook case of how external assistance can be co-opted by an authoritarian governance system in order to promote centralisation and undermine civil society, democracy and the rule of law.

And in the case of Southern Sudan, it is uncertain how much US assistance even supported the SPLA's own administrative and military capacity. This points to perhaps the greatest problem with the policy: it risked replicating the failures of the 1980s, when generous and uncritical US assistance to regimes such as Siyaad Barre, Samuel Doe and Jaafar Nimeiri promoted a clientelistic style of governance that eroded legitimacy and capacity.

By the summer of 1998, it was time for the Clinton Administration to reconsider its Sudan policy. But there was no turning back. No-one could admit that al Shifa was a mistake—especially as the evidence for *some* chemical weapons manufacture was so strong. Susan Rice was personally committed to the policy, and the Administration's policy was becoming intimately aligned with a pro-SPLA constituency in Washington. The policy stagecoach having lost its Ethiopian and Eritrean horses, it now acquired a set of powerful and wild steeds: the Congressional anti-Khartoum lobbies. These proved capable of making a lot of noise and rendering it impossible to steer the wagon, but they could not pull it down the road to an alternative government. A coalition of some liberal human rights activists, the Congressional Black Caucus and the religious right (the latter by far the most powerful) brought serious political pressure to bear on the Clinton Administration and then its successor for a hard-line anti-Khartoum policy. This lobby is also well-connected to faith-based humanitarian agencies operating in Southern Sudan, some of them involved in activities such as slave redemption. This environment was a leading factor in determining the implementation of STAR, notably its close relationship with the SPLA. The lobby drafted a Sudan Peace Bill, aiming to provide massive support directly to the SPLA and sanction Khartoum.[34]

---

[34] When finally passed into law in 2002, the Sudan Peace Act was substantially watered down. The assistance authorised was for SPLA-controlled areas rather than the SPLA

The increasing role of the Congressional lobbies shifted the terms of the policy, away from a liberal secularist framework founded on a vision for the 'Greater Horn' to an agenda driven by moral imperative and Christian solidarity. The common basis was recognition of the historical injustice and contemporary suffering undergone by the people of Southern Sudan and the Nuba Mountains. The convergent aim was a change in government in Khartoum. In other respects, the policy had in fact changed. It was in danger of becoming a crusade. And whereas the State Department or NSC can revise its position as circumstances change, a morally-driven lobby is very slow to do so. Relying on the SPLA plus the United States' own policy instruments alone, the policy of confrontation with Khartoum was doomed to fail.

Over the 1990s the United States did however achieve its minimum aim of making it impossible for Sudan to remain as a state sponsor of terrorism. By the late 1990s it was simply too difficult for Sudan to exist as a state and protect terrorists. But, as always in Khartoum, it was difficult for an executive decision to be translated into policy. It was made doubly difficult because certain individuals high up in the state apparatus were personally implicated in support for a number of organisations including al Qa'ida, while the military industrial corporations retained links with Iraq. Between late 1999 and early 2001, some NIF hardliners were dismissed and jailed, and others died in a plane crash. In the summer of 2001, American counter-terrorists concluded that Sudan had passed its test. For Sudan, the bar was raised higher than it had been for countries such as Syria, and there was the additional complication that there was a very powerful Congressional lobby hostile to Khartoum, including the religious right as well as the Black Caucus and human rights activists. By the end of August the United States had decided to abstain at the UN Security Council vote on lifting the UN sanctions on Sudan, scheduled for 17 September. Events, again, intervened.

Conclusion

The basic story of this chapter is that state interest prevailed in the Horn of Africa in the 1990s, and while *jihad* may occasionally be a useful tool, it is ultimately incompatible with the consistent pursuit of state interest. But, nested within this narrative is a contrary sub-plot, which is that local-

---

itself. Capital market sanctions against companies doing business in Sudan were also dropped.

ised grievance and resistance can embrace *jihad* if this obtains it an external sponsor. It is in fact a typically intricate story of a regional conflict,
with a mix of *Realpolitik*, ideology, vision and stupidity, and woven through
with ironies and surprises. In 1991, Sudan and several of its main east
African neighbours were ruled by visionaries, and later in the decade, US
policy adopted some of this visionary outlook. By the end of the decade,
all in the region were concerned overwhelmingly with the calculus of
power, and were ready to compromise principle for the sake of maintaining their grip. Militancy in the Horn of Africa is localised. Ideas of universal *jihad* are alien to the region and were merely passing through in the
1990s. Only in Washington, through the political accident of the religious right fastening onto the Southern Sudanese agenda, was ideology
in the ascendant.

The 1990s in the Horn of Africa also demonstrates that the United
States is ultimately so powerful that its basic interests prevail even when
its policies are poorly-implemented or are founded on unsustainable pre-
mises. America's strategy of fighting terrorism by pressuring its state
sponsors worked in north-east Africa.

The decade also witnessed the coincidence that Islamism's most formidable adversary, leftist revolutionary militarism, rose and fell in syn-
chrony. Just as the Islamist project fell apart, so did the opposing alliance
of former liberation fronts. This is another intriguing parallel between
revolutionary leftism and militant Islamism.

7

AFRICA, ISLAMISM AND AMERICA'S 'WAR ON TERROR'

Alex de Waal and A. H. Abdel Salam

After September 11, 2001, much has changed and much has remained the same. The story of the succeeding eighteen months in north-east Africa is in part one of the conflicts and uprisings that did not happen. As with the Middle East, the governments of the region stayed in place, scarcely ruffled by any popular discontent. The Israeli offensives of early 2002 also failed to disturb the calm, even in Egypt, further building Washington's confidence that America could impose yet more ambitious plans on the Muslim world without significant hindrance.

But we would be foolish to ignore the long-term implications of the unfolding conflict between America, its 'terrorist' enemies, and Iraq. The confrontation has exposed, more clearly than ever, the true nature of power relations between the United States and the Arab world and Africa. Much of this relationship pre-dated September 11, and an increasing number of young Muslims in the region look back at Usama bin Laden's declarations of war on America as prophetic. The terrorist crime of September 11 and the US response have set in train further processes that have transformed the politics of the region and the trajectory of Islamism. One of the lessons of al Qa'ida that the United States seems to have ignored in its calculations for the regional fallout of a war with Iraq is that young people can act independently of state power.

Other than Egypt, north-east Africa is marginal to this confrontation. In 2001, political Islam in was in retreat: paralysed internally and stalemated externally. Those who wrote of its failure were justified. The perspective of early 2003 was very different. A new militant Islam had been brought to life by war. In the competition for positive political projects,

231

political Islam failed, but in the competition for allegiance in war it thrived. Militant Islamists will find their task more difficult in north-east Africa than elsewhere, because of the war-weariness of the region, the weakness of the Islamist constituency, and the discrediting of political Islam by its decade in power in Sudan. But the fate of the region will be powerfully influenced by the wider confrontation between America and those who resist its hegemony.

This concluding chapter is structured around two interlinked stories, which form the underlying narrative for what has happened in north-east Africa between September 11, 2001 and early 2003. One is the 'local' story of how Islamism and its enemies in north-east Africa had fought each other to a standstill in the 1990s, and were now living with the aftermath of this stalemate. Neither could destroy the other, and each was internally divided and paralysed. The grand confrontation between Islamism and revolutionary militarism of the mid-1990s degenerated into internecine strife within each camp. The Islamists in Sudan, Egypt and Somalia were hanging on to what they had won. And they had won much ground: most of the social and political terrain had been Islamised.

The second narrative is the 'global' picture of unprecedented world domination by American military and economic power. Throughout the 1990s the United States had been emerging as a new focus for militant Islamist anger. While states adapted to the reality of US domination, their citizens were repeatedly outraged by the insults bestowed upon them by the global order, symbolised by the fate of the Palestinians, poverty and famine in Africa, and the US readiness to bully the world into acquiescing in an attack on Iraq. Militant Islamism has consistently shadowed its enemies, producing political and ideological agendas that reflect them. Exhausted by their failed attempts to create a new order in Muslim countries, including north-east Africa, jihadists now face America itself. The agenda is now solely a negative one of resistance and destruction. For a militant Muslim, the choice is between joining al Qa'ida to (perhaps) engage in an act of senseless violence that brings martyrdom, and standing on the sidelines and applauding. Al Qa'ida's agenda of resistance may be sufficient to create for it a constituency where beforehand it had done.

Africa is marginal in this global confrontation. In his speech to the Labour Party conference shortly after September 11 Tony Blair bravely argued that poverty in Africa was not only a scar on the conscience of the world but also a strategic threat insofar as poverty and frustration could breed terrorism. Blair's personal commitment to Africa may be genuine, and his role in supporting the New Partnership for Africa's Development (NEPAD) is noble, but the link between poverty and international terrorism is spurious (cf. Pipes 2001/02). North-East Africa is where terrorism and militant Islamist jihadism should have the best chance of combining. To date, they do not. There are plenty of good reasons, both humanitarian and self-interested, for the Western powers including America to be concerned with Africa's plight. But fear of terrorism born of poverty should not figure high on the list.

The 'war on terror' is not Africa's war. Instead the American confrontation with al Qa'ida is being occasionally fought in Africa, but not by Africans and not for Africa. This was illustrated in November 2002 by the terrorist attack on the Paradise Hotel in Mombasa. The targets were Israeli tourists, of whom three were killed. Ten Kenyans died, victims of the fact that al Qa'ida prefers to attack Israelis abroad rather than at home. Meanwhile the new US military base in Djibouti has a watching brief over the Horn, but its main function is as a base for airborne operations in Yemen. What is most striking about the region since September 11 is not the terrorist attack or the presence of US forces, but what has *not* happened. There has been no militant insurrection or uprising in Egypt and no US military action in Somalia, and the Sudan government has sought, and partly obtained, a rapprochement with America.

The United States and Africa

The overwhelming global reality since September 11, 2001, has been the extent of US global domination, military and economically, and hence politically. With appropriate irony it took a display of apparent American vulnerability for the extent of this power to be revealed.

The United States is so powerful that it no longer needs to know much about the rest of the world and adapt its power to local realities. More than anywhere else in the globe, this is true of Africa. The inequity between US power and Africa is illustrated by a simple financial statistic. In 2002/3 the budget of the US Department of Defense surpassed $360 billion, compared to a gross continental product for Africa of about $540 billion.[1] Of this over $200 billion is provided by the five north African states, and $140 billion by South Africa, while the remaining forty-plus countries contribute $200 billion between them. In 2001 the revenue of

---

[1] World Bank figures for 2001. Spain's GDP is about $ 580 billion. If purchasing power parity is used, the GDP figures for Africa are substantially larger. South Africa's PPP GDP is about $370 billion.

the world's largest oil company, ExxonMobil, was $191 billion. Alongside the sheer scale of US might is the administration's readiness to use it: the new national security strategy, published in September 2002, defines for the first time America's assumed right to take pre-emptive military action against emergent threats.

American power means that all autonomous political projects elsewhere in the world are in jeopardy. This is most sharply the case for Africa, the poorest and most vulnerable continent. The principle of 'African ownership' of the goals and strategies for development, one of the pillars of the NEPAD, is in reality rather modest. No African country can attempt to chart an economic course that does not correspond to the orthodoxies of the Washington-based international financial institutions, and prevail. The latitude for action of African governments is vanishingly small. The prospects for sub-Saharan Africa achieving the 'millennium development goals' of halving poverty by 2015 are meagre. Even before the HIV/AIDS cataclysm, life expectancy was faltering. For a generation of young people, the chances of achieving reasonable ambitions for career, family and community are receding into the indefinite future.

In the days and weeks following September 11 African governments hurried to show their support for the United States. Some leaders, such as Kenya's President Daniel arap Moi, were quick to point out that their countries too had been victims of terrorism. Some of Washington's closest friends in the region, including Nigeria and Senegal, hastily convened a summit on terrorism in Dakar on 17 October. The host, President Abdoulaye Wade, had hoped that the summit would help Africa 'team up with the world coalition against this evil' (Malan 2002: 57). The result was more modest. The twenty-seven heads of state and government who attended did not adopt a new Convention, but rather reaffirmed their commitment to the OAU's 1999 Algiers Convention on Terrorism. Their main concern was to ensure that the US 'war on terror' would (in the words of their declaration) 'have the least possible adverse impact on the development of Africa'. A meeting of the OAU's Mechanism for Conflict Resolution, convened in New York at the request of Sudan on 11 November, had a similar outcome, namely a reiteration of existing commitments.

Encouraged by Nelson Mandela, former liberation fighters in Africa expressed their unease with US definitions of terrorism that would have concurred with (among others) white Rhodesia and Apartheid South Africa in branding their former struggles as 'terrorism'.[2] The Algiers

---

[2] 'African leaders wary of evolving US definition of "terrorist"', *Christian Science Monitor*, 20 May 2002.

Convention definition of 'terrorism' had been careful to exclude national liberation movements, and leaders who had won independence so recently and so bitterly, and continued to support the Palestinian cause, were not ready to surrender so readily to US neo-imperialism. Article 3 (1) of the Convention reads:

The struggle waged by peoples in accordance with the principles of international law for their liberation or self-determination, including armed struggle against colonialism, occupation, aggression and domination by foreign forces, shall not be considered as terrorist acts.[3]

Civil liberties were another concern. As noted by Cilliers and Sturman (2002:15): 'The dilemma for Africa is the need to act against terrorists as a national security risk without destroying the often tenuous rule of law that exists in many of our constituent states.' The State Department was well aware of this problem, and especially the readiness of many African rulers to justify repressive actions with reference to fighting terrorism.

But the United States achieved what it wanted in Africa very quickly. Conscious that America was ready to use its power with full force and little warning, governments rushed to cooperate. In all key areas, African states fell into line. The first was cooperation in counter-terrorism. The United States already had good cooperation with all states in north-east Africa except Sudan, and within days of September 11 Khartoum had opened many of its files to US counter-terrorist specialists.

The second was allowing military bases and overflights, if necessary for military action in Somalia. Kenya and Djibouti already provided America with facilities, and air patrols of the Somali coast began almost immediately. In the last months of 2001 US military action in Somalia seemed possible, but as intelligence investigations drew a blank, this option receded (see below). Rather than being concerned about al Qa'ida bases in north-east Africa, America became worried that the 'vacuum' in Somalia and the weak governance of other countries made them attractive hiding places for al Qa'ida assets, whether human, military or financial. The broad assumption was that Africa does not create al Qa'ida terrorists, but may unwittingly host them. A longer-term strategy emerged in 2002. By October a major US base at Djibouti was operational. The main concern of the 800 Marines stationed there, and of the associated command centre, was not the Horn of Africa at all; it was for operations in Yemen and possibly elsewhere in the Arabian peninsula. A Djibouti-

---

[3] The Organisation of the Islamic Conference, meeting in Kuala Lumpur in April 2002, adopted a similar definition (Hiro 2002: 412).

based unmanned drone killed an alleged al Qa'ida leader in Yemen. A secondary concern was to prevent al Qa'ida gaining access to Somalia, by serving as a coordinating centre for coastal surveillance to seal off the region. This command base indicated that the United States was in the region for the long haul, which in turn has implications for its policy in the Horn.

The choice of Djibouti for the base disappointed Eritrea, which had lobbied hard for the Americans to come there instead. In October 2002 the Eritrean government circulated a paper in Washington entitled *Why Not Eritrea?*, and hired a public relations firm to beg for a close alliance with the United States.[4] It was a sad comedown for a government that had boasted its proud independence just a few years earlier. It reflected the Eritrean President's increasingly desperate search for political legitimacy, as well as income. One of the interesting features of the paper is the Eritrean argument that it is the sole non-Arab country on the Red Sea, save Israel. The same month, Isseyas Afewerki had argued for Eritrean admission to the Arab League, on the basis of the country's long ties with its Arab neighbours.

The Department of Defense finds Eritrea an attractive proposition, with its strategic location, long coastline, two good ports, airfield facilities, and pleasant highland climate. The State Department is suspicious of the erratic and bellicose tendencies of the president, and the fact that two Eritrean nationals employed by the US embassy were in prison for more than a year without charge is a significant impediment to closer relations. But should US security concerns appear to be a serious consideration, the Pentagon will undoubtedly win out. In this context, US concerns also focus on preventing any future conflicts in the subregion, by preserving stability in Ethiopia and Sudan and discouraging any resumption of the Ethiopian-Eritrean border conflict. The impact on Sudan is discussed below.

The third plank of the US strategy was financial scrutiny of Islamic charities, banking systems and financial houses. Several were named and closed down. Many of the charities in particular were Salafi agencies based in and funded from Saudi Arabia, but with operations in Africa. The scaling back of their activities will certainly diminish Salafi evangelism and influence in Africa. Tightening up the financial sector to close loopholes used by terrorists proved more difficult to operationalise, in metropolitan countries and Africa alike. OECD countries were unable to

[4] Judy Sarasohn, 'Eritrea Pushes to Get U.S. Base', *Washington Post*, 21 November 2002.

meet a June 2002 deadline for effective anti-terrorist financial regulations.[5] Evidence for al Qa'ida involvement in the illicit West African
diamond trade had emerged as early as 1998, when the organisation reportedly used its funds to buy diamonds partly so as to escape a financial
crackdown after the embassy bombings. Liberia and Burkina Faso were
implicated. Allegations were made that al Qa'ida had also profited from
the trade in tanzanite, a precious stone mined in Tanzania. In Africa, the
basic problem is not financial regulation as such but enforcement of those
regulations, and some finance ministries hoped for technical assistance in
building their capacities. Police forces similarly hoped for support in
combating organised crime. Thus far, they have been disappointed. The
links between financial governance in Africa and counter-terrorism are
either not understood by the US government, or not thought significant.

   A related agenda is closing off terrorist access to 'failed states'. Part of
this involves supporting the settlement of ongoing wars (Angola, Congo
and especially Sudan), knowing that war economies provide niches for
terrorists to hide their assets and obtain weaponry. The British military
involvement in Sierra Leone could thus have a strategic significance: it
plugs one of al Qa'ida's potential bolt-holes and makes it more difficult
for it to buy diamonds. Angola has been another beneficiary of the
American preference for the restoration of old-fashioned territorial control by states. The greatest fear is that al Qa'ida could obtain a nuclear
weapon from Pakistan or a former Soviet republic. It reportedly tried to
buy one in Khartoum in 1994. In opportunistic ways, as for example in
Sudan, this agenda may support the resolution of some of Africa's conflicts. But it does not provide a framework for resolving the problems that
give rise to these conflicts. On the contrary, it is more likely to connive in
the abuse of state power.

   Fourthly, as America sought to lessen its dependence on Middle Eastern oil, the rapidly expanding oilfields along the West African coast
became a strategically important asset to the United States. Countries
such as Equatorial Guinea, Gabon and São Tomé and Príncipe are rapidly becoming middle-order oil producers, situated an ocean nearer to
America than the Middle East, and whose oil is situated conveniently off-
shore. Within ten years, America may be importing more oil from Africa
than from the Middle East. However, owing to the power of the anti-Khartoum Congressional lobby, the sole oil producer in the Horn of Africa,
Sudan, has been unable to benefit from this. A high-profile human rights

[5] Jimmy Burns, 'Tracking of terrorist finances obstructed', *Financial Times*, 9 June 2002.

campaign aimed at the Canadian oil company Talisman, the leading Western corporation involved in extracting Sudanese oil, caused immense damage to its public image and also hurt its share price. Congress even threatened the unprecedented step of capital market sanctions against companies operating in Sudan (a measure that generated strong opposition from the Treasury). In November 2002 Talisman sold its stake in the Sudanese oilfields to the Indian state oil and gas company. Under these circumstances, no American oil company seriously considered doing business in Sudan.

Lastly, the United States has sought to share the burdens of maintaining security and containing terrorism. In the Sudan peace process, Kenya has been in the lead and European governments have taken on many tasks, including assisting with the mediation (Britain and Norway), negotiating and monitoring ceasefires (Switzerland and others), and making scaled-up development assistance conditional on progress towards peace (the European Union). The Djibouti-based operations to patrol the Somali coast have been assisted by German air force overflights. Implicitly, America has also placed the burden of peacekeeping upon Europe, South Asia and Africa (Malan 2002). American forces have taken the lead in military offensives against the Taliban, al Qa'ida and Iraq, leaving the rest of the world to do most of the peacekeeping, humanitarian assistance and reconstruction.

Notable by its low profile in US engagement is a concern with the supposed 'root causes' of terrorism or Islamist militancy. One might expect substantially expanded foreign assistance and a new expanded mission for USAID, but American aid policies have continued to be parsimonious and short-sighted. American support for the peace process in Sudan may be the exception to this neglect. Peace in Sudan would decisively shut the door to state sponsorship of jihadism and thus help achieve a major US foreign policy goal. But this is not the public rationale for US Sudan policy and it does not treat most other state sponsors or hosts of terrorism this way.

Meanwhile, African governments have tried to utilise the threat of terrorism for their own internal ends. The Eritrean President, having locked up his more democratically-minded former colleagues, branded then 'terrorists' and tried, absurdly, to link them to Islamic militancy. Zimbabwe's Robert Mugabe tried a similar trick, equally unconvincingly. The trick is so transparent that few tried it in such a crude manner. However, the Ugandan government succeeded in having the Lord's Resistance Army put on the US list of 'terrorist' organisations.

Africa is likely to remain a sideshow in the 'war on terrorism'. That is one of the few blessings of the continent's marginalisation. The American base in Djibouti will be a tempting target for al Qa'ida attacks, and its very presence will generate a need for US surveillance. But vibrant militant Islamist movements that could incubate al Qa'ida terrorism no longer exist in the Horn. They are exhausted and their erstwhile state sponsor in the region, Sudan, has given up on their cause.

Egypt: still paralysis

The most remarkable thing about Egypt after September 11 is that nothing significant happened. The Egyptian security forces had defeated organised militancy in 1997, and that victory remained intact. The modest lightening of pressure on militant Islamists abruptly ended, with renewed crackdown. There was a high-profile trial of twenty-two Muslim Brothers detained on the grounds that their publications 'looked suspicious' (see chapter 2). But the tide of political Islam in the Egyptian state did not ebb. If anything, President Mubarak became more publicly devout.

Egypt had long been a favoured US ally in the region. But the Bush administration has been sufficiently confident of its supremacy that it has ridden roughshod over Egyptian sensitivities. Egypt has been humiliated over US support for Israel against the Palestinian Authority, over US insistence on confronting Iraq, and over US readiness to support self-determination for Southern Sudan. In retaliation Egypt snubbed America by detaining and prosecuting the US-Egyptian professor Saad Eddin Ibrahim in the Supreme Security Court on charges of espionage, distributing propaganda, harming Egypt's reputation, voter registration fraud and receiving funds illegally from abroad. Anti-Semitism has reached new levels of official endorsement, with a thirty-part series based on the notorious Tsarist Russian forgery, the *Protocols of the Elders of Zion*, produced by Arab Radio and Television in Egypt (see Evans 2002).

The Egyptian state is exhausted and uses issues such as Palestine and other struggles as symbols, not least to deflect attention from its own record. It is trapped between its reliance on the army and its incremental Islamisation. This buys stability, but at the price of paralysis. However, Egypt cannot continue this game indefinitely. It is not delivering on the aspirations of its people, and in practice it is doing nothing for the Palestinians. The level of repression and abuse in the Occupied Territories will sooner or later unleash a violent reaction that will be difficult to control.

The deepest problem that Egypt faces is the way in which Islamism, in both government institutions and opposition, is stifling free thought.

Conservatism and coercion have been placed at the heart of political and cultural life in Egypt, as they have in a range of other Arab countries. Intellectuals have been assassinated or intimidated for their views that opposed Islamist neo-fundamentalism, and among the victims have been devout Muslims. However, there are always hints of contrary trends: some Egyptian writers have been reported publicising the *fatwas* against them in order to gain publicity and sales from a sophisticated reading public. (Mostyn 2002: 152)

Egypt is the clearest case of the way in which political Islam has posed a severe and creeping threat to rational and scientific thinking in the arena of political life. Egypt's modern civil society, which emerged in the 1980s, is still seeking legitimacy with respect to both the state and the populace. The Egyptian human rights movement's quest for popular legitimacy led it to concentrate on collective rights, principally the collective rights of the Palestinians. As for facing down the threats on the freedom of thought and freedom of expression that the Islamists pose with their machinery of character and physical assassination, most of the human rights groups avoid direct confrontation. Instead they try to encourage dialogue with the less hard-line elements among the Islamists, hoping that this policy will lead the Islamists to adopt human rights norms in the future. Civil society as the fulcrum for new thinking and creativity is eclipsed. The key issue of the antagonism between Islamism and political modernity is unaddressed. However, this deadening of intellectual life is not an inevitable or necessary feature of Islam or even Islamism. The vigorous theoretical debates that characterise contemporary Iran show that political Islamism can coexist with free expression. Egypt's challenge is to re-establish that confidence and recreate that space.

The Sudan peace process

Prospects for peace in Sudan were a surprise beneficiary of the conjuncture of events in September 2001.[6] Sudan has been an anomaly in the 'war on terror': a state with a well-documented history of alignment with al Qa'ida, now cooperating with America, an oil-producer that is not courted by US oil companies, and a country in which the weight of US domination may just be used to bring about peace. This has coincided with a vigorous debate within Sudan about the political direction of the country, including the future of Islamism.

[6] On the twists and turns of the peace process, see the Justice Africa monthly briefing, *Prospects for Peace in Sudan*, September 1999-present.

Just five days before September 11 President George W. Bush appointed Senator John ('Jack') Danforth as Special Envoy for Sudan. On 17 September the UN Security Council was due to deliberate on renewing the limited diplomatic sanctions on Sudan imposed after the June 1995 assassination attempt on Husni Mubarak. The United States had decided not to vote to continue the sanctions: it had decided to do business with Sudan. But meanwhile, a well-organised coalition spearheaded by the 'religious right' had pushed through the House of Representatives a very strong bill that included capital market sanctions against companies doing business in Sudan and promised support to the SPLA. The bill was due to go to the Senate shortly: the stakes had been raised. The timing was fortuitous.

The United States had unusually strong leverage in Khartoum because Sudan wanted to normalise relations, specifically with the aim of neutralising the Congressional coalition that wanted to overthrow it. In addition, the State Department could blackmail several leading Sudan government and security officials over their past links to al Qa'ida and Iraq. In short, Khartoum knew that Washington had both motive and evidence to put it in the same category as Afghanistan and Iraq. The Sudan government needed to act fast, which it did. It provided important counter-terrorist intelligence and agreed to negotiate for peace more seriously than ever before. These concessions were enough to stop the Administration from militarily backing the SPLA, although Congress still succeeded in passing the Sudan Peace Act, in watered down form, a year later.

Since 1998 the United States had become the principal backer of the SPLA, through USAID and Congress. This gave it considerable leverage over the SPLA as well, but effective use of this power was limited by the fact that State Department messages were frequently contradicted by Congressional vows of solidarity, keeping SPLA hopes alive that Washington would decide to turn the SPLA into Sudan's version of the Afghan 'northern alliance' and bring John Garang to power. In this tussle, the position of the Pentagon is crucial. Should hardliners in the Department of Defense wish to punish Khartoum, they will find a ready political constituency. Should it instead calculate that stability in Sudan is more strategically important—and with a conflict in Iraq and continuing al Qa'ida presence in Yemen, a resumed war in Sudan would run the risk of pushing Khartoum into collaborating with America's declared enemies— then the DoD will support State and push for peace. At the time of writing (February 2003), it seems clear that the DoD is strongly in favour of peace and a continuation of the Bashir government in power, for precisely these reasons. Whether or not the SPLA leadership reads these signs correctly is a different question.

Senator Danforth's approach was to zero on the key issues and key parties. He immediately identified military power as the central factor, and designed four 'tests' for the parties, two of which would focus attention on military command and control on each side. These two tests were a ceasefire in the Nuba Mountains and a monitored cessation of attacks on civilians in the South, including aerial bombardment. Tough US reactions to government violations of the latter test, notably at Rieh in February 2002, ensured that President Bashir was forced formally to centralise command so that he could no longer excuse violations as the work of out-of-control officers. (The other two tests were an impartial investigation into slavery, and a ceasefire for vaccination programmes.) Danforth identified peace as the prerequisite for achieving other desirables such as democracy, and thus narrowed the protagonists to the Sudan government and SPLA, sidelining the NDA (which was increasingly divided and ineffectual). At a regional level, he consulted Kenya (as chair of the IGAD Sudan Peace Secretariat) and Egypt, and at an international level he worked with the informal troika of America, Britain and Norway.

In March 2002 Senator Danforth submitted his report: America should engage. The State Department took over, and followed the same approach (with the significant difference of taking a more flexible stand on self-determination for Southern Sudan, which Danforth had not supported). This 'two plus two plus three' formula was sufficiently streamlined to work: a new round of IGAD peace talks began at the Kenyan town of Machakos, and the two sides signed a preliminary Protocol agreement in July. This was essentially a 'one country two systems' approach that recognised Islamic law in Northern Sudan and set a date for a Southern referendum on self-determination after a six year interim period.

Neither of the parties in Sudan was truly energetic or committed to peace. This was demonstrated by the naïve positions that each presented to the mediators at the revived IGAD forum, under Kenyan chairmanship but with the troika exercising most leverage. However, each side was sufficiently serious about other issues, such as international standing, which could be used as leverage by the facilitators. Hence the reinvigorated peace process was dependent on the US administration's focus and the ad hoc multilateralism that brought in an array of other international actors. Early in 2003 the international coalition in favour of peace had succeeded in weathering potential storms including the change of government in Kenya, the distractions of an approaching war on Iraq, and continuing determination by the Congressional 'religious right' to bring down the Sudan government.

The basic logic of the negotiations was that the mediators developed positions based on their own assessments of the problems and the 'literature of accord'—the history of agreements signed by various parties during the previous decade—and got the two parties to agree to a common text. In that sense it was an attempt at an imposed settlement, based on what the parties have already agreed. The key factor was not the readiness of the two parties to achieve a compromise or to trust one another, but the energy, patience and leverage of the mediators. In this respect hegemonic US power was the critical element, although the diplomatic finesse of the British Special Envoy, Alan Goulty, was also instrumental.

But it was still vulnerable to the calculations and miscalculations of the two parties. President Bashir had a difficult task in creating consensus behind the July 2002 Machakos Protocol, which had been signed without the prior agreement of senior members of the government, including Vice President Ali Osman Mohamed Taha and Foreign Minister Mustafa Ismail. The latter had personally assured the Egyptian President that no agreement would be signed that included reference to self-determination. This coalition forced Bashir to withdraw from the IGAD peace process in September, the final spark being an SPLA offensive that captured the Southern town of Torit. The negotiations had been ongoing without a concomitant general ceasefire, so such attacks were to be expected, and indeed the Sudan government had launched several in June and July. But the SPLA attack on Torit seemed designed to provoke Khartoum, and it succeeded. Most significantly, it destroyed the nascent confidence that Bashir had been vesting in Garang, after the two had met for the first time in Kampala in July. With an unprecedented level of mobilisation, made possible by oil revenue, the Sudan government regrouped and recaptured Torit in October. While this was in train, the SPLA and Eritrean forces launched a major operation in eastern Sudan, briefly capturing the town of Hamush Koreb. With honour satisfied on both sides, and much arm-twisting by the facilitators, the two sides returned to Machakos on 17 October, and signed a ceasefire for the duration of the talks. This time, for the first time, the ceasefire was not quickly violated.

At the time of writing, the outcome of the peace process remains in the balance. The mediators are planning to corral the parties into signing an agreement during 2003, essentially by adopting a process of arbitration:

assessing the parties' positions, finding a middle way, and pressuring them to accept. This is akin to a peace imposed by an 'external leviathan', and some Sudanese commentators are hopeful that such an approach, despite violating many of the standard precepts of peacemaking, could actually work. (Ef-Affendi 2002) However, the Sudan government is still tempted by the logic of its military ascendancy over the SPLA due to oil revenue, and its strengthened diplomatic position in the region. The SPLA leadership on its side is tempted by the promise made by powerful individuals in Washington, and made concrete in the Sudan Peace Act, that it can win the military jackpot with US assistance.

What does this mean for Islamism? In Northern Sudan, Islamism is both triumphant and exhausted. It has succeeded in changing the colour of political discourse in the country to an unparalleled degree. Not only are the traditional sectarian parties Islamist, but even the erstwhile secular forces such as the Communist Party have adopted Islamist discourse. For example, the veteran Communist leader Mohamed Ibrahim Nugud has written explaining his preference for the term 'civil state' rather than 'secular state'.[7] Having called for a democratic state, not based upon religion, Nugud felt obliged to give assurances to his readership that he did not mean the Western style of secularism. Rather, he explained, secularism need not follow one model, and under his conceptualisation,

[the 'civil' state] does not turn a blind eye to the forms of decadence and moral degradation in society. It does not allow society to turn into a bar for drunks or a brothel. It does not allow the youth to fall into holes of waste. But its means to guarantee this are not the Public Order Police and Courts, the method used currently by the National Salvation Regime. Instead its tool is the restraint provided by upbringing and religion, ethics and the good example of family and society. After that, certainly not before it, comes enforcement by law.

Most of what he says would be endorsed by Islamists. Whether this Islamisation of the social terrain has occurred through intimidation or through the long term Islamisation of education and social mores, it has become a reality. Meanwhile, the project of building a militant Islamic state has come to a halt. The Islamists are divided and acrimonious, and their overriding concern is hanging on to power. There is an increasingly vigorous debate about the future of the country, but it is conducted overwhelmingly at the level of tactical political concerns, interspersed with threats of violence, largely against one another. Theoretical issues are

[7] Mohamed I. Nugud, 'The Solution to Sudan's Dilemma is Represented in a Civil State', *al-Baian*, 28 August 2002, Dubai.

discussed, but primarily in the framework of reiterating existing points of view.

When confronted with points of Islamist principle, President Bashir cannot compromise: it is ruled out by the logic of neo-fundamentalism. For example, the SPLA demand that the national capital be under secular law is a logical implication of the federal or confederal arrangement accepted by the government. But to abandon an Islamic Khartoum is simply inconceivable to most Islamists. Any compromise formula will be exceptionally hard for Bashir to swallow, and may provoke serious infighting within the Islamist movement. Similarly the Northern Sudanese political establishment cannot conceive of a non-Muslim heading the Sudanese state. Evasive formulae such as 'citizenship alone shall be the basis of all rights' are acceptable. But for the SPLA, representing the South and other marginalised peoples, whose experience has been one in which Khartoum has repeatedly dishonoured agreements (cf. Alier 1990), such a formulation provides no guarantees. Thus far, neither Bashir nor Garang has displayed the leadership qualities necessary to make peace a reality. Signing an agreement is only part of the story: making it work will be more difficult.

If peace in Sudan is achieved, the credit will go overwhelmingly to the mediators, whose persistence and readiness to use their leverage will have delivered two reluctant warmakers to a settlement. Khartoum and the SPLA, having long engaged in a conflict that has allowed each leadership to consolidate its power and wealth, and repress opposition, will need to formalise their mutual accommodation. In contrast to, say, Algeria or Egypt this accommodation will be ideologically difficult because of the absence of compromise in the Islamist political vocabulary and the SPLA's insistence on secular rule in at least a substantial part of the country. Peace is a destabilising prospect for both parties. Hopefully, the Sudanese people will use the opportunity of the belligerents' weakness and disorientation to promote human rights, democracy and a fairer distribution of the national wealth.

If the talks collapse, or the settlement unravels, there will be acrimony all round. Doubtless the mediators' tradecraft will be criticised. But the blame will fall chiefly on the leaders on both sides, notably on the Islamists' blackmail of any compromise and on Garang's vaulting ambitions, sustained by the American anti-Khartoum lobbies. The two leaderships' comfort with unending conflict will be illustrated: the Islamist project and its enemies' mutual need for one other. Any failure will also demonstrate the limits of US power, and especially that power's greatest weakness, the contradictions between its different domestic constituencies.

The Horn: local politics prevails

Next to Afghanistan, Somalia seemed the most likely location for US military action in the autumn of 2001. It did not occur, and the reasons for this show much about the nature of militant Islam in the region, and how matters had changed from five years earlier. Somalia seemed to be an ideal candidate for an al Qa'ida base: a collapsed state without central authority and a known site for jihadism, in the form of al Itihaad al Islami, which had past links to al Qa'ida. But there the parallels with Afghanistan ended. Somalia is an open economy with an active and internationally mobile trading class. There are few secrets in the country, and certainly nothing the size of a terrorist base could be hidden. The best candidate, a camp at Ras Komboni at the southern tip of Somalia on the Kenyan border, was quickly investigated and found to be abandoned. Above all, there was no neighbouring state playing the role of protector of extremism, as Pakistan had been doing for the Taliban.

The US's first action was perhaps its most effective. It began naming the Somali individuals, mostly businessmen, whom it suspected of terrorist links. Somali businessmen cannot disappear or go underground: they must travel and trade. The next action, on 7 November 2001, was to freeze the assets and suspend the international operations of Somalia's largest finance house, al Barakaat. This was the financial equivalent of carpet bombing, and thousands of Somalis, especially in the diaspora, lost savings and the ability to remit money back home. Military action was also threatened, and reconnaissance flights (by the German air force) began along the coast, to intercept arms shipments and terrorist suspects. The legal justification for the latter was the 1991 UN arms embargo imposed on Somalia.

Virtually nothing was turned up by any process of investigation. Asked by a journalist what were the specific ties between al Itihaad and al Qa'ida, a 'senior official' at the Pentagon said at the 8 March 2002 press briefing:

'While bin Laden would be kind of a corporate model, extreme AIAI [al Itihaad al Islami] members, violent AIAI members may be a kind of a franchise element that share that world view that bin Laden has articulated, so whatever the connections, they certainly share the same kind of perspective regarding the West, some extreme factions.... [As for terrorist activities, he conceded:] To my knowledge, extreme AIAI members really have not engaged in acts of terrorism outside Somalia. [He had earlier referred to possible al Itihaad involvement in the kidnapping of an aid worker inside Somalia.]'[8]

[8] US Department of Defense, News Briefing, 'Background Briefing on the Terrorist Threat in the Horn of Africa', 8 March 2002.

The phrasing 'extreme AIAI members' is instructive: America was concerned about individuals, not the organisation itself. By June 2002 overflights were scaled back. They had found nothing. Neither was any evidence found of the existence of connections between al Barakaat and terrorism,[9] and the company was taken off the blacklist in August. But meanwhile, there were a number of warnings that terrorists were transshipping arms and operatives through Somalia.[10] After the November terrorist attack in Mombasa, these were re-examined, and suspicions again fell on al Itihaad.

Throughout the region, the labels 'terrorist' and *'jihad'* have become common currency, often with little reference to political realities, and with the intent of closing down the prospects for political dialogue and compromise. There is no theoretical discussion about Islamism worthy of the name, but rather a continuing concern with tactical manoeuvring and the local logic of power.

For example, the Ugandan Lord's Resistance Army (LRA) was the first African organisation to be formally labelled a terrorist organisation by the United States. Though it has been supported by Sudan, the LRA is in no sense Islamist. This label was important in enabling the Ugandan government to negotiate an agreement with Sudan whereby it could operate inside Southern Sudan to destroy the LRA. 'Operation Iron Fist' began in March 2002, with grand promises from Kampala that the LRA would be rapidly crushed and its leader Joseph Kony killed or captured. An early incident in which Sudanese officers supplied intelligence to the LRA, and Ugandan soldiers were ambushed and killed, rebounded on the conspirators: Sudan was compelled to cooperate more effectively. But the LRA proved far more difficult to defeat than Ugandan generals had bragged. It not only evaded the Ugandan operations but mounted vicious attacks into northern Uganda, even shooting down a helicopter (a claim denied by the Ugandan government, which closed down the newspaper that reported it). In 2003 there is no end to the conflict in sight.

The label 'terrorist organisation' may have been tactically useful in forcing Sudan to end its military sponsorship of the LRA. But it has proved a strategic drawback, by encouraging the Ugandan leadership to believe that it cannot negotiate with the LRA, and the LRA leadership to believe that it has nothing to lose by continuing to fight. The roots of the

9 Tim Golden, Bill Berkeley and Donald G. McNeil, '5 Months After Sanctions Against Somali Company, Scant Proof of Qaeda Tie', *New York Times*, 13 April 2002.
10 'Israel "Knew Kenya was Target"', *Daily Nation*, Nairobi, 3 December 2002.

insurgency lie in the profound traumatisation of Acholi society due to the excesses of the Obote regime in the early 1980s and the incapacity of the Museveni government to heal the wounds. Labelling a protagonist, albeit a peculiarly vicious one, 'terrorist' has not proved helpful in the search for a political solution.

The (mis)use of the label 'terrorist' is also evident in the conflicts surrounding the political implosion of Eritrea. Following its defeat in the 1998–2000 war with Ethiopia (both war and defeat in large measure the responsibility of the President and his closest advisers), Eritrea reverted rapidly to a paralytic dictatorship. Isseyas Afewerki became even more erratic and egotistic than before, and by mid-2002 had summoned up a broad coalition of Eritrean opposition forces, based in the diaspora, in Sudan (most of them veterans of the Eritrean Liberation Front) and increasingly in Ethiopia. Eritrea continued its proxy war against Ethiopia by training Oromo Liberation Front fighters and despatching them into Ethiopia, via Somalia and Sudan, and Ethiopia began to reply in kind. The military incursion into Sudan in October, alongside the SPLA, was the spark for this regional confrontation to move to a different level. The leaders of Ethiopia and Sudan flew to Yemen for a regional summit, and moves were accelerated to bring the disparate Eritrean guerrilla forces under a central political command. Among the groups that formed the coalition was Eritrea Jihad, an Islamist group that was unwavering in its commitment to creating an Islamic state in Eritrea. President Isseyas had no hesitation in labelling the opposition 'terrorist'. This illustrates the extent to which the word 'terrorist' has just become a card to play in propaganda wars, no longer possessing any credibility.

Alongside the domestic Sudanese process of 2001–3 has proceeded a normalisation of relations between Sudan and its neighbours (with the exception of Eritrea, for which Khartoum and Addis Ababa seem to have decided that normalisation is not possible). Having achieved its goals in containing Islamist destabilisation, Ethiopia has moved quietly but determinedly towards closer relations with Sudan. Uganda has done the same, though the relationship is vulnerable to the side-effects of the ongoing LRA insurgency. Egypt was, of course, the first to normalise relations, but tensions have emerged over the Machakos peace process and its provisions for self-determination for Southern Sudan. These tensions have nothing to do with the Islamist project. They reflect the oldest and most vested of Egypt's interests, the River Nile, and Egypt's fear of revisiting the 1959 Nile Waters Agreement, which would be necessary if Southern Sudan were to become an independent state.

More widely, Islamism's enemies in north-east Africa have fallen further into internal dissension. The backwash from the collapse of the
grand alliance of the Asmara-to-Kigali axis in 1998 has left the former
leftist liberation movements in disarray. Political Islam in north-east
Africa and its most formidable adversary, leftist militarism, not only rose
in parallel but decayed and fragmented in parallel as well.

Islamism and the HIV/AIDS crisis

How will Islamism and its enemies respond to the single greatest threat to
human well-being, development and governance in Africa, namely the
HIV/AIDS epidemic? At present, Africa's generalised HIV/AIDS epidemics have chiefly afflicted southern and eastern Africa. A number of
factors, historical, socio-cultural and socio-biological (male circumcision
helps protect against HIV transmission) mean that principally-Muslim
societies are as yet less afflicted. But, as Malik Badri, one of the few Islamist thinkers to address the HIV/AIDS crisis in a thoughtful way notes,
Muslim societies should not succumb to a 'false complacency' that they
are somehow immune to the disease (Badri 1997: 288). One of the main
reasons why high HIV prevalence has not been found in countries such as
Sudan has been that proper surveillance has not yet been undertaken.

HIV/AIDS appears to fit an Islamist eschatology well. It is readily portrayed as Divine retribution, a punishment on decadent Western societies
and their promiscuity, homosexuality and drug and alcohol abuse.
Islamists even cite a *hadith* in support of this: 'If fornication and all kinds
of sinful sexual intercourse become rampant and openly practised without inhibition in any group or nation, Allah will punish them with new
epidemics and new diseases which were not known to their forefathers'
(cited in Badri 1997: v). The Islamist intolerance of homosexuality and
insistence on the subordinate but protected status of women contribute to
this mindset. Indeed, attitudes to gender and sexuality are perhaps the
area of the most marked divergence between Islamic and Western societies (Inglehart and Norris 2003). Another, more 'merciful' interpretation
of Divine retribution is sending a plague as a means of protecting humanity from something worse. This is one interpretation of God's punishment on the people of Sodom: it protected humanity from what is seen
as a particularly heinous sin and its consequences (Badri 1997: 209).

The Islamist response to HIV/AIDS captures both the strengths and
weaknesses of political Islam and Islamist voluntarism. To begin with the
strengths, Islamism's comprehensive philosophy is well-suited to addressing

HIV/AIDS. Most Western HIV/AIDS programmes have focused on the biological and behavioural determinants of HIV infection, neglecting the wider social environment. But it is increasingly evident that economic inequality and lack of social cohesion are important predisposing factors that put certain environments at high risk for HIV (Barnett and Whiteside 1999). It follows that social control and cohesion including a reversion to conservative sexual morality can serve to prevent and contain the epidemic. In Senegal this has happened, through the liberal Islamism of the government and religious authorities. The Islamist approach, focusing on social reform, may converge with this. Moreover, unlike many Christian teachings, Islam recognises that sex should give pleasure to both men and women. Islamists have few problems with condoms (which are produced by government factories in Iran), and compassion for the sick and orphans is a feature of Islamic humanitarianism.

There are three main weaknesses in the Islamist response to HIV/AIDS. The first is denial and stigmatisation. If the disease is seen as a Western import (or worse, as a Western conspiracy), and also a punishment from God, it will be extraordinarily difficult to obtain public recognition of the problem, and humane treatment of sufferers from it. Related to this is the Islamist tendency of diagnosing social problems as manifestations of personal vices. This puts Islamist humanitarians on a slippery slope: how can human compassion prevail in the face of religiously-sanctioned judgementalism? For many Islamists, the priority is not combating HIV/AIDS, but furthering their own political-religious agendas, which entails resisting an objective assessment of the science and epidemiology of the disease.

The second weakness is gender inequality. The low status of women and girls is perhaps the single most important factor in the escalation of the HIV/AIDS epidemic in the continent. Islam formalises this low status, making it extraordinarily difficult for women to negotiate safer sex, escape from abusive husbands, or make accusations against the perpetrators of sexual violence. However, among educated women there may be protected spaces in which information on sexual and reproductive health can be circulated away from male scrutiny.

The final problem is a version of the familiar problem that Islamists face in moving from the moderately successful pursuit of micro-solutions to the failed attempt at resolving big problems. Chanting that 'Islam is the answer' is no response to HIV/AIDS. Islamist moralism is not up to the task. Islamists—including humane psychologists such as Badri—find themselves supporting Zimbabwean President Robert Mugabe's persecution of homosexuals and the imposition of Islamic law in Sudan. This reflects the deeper problem that while Islamist mobilisation may forge social cohesion at a very local level, Islamist politics creates divisiveness and social crisis at a national level. The social cohesion that can provide a framework for rolling back HIV/AIDS is in fact undermined by the realities of the Islamist project.

Another dimension of the relationship between Islamism and HIV/AIDS demands attention. Vicious interactions between HIV/AIDS and terrorism are feared (Fidas 2002). There has been speculation that individuals who know that they are living with HIV, and thus believe they have been handed a death sentence, may be ready to become suicide bombers. However, while there are examples of criminal and destructive behaviour by some individuals living with HIV and AIDS, there is no obvious convergence between this mindset and that of a committed *mujahid*.

Much more probable is that governance crises associated with the impact of HIV/AIDS will provide an environment for extremism or terrorism. One scenario is a governance vacuum that could be exploited by al Qa'ida. Such a crisis in a large African country is much feared in the US Administration. HIV rates in Ethiopia and Nigeria are rising rapidly, and the US National Intelligence Council has identified these countries as part of the 'second wave' of AIDS-impacted countries, where the epidemic threatens political instability in the coming decade (National Intelligence Council 2002). In Uganda HIV/AIDS decimated the senior ranks of the armed forces, leading to a serious decline in military capacity and discipline. If replicated more widely, this could be a major threat to regional peace and security. Recognising this threat, Ethiopia implemented an early and relatively successful campaign in its army, but this remains exceptional. In Sudan there is the possibility that peace and the return of refugees and displaced people to their homes may be followed by an escalation of the AIDS epidemic. This might in turn contribute to a breakdown, or failure to develop, of key governing institutions, especially in the South, which could in turn hinder the reconstruction and political stabilisation of the country.

Another scenario is the emergence of religious extremism of any colour, in societies subjected to the existential crisis of mass adult mortality. Currently Christian fundamentalism is the most likely manifestation of this, although this may in turn provoke a reaction by Islamists.

Where next for jihadism and its enemies?

Both the objective and subjective conditions exist for a global jihadist insurgency. This may be waged by Usama bin Laden and al Qa'ida, or by their successors. Through their audacious propaganda of the deed, they have shown that the theorising of their predecessors, and the struggles of their predecessors to establish Islamic states and societies in small countries like Sudan and Afghanistan, should be superseded by a global confrontation in which victory remains carefully undefined.

In the context of the failure of militant Islamism as a political programme with concrete goals for its host societies, it has mutated to a project of simply resisting and destroying American power. As this book has sought to show, militant Islam in north-east Africa has historically resembled its adversaries, both in its political strategies and in its ideological constructs. In Egypt in the 1930s and '40s Islamism was a product of the struggle against colonial rule, and an ideological sibling of both fascism and communism. In the 1960s and '70s modernist Islamism competed for political and ideological space with Arab nationalism and state socialism, a struggle that culminated in the anti-communist international *jihad* in Afghanistan. For this reason, among others, it was a 'modernist' project, and Islamist social and political organisation still bears this imprint. In the 1990s neo-fundamentalism's prime global adversary became Westernised capitalism. In Algeria the Islamist militants fought an ideologically bankrupt militarised state, with each party ultimately benefiting from the political and economic rewards of war. In the Horn of Africa it took a different path to a similar outcome, as the Islamist state in Sudan has faced secular revolutionary militarism in the form of the SPLA and the governments of neighbouring states. Each consolidated its power and built its economic base under conditions of protracted war. Sudan is a textbook example of how enemies can simultaneously fight one another and need one another, and how *jihad* and liberation can each be subverted to political and economic instrumentality. In a historical irony, the Sudanese revolutionary Islamist project began to collapse under internal contradictions and external economic and military pressures, just as the liberation regimes in Eritrea, Ethiopia, Rwanda and Uganda themselves became exhausted and started fighting one another. The recourse to violence, so readily and at so many levels, reflects the pervasive influence of a militarised political imagination. (Martinez 2000, de Waal 2002)

Militant Islamism now confronts its nemesis: US global neo-imperialism.[11] So far, it has accommodated effectively to this enemy, using its technology and financial systems, exploiting its fears and symbols.

---

[11] For a comparable analysis of Islam and France, see Burgat 2003. He writes: 'The Muslims of tomorrow's France will be those we have taken part in shaping.' (p. 20)

The Bush Administration did not seek the war nor start it. But it is moulding the conflict for its political purposes. The Republicans' electoral ascendancy in 2002 would have been improbable if the leading political issue had been domestic economic management. Moreover, the dimensions of the 'war on terror' have been drawn with a studious lack of clarity, leaving the Administration with enormous discretion about when if ever it will declare victory, and when it prefers to insist that the war must continue or be escalated. Speaking at Washington's National Cathedral on 14 September President Bush himself said: 'This conflict was begun on the timing and terms of others. It will end in a way, at an hour, of our choosing.' Bob Woodward comments: 'A war speech in a cathedral was jarring, even risky, but it delivered the message Bush wanted.' (Woodward 2002: 67) At the time of writing, it is unclear whether the primary US war aims are to destroy 'terrorism' as a general phenomenon, to destroy al Qa'ida and its jihadist allies specifically, or to use the 'war on terror' also as an opportunity to resume the older confrontation with pre-existing adversaries such as Iraq, Iran and North Korea—Bush's 'axis of evil'. Moreover, it is unclear to what extent the strategy extends beyond military domination to include tackling the 'root causes' of terrorism, however these may be diagnosed. Lastly, it is important to bear in mind that the US war strategy is as much about building domestic coalitions and winning elections as it is about defeating an external enemy. The administration has evidently included a wide range of views on whom to attack and how to conduct the 'war on terror'. Christian fundamentalism, in alliance with the Israeli lobby, plays an important role in determining US policies in this regard.

These ambiguities are not accidental. For the United States we can be confident that the 'victory' will be instrumental as well as the 'war', and that politics of the world will have undergone some important transformations by the time that 'victory' is declared, if ever.

On the Islamist side, what is the instrumentality and the prospect of victory? Here, we must distinguish between al Qa'ida and the wider Islamist movement. Usama bin Laden is explicit about his war aims: he wants America to leave the Arabian peninsula, Israel to be destroyed, and the 'hypocritical' Arab governments to be overthrown to be replaced by Islamic states. He seems to believe that achieving these goals will require the destruction or surrender of the US. How is this to be achieved? Since his first declarations of *jihad* against America, bin Laden seems to have wanted a protracted war on terrain favourable to al Qa'ida and its allies: 'I want the Americans to proceed toward Afghanistan, where all their misconceptions and illusions will be removed.' (Anonymous 2002: 155) But, Usama bin Laden has not clarified how he will translate a battlefield success into the establishment of the *khilafa*. Perhaps this stems from the lack of Islamist political theory. Perhaps it reflects an enthusiasm for *jihad* as an end in itself. Vagueness of war aims suits al Qa'ida's leadership as much as it suits the Pentagon and White House. After the 1998 missile attack on Afghanistan, Usama bin Laden said, 'God is the real superpower, so there is no need to be afraid of the US. We will die at the will of God, not at the will of the US.' (quoted in Anonymous, 2002: 155)

For Islamists who do not wish to join Usama's indefinite *jihad*, the option of military resistance is limited. The United States will not give up after a dozen fatalities (as in Somalia) or even a few hundred (as in Lebanon). Islamists cannot follow the example of Shukri Mustafa in the 1970s and try to separate from the rest of the world. The attempt by the Saudi Arabian elite to buy immunity from the political logic of modernity has failed, and it is likely that the US imperium will be unforgiving of the Saudi role in paying neo-fundamentalists protection money. Nor can Islamists seek out alternative alignments in global politics: there is no contemporary counterpart of the defunct Soviet Union to balance US power. And the Israeli-style option of building a power base within the US democratic system is closed: it is too late to start such a strategy when the war has already started.[12] The conclusion is evident: Islamists in particular and Muslims in general will be losers in this confrontation.

Immediately after September 11, there was popular confusion across Africa. Many columnists were ready to blame Serbs or Israelis for the attack. The subjective conditions for popular Islamist insurrection seemed propitious. In some places, such as northern Nigeria, militant Islam stood as a symbol of resistance to the US imperium. In demonstrations, notably in Kano on 13 October, Usama bin Laden's image was held up by demonstrators opposing the United States and those who are seen as its clients—notably President Obasanjo. There was a growing exhilaration, a sense that Muslims had hit back at the global bully. Usama bin Laden became a cult figure, with boys named after him and T-shirts printed with his face, or with pictures of planes crashing into skyscrapers. These emotions are not channelled. But they should not be dismissed.

The global Salafi jihadists who instigated this war have much to gain, and not only in the next world. The ideological and charismatic leader-

---

[12] C. f. Ali Mazrui, 'Africa in the Shadow of the New Global Alignments: Between Hope and Peril', lecture delivered in Addis Ababa, Development Policy Management Forum and Inter Africa Group, 3 December 2002.

ship of al Qa'ida in the militants' struggle is now undisputed. Militancy's middle ground has vanished: jihadist activists and Salafi rulers are either with al Qa'ida, or with its enemies. As with the Groupement Islamique Armé and its enemy the Algerian state, there is 'no dialogue, no reconciliation, no truce'. Those who sought to conduct *jihad* as political activism by other means have found themselves with no political space to defend. And the rulers of Saudi Arabia have had their hypocrisy exposed, though the immediate instrument of their demise is more likely to be their erstwhile American ally than their disinherited son, Usama bin Laden.

The lack of a organised popular reaction to the US attack on Afghanistan and the Israeli attacks on Palestine should not delude us that mass mobilisation is dead. The consequences of the US war on Iraq, in the short term, may not be great. But the longer-term consequences may be enormous. The impact on public opinion of the continued and increasing Israeli repression of the Palestinians should not be underestimated. These events can only radicalise Muslims across the world. The US Administration may judge that Arab states' support for the Palestinian cause is only symbolic and superficial, but one of the lessons of al Qa'ida is that frustrated young people have means of acting beyond the reach of states. We are likely to face widespread violent resistance against American domination.

Jihadism's weaknesses may prove its strengths. It can cope with adversity and defeat. It can lose wars but still win hearts and minds. Usama bin Laden and al Qa'ida may be defeated. But they may be followed by others with comparable ambition. The structural conditions exist for a protracted global insurgency.

Where next for civil Islamism?

Most analyses of extremist or jihadist Islamism have centred on how far or how close jihadist Islamism is to 'real Islam'. This is misleading, as there is no such thing that can be construed as 'real Islam'. All depends upon the interpretation of Islam, and the different factors that influence the interpretation, consciously or unconsciously. The Fourth Rightly-Guided Caliph, Ali ibn Abu Talib, who was described by the Prophet as 'the door to the city of knowledge', said: 'The Qur'an is a script bound between two covers. It does not utter, but men speak of it.'

The fact remains that the Prophet Mohamed succeeded in his lifetime in transforming scattered nomadic tribes and some few urban centres in the Arabian peninsula into a strong nation that was capable of defeating the two powers of the time, namely the Persian and Roman Empires. Whether this happened because of the historical conditions of the time or because of God's intervention is a matter of belief. However, Islam undoubtedly provided the ideology that brought the Arabs together and built the empire. Many Muslim leaders have subsequently tried to repeat this feat, and rebuild that model. From Islamist groups such as Hezb al Tahrir, which does not believe in the nation state and calls instead for the restoration of the *khilafa*, to those that act solely within nationalist perimeters, to al Qa'ida which has a global scope but no declared programme, all believe that the way forward for Muslims is to repeat this experience. Such views can prevail only in extraordinary historical circumstances, but it appears that the combination of repression, demoralisation, intellectual terrorism by neo-fundamentalists, and now confrontation with the United States, has created precisely these circumstances.

In addition, the ability of Islamists to snatch 'little solutions' will continue to nourish Islamism in various forms. Whatever happens to its 'big project', Islamism will remain as an attempt at local social mobilisation, trying to establish a space and means for Muslims to build a community based on piety and justice. Islamic humanitarianism is more needed than ever, but its Salafist version is badly damaged by links to militancy including al Qa'ida, and will be trampled in the emergent global confrontation. Many Islamist civil society organisations are similarly needed but compromised. As argued in chapters 1 and 2, the 'Islamic civil society' that emerged in the Nile Valley is an inherently limited notion that has frequently served to impede freedom of expression and intellectual creativity. This is inherent in neo-fundamentalist Islamism, marked as it is by anti-intellectualism. But, as the vigorous debate in Iran demonstrates, such mental closure is not inherent in Islamism itself, let alone Islam. There is no reason why Sunni Muslims should not match their famously argumentative Shi'a co-religionists in readiness to stretch the limits of their political imagination.

There is an intellectual ferment in Sudan too. Hassan al Turabi's students are challenging their master, not only politically but intellectually too. The writings of Abdel Wahab El-Affendi, cited at various points in this book, demonstrate a readiness to assess the dilemmas of Islamism with remarkable honesty. We may criticise El-Affendi's attempted answers, but we must applaud both his readiness to pose the questions, and his support for the Sudanese peace process and an associated commitment to tolerance, pluralism and democracy. We may also criticise El-Affendi's earlier role as spokesman for the Sudan government, but this history is surely pivotal to his current position as critic and peace advocate. He has learned from experience. Most Sudanese writers' concern is overwhelmingly with short-term politics, but within these debates there is the kernel of a more fundamental reassessment of identity and the role of faith.

What Iran and Sudan have in common is the *experience* of trying to use state power to build an Islamic state. Experience is the great tutor, and Islamists are nothing if not adaptable. It is in perpetual opposition, trapped in the paralytic impasse of being unable to deliver sustainable 'little solutions' and being unable to progress in a 'big struggle' and confront Islamism's shortcomings, that the principle of *takfir* and its visceral intolerance flourish. For the struggle against neo-fundamentalist intolerance to succeed, there are two main preconditions. The most important is the intellectual leadership of Muslims, to create a civil society in the broader and more fundamental sense of an open society, that welcomes debate and is ready to debate subversive and even heretical ideas. The onus falls on secularist writers to be courageous in putting their views in an unapologetic manner, and enforce their rights through exercising them. The human rights community should advocate a real freedom of religion, which includes the right to change one's faith and the right to be without any faith at all. Any attempt to avoid provoking the neo-fundamentalists by compromise will only encourage the latter to ask for complete commitment to their views. This will require honest reflection upon recent history. It will demand the wider and more reflective teaching of the social sciences in Muslim universities. It will not be an easy struggle: neo-fundamentalists will resist with intimidation and violence, to compensate for their inadequate intellectual armoury. In north-east Africa the debate has its own unique dimensions, because of the region's extreme poverty, the eclipsed rivalry of revolutionary militarism, emergent Christian fundamentalism in Southern Sudan, and the dominance of concepts of 'development' and 'civil society' deployed by the World Bank and other major donors.

The second requirement for an open, civil Islamism is that the external adversaries of Islamism—most particularly the US government—provide the space for this debate to flourish. Confrontation will only nurture intolerance, jihadism may again become the sorcerer's apprentice of war.

BIBLIOGRAPHY

Abdel Rahim, Mudathir, 1969, *Imperialism and Nationalism in the Sudan*, London: Oxford University Press.

Abdel Rahman, Maha, 2001, 'State and Civil Society in Egypt', The Hague: Institute of Social Studies, PhD thesis.

Abdel Salam, A.H., and Alex de Waal (eds), 2001, *The Phoenix State: Civil Society and the Future of Sudan*, Lawrenceville, NJ: Red Sea Press.

Abdi Sheykh Abdi, 1992, *Divine Madness. Mohammed Abdulle Hassan (1856–1920)*, London: Zed Press.

Abdo, Geneive, 2000, *No God But God: Egypt and the Triumph of Islam*, Oxford University Press.

Aboagye, A., 1988, *The Informal Sector in Mogadishu: An Analysis of the Survey*, Addis Ababa: ILO/JASPA.

Abou El Fadl, Khaled, 2000, 'The Use and Abuse of "Holy War"', *Ethics and International Affairs*, 14, 133–40.

Abrahamsen, Rita, 2000, *Disciplining Democracy: Development Discourse and Good Governance in Africa*, London: Zed Books.

Abu Amud, Mohamed Saad, 1992, *The Associations of Political Islam and Violence in the Arab World*, Cairo: Al Ma'arif, October Books (in Arabic).

Abu Zaid, Nasr Hamed, 1992, *Critique of the Religious Discourse*, Cairo: Sina Publishing (in Arabic).

———, 1996, 'The Case of Abu Zaid', *Index on Censorship*, 4, 30–9.

Aburish, Saïd K., 1994, *The Rise, Corruption and Coming Fall of the House of Saud*, London: Bloomsbury.

———, 1997, *A Brutal Friendship: The West and the Arab Elite*, London: Indigo.

Adam, Hussein M., 1995, 'Islam and Politics in Somalia', *Journal of Islamic Studies*, 6 (2).

Africa Watch, 1990, *Somalia: A Government at War with its Own People*, London and New York: Africa Watch, January.

———, 1991, *Evil Days: Thirty Years of War and Famine in Ethiopia*, London and New York: Human Rights Watch.

African Rights, 1995a, *Sudan's Invisible Citizens: The Policy of Abuse against the Displaced People in the North*, London: African Rights.

———, 1995b, *Facing Genocide: The Nuba of Sudan*, London: African Rights.

———, 1997, *Food and Power in Sudan: A Critique of Humanitarianism*, London: African Rights.

Afrobarometer, 2002, 'Islam, Democracy and Public Opinion in Africa', Afrobarometer Briefing Paper no. 3, September, www.afrobarometer.org.

Ahmed, Khurshid (ed.), 1980, *Studies in Islamic Economics*, Leicester: The Islamic Foundation.

Ajami, Fouad, 1999, *The Dream Palace of the Arabs: A Generation's Odyssey*, New York: Vintage Books.

Ajawin, Yoanes, and Alex de Waal (eds), 2002, *When Peace Comes: Civil Society and Development in Sudan*, Lawrenceville, NJ: Red Sea Press.

Akbar, M.J., 2002, *The Shade of Swords: Jihad and the Conflict between Islam and Christianity*, London: Routledge.

al Banna, Hassan, 1990, *Collection of the Martyr Imam Hassan al Banna's Messages*, Alexandria: Al Da'wa House (in Arabic).

Alier, Abel, 1990, *Southern Sudan: Too Many Agreements Dishonoured*, Exeter: Ithaca Press.

al Jindi, Amina, 1989, 'Extremism among Youth: How the Egyptian University Student Leaders Think', *Manar Magazine*, 51, March 1989 (in Arabic).

al Karsani, Awad Al Sid, 1993, 'Beyond Sufism: the Case of Millennial Islam in Sudan' in Louis Brenner (ed.), *Muslim Identity and Social Change in Sub-Saharan Africa*, Bloomington: Indiana University Press.

al Qaradawi, Yusuf, 1981, *Economic Security in Islam*, Lahore: Kazi Publications.

———, 1987, *Islamic Awakening: Between Rejection and Extremism*, London: Zain International.

al Sadiq al Mahdi, 1983, 'Islam—Society and Change' in John L. Esposito (ed.), *Voices of Resurgent Islam*, Oxford University Press.

———, 2000, 'Second Birth in Sudan in the Cradle of Sustainable Human Rights', Cairo: Umma Party (paper presented at Kampala Conference, 'Human Rights in the Transition in Sudan', February 1999).

al Said, Rifaat, 1972, *Hassan al Banna—When, How and Why?* Cairo: Matbouli Bookshop (in Arabic).

al Tilmisani, Omer, 1982, 'Third Supreme Guide', interview in Cairo magazine *Al Musawar* 29 (89), 22 January (in Arabic).

al Turabi, Hassan, 1983, 'The Islamic State' in John L. Esposito (ed.), *Voices of Resurgent Islam*, Oxford University Press.

———, 1992, 'Islam as a Pan-National Movement and Nation States: An Islamic Doctrine on Human Association', London: Royal Society of Arts, Nationhood Lecture, 27 April.

———, 2001, *The Islamic Movement: The Lesson of the Journey of the Last Twelve Years*, Khartoum: Popular National Congress (in Arabic).

———, 2002, *The Phenomenon of Political Terrorism and the Evaluation of the September Incident in America*, Khartoum: pamphlet (in Arabic, originally published in *al Hayat*, 18–20 January 2002).

An-Na'im, Abdullahi Ahmed, 1990, *Towards an Islamic Reformation: Civil Liberties, Human Rights, and International Law*, Syracuse University Press.

Anderson, Lisa, 1983, 'Qaddafi's Islam', in John Esposito (ed.), *Voices of Resurgent Islam*, Oxford University Press.

Anonymous, 2002, *Through Our Enemies' Eyes: Osama Bin Laden, Radical Islam, and the Future of America*, Washington, DC: Brassey's.

Aqli, Abdirisaq, 1993, 'Historical Development of Islamic Movements in the Horn of Africa', paper delivered at the first conference of the European Association of Somali Studies, London, September.

Argenti, Nicolas, 2002, 'Youth in Africa: A Major Resource for Change' in Alex de Waal and Nicolas Argenti (eds), *Young Africa: Realising the Rights of Children and Youth*, Lawrenceville, NJ: Africa World Press.

Ariff, Mohamed (ed.), 1991, *The Islamic Voluntary Sector in Southeast Asia*, Opanjang: Institute of Southeast Asian Studies.

Armstrong, Karen, 2000, *The Battle for God*, New York: Ballantine Books.

Ataul Karim, Mark Duffield *et al.*, 1996, *OLS Review*, University of Birmingham, Centre for Urban and Regional Studies.

Auda, Gehad, 1991, 'An Uncertain Response: The Islamic Movement in Egypt', in James Piscatori (ed.), *Islamic Fundamentalisms and the Gulf Crisis*, Washington, DC: American Academy of Arts and Sciences.

Awad, Mohamed Hashim, 1984, 'Economic Islamisation in the Sudan: A Review', University of Khartoum: Development Studies Research Centre, Seminar no. 50, October.

Ayoob, M. (ed.), 1981, *The Politics of Islamic Reassertion*, London: Croom Helm.

Badri, Malik, 1997, *The AIDS Crisis: An Islamic Socio-cultural Perspective*, Kuala Lumpur: International Institute of Islamic Thought and Civilization.

Baer, Robert, 2002, *See No Evil: the True Story of a Ground Soldier in the CIA's War Against Terrorism*, New York: Random House.

Bahey el Din Hassan (ed.), 2000, *Arabs Caught between Domestic Oppression and Foreign Injustice*, Cairo Institute for Human Rights Studies.

Bannerman, T., 1988, *Islam in Perspective: A Guide to Islamic Society, Politics and Law*, London: Routledge.

Barkindo, B.M., 1993, 'Growing Islamism in Kano City since the 1970s: Causes, Form and Implications' in L. Brenner (ed.), *Muslim Identity and Social Change in Sub-Saharan Africa*, London: Hurst.

Barnett, Tony, and Alan Whiteside, 1999, 'HIV/AIDS and Development: Case Studies and a Conceptual Framework', *European Journal of Development Research*, 11/2, 200–34.

Bassam Tibi, 1998, *The Challenge of Fundamentalism: Political Islam and the New World Disorder*, Berkeley: University of California Press.

Benjamin, Daniel, and Steven Simon, 2002, *The Age of Sacred Terror*, New York: Random House.

Benthall, Jonathan, 1997, 'The Qu'ran's Call to Alms', *Times Higher Education Supplement*, 3 January, 15–16.

Berdal, Mats and David M. Malone, 2000, *Greed and Grievance: Economic Agendas in Civil Wars*, Boulder, CO: Lynne Rienner.

Bergen, Peter, 2002, *Holy War Inc.: Inside the Secret World of Osama bin Laden*, London: Weidenfeld.

Biobaku, Saburi, and Mohammed al Hajj, 1966, 'The Sudanese Mahdiyya and the Niger-Chad Region' in I. M. Lewis (ed.), *Islam in Tropical Africa*, Oxford University Press for International African Institute.

Bodansky, Yossef, 1999, *Bin Laden: The Man who Declared War on America*, New York: Forum.

Boisard, Marcel A., 1985, *L'Humanisme de l'Islam*, Paris: Albin Michel.

Bowden, Mark, 1999, *Black Hawk Down*, London: Bandam Press.

Brenner, Louis, 2000, 'Muslim Schooling, the State and the Ideology of Development in Mali' in T. Salter and K. King (eds), *Africa, Islam and Development*, Centre of African Studies, University of Edinburgh.

———, 1993, 'Constructing Muslim Identities in Mali', in Louis Brenner (ed.), *Muslim Identity and Social Change in Sub Saharan Africa*, London: Hurst and Co.

Burgat, François, 2003, 'Veils and Obscuring Lenses' in John L. Esposito and François Burgat (eds), *Modernizing Islam: Religion and the Public Sphere in Europe and the Middle East*, London: Hurst.

Cassanelli, Lee, 1975, 'Migrations, Islam and Politics in the Somali Benaadir (1500–1843)' in H. Marcus (ed.), *Proceedings of the First US conference on Ethiopian Studies*, East Lansing: Michigan State University Press.

———, 1982, *The Shaping of Somali Society, 1600–1850*, Philadelphia: University of Pennsylvania Press.

Castagno, A., 1964, 'The Somali Republic', in J. Coleman and R. Rosberg, *Political Parties and National Integration in Tropical Africa*, Berkeley and Los Angeles: University of California Press.

Červenka, Zdenek, 1977, *The Unfinished Quest for Unity: Africa and the OAU*, London: Julian Friedmann.

Chaliand, Gérard, 1985, *Terrorism: From Popular Struggle to Media Spectacle*, London: Saqi Books.

Chapra, M.U., 1992, *Islam and the Economic Challenge*, Leicester: Islamic Foundation and International Institute of Islamic Thought.

Choueiri, Youssef M., 1990, *Islamic Fundamentalism*, London: Pinter.

———, 1996, 'The Political Discourse of Contemporary Islamist Movements', in Abdel Salam Sidahmed and Anourshiravan Etheshami (eds), *Islamic Fundamentalism*, Boulder, CO: Westview Press.

———, 2000, *Arab Nationalism: a History*, Oxford: Blackwell.

Chouldhury, M.A., 1986, *Contributions to Islamic Economic Theory*, Basingstoke: Macmillan.

Cilliers, Jakkie, and Kathryn Sturman, 2002, *Africa and Terrorism: Joining the Global Campaign*, Pretoria: Institute for Security Studies, Monograph Series no. 74.

Cizakca, M., 2000, *A History of Philanthropic Foundations: the Islamic World from the Seventh Century to the Present Day*, Istanbul: Bogazic University Press.

Clausewitz, Carl von, 1968, *On War*, Harmondsworth: Penguin.

Commins, David, 1994, 'Hasan al-Banna (1906–1949)' in Ali Rahnema (ed.), *Pioneers of Islamic Revival*, London: Zed Press.

Compagnon, D., 1990, 'The Somali Armed Oppositional Fronts', *Horn of Africa*, 1 & 2.

Constantin, F., 1995, 'The Attempts to Create Muslim National Organisations in Tanzania, Uganda and Kenya', in H. B. Hansen and M. Twaddle (eds), *Religion and Politics in Africa*, London: James Currey.

Cooley, John K., 2000, *Unholy Wars: Afghanistan, America and International Terrorism*, London: Pluto Press, 2nd edn.

Creevey, L.E., 1980, 'Religion and Modernisation in Senegal' in J. L. Esposito (ed.), *Islam and Development*, Syracuse University Press.

de Waal, Alex, 1993, 'Sudan: Searching for the Origins of Absolutism and Decay', *Development and Change*, 24/1, 177–202.

———, 1994, 'Starving out the South', in Martin Daly and A. Alsikainga (eds), *Civil War in Sudan*, London: I. B. Tauris.

———, 1997a, *Famine Crimes: Politics and the Disaster Relief Industry in Africa*, Oxford: James Currey.

———, 1997b, 'Contemporary Warfare in Africa' in Mary Kaldor and Basker Vashee, *Restructuring the Global Military Sector*, vol. 1: *New Wars*, London: Pinter.

———, 2000a, 'Contemporary Islamic Humanitarianism in Sudan', in Thomas Salter and Kenneth King (eds), *Africa, Islam and Development*, University of Edinburgh, Centre of African Studies.

———, (ed.), 2000b, *Who Fights? Who Cares? War and Humanitarian Action in Africa*, Lawrenceville, NJ: Africa World Press.

———, 2002, *Demilitarising the Mind: African Agendas for Peace and Security*, Lawrenceville, NJ: Africa World Press.

———, 2003, 'How Will HIV/AIDS Transform African Governance?', *African Affairs*, 102, 1–24.

———, and Nicolas Argenti (eds), 2002, *Young Africa: Realising the Rights of Children and Youth*, Lawrenceville, NJ: Africa World Press.

Doran, Michael Scott, 2002, 'Somebody Else's Civil War', *Foreign Affairs* 81/1, January/February, 22–42.

Dorsey, J., 2002, 'Saudis Monitor Key Bank Accounts for Terror Funding at U.S. Request', *the Wall Street Journal*, 6 February.

Duffield, Mark, 2001, *Global Governance and the New Wars: The Merging of Development and Security*, London: Zed Press.

Edge, I. (ed.), 1996, *Islamic Law and Legal Theory*, New York University Press.

El-Affendi, Abdelwahab, 1990, 'Discovering the South: Sudanese Dilemmas for Islam in Africa', *African Affairs*, 89, 371–89.

———, 1991a, *Turabi's Revolution: Islam and Power in Sudan*, London: Grey Seal.

———, 1991b, *Who Needs an Islamic State?* London: Grey Seal.

———, 1999, 'The Sudanese Experiment and the Crisis of the Modern Islamist Movement: Lessons and Significance,' *al Quds al Arabi*, 29 December.

———, 2002, 'For a State of Peace: Conflict and the Future of Democracy in Sudan', London: University of Westminster, Centre for the Study of Democracy.

Ellis, Stephen, 2002, 'Writing Histories of Contemporary Africa', *Journal of African History*, 43, 1–26.

Esposito, John L., 1980, *Islam and Development*, Syracuse University Press.

———, 1995, *The Islamic Threat: Myth or Reality?*, Oxford University Press.

———, 1998, *Islam the Straight Faith*, Oxford University Press, Third Edition.

Evans, Harold, 2002, 'The Voice of Hate', *Index on Censorship*, 4/02, 5–15.

Fanon, Frantz, 1967, *The Wretched of the Earth*, Harmondsworth: Penguin.

Fazlur Rahman, 1982, *Islam and Modernity: Transformation of an Intellectual Tradition*, University of Chicago Press.

————, 2000, *Revival and Reform in Islam: A Study of Islamic Fundamentalism*, Oxford: One World.

Fidas, George, 2002, 'AIDS and Political Instability', presentation to conference, Yale University School of Law, October.

————, 2002, 'HIV/AIDS, National Security, and Policy Responses', Paper presented at the International Conflict Research Group Conference, 'HIV/AIDS as a Threat to Global Security', Yale University School of Law, 9 November.

Flores, Alexander, 1997, 'Secularism, Integralism, and Political Islam: The Egyptian Debate', in Joel Beinin and Joe Stork (eds), *Political Islam: Essays from Middle East Report*, London: I. B. Tauris.

Fromkin, David, 1989, *A Peace to End All Peace: The Fall of the Ottoman Empire and the Creation of the Modern Middle East*, New York: Avon Books.

Gerholm, Thomas, 1997, 'The Islamization of Contemporary Egypt', in David Westerlund and Eva Evers Rosander (eds), *African Islam and Islam in Africa: Encounters Between Sufis and Islamists*, London: Hurst and Co.

Gifford, Paul, 1998, *African Christianity: Its Public Role*, London: Hurst.

Gilsenan, Michael, 1982, *Recognizing Islam: Religion and Society in the Modern Middle East*, London: Croom Helm.

Golden, Daniel, 2002, 'Western Scholars Play Key Role in Touting "Science" of Koran', *Wall Street Journal*, 23 January.

Grossman, Lt.-Col. Dave, 1995, *On Killing: The Psychological Cost of Learning to Kill in War and Society*, Boston, MA: Back Bay Books.

Guevara, Che, 1998, *Guerrilla Warfare*, Lincoln: University of Nebraska Press.

Gunaratna, Rohan, 2002, *Inside Al Qaeda: Global Network of Terror*, London: Hurst; New York: Columbia University Press.

Haddad, Y.Y., 1983, 'Sayyid Qutb: Ideologue of Islamic Revival' in John L. Esposito (ed.), *Voices of Resurgent Islam*, Oxford University Press.

Haider, Ali, 1996, *The Islamic Trend and the Case of Democracy*, Cairo: Centre for Arab Unity Studies (in Arabic).

Hale, Sondra, 1997, *Gender Politics in Sudan: Islamism, Socialism and the State*, Boulder, CO: Westview Press.

Hamad, Ordesse, 1995, 'On NIF Ideological Indoctrination and Islamist Education Programmes', *Alwah*, Journal of Sudanese Writers and Journalists in UK, May (in Arabic).

Hansen, Holger Bernt, and M. Twaddle (eds), 1995, *Religion and Politics in Africa*, London: James Currey.

Hassan Makki Mohamed Ahmed, 1989, *Sudan: The Christian Design: A Study of the Missionary Factor in Sudan's Cultural and Political Integration 1843–1986*, Leicester: Islamic Foundation.

Helander, Bernard, 1999, 'Somali Islam as World View and Unifying Factor' in David Westerlund and Ingvar Svanberg (eds), *Islam outside the Arab World*, Richmond: Curzon Press.

Hersi, Ali Abdirahman 1977, 'The Arab Factor in Somali History: The Origins and Development of Arab Enterprise and Cultural Influence on the Somali Peninsula', PhD thesis, University of California, Los Angeles.

Hiro, Dilip, 2002, *War Without End: the Rise of Islamist Terrorism and Global Response*, London: Routledge.

Horne, Alistair, 1977, *A Savage War of Peace: Algeria, 1954–1962*, London: Macmillan.

Hunter, Shireen, 1998, *The Future of Islam and the West: Clash of Civilizations or Peaceful Coexistence?* Westport, CT: Praeger.

Hunwick, John, 1997, 'Sub-Saharan Africa and the Wider World of Islam: Historical and Contemporary Perspectives', in David Westerlund, and Eva Evers Rosander (eds), *African Islam and Islam in Africa: Encounters Between Sufis and Islamists*, London: Hurst.

Ibrahim, Saad Eddin, 1995, 'Civil Society and the Prospects for Democratization in the Arab World', in Augustus Norton (ed.), *Civil Society in the Middle East*, Leiden: E. J. Brill.

———, 2002, *Egypt, Islam and Democracy: Critical Essays*, Cairo and New York: American University in Cairo Press.

Imam, Zakaria Bashir, 1996, 'From the Laws of Dynamism in the Holy Koran: Social and Economic Planning,' *Al Inqaz al Watani*, 30 May (in Arabic).

Indyk, Martin, 2002, 'Back to the Bazaar', *Foreign Affairs* 81/1, Jan./Feb./May, 75–88.

Inglehart, Ronald, and Pippa Norris, 2003, 'The True Clash of Civilizations', *Foreign Policy*, March/April, 62–71.

Iyob, Ruth, 1995, *The Struggle for Eritrean Independence: Domination, Resistance, Nationalism, 1941–1993*, Cambridge University Press.

Jamal, Vali, 1988, 'Somalia: Understanding an Unconventional Economy', *Development and Change*, 19.

Jansen, J.J.G., 1997, *The Dual Nature of Islamic Fundamentalism*, London: Hurst.

Jardine, D., 1923, *The Mad Mollah of Somaliland*, London: Herbert Jenkins.

Jenkins, Rob, 2002, 'Mistaking "Governance" for "Politics": Foreign Aid, Democracy and the Construction of Civil Society', in Sudipta Kaviraj and Sunil Khilnani (eds), *Civil Society: History and Possibilities*, Cambridge University Press.

Jomo, K.S. (ed.), 1992, *Islamic Economic Alternatives*, Basingstoke: Macmillan.

Kaldor, Mary, 1999, *New and Old Wars: Organized Violence in a Global Era*, London: Polity Press.

Kapteijns, Lidwien, 1985, 'Mahdist Faith and the Legitimation of Popular Revolt in Western Sudan,' *Africa*, 55, 390–9.

Karam, Azza M., 1997, 'Women, Islamisms and the State: Dynamics of Power and Contemporary Feminisms in Egypt', in C. J. Hamelink (ed.), *Ethics and Development: On Making Moral Choices in Development Co-operation*, Kampen Uitgeverij.

Karrar, Ali Salih, 1992, *The Sufi Brotherhoods in the Sudan*, London: Hurst.

Keane, John, 1998, *Civil Society: Old Images, New Visions*, London: Polity Press.

Keddie, Nikki R., 1994, 'Sayyid Jamal al-Din "al-Afghani"', in Ali Rahnema (ed.), *Pioneers of Islamic Revival*, London: Zed Press.

Keen, David, 1998, 'The Economic Functions of Violence in Civil Wars', London: International Institute for Strategic Studies, Adelphi Paper no. 320.

Keen, David, 2000, 'Incentives and Disincentives for Violence' in Mats Berdal and David Malone (eds), *Greed and Grievance: Economic Agendas in Civil Wars*, Boulder, CO: Lynne Rienner.

Kepel, Gilles, 1993, *Muslim Extremism in Egypt: The Prophet and the Pharaoh*, Berkeley: University of California Press, 2nd edn.

———, 2002, *Jihad: The Trail of Political Islam*, Cambridge, MA: Belknap Press.

Kolho, Gabriel, 1994, *Century of War: Politics, Conflicts, and Society since 1914*, New York: The New Press.

Kotb, S. [Sayyid Qutb], 1953, *Social Justice in Islam*, Washington, DC: American Council of Learned Societies.

Kukah, M.H., 1993, *Religion, Politics and Power in Northern Nigeria*, Ibadan: Spectrum.

———, and T. Falola, 1996, *Religious, Militancy and Self-Assertion: Islam and Politics in Nigeria*, Aldershot: Avebury.

Kuran, T., 1986, 'The Islamic Economic System in Contemporary Islamic Thought', *International Journal of Middle East Studies*, vol. 18.

Laitin, D., 1977, *Politics, Language and Thought. The Somali Experience*, University of Chicago Press.

Lam Akol, 2001, *SPLM/SPLA: Inside an African Revolution*, Khartoum University Press.

Lan, David, 1985, *Guns and Rain: Guerrillas and Spirit Mediums in Zimbabwe*, London: James Currey.

Laqueur, Walter, 1977, *A History of Terrorism*, New York: Little, Brown.

———, 1999, *The New Terrorism: Fanaticism and the Arms of Mass Destruction*, London: Phoenix Press.

Laremont, Ricardo René, 2000, *Islam and the Politics of Resistance in Algeria, 1783–1992*, Lawrenceville, NJ: Africa World Press.

Last, Murray, 1992, 'The Power of Youth, Youth of Power: Notes on the Religions of the Young in Northern Nigeria', in Hélène d'Almeida-Topor, Catherine Coquéry-Vidrovitch, Odile Goer and Françoise Guitart (eds), *Les jeunes en Afrique. La Politique et la Ville*, Paris: L'Harmattan.

Leenco Lata, 1999, *The Ethiopian State at the Crossroads: Decolonization and Democratization or Disintegration?* Lawrenceville, NJ: Red Sea Press.

LeShan, Lawrence, 2002, *The Psychology of War: Comprehending its Mystique and its Madness*, New York: Helios Press.

Lewis, Ioan, 1986, *Religion in Context: Cults and Charisma*, Cambridge University Press.

———, 1988, *A Modern History of Somalia*, Boulder, CO: Westview Press.

———, 1998, *Saints and Somalis: Popular Islam in a Clan-Based Society*, Lawrenceville, NJ: Red Sea Press.

Lissner, J., 1977, *The Politics of Altruism*, Geneva: Lutheran World Federation.

Mao Tse-Tung, 2000, *On Guerrilla Warfare*, trans. Samuel B. Griffith, Urbana: University of Illinois Press.

Malan, Mark, 2002, 'The Post-9/11 Security Agenda and Peacekeeping in Africa', *African Security Review*, 11/3, 54–66.

Marchal, Roland, 1993, 'Les Mooryaan de Mogadishu: recomposition urbaine dans un espace en guerre', *Cahiers d'Études Africaines*, 131.

———, 2000, 'Mogadiscio dans la guerre civile. Rêves d'État', *Les Études du CERI*, 69, October.

———, and C. Messiant, 1997, *Les chemins de la guerre et de la paix*, Paris: Karthala.

Markakis, John, 1987, *National and Class Conflict in the Horn of Africa*, Cambridge University Press.

Marshall, R., 1995, ' "God is Not a Democrat"; Pentecostalism and Democratisation in Nigeria', in P. Gifford (ed.), *The Christian Churches and the Democratisation of Africa*, Leiden: E. J. Brill.

Martinez, Luis, 2000, *The Algerian Civil War, 1990–1998*, London: Hurst.

Marty, Martin E., and R. Scott Appleby (eds), 1994, *Accounting for Fundamentalisms: The Dynamic Character of Movements*, University of Chicago Press.

——— (eds), 1995, *Fundamentalisms Comprehended*, University of Chicago Press.

Mayer, A.E., 1985, 'Sudanese Laws Affecting the Private Sector and the Economy: Assessment of Legal Developments From 1983 to Mid-1985', USAID, Khartoum: 1985, cited in Richard Brown, *Public Debt and Private Wealth: Debt, Capital Flight and the IMF in Sudan*, London: Macmillan, 1992.

Medhane Tadesse, 2002, *Al-Ittihad: Political Islam and Black Economy in Somalia*, Addis Ababa: Meag Printing Enterprise.

Mehmet, O., 1990, *Islamic Identity and Development: Studies in the Islamic Periphery*, London and New York: Routledge.

Moosa, Ebrahim, 2000, 'Introduction' to Fazlur Rahman, *Revival and Reform in Islam: A Study of Islamic Fundamentalism*, Oxford: One World.

Mostyn, Trevor, 2002, *Censorship in Islamic Societies*, London: Saqi Books.

Muhammed Mahmoud, 1997, 'Sufism and Islamism in the Sudan' in David Westerlund and Eva Evers Rosander (eds), *African Islam and Islam in Africa: Encounters Between Sufis and Islamists*, London: Hurst.

Mukhtar, Mohamed Haji, 1995, 'Islam and Somali History', in Ali Ahmed Jimale (ed.), *The Invention of Somalia*, Lawrenceville, NJ: Red Sea Press.

Mutalib, H. and Taj ul-Islam Hashmi (eds), 1994, *Islam, Muslims and the Modern State*, Basingstoke: Macmillan Press.

NAFIR, 1997, 'The History of the Battle of Tullishi Mountain', *NAFIR: The Newsletter of the Nuba Mountains, Sudan*, Nuba Mountains Solidarity Abroad, 3/3, October, 6–8.

National Intelligence Council, 2002, 'The Next Wave of HIV/AIDS: Nigeria, Ethiopia, Russia, India and China', Washington, DC: Intelligence Community Assessment 2002–04-D, September.

Nelson, H. (ed.), 1982, *Somalia: a Country Study*, Washington, DC: US Government.

O'Toole Salinas, Anne, and Brian C. D'Silva, 1999, 'Evolution of a Transition Strategy and Lessons Learned: USAID Funded Activities in the West Bank of Southern Sudan, 1993 to 1999', Washington, DC, and Nairobi: USAID, AFR/SD and REDSO/ESA.

Olawale, A., 1997, 'Kano: Religious Fundamentalism and Violence' in G. Herault and P. Adesanmi (eds), *Youth, Street Culture and Urban Violence in Africa*, IFRA.

Perinham, B. Marie, 1982, *Holy Violence: The Revolutionary Thought of Frantz Fanon*, Washington, DC: Three Continents Press.

Pipes, Daniel, 2001/02, 'God and Mammon: Does Poverty Cause Militant Islam?', *The National Interest*, 66, 14–21.

Piscatori, James, 1991, 'Religion and Realpolitik: Islamic Responses to the Gulf War' in James Piscatori (ed.), *Islamic Fundamentalisms and the Gulf Crisis*, Washington, DC: American Academy of Arts and Sciences.

Proctor, J.H. (ed.), 1965, *Islam and International Relations*, London: Pall Mall Press.

Procyshen, Crystal, 2001, 'Islam, Institutions and Insurgency: Territorial and Network Jihad', *Conflict, Security, Development*, 1/3, December, 33–53.

Qaoud, Ala, 2000, *Towards Reform of Religious Sciences: The Model of Azharic Education*, Cairo Institute for Human Rights Studies, Human Rights Studies Series no. 7 (in Arabic).

Qutb, Sayyid, 1990, *Milestones*, Plainfield, IN: American Trust Publications.

Reeve, Simon, 1999, *The New Jackals: Ramzi Yousef, Osama bin Laden and the Future of Terrorism*, London: André Deutsch.

Reichmuth, S., 1993, 'Islamic Learning and its Interaction with Western Education in Ilorin, Nigeria' in L. Brenner (ed.), *Muslim Identity and Social Change in Sub-Saharan Africa*, London: Hurst.

Reno, William, 1998, *Warlord Politics and African States*, Boulder, CO: Lynne Rienner.

Rifat Sid Ahmed, 1989, *The Islamic Anger Organisations in the Seventies*, Cairo: Madbuli (in Arabic).

Roff, W.R., 1987, *Islam and the Political Economy of Meaning*, London: Croom Helm.

Rosander, Eva Evers, 1997, 'Introduction: The Islamization of "Tradition" and "Modernity"' in David Westerlund and Eva Evers Rosander (eds), *African Islam and Islam in Africa: Encounters Between Sufis and Islamists*, London: Hurst.

Roy, Olivier, 1999, *The Failure of Political Islam*, London: I. B. Tauris.

Said, Edward W., 1991, *Orientalism: Western Conceptions of the Orient*, Harmondsworth: Penguin.

Salih, M. A. Mohamed, 1995, 'Resistance and Response: Ethnocide and Genocide in the Nuba Mountains, Sudan', *GeoJournal*, 36, 71–8.

——, 1998, 'Political Narratives and Identity Formation in Post 1989 Sudan' in M. A. Mohamed Salih and John Markakis (eds), *Ethnicity and the State in Eastern Africa*, Uppsala: Nordiska Afrikainstitutet.

——, 2000, 'Islamic Ethics and Sustainable Development: An African Perspective' in T. Salter and K. King (eds), *Africa, Islam and Development*, Centre of African Studies, University of Edinburgh.

——, 2001, *African Democracies and African Politics*, London: Pluto Press.

Samatar, Ahmed, 1988, *Socialist Somalia: Rhetoric and Reality?*, London: Zed Books.

Samatar, Said, 1992, *In the Shadow of Conquest. Islam in Colonial Northeast Africa*, Lawrenceville, NJ: Red Sea Press.

Sidahmed, Abdel Salam, 1996, 'Sudan: Ideology and Pragmatism' in Abdel Salam Sidahmed and Anourshiravan Eteshami (eds), *Islamic Fundamentalism*, Boulder, CO: Westview Press.

Simons, Anna, 1995, *Networks of Dissolution: Somalia Undone*, Boulder, CO: Westview Press.

Sperling, D.C., 1993, 'Rural Madaris of the Southern Kenyan Coast 1971–1992', in L. Brenner (ed.), *Muslim Identity and Social Change in Sub-Saharan Africa*, London: Hurst.

Starrett, Gregory, 1998, *Putting Islam to Work: Education, Politics and Religious Transformation in Egypt*, Berkeley: University of California Press.

Steed, Christopher and David Westerlund, 1999, 'Nigeria' in David Westerlund and Ingvar Svanberg (eds), *Islam Outside the Arab World*, Richmond: Curzon Press.

Stork, Joe, 2002, 'The Human Rights Crisis in the Middle East in the Aftermath of September 11', Paper presented at Cairo Institute of Human Rights Studies conference, 'Terrorism and Human Rights', 26–28 January.

Sudan Rights Programme, 1998, 'What Islam? Destruction of Mosques and Islamic Schools by the Government of Sudan', Addis Ababa: Inter Africa Group, *Sudan Rights Bulletin* no. 2, September.

Sullivan, Denis J., 1994a, 'Islam and Development in Egypt: Civil Society and the State' in H. Mutalib and Taj ul-Islam Hashmi (eds), *Islam, Muslims and the Modern State*, Basingstoke: Macmillan.

———, 1994b, *Private Voluntary Organisations in Egypt: Islamic Development, Private Initiative and State Control*, Gainesville: University Press of Florida.

———, and Sana Abed-Kotob, 1999, *Islam in Contemporary Egypt: Civil Society vs. the State*, Boulder, CO: Lynne Rienner.

Taha, Mohamed Mahmoud, 1990, *The Second Message of Islam*, trans. Abdullahi an-Naim, Syracuse University Press.

Taji-Farouki, Suha, 1996, 'Islamic State Theories and Contemporary Realities', in Abdel Salam Sidahmed and Anoushiravan Eteshami (eds), *Islamic Fundamentalism*, Boulder, CO: Westview Press.

Taleghani, A.S.M., 1982, *Society and Economics in Islam*, Berkeley: Mizan Press.

Touval, S., 1964, *Somali Nationalism*, New York: Praeger.

Tozy, Mohamed, 1996, 'Movements of Religious Renewal' in Stephen Ellis (ed.), *Africa Now: People, Policies, Institutions*, Oxford: James Currey.

Trimingham, J., 1965, *Islam in Ethiopia*, London: Frank Cass.

Tripp, Charles, 1994, 'Sayyid Qutb: The Political Vision' in Ali Rahnema (ed.), *Pioneers of Islamic Revival*, London: Zed Press.

———, 1996, 'Islam and the Secular Logic of the State in the Middle East', in Abdel Salam Sidahmed and Anoushiravan Eteshami (eds), *Islamic Fundamentalism*, Boulder, CO: Westview Press.

Tuchman, Barbara, *The March of Folly: From Troy to Vietnam*, London: Abacus, 1984.

Umar, Muhammed Sani, 1993, 'Changing Islamic Identity in Nigeria from the 1960s to the 1980s: From Sufism to anti-Sufism' in Louis Brenner (ed.), *Muslim Identity and Social Change in Sub-Saharan Africa*, London: Hurst.

Ushari Mahmoud and Suleiman Baldo, 1987, *El-Diein Massacre and Slavery in the Sudan*, Khartoum.

Utvik, Bjørn Olav, 2003, 'The Modernizing Force of Islam' in John L. Esposito and François Burgat (eds), *Modernizing Islam: Religion and the Public Sphere in Europe and the Middle East*, London: Hurst.

Van Crefeld, Martin, *On Future War*, London: Brassey's, 1991.

Vergès, Meriam, 1997, 'Genesis of a Mobilization: the Young Activists of Algeria's Islamic Salvation Front', in Joel Beinin and Joe Stork (eds), *Political Islam: Essays from Middle East Report*, London: I. B. Tauris.

Warburg, G., 1978, *Islam, Nationalism and Communism in a Traditional Society: The Case of Sudan*, London: Frank Cass.

Ward, K., 1999, 'Africa' in Adrian Hastings (ed.), *A World History of Christianity*, London: Cassell.

Watt, W.M., 1988, *Islamic Fundamentalism and Modernity*, London and New York: Routledge.

Weaver, Mary Anne, 1999, *A Portrait of Egypt: A Journey through the World of Militant Islam*, New York: Farrar, Straus and Giroux.

Westerlund, David, 1997, 'Reaction and Action: Accounting for the Rise of Islamism' in David Westerlund and Eva Evers Rosander (eds), *African Islam and Islam in Africa: Encounters Between Sufis and Islamists*, London: Hurst.

———— and Eva Evers Rosander (eds), 1997, *African Islam and Islam in Africa: Encounters Between Sufis and Islamists*, London: Hurst.

Wickham, Carrie Rosefsky, 1997, 'Islamic Mobilization and Political Change: The Islamic Trend in Egypt's Professional Associations' in Joel Beinin and Joe Stork (eds), *Political Islam: Essays from Middle East Report*, London: I. B. Tauris.

William, John Hanna and J. Lynne Hanna, 1971, *Urban Dynamics in Black Africa: An Interdisciplinary Approach*, Chicago: Aldine, Atherton.

Woodward, Bob, 2002, *Bush at War*, New York: Simon and Shuster.

Zineldin, M., 1990, *The Economic of Money and Banking: A Theoretical and Empirical Study of Islamic Interest-free Banking*, Stockholm: Almqist and Wiksell.

Zubaida, Sami, 1997, 'Religion, the State and Democracy: Contrasting Concepts of Society in Egypt' in Joel Beinin and Joe Stork (eds), *Political Islam: Essays from Middle East Report*, London: I. B. Tauris.

————, 2001, 'Civil Society, Community and Democracy in the Middle East' in Sudipta Kaviraj and Sunil Khilnani (eds), *Civil Society: History and Possibilities*, Cambridge University Press.

INDEX

Aba *Island* 162
Abane, Ramdane 28
Abdel Hafiz, Ibrahim 90–1, 94, 95, 96, 97, 99
Abdel Kader, Amir 64
Abdel Karim, Khalil 60
Abdel Rahman, Omar 25, 45, 191, 218
Abdille Hassan, Mohamed 65
Abduh, Mohamed 5, 26, 42
Abgaal 130n, 132, 133
Abu Hamza, Imam 7
Abu Nidal 194
Abu Zaid, Nasr Hamid 16, 60, 61
Acholi 198, 248
Adabiyya Muslim Society 163
Addis Ababa 202, 205, 206, 207
Afghani, Jamal al Din al 5, 26, 36n
Afghanistan: 8, 13, 14, 24, 38, 40–1, 43, 45, 46–7, 50, 68, 94, 100, 105, 169, 175, 176–7, 191, 193, 199, 216, 218, 221, 241, 246, 252, 253–4, 255; Arab volunteers in 8, 43, 44, 45, 46–7, 73n, 126, 139, 196, 201, 252
Aflaq, Michel 59
Afrah, Mahamed Qanyere 136
African National Congress 67
African Union 67; *see also* Organisation of African Unity
Aga Khan and Aga Khan Foundation 173–4
Agab, Mansur el 72
Ahle Sunna wa Jama'a 124
Ahmadiyya 124, 160
Ahmed, Abdullahi Yuusuf 129
AIDS and HIV 24, 198, 234, 249–51

Ajami, Fouad 62–3
Akol, Lam 207, 210
Al Qaida 8, 19–20, 22, 40–1, 45–50, 68, 114, 139, 172, 194, 196, 199–200, 206, 213, 223, 226, 229, 231–9, 240–1, 246, 251, 253–6
Al-Haramain Foundation 175
Albania 193
Albright, Madeleine 220
Algeria 9, 24, 28–9, 32, 38, 44, 46, 58, 67, 68, 190n, 193, 255
Algiers Convention on Terrorism 234–5
Allied Democratic Forces (ADF) (Uganda) 198–200, 208–9
Amal Trust 227
Amin, Idi 199, 200
Amin, Qaasim 5
Angola 154, 237
Ansar 4, 76, 79, 162
Ansar al Sunna 82, 111, 125
Ansar al-Islam Society 163
Ansar e Sunna a Wahhabi 125
Ansarul Din 160
'Arab Afghans', *see* Afghanistan, Arab volunteers in
Arab Bank for Economic Development in Africa 68
Arab League 83, 118, 190, 236
Arafat, Yasser 29
Arta conference 127, 138–9
Asmara 200, 201, 210
Asosa, *Asosa Operation* 187–9, 201
Asyut 43
Ataturk, Mustafa Kemal 25
Auda, Salman al 36
Awad, Mohamed Hashim 94

271

'Awwa, Mohamed Salim al 6, 38–9, 42, 88
Aydiid, Hussein 142n
Aydiid, Mahamed Faarah 122, 128–31, 132–3, 134–5, 140, 145
Azhar, al 16, 27, 51, 52, 59, 61, 66, 84, 118
Azzam, Abdalla 25, 45, 47, 49, 56n, 73n

Ba'ath party 59
Badri, Malik 249, 250
Baggara Arabs 99
Baghdad 25, 191
Bakool 131
Bamiyan Buddhas 38, 100
Bangladesh 94, 169
banks 94, 154, 177–8
Banna, Hassan al 24, 26–7, 54–5, 127
Banshiri, Abu Ubaida al 199–200
Baraawe 127, 128
Barakaat, al 19, 114–15, 140–4, 246–7
Bashir, Omer al 72, 82, 85, 97, 99, 100, 105, 106–9, 183, 189, 190, 197, 203–4, 206, 210, 223, 226, 242, 243, 245
Bay *region, Somalia* 131, 213
Beja 73, 99, 214, 227
Beja Congress 82n, 201
Benaadir 142
Beni Shangul Liberation Front 204, 205
Benin 172
Berti 99
Betai, Ali 82
Betelco 140
Bin Baz, Shaikh 36
Bin Laden, Usama 1, 8–9, 19–20, 25, 40–1, 45–50, 68, 82, 94, 111, 114, 140, 176–8, 192, 194, 195n, 199, 216, 221–2, 226, 231, 251, 253–4
Bishri, Tariq al 51–2
Blair, Tony 232–3
Bod, Hussein Haji 124
Bolad, Daoud 98–9, 108
Bongo, Omar 69

Boosaaso 127
Bosnia 13, 14, 105, 193
Boumedienne, Houari 28–9
Britain 4, 26, 29, 59, 66, 71–2, 116–17, 168, 178, 232–3, 237, 238, 242, 243
Burco 119
Burkina Faso 237
Burundi 168, 169, 171
Bush, George W. 182, 223, 226, 241, 253
Bush, George (senior) 219
Buulo Haawa 128, 138

Cairo 51, 64, 66, 135, 161
Caliphate/*khilafa* 5, 25, 26, 27, 43, 48–9, 254, 256
Cameroon 175
Canada 220, 238
Casablanca Group 66
Catholic Church 120, 165
censorship 52, 61, 62, 240
Central African Republic 99
Chad 67, 99, 154, 172, 173, 183, 197, 209n
Chechnya 194
China 31, 33
Christianity 14, 26, 59, 65, 97, 117, 153, 164, 165, 172, 229, 250, 251, 253, 257
CIA 36, 217, 218
civil society 10–13, 56, 110, 180, 257
Clausewitz, Carl von 29–30, 33, 34, 44
Clinton, Bill 217, 220, 222n, 224, 225, 228
Communism 54, 56, 59–60, 79, 118, 195, 244
'comprehensive *da'wa*' 10, 12, 89–97, 100, 195
Congo (Democratic Republic)/ Congo/Zaire 99, 168, 183, 197, 199–200, 202, 207–9, 210, 219, 220–1, 237
Copts 26, 43, 100

Counter-Terrorism Bureau (US) 218, 222

da'wa 10, 13, 14, 18, 30, 66, 68, 69, 89–100, 103–5, 146, 165, 167, 172, 179, 184, 191, 195
Da'wa al Islamiyya, al 69
Daarood 121, 122, 129
Dallah al Baraka Group 141n
Damazin 90–91, 97, 209–10
Danforth, John 226, 241, 242
Dar Masalit 77, 99
Darfur 77, 78, 98–9
See also, Fur
Democratic Unionist Party (DUP) 98, 109, 207
Deng, William 79
Dheere, Sheykh Ali 134
Diwan al Zakat 92–3
Djibouti 126, 127, 137, 142, 143, 233, 235–6, 238, 239
Dolo 207
Dubai 115, 118, 142, 143

East Africa, *see also* names of countries 158–9, 163, 164, 172, 174
East African Muslim Welfare Society 174
education 52–4, 57–8, 66, 78, 118, 158–68
Egypt: 3, 5, 10, 16, 17, 22, 23, 26–8, 39–40, 42–3, 45, 46, 48, 51–63, 64, 66–7, 68, 69, 70, 75, 76, 84, 94, 111, 138, 161, 162, 168, 169, 182–4, 190–3, 194, 195, 203, 206, 214–16, 222, 231, 233, 239–40, 242, 243, 248, 250, 252; education 52–4, 57–8; Islamic Trend 5, 52, 57, 60
El-Affendi, Abdelwahab 50–1, 65, 81, 88, 98, 191, 256–7
El Obeid 72, 74, 102
Equatoria province 185, 206–7, 209
Equatorial Guinea 237
Eritrea 24, 30, 33, 67n, 138, 163, 183–4, 195, 197, 200–8, 210–20, 224, 226, 228, 236, 238, 248, 252

Eritrea Jihad 201, 248
Eritrean Liberation Front 248
Eritrean Liberation Front-Revolutionary Command 201
Eritrean Peoples Liberation Front (EPLF) 187–9, 200–1, 222n
Erwa, El Fathi 221–2
Ethiopia 3, 24, 67, 97, 105, 115, 118, 119, 121, 125, 128, 138–9, 140, 154, 156, 182–4, 196n, 197, 200–20, 222n, 224, 226, 228, 236, 248, 252, 252
Ethiopian Peoples Revolutionary Democratic Front (EPRDF) 187–9, 196n, 197, 202–5, 222n
European Union 238

Fadl, Mohamed el Tayeb 102
Fahd, King 190, 193, 221
Falashas 222n
Fanon, Frantz 29
Faraah, Hassan Abshir 138
Farag, Abdel Salam 25, 39–40, 42–3, 45, 49
Fazlur Rahman 16, 42, 51
FBI 14, 172, 175, 178, 217, 218, 223
Fellata 77, 78, 96, 97, 99
FIS (Front Islamique du Salut) 44
FLN (Front de Libération Nationale) 28, 34, 44
Foda, Farag 16, 60, 61, 215
Fodio, Uthman dan 64
France 28–9, 59, 75, 178, 220, 222
Funj 96, 97
Fur 78, 99

Gabon 69, 237
Gaddafi, Col. Muammar 69
Galeyr, Ali Khalif 138, 142
Galgadud 129
Gam'a al Islamiyya, al 25, 43, 45, 60, 100, 194, 206, 215, 216
Gambella 202–3, 211
Gambia, The 172
Garang, John 81, 202, 209, 220, 241, 243, 245

Garissa 165
Ganyaare, Sheykh Mohamed Ahmed 119
Gedo 128, 129, 132, 139
Germany 46, 238, 246
Gezira, al (TV station) 47
Ghana 66, 172
GIA (Groupement Islamique Armé) 44, 255
Great Islamic Encyclopaedia 173
Guevara, Che 33, 34, 98
Guinea 168, 173
Gulf states 13, 35, 53, 68, 81, 94, 115, 118, 126, 127, 191, 205
Gulf War (1991) 24, 46, 68, 190–3, 217
Gumi, Shaikh Abubakar 160–61

Habbash, George 29, 193
Halaib 251
Hamas 45, 193, 194
Hamdi, Abdel Rahim 196
Hargeysa 119, 142
Harti 128
Hassan, Abdiqassem Salad 137
Havel, Vaclav 11–12
Hawali, Safar al 36
Hawiye 122
Hezb al Tahrir 39, 256
Hezbe Itihaad al Islaami 120
Hezbollah 36, 194
Hitaab agreement 133
humanitarianism, Islamic 13–15, 68, 103–5, 115, 144, 146–81, 161, 195, 202
Hussein, Abdel Majid 207
Husseini, Haj Amin el 29
Husseini, Lt. -Gen. Abdel Karim 72,
Husseini, Sayed Abdel Karim al 102

Ibrahim Bin Abdul Aziz Al Ibrahim Foundation 175
Ibrahim, Saad Eddin 11, 239
Ibrahim, Tayeb 99
IGAD (Intergovernmental Authority on Development) 203, 210, 212,

216, 218, 219, 222, 225, 226, 242, 243
India (and Indian Subcontinent) 27n, 172, 173, 174, 198, 238
Indonesia 169
Ingenessa 95–6
International Islamic *Da'wa* Society (Libya) 167; *see also* World Islamic Call Society
International Islamic Relief Organisation (IIRO) 168–72, 175, 179
Iran 2, 5, 15, 17, 24, 36, 46, 77, 101, 116, 117, 118, 190, 191, 199, 240, 250, 253, 257
Iraq 2, 24, 46, 47, 59, 171, 190–3, 229, 238, 241, 243, 253
Islaah, al 126–7, 135, 136, 137
Islamic African Relief Agency 68, 154
Islamic Charter Front 79
Islamic Commission for Economic, Cultural and Social Affars (ISCECSA) 167
Islamic Committee of the International Crescent 167
Islamic Development Bank 68, 156, 171
Islamic Front for the Liberation of Oromia 204, 205
Islamic Jihad (Palestine) 194
Islamic justice in Somalia 132–7, 142, 144
Islamic Relief 14
Islamic Trend (Egypt) 5, 52, 57, 60
Ismail, Mustafa 193, 243
Ismailis 173–4
Israel 8, 29–30, 49, 59, 63, 66, 67, 231, 233, 236, 239, 253, 254, 255
Isseyas Afewerki 201, 202, 212, 220, 236, 238, 248
Islambuli, khalid al- 42–3
Italy 116–17, 118
Itihaad al Islaami, al 114, 125, 126, 127, 128, 129, 135, 136, 138, 139–40, 204, 205, 207, 212–13, 224, 246–7

Jama'at Ahlal Islami 119
Jama'at Islah 119
Jamaat Izalat al Bidi'wa Iqamat al
  Sunna 160–61
Jamaatu Muslemeen Council 160
Jamaatu Nasril Islam 160, 161
Jandel agricultural scheme 96–7
Jaz, Awad al 196
Jeddah 141
jihad 7–10, ch. 2, 14, 17, 19, 21–70,
  77, 79, 89, 92, 100–6, 112, 158,
  159, 162, 179, 229–30, 252, 253–4
Jordan 190n, 191
Juba 197, 198, 200, 209, 217

Kabila, Laurent 208, 211, 221
Kadugli 102, 104–5
Kaduna 160
Kagame, Paul 202, 207–8, 220
Kamal ud-Din 163
Kampala 73, 158, 185, 199, 243
Kano 19, 160, 164, 154
Kassala 162, 210, 212
Kenya 3, 115, 139, 143, 156, 159,
  164, 165, 168, 172, 175, 196, 204,
  212, 213, 219n, 233, 234, 235, 242,
  219n, 238, 242, 243, 246, 247
Kerubino Kuanyin 189
kharaj 149
Khartoum 78, 82, 194, 218, 223, 226
Khatmiyya 76, 162
Khomeini, Ayatollah 15, 36, 77
Kismaayo 122, 127–8
Kivu 208, 220
Kordofan 72, 99, 101–5, 207
Korea, North 253
Kurmuk offensives 185, 186 9
Kuwait 68, 119, 126, 168, 190
Kyrgyzstan 169

Lebanon 36, 194, 254
Liberia 228, 237
Libya 67, 69, 156, 167, 168, 190, 191,
  216
Lord's Resistance Army 19, 195, 198,
  199, 200, 238, 247–8

Luuq 128, 131, 138, 207, 213, 224
Luxor 43

Machakos Protocol 243–4, 248
Machar, Riek 210
Mahdi Mahamed, Ali 122, 124, 132–4
Mahdi, Mohamed Ahmed al 64
Mahdi, Sadiq el 76–7, 79, 81, 99,
  113, 210, 216, 217
Mahdi, Sayyid Abdel Rahman al 4, 162
Mahdism 4, 64, 75–6
Mahfouz, Naguib 52–3, 61
Majerteen 128
Majma al Islam, al 125
Makki, Hassan 65, 95, 97
Malawi 168
Mali 67, 159, 163, 164, 169, 172, 173
Malik Agar 95–6
Mao Zedong 32, 33, 34
Mareehaan 129
Mas'ari, Mohamed al 36
Massawa 187, 188, 212
Mauritania 156, 159, 163, 169, 190n
Mawdudi, Abu al A'la al 37, 83, 86,
  87, 119, 127
Mbale Islamic University 167
Mekki, Yousif Kuwa 96
Meles Zenawi 138, 209n
Mengistu Haile Mariam 188, 202–3,
  207, 227
Menza 185, 187
Mercy International 175, 178
Merka 127, 128, 137, 142
Mirghani family 76, 162
Moallim, Sheykh Mahamed 119
Mogadishu 24, 115, 116, 119, 120,
  121 7, 128 30, 132–7, 139, 141–4
Moi, Daniel arap 175, 234
Mombasa 233, 247
Mongols/Tartars 25, 39
Morocco 64, 67, 168
Mozambique 154, 156, 168, 171,
  198, 219n
Mubarak, Husni 46, 52, 57, 59, 60,
  67, 105, 194, 195, 206, 214, 216,
  239, 243

Mudawwi, Osman al 196
Mudullod 130n, 132, 134
Mugunga 208, 209
Muse, Mohamed Abshir 120
Museveni, Yoweri 197, 209n, 248
Muslim Brothers 3, 5, 10, 17, 22, 24,
  26–8, 44, 53–7, 69, 75–7, 79, 81,
  119, 160, 190, 239
Mustafa, Shukri 254
Mwanboga, Shaikh Muhammad Ali
  164

Nabhani, Taqi al Din al 39
Nairobi and Dar es Salaam bomb at-
  tacks (1998) 139, 172, 174–6, 178,
  224, 225, 237
Nasser, Gamal abd al 23, 24, 28, 35,
  36, 37, 54, 59, 66, 79, 89
Nation of Islam 194
National Army for the Liberation of
  Uganda 200
National Congress Party (Sudan) 107,
  109
National Democratic Alliance (Sudan)
  201, 210, 212, 216, 219, 220, 226,
  242
National Islamic Front (NIF) 78, 81–
  2, 84, 89–93, 95, 96, 98–9, 110–11,
  112, 155, 184, 190, 203, 205, 229
NEPAD (New Partnership for Africa's
  Development) 233, 234
Netherlands 61
NGOs, Islamic 11–12, 13, 57, 68, 90,
  115, 126, 127, 130–1, 146–81 (list,
  170–1)
NGOs, Western 115, 130–31, 146,
  153–5, 227–8
Niassiya 68
Niger 159, 163, 173
Nigeria 19, 35, 50, 67, 160–1, 163,
  168, 172, 173, 203, 234, 251, 254
Nile, River 66, 97, 203, 215, 248
Nimeiri, Jaafar 60, 79–81, 92, 109,
  195, 228
Non-Aligned Movement 66
Norway 238, 242

Nuba Mountains 72–3, 89, 92, 96,
  100–5, 106, 155, 226, 229, 242
Nugud, Mohamed Ibrahim 244

Obasanjo, Olusegun 19, 254
Ogaden 118, 125, 138
Ogaden National Liberation Front
  (ONLF) 138–9, 140, 204, 205, 207,
  213
oil 35, 67, 68, 81, 106, 108, 111, 112,
  149, 154, 207, 211–12, 237–8, 240,
  243
Oman 116
Omdurman 162, 166
Operation Lifeline Sudan 226–7
Organisation of African Unity 66,
  206, 234; *Also see: African Union*
Organisation of the Islamic Confer-
  ence (OIC) 83, 158, 167, 176, 191,
  192
Orientalism 15, 18
Oromo Liberation Front (OLF) 138–
  9, 140, 187–8, 204–5, 207, 210,
  213, 248
Ottoman empire 5, 64, 65

Pakistan 16, 47, 50, 126, 143, 174,
  198, 199, 226, 237, 246
Palestine 24, 26, 29–30, 32, 34, 35,
  45, 49, 50, 61, 66, 67, 191, 232,
  235, 239, 240, 255
Peshawar 8, 46, 47
Philippines 35, 169
PLO 67
Popular Arab and Islamic Conference
  74, 82, 193–4
Popular Defence Forces (Sudan) 90,
  93, 96, 100, 102, 104–5, 195
Popular Front for the Liberation of
  Palestine 193
Popular Islamic Conference 191, 193
Popular National Congress 109
Puntland 123, 139

Qadiriyya 119, 124, 173
Qaida, al, *see* Al Qaida

Qaradawi, Yusuf al 6, 38, 42, 151–2
Qatar 224
Qutb, Sayyid 5, 17, 23, 24–5, 28, 30–
  8, 40, 42, 44, 47, 50, 52, 59, 66, 83,
  86, 87, 112, 127

Rahanweyn Resistance Army 131,
  138, 213
Rahman Ali, Abdel Wahab Abdel 102
Ras Komboni 213, 246
refugees 13, 169, 171
Republican Brothers 77, 81
Rice, Susan 218, 219n, 224, 228
Rida, Rashid 5, 26
Riyadh 141, 194, 221
Roseires 97
Rushdie, Salman 15
Rwanda 29, 169, 171, 183, 185, 202,
  207–9, 219, 220–1, 252
Rwandese Patriotic Front 198, 207–8

sadaqat 148–50
Sadat, Anwar 25, 35, 39, 42–3, 46
Saddam Hussein 47, 82, 190
Salafis, Salafism 4–5, 6–7, 13, 23, 26,
  35, 36, 37, 42, 45–50, 64, 66, 67,
  68–9, 103, 105, 119–20, 124, 141,
  193, 236, 254–5, 256
Salih, Zubeir Mohamed 102
Sanchez, Illich Ramirez ('Carlos')
  201–2, 206, 222
São Tomé and Príncipe 237
Saud, Abdel Aziz al 35
Saudi Arabia 7, 22–3, 35–6, 45, 46–8,
  49, 61, 64, 66, 67–8, 69, 103, 115,
  119–20, 121, 125, 138, 141, 160,
  161, 168, 172, 173, 178, 184, 190–
  5, 205, 216, 218, 221–2, 236, 254,
  255
Saudi Islamic Relief Association 161
Senegal 163, 168, 175, 234, 250
September 11, 2001 attacks 8, 22,
  40–1, 45n, 48–50, 62, 68, 114,
  176–8, 222, 224, 225, 231–4, 241,
  254
'September Laws' (Sudan) 80–1

Shagari, Shehu 161
Shams el Din, Ibrahim 184, 189, 223,
  224
Shari'a Support Fund 92–3
Shari'ati, Ali 5, 29, 36
Shi'a Islam 17, 36n, 75, 82, 100n,
  160, 173, 256
Shifa, al (factory, Sudan) 225–6, 228
Sierra Leone 156, 168, 171, 173, 237
Siyaad Barre, Mahamed 115, 118–
  21, 128, 228
Soba 201
Sokoto Caliphate 77
Sokoto, Sultan of 160, 161
Somali language 117–8
Somali National Front (SNF) 129
Somali National Movement (SNM)
  34, 119, 121
Somali Reconciliation and Rehabilita-
  tion Council (SRRC) 138, 139
Somali Salvation Democratic Front
  (SSDF) 120
Somali Youth League (SYL) 117
Somalia: 2, 6, 19, 34, 64, 67, 114–45,
  154, 159, 168, 169, 177, 196–7,
  204, 205, 207, 212–14, 232, 233,
  235–6, 246–7, 248, 254; Islamic
  justice 132–7, 142, 144; Transi-
  tional National Government 127,
  138–9, 142, 143, 214; US-UN in-
  tervention 128, 129–32, 140, 196–7
Somaliland 114n, 116, 139, 140
South Africa 67, 156, 168, 176, 233,
  234
Southern Blue Nile Province 73, 90–
  7, 99, 106, 185, 186–9, 207
Southern Sudan 65–6, 72–3, 78, 89,
  92, 106, 155, 172, 184–9, 200–4,
  205–7, 209–12, 216, 217–20, 227–
  30, 237–8, 240–5, 247, 248, 251,
  257
Soviet Union 8, 41, 43, 54, 191, 254
SPLA-United 210
Sri Lanka 169
Southern Sudan Independence
  Movement (SSIM) 210

Sudan 1–2, 4, 8, 9, 10, 11, 14, 17–18, 25, 47, 50, 63, 64, 65–6, 68–9, 71–113, 118, 139, 154, 155, 156, 159, 163, 168, 175, 177, 182–207, 209–16, 217–30, 232, 234, 235, 236, 237, 239, 240–5, 247, 248, 249, 251, 256–7; civil war 72–4, 79, 89–92, 95–96, 97, 98–9, 100–6, 108, 184–9, 197–207, 209–12, 216, 217–20, 222, 226–30, 240–5, 247, 248, 256–7; Constitution 85–9, 107, 108; National Assembly 90, 107–8; Revolutionary Command Council 84, 85, 87, 107
Sudan African National Union 79
Sudan Alliance Forces 97, 207, 211, 227
Sudan Peace Act 228, 241, 244
Sudan People's Liberation Army (SPLA) 72–3, 79, 95, 97, 98–9, 101–3, 110–11, 184–9, 197–8, 201, 202–4, 206–7, 209–12, 218, 220, 226–9, 241, 248, 252
Sudan Socialist Union 109
Sudan Transitional Assistance and Relief (STAR) 226–8
Sudan, southern, *see* Southern Sudan
Sufism 3, 4, 13, 36, 64, 66n, 67, 68, 70, 75–6, 77, 82, 161, 163, 178
Switzerland 174, 178, 238
Syria 59, 229

Tablighi Jamaat 198
Tablik youth movement (Uganda) 176, 198–9
Tabliq, al (Somalia) 126
Taha, Ali Osman Mohamed 84, 89–90, 108, 113, 243
Taha, *Ustaz* Mahmoud Mohamed 60, 77, 81
Taimiyya, Taqi el Din Ibn 25, 35, 36, 39
Taju l-Adab, Shaikh Muhammad al-Labib 163
Takfir wa al Hijra 10, 111, 119

Taliban 38, 40–1, 73, 82, 100, 221, 238, 246
Talisman 238
Tanzania 139, 159, 168, 171, 175, 237
Tanzim al Jihad 42–3, 45, 194, 199, 215
Tawhid Islamic Association 158–9, 167
taxation 92–3, 94, 136–7, 148–9, 150–2
Tayeb, Omer Mohamed al 80
Tehran 167
Tigray 187, 219
Timbuktu 164
Tokar 210
Torit 243
Tuareg 169
Tullishi mountain, battle of 101
Tunisia 118, 173
Turabi, Hassan al 7, 8, 17–18, 22, 25, 40–2, 63, 66, 71–7, 79–86, 89, 98, 99, 100, 105, 106–13, 184, 190–5, 199, 210, 211, 216, 217, 223, 224, 256
Turkey 64

Uganda 19, 24, 33, 115, 154, 155, 156, 158–9, 166–7, 168, 175, 176, 183, 196–7, 217–20, 226, 238, 247–8, 251, 252
Uganda National Rescue Front 200
Umma Party 75–7, 109, 207
Unionist Party 75–6
United Arab Emirates 118, 121, 138
United Nations: 14, 90, 103, 114, 137, 215, 226, 227, 229; agencies 14, 169, 171
United Somali Congress (USC) 121, 122, 128
University of Holy Qur'an and Islamic Sciences 166–7
Upper Nile Province 93
United States of America 1, 8, 14, 18, 19, 22, 30, 36, 40–1, 45, 47, 49, 50, 53, 63, 68, 92, 114, 128, 139–45,

160, 174–8, 190–4, 196–7, 210, 211–30, 231–57
USAID 92, 217, 227, 238, 241
USSR *see* Soviet Union

Wade, Abdoulaye 234
Wafd 26
Wahab, Mohamed Ibn Abdel 35
Wahdat Shabad al Islami (Waxda) 119
Wahhabis 4–5, 6–7, 35–6, 39, 68, 77, 82, 120, 161
'War on Terror' (US) 1, 19, 139–40, 231–57
Weliye, Hassan 141
West Nile Bank Front 200
Western Sahara 67
World Bank 195n, 257
World Islamic Call Society 167, 168, 172–3; *see also* International Islamic Da'wa Society

World Trade Center, *see also* September 11, 2001 22, 25, 48–9, 218
World War, First 25

Yabus 206
Yasin, Ahmed 45
Yei 209, 210
Yemen 67n, 115, 116, 138, 142, 190n, 233, 235–6, 241, 248
Young Muslim Association (Kenya) 165

Zaghlul, Saad 26
Zaire, *see* Congo, Democratic Republic
Zak Zaky 160
zakat 147–52
Zamfara State (Nigeria) 177
Zanzibar 116, 117
Zawahiri, Ayman al 45
Zenawi Meles *see* Meles Zenawi
Zimbabwe 238, 250